TIP-OF-THE-TONGUE STATES AND RELATED PHENOMENA

When the memory retrieval process breaks down, people wonder exactly why and how such a thing occurs. In many cases, failed retrieval is accompanied by a "tip-of-the-tongue state," a feeling that an unretrieved item is stored in memory. Tip-of-the-tongue states stand at the crossroads of several research traditions within cognitive science. Some research focuses on the nature of the retrieval failure. Other research tries to determine what tip-of-the-tongue states can tell us about the organization of lexical memory – that is, what aspects of a word we can recall when we are otherwise unable to do so. Still other research focuses on the nature of the experience of a tip-of-the-tongue state. Each of these perspectives is represented in this book, which presents the best theoretical and empirical work on these subjects. Much of the work is cross-disciplinary, but what unifies the topics in this book is that they concern strong phenomenological states of knowing that are not accompanied by recall or recognition of the desired information.

Bennett L. Schwartz is professor of psychology and Fellow of the Honors College at Florida International University. He received his PhD in cognitive psychology from Dartmouth College in 1993. He is the author of more than 50 publications, including journal articles, book chapters, edited books, and textbooks. He has published papers on animal memory, the language of thought, and adaptation and memory, but has worked most consistently on the tip-of-the-tongue phenomenon and issues of metacognition. He sits on the editorial board of several journals and is associate editor of the *Journal of Applied Research in Memory and Cognition*.

Dr. Alan S. Brown is a professor in the Psychology Department at Dedman College at Southern Methodist University. He received his BA from the College of Wooster and his PhD in human memory from Northwestern University in 1974. Dr. Brown has published more than 70 professional articles, as well as six books, on basic and applied areas of human memory and cognition. His primary interest is on investigating different varieties of memory dysfunction, such as the tip-of-the-tongue experience, déjà vu, inadvertent plagiarism, and retrieval interference. He has refereed journal articles submitted to more than 30 journals, and he currently serves as consulting editor for *Memory and Cognition*.

Tip-of-the-Tongue States and Related Phenomena

Edited by

Bennett L. Schwartz

Florida International University

Alan S. Brown

Southern Methodist University

CAMBRIDGE
UNIVERSITY PRESS

CAMBRIDGE
UNIVERSITY PRESS

32 Avenue of the Americas, New York, NY 10013–2473, USA

Cambridge University Press is part of the University of Cambridge.

It furthers the university's mission by disseminating knowledge in the pursuit of education, learning, and research at the highest international levels of excellence.

www.cambridge.org
Information on this title: www.cambridge.org/9781107035225

© Cambridge University Press 2014

First published 2014

Printed in the United States of America

A catalog record for this publication is available from the British Library.

Library of Congress Cataloging in Publication data
Schwartz, Bennett L.
Tip-of-the-tongue states and related phenomena / Bennett L. Schwartz, Florida International University, Alan S. Brown, Southern Methodist University.
pages   cm
Includes bibliographical references and index.
ISBN 978-1-107-03522-5 (hardback)
1. Memory disorders.   2. Metacognition.   3. Recollection (Psychology)
I. Brown, Alan S., 1948–   II. Title.
BF376.S393   2014
153.1′25–dc23   2014002249

ISBN 978-1-107-03522-5 Hardback

Contents

Contributors

MELISA AKAN, Boğaziçi University, Istanbul, Turkey

ELISABETH BACON, INSERM, Strasbourg, France

ROSEMARY BRADLEY, University of Leeds, England, UK

ALAN S. BROWN, Southern Methodist University, TX, USA

SARAH BUCHANAN, University of Leeds, England, UK

ANA BUJÁN, University of Santiago de Compostela, Santiago de Compostela, Spain

ANNE M. CLEARY, Colorado State University, CO, USA

KATIE CROFT CADERAO, Southern Methodist University, TX, USA

FERNANDO DÍAZ, University of Santiago de Compostela, Santiago de Compostela, Spain

ANASTASIA EFKLIDES, Aristotle University of Thessaloniki, Greece

DAVID FACAL, University of Santiago de Compostela and INGEMA Foundation, San Sebastián, Spain

SANTIAGO GALDO-ÁLVAREZ, University of Santiago de Compostela, Santiago de Compostela, Spain

J. RICHARD HANLEY, University of Essex, England, UK

TREVOR A. HARLEY, University of Dundee, Scotland, UK

MARIE IZAUTE, Blaise Pascal University, Clermont-Ferrand, France

FREDRIK U. JÖNSSON, Stockholm University, Stockholm, Sweden

ONÉSIMO JUNCOS-RABADÁN, University of Santiago de Compostela, Santiago de Compostela, Spain

DILAY ZEYNEP KARADOLLER, Boğaziçi University, Istanbul, Turkey

KIMBERLY R. KLEIN, Colorado State University, CO, USA

ASHER KORIAT, University of Haifa, Haifa, Israel

MÓNICA LINDÍN, University of Santiago de Compostela, Santiago de Compostela, Spain

SIOBHAN B. G. MACANDREW, School of Health and Social Sciences, University of Abertay, Dundee, UK

JANET METCALFE, Columbia University, NY, USA

CHRIS J. A. MOULIN, University of Bourgogne, Dijon, France

RAVIT NUSSINSON, Open University of Israel, Ra'anana, Israel

JUSTIN D. OH-LEE, Central Michigan University, MI, USA

HAJIME OTANI, Central Michigan University, MI, USA

ARTURO X. PEREIRO, University of Santiago de Compostela, Santiago de Compostela, Spain

BENNETT L. SCHWARTZ, Florida International University, FL, USA

CELINE SOUCHAY, University of Bourgogne, Dijon, France

SHELLY R. STALEY, Colorado State University, CO, USA

RICHARD J. STEVENSON, Macquarie University, Sydney, Australia

Why Tip-of-the-Tongue States Are Important

ALAN S. BROWN AND BENNETT L. SCHWARTZ

The tip-of-the-tongue (TOT) state is endlessly fascinating to the editors and authors of this volume, as well as to the public at large. The perennial popularity of television shows such as *Jeopardy* and of trivia board games attests to the broad appeal of word finding as entertainment, and the associated "almost retrievals" are part of the engagement of the experience. Although it is one of the most commonplace and harmless cognitive experiences, it packs a considerable amount of drama for people experiencing it and for researchers studying it. William James expressed this most poetically more than 120 years ago, and others have frequently quoted him ever since. Speaking of the cognitive "gap," James writes:

> A sort of wraith of the name is in it, beckoning us in a given direction, making us at moments tingle with the sense of our closeness, and then letting us sink back without the longed-for term. If wrong names are proposed to us, this singularly definite gap acts immediately so as to negate them. They do not fit into its mould.... The rhythm of a lost word may be there without a sound to clothe it; or the evanescent sense of something which is the initial vowel or consonant may mock us fitfully, without growing more distinct. (1893, pp. 163–164)

The two editors of this volume have been long-term fans of the TOT experience, and have tag-teamed reviews of the literature every decade (Brown, 1991, 2012; Schwartz, 2002). We are not alone in our intense and abiding interest in this phenomenon. The pace of scientific investigation has picked up considerably, from less than one article per year in the 1970s to approximately one published report appearing every two months through the 2000s (Brown, 2012). A recent check of articles published from 2010 to 2012 reveals that this pace has not slackened. The TOT experience has spawned research on a rich variety of corollary topics in such diverse areas as philosophy, neuroscience, linguistics, and cognitive psychology. The current edited volume is a testimony to the way this mysterious experience can stimulate thought and feed theoretical speculation in many related topic areas. In this book, we hope to give you a better idea of why the TOT experience has engaged such a broad range of interest in the professional community.

WHY IS THE TIP-OF-THE-TONGUE STATE IMPORTANT?

It is important to convey exactly why the TOT state is so compelling to researchers. On one hand, the TOT experience appears so amorphous and subjective that it looks like trying to grab cognitive cotton candy, exactly the kind of mental phenomenon that behaviorists might have had us avoid. However, it is just this evanescence that allows enormous latitude in scientific approach and speculation. Indeed, researchers have devised a number of important ways of bringing the TOT into the lab and studying it scientifically.

Window on word retrieval. Aside from the personal fascination surrounding the TOT, the experience provides a potential portal to our understanding of how retrieval works. As noted before, during the TOT experience there is a sense that retrieval is momentarily slowed down or suspended, as if we slip into an altered cognitive state (see Díaz, Lindín, Galdo-Álvarez, & Buján, Chapter 10, this volume; Hanley & Chapman, 2008; Harley & MacAndrew, Chapter 6, this volume). James characterized this aptly in his quote by describing a friendly jousting match between ourselves and the missing word. The sought-after information has the capacity to make us tingle, as well as beckoning and mocking us. It is this suspension of routine, automatic and unaware cognitive processing, that allows us to take a closer look at what is happening during word access. In this sense, the TOT allows us to examine word retrieval in slow motion (Brown, 1991).

Case study of human phenomenology. The TOT experience is common enough that it allows an unusual opportunity to isolate individual experiences as they happen. Indeed, unlike judgments of learning or remember/know judgments, the term TOT derives from the commonly understood label given its everyday occurrence. Because most TOT states last a half minute or longer, even an untrained observer can gather considerable detail on the dynamics of his or her personal experience. There exists a number of early personal descriptions full of rich descriptive detail (Angell, 1908; James, 1893), and the first solidly scientific study of the TOT experience evolved from the authors' personal introspections (R. Brown & McNeill,

1966). In the empirical literature, TOTs offer an excellent case study on phenomenological experience because they are easy to induce in the lab and have a clear objective referent, namely the word that cannot be retrieved (Schwartz & Metcalfe, 2011, Chapter 2, this volume).

Easy-to-understand metamemory judgment. Many of our personal subjective experiences feel dense and difficult to assess, such as why minor chords sound sad or why we keep forgetting where we parked our car. More specifically, it is hard to have a naïve understanding of how we remember facts and dates, and to predict why and when we lose that same information. As those who have done research in this area can appreciate, it takes quite some time and effort to explain to participants the difference between "remember" and "know" in recognition experiments. However, the TOT experience presents a short, simple, and dramatic personal experience in which the laboratory version feels much like everyday examples. Even more helpful, it is immediately apparent when a TOT is happening to us, unlike identifying the moment when a fact is solidly implanted in memory or the precise time that a name is forgotten forever. And because there is an objective referent, the accuracy of this TOT can be verified against later recall or recognition of the missing target.

HISTORY OF THE TOT

We will present a brief historical background on empirical research on TOTs so that readers can see where this research has come from and appreciate where it is heading. Whereas sporadic descriptions of the TOT experience have appeared in various general psychology books since the late 1800s (e.g., James, 1893), the scientific method was never applied to the phenomenon until more than half a century later.

Brown and McNeill's investigation. The modern era was initiated by Roger Brown and David McNeill's (1966) thorough research study on the TOT experience. The vast majority of researchers over the past 50 years have heavily drawn on Brown and McNeill's methodology, which they referred to as "prospecting." Moreover, Brown and McNeill provided an impressive model of methodology for undertaking the scientific study of a psychological experience. As the first step, they gathered anecdotal and personal experiences over a period of months to help them clarify exactly what comprises the TOT experience and to guide them toward potentially important empirical and theoretical issues. For example, they anecdotally observed that when in a TOT state, they often recalled words that sounded like the word they were trying to recall but failing at. Indeed, much research has documented the importance of retrieving similar-sounding words (Jones, 1989). Next, based on this information, they designed a pilot investigation with a handful of subjects to design, test, and refine their empirical procedures. Finally, they undertook a full-scale study with a substantial number of participants. This investigation was unprecedented, as they ran a large group of subjects and would call a temporary halt to the procedure whenever someone would declare that a TOT experience was occurring. All others in the group would wait patiently so that the TOT-stricken individual(s) could answer a series of questions about their present state of retrieval uncertainty. While later researchers would test people individually, their methodology has proven very successful in investigating TOTs.

The fact that different words elicited TOTs at different rates and in different individuals created a challenge to traditional statistical procedures, an issue that Brown and McNeill referred to as the "fragmentary data problem." Their creative and detailed solution to this problem was an important factor in allowing subsequent research to probe the TOT to move forward. Among their findings, Brown and McNeill found that participants in TOTs were indeed more likely to possess partial or related information and often spontaneously recalled the target word.

Once this study was conducted, Brown and McNeill (1966) took great pains to analyze their data in many different ways, using different statistical procedures, especially as they found few available analogs to their prospecting method. To illustrate their anomalous approach, they analyzed subjects' guesses on the number of syllables in the intended target word in several different ways. For example, they were concerned that some participants reported more TOTs than others. Thinking that these participants might unduly influence the results, they looked at syllable reports both with item and with participant as the unit of analysis. Most impressively, Brown and McNeill were not dogmatic about their design, findings, or conclusions, but constantly reminded the reader of the limitations of collecting and analyzing data from their semi-experimental design. Even now, this study presents an excellent model of how to approach the scientific exploration of a new phenomenon, alerting subsequent researchers to the pitfalls and limitations of the research.

Interestingly, in 1966, TOTs were part of the zeitgeist. Coeditor Schwartz was born, coeditor Brown started college, Brown and McNeill published their paper, and as often happens in science, another group of researchers was turning its attention to TOTs as an empirical phenomenon, and published its paper the same year (Freedman & Landauer, 1966). In these scholars' investigation, when subjects could not answer a general information item, they rated how confident they were that they knew the answer. Freedman and Landauer did not define the TOT experience for their participants, but rather used the scale point of *"definitely know it"* as a substitute. Subsequent investigators have employed this methodology (e.g., Goodglass, Kaplan, Weintraub, & Ackerman, 1976; Kikyo, Ohki, & Sekihara, 2001; Vigliocco et al., 1997), but most find it essential to have participants report TOTs rather than to infer the presence of TOTs from other responses (see Schwartz, 2006).

The 1970s and 1980s saw a continued but slow growth in research on TOTs. Most of the interest in the 1970s came from researchers interested in aphasiology (e.g., Barton, 1971; Bruce & Howard, 1988; Goodglass et al., 1976) and metacognition (e.g., Koriat & Lieblich, 1974; Wellman, 1977), and in the 1980s from those interested in models of forgetting (Jones, 1989; Reason & Lucas, 1984). TOT research became big business in 1991 and entered its modern age with the publication of two landmark papers. The first was an exhaustive review of the work done on TOTs in the 25 years since R. Brown and McNeill (A. Brown, 1991). In that same year, Burke and her colleagues published a major empirical and theoretical work on TOTs, delineating perhaps the most popular and lasting model to explain TOTs and retrieval failure, based on the transmission deficit hypothesis (Burke, MacKay, Worthley, & Wade, 1991). Nearly 25 years after these publications, Brown's review continues to define the field and the issues studied, and Burke and her colleagues' model continues to drive research in the field (see Díaz et al., Chapter 10, this volume; Hanley, Chapter 4, this volume), particularly investigations on word retrieval during TOTs. Following these two landmark papers, there has been a steady rise in the work on the TOT phenomenon from a number of perspectives.

The most recent evolution in TOT research involves cognitive neuroscience. In 2001, two groups of researchers published data supporting speculation that TOTs arise out of processes in the prefrontal lobe, including the anterior cingulate (Kikyo et al., 2001; Maril, Simons, Weaver, & Schacter, 2001). We see this focus on the neuroscience approach to TOTs represented in three chapters contained in the present volume: Díaz and colleagues (Chapter 10); Izaute and Bacon (Chapter 9); and Juncos-Rabadán, Facal, and Pereiro (Chapter 7).

COLLECTING AND ANALYZING TOTS

Brown and McNeill's (1966) term for their technique, *prospecting*, is certainly appropriate. Finding TOT experiences resembles the physical experience of digging for nuggets of gold in a mountain stream. Like the '49ers, researchers know the general "cognitive area" where TOTs can be found (e.g., obscure words, the faces of second-tier celebrities), but do not know exactly where the TOTs will be on any given person at any given time. The experience cannot be reliably produced by one particular item. A given word will elicit a TOT in some participants, but not others. Likewise, a particular word may elicit a TOT in a person on one occasion, but not on another. Research does suggest that people get into a rut and experience TOTs for the same item repeatedly even after they relearn it (Brown & Croft Caderao, Chapter 3, this volume; Warriner & Humphreys, 2008). So the alternative is to be prepared to grab the experiences whenever (and in whomever) they show up.

Prospecting method. The typical laboratory design involves individually presenting a large set of pictures, general information questions, or definitions of words and having participants self-identify when a TOT happens. Usually, the participant answers additional questions in the moment, such as what is the first letter of the intended word, how many syllables does it contain, and what other words come to mind that resemble this missing word. Other requests might include generating words that are similar in sound or meaning to the target, or information related to the target word (such as where one finds the object), or the strength of the TOT being experienced. Given that the TOT is purely subjective, depending solely on the individual's personal assessment, it is essential to carefully define and instruct the participants about the experience. This instruction ensures that all participants are using the same criteria and that results across studies are comparable. This definitional challenge is one of the primary reasons the systematic research on TOTs has been so slow to develop. The absence of a clearly observable behavior in TOT research flew in the face of the behaviorist tradition that ruled scientific psychology research for more than 50 years, through the 1960s. The remedy for this problem proved to be correlating TOT with subsequent behavior, such as performance on a subsequent recognition test. Brown and McNeill (1966) failed to do this, but the practice became common in work starting in the 1980s (e.g., Hart, 1965, 1966; Yaniv & Meyer, 1987). In all studies, self-rated TOTs correlate with later recall and recognition accuracy (Brown, 2012), supporting the idea that when participants experience TOTs they do have knowledge of the missing target word.

Diary studies. An alternative way to study TOTs is to have individuals keep a diary over several weeks. Participants record TOTs as they occur, and then answer questions about the experience as it actually occurs

(Burke et al., 1991; Reason & Lucas, 1984). Participants can also later add if they eventually recalled the missing target word. The diary approach is considerably more efficient for the experimenter, given that most laboratory trials are discarded because TOTs only happen with a small fraction of words. Diaries also give us a better picture of the kinds of words that elicit TOT experiences in day-to-day living. In the prospecting technique, the researcher brings in assumptions as to what kinds of items will induce TOTs, but in diary studies participants report naturally occurring TOTs, which are predominantly proper nouns (Burke et al., 1991). In addition, this technique allows us to estimate the rate with which TOTs naturally occur on a daily basis. Of course, as with the laboratory investigation, there is the problem of whether the participants are using an accurate and consistent definition to identify TOT states. An additional problem, unique to diary research, pertains to whether participants remember to record all of their experiences, given that TOTs may occur in inconvenient circumstances without a notebook handy, leaving record keeping vulnerable to the standard nemesis of forgetting to record the experience.

Classifying TOTs by outcome. From the beginning of research on TOTs, there have been issues about how to classify TOTs. This stems from two concerns, one of which is the behavioral concern – if a TOT is not accompanied by partial information or subsequent recognition, how do we know if it is really a TOT? The second concern is based on curiosity as to whether there are different kinds of TOTs. For example, can we identify phenomenological differences between those TOTs that are eventually resolved accurately, and those that are neither recalled nor recognized?

Brown and McNeill (1966) addressed this issue by dividing TOTs into two categories, positive or negative, based on whether the participant recognized the word provided as the one for which he or she was experiencing a TOT (also see Vigliocco et al., 1997. Brown and McNeill (1966) also distinguished between "nearer" TOTs, in which the target word was recalled during the TOT state, and "farther" TOTs, when the target was not produced before the experimenter provided it. In a more fine-grained classification scheme, Koriat and Lieblich (1974) divided TOTs into nine different categories based on whether the target word was eventually retrieved, correctly recognized, or not recognized. Burke and colleagues (1991) also defined some TOTs as proper TOTs, which were followed by successful recognition. Similarly, Jones and Langford divided TOTs into ones that were objective, for which target information was accessible, versus subjective, for which no verifiable information was retrieved. Schwartz, Travis, Castro, and Smith (2000) subdivided TOTs along phenomenological lines, including those in which recall felt imminent versus those for which it did not, and TOTs that were accompanied by emotion versus those that were not. Finally, some researchers have used subjective strength to divide TOTs into "strong" and "weak" categories (Gardiner, Craik, & Bleasdale, 1973; Schwartz et al., 2000). Several of the chapters in this volume make use of such TOT classification systems (e.g., Díaz et al., Chapter 10; Hanley, Chapter 4).

Measuring TOT accuracy – recall or recognition. Most researchers define the TOT in terms of the feeling that recall is about to occur – also known as *imminence*. This corresponds to people's subjective experience of TOTs, in which they feel like the word is elusive but just about to come to mind. However, for the sake of expediency, TOT accuracy is often measured by asking participants to recognize the correct response among alternatives. For a researcher interested in the TOT as phenomenology or as a meta-cognitive state, this question is important. Our experience is only adaptive, and our metacognition functional, if it predicts how we will respond in the future. Indeed, every study that has compared recognition performance for TOTs and unrecalled non-TOTs has found a recognition advantage for TOTs (Brown, 2012). Although many studies have shown that many TOTs are successfully resolved via eventual target word retrieval, only a few have examined resolution rates for non-TOTs (or n-TOT) items. Smith (1994) and Schwartz (1998) both confirmed higher resolution rates for TOTs than for n-TOTs, further supporting the assertion that TOTs reflect successful memory monitoring by correctly indicating the presence of information in memory and the likelihood that we will recall it eventually.

Issues in measurement – how do you determine TOT rates? As noted earlier, the assessment of whether one is experiencing a TOT is inherently subjective. Although there are features of TOTs that are attention grabbing, there is not a clearly defined and universally understood line between what rates a TOT label and what does not. Given that laboratory studies always have a fixed set of cue stimuli, TOTs are directly affected by the number of successful retrievals. The more successes one has (correct retrievals), the fewer opportunities exist to have TOTs. Thus, performance differences across individuals or groups need some correction factor to adjust for opportunity. One way to make this adjustment is to divide TOTs by all errors, or non-correct trials (Brown, 1991). From this perspective, the TOT is considered a variety of retrieval failure. This is the preferred method in studies interested in TOTs as metacognition (Schwartz & Metcalfe, 2011). However, there is another way to view TOTs. Perhaps they are more aptly represented as a form of retrieval success, albeit insufficient and incomplete. That is, a TOT represents an attempt at word access that is nearly successful

(Burke et al., 1991). A different adjustment that is based on this second perspective is to adjust TOTs against a baseline of correct retrievals (Gollan & Brown, 2006). This latter type of adjustment is the preferable one for those using TOTs to measure lexical retrieval failures. This is the case because in this research, one is interested in why known items are not retrieved rather than why people experience TOTs.

Although this may sound like a philosophical quibble – is the glass half full or half empty? – this difference in adjustment can have a profound effect on the interpretation of group performance differences. More specifically, with the error-trial adjustment, older adults consistently show higher TOT rates than do young adults. However, with the correct-trials adjustment, older adults do not differ from younger adults (Gollan & Brown, 2006). The reason for this is that older adults almost always know more words than younger adults in any given study. With fewer error trials to use for the baseline comparison, older adults will have a higher ratio of TOTs. In contrast to this, when older adults' larger pool of correct retrievals is used as a basis of comparison, this inequity drastically shrinks or vanishes. This suggests that older adults do not have a higher probability of a TOT per retrieval effort, but that they have more TOTs because of greater opportunity – they simply know more words. This ought to console older adults who are concerned about word-finding difficulties. The problem does not result from a deficiency, but rather an overabundance (word store) (Dahlgren, 1998).

Partial information and assessing accuracy. One of the most curious and compelling aspects of the TOT experience is having bits and pieces of the target word come to mind as one is feverishly searching to find the complete word. This peripheral information can also include images or sounds related to the named person/object, or words close in meaning or sound to the one that you want to find. James (1893) richly described this fascination in the quote presented earlier in this chapter, and the sporadic accessibility of such fragmentary word data provided one of the primary motivations for Brown and McNeill's (1966) first empirical exploration of the subject. A considerable portion of Brown and McNeill's article was devoted to dissecting the nature of these related words and word fragments, and much subsequently has been published on the topic (Brown, 2012; Schwartz, 2002).

Most of the research has focused on the accessibility of letters or phonemes, and syllable information (number, accent) has been investigated to a lesser degree. It is relatively clear that we have some, above-chance, knowledge of what a word begins with, and, to a lesser degree, how it ends. The evidence for a syllabic understanding of the missing word is less clear. Although many investigations indicate some sensitivity to this (Brown,

2012), these data are not strong or consistent (cf. Brown, Burrows, & Croft Carderao, 2013). There has been investigation into the accessibility of grammatical features of the missing target word, and this research shows a generally consistent ability to access the gender of the word (in Italian, for example, Miozzo & Caramazza, 1997; Vigliocco, Antonini, & Garrett, 1997), as well as its numerosity (Vigliocco et al., 1999). The numerosity study showed that English speakers were able to correctly predict if an unrecalled noun referred to "mass" or something that cannot be counted in individual units (e.g., "beer," "gold"), versus "count," which can be counted in individual units (e.g., "bottles," "rings"). Vigliocco and colleagues interpreted these results to mean that participants have access to grammatical features of unrecalled words while in TOTs, a finding also important in determining the time course of the stages of lexical retrieval (see Vigliocco et al., 1999).

It is important to note that important cautions are associated with data gathered on partial information accessibility. They tend to be selective, in that many investigations ask individuals to report such information if it happens to come to mind. Thus, it is often difficult to construct an accurate picture of how frequently such information is accessible, because these reports are up to the discretion of the participant. In many investigations, although the accuracy of first letter guesses may be high, there are often only a handful of TOT trials in which the participant ventures one. It is also difficult to establish chance guessing rate for comparison purposes (e.g., Koriat & Lieblich, 1974). This issue becomes even more problematic given research that indicates that individuals have above-chance access to first letter information about inaccessible words even when they claim not to know the defined word (Brown et al., 2013; Koriat & Lieblich, 1974). So perhaps we routinely have such information available, but are only motivated to access it when we are experiencing retrieval desperation.

Overall organization of this book. Our initial motivation in organizing the current set of chapters was to broaden the perspective on TOT research. As the literature has evolved, the TOT state has become important beyond memory researchers, and has grown into a useful tool for studying philosophical issues about the mind, metacognition, phenomenology, the structure of language, and bilingual linguistic functions, to name just a few (Brown, 2012; Schwartz & Metcalfe, 2011). Our purpose is to pull in additional perspectives and cognitive phenomena that relate to the TOT experience, such as déjà vu and recognition without identification. We are also excited about new developments in understanding the brain mechanisms involved in retrieval and TOTs.

We have claimed that TOTs are an excellent case study in a number of areas of cognitive psychology, but our insight into TOTs should generalize to other phenomena at the margin of knowledge and retrieval. Thus, Cleary describes her fascinating research that brings the déjà vu phenomenon under experimental control using a research paradigm grounded in TOT investigations. Moulin and his colleagues also investigate the déjà vu experience, discussing how aging and neurological disorders relate to the phenomenon. One of the more problematic manifestations of the TOT experience relates to olfactory cues. Jönsson and Stevenson discuss this tip-of-the-nose phenomenon, the feeling that you know a presented odor but cannot name it. In addition, Efklides presents the "blank-in-the-mind" state, the feeling one gets when one forgets what one was about to do. In each of these phenomena, the research effort benefits from a half century of empirical TOT research.

There is also an assortment of chapters on drilling deeper about specific topics in the TOT literature, investigating the nature of phenomenological experience in the TOT, its relation to word retrieval failures and forgetting, and its relation to those that are impaired neurologically. Several chapters explore the theoretical underpinnings of TOTs and their relation to lexical retrieval. Hanley, for example, takes issue with the majority of TOT studies, which use word definitions or general information questions as stimuli. He argues that most real-world TOTs arise from failing to retrieve the name of a familiar face, and uses models of face recognition to explore this phenomenon. Harley and MacAndrew introduce a model of lexical memory and discuss how TOT data support this conceptualization. Brown and Croft Caderao explore how certain items elicit TOT again and again and why they do so.

Another group of chapters extends the research on TOTs into special populations. Oh-Lee and Otani explore TOTs and related metamemory judgments in Parkinson's patients, whereas Juncos-Rabadán, Facal, and Pereiro explore lexical retrieval models of TOTs in patients with mild cognitive impairment. Using normal participants but testing them under unusual circumstances, Izaute and Bacon explore how benzodiazepines affect both TOTs and memory.

A final group of chapters includes that presented by Díaz and colleagues, who examine the neurological underpinnings of TOTs and interrupted recall. Díaz and colleagues employ both EEG and MEG technology to look at the neurological correlates of successful recall, TOTs, and don't know states. Schwartz and Metcalfe tout the metacognitive approach to TOTs. They are particularly interested in whether TOTs serve a control function, that is, whether experiencing a TOT directs one toward successful retrieval. Finally, Cleary, Staley, and Klein demonstrate another control function of TOTs, finding that when people experience TOTs they are more likely to indicate that they have recently studied that item compared to when they are not in a TOT. In summary, taken in total, these chapters represent the very best of new research explorations on TOTs from a wide variety of perspectives.

REFERENCES

Angell, J. R. (1908). *Psychology*. New York: Henry Holt.

Barton, M. I. (1971). Recall of generic properties of words in aphasic patients. *Cortex, 7*, 73–82.

Brown, A. S. (1991). A review of the tip-of-the-tongue experience. *Psychological Bulletin*, 109, 204–223.

(2012). *Tip of the tongue state*. New York: Psychology Press.

Brown, A. S., Burrows, C. N., & Croft Caderao, K. (2013). Partial word knowledge in the absence of recall. *Memory & Cognition*, 41, 967–977.

Brown, R., & McNeill, D. (1966). The "tip of the tongue" phenomenon. *Journal of Verbal Learning and Behavior*, 5, 325–337.

Bruce, C., & Howard, D. (1988). Why don't Broca's aphasics cue themselves? An investigation of phonemic cueing and tip of the tongue information. *Neuropsychologia*, 26, 253–264.

Burke, D. M., MacKay, D. G., Worthley, J. S., & Wade, E. (1991). On the tip of the tongue: What causes word finding failures in young and older adults? *Journal of Memory & Language*, 30, 542–579.

Cleary, A. M., Brown, A. S., Sawyer, B. D., Nomi, J. S., Ajoku, A. C., & Ryals, A. J. (2012). Familiarity from the configuration of objects in 3-dimensional space and its relation to déjà vu: A virtual reality investigation. *Consciousness and Cognition*, 21, 969–975.

Dahlgren, D. J. (1998). Impact of knowledge and age on tip-of-the-tongue rates. *Experimental Aging Research*, 24, 139–153.

Freedman, J. L., & Landauer, T. K. (1966). Retrieval of long-term memory: "Tip-of-the-tongue" phenomenon. *Psychonomic Science, 4*, 309–310.

Gardiner, J. M, Craik, F. I. M., & Bleasdale, F. A. (1973). Retrieval difficulty and subsequent recall. *Memory & Cognition*, 1, 213–216.

Goodglass, H., Kaplan, E., Weintraub, S., & Ackerman, N. (1976). The "tip-of-the tongue" phenomenon in aphasia. *Cortex*, 12, 145–153.

Gollan, T. H., & Brown, A. S. (2006). From tip-of-the-tongue (TOT) data to theoretical implications in two steps: When more TOTs means better retrieval. *Journal of Experimental Psychology: General*, 135, 462–483.

Hanley, J. R., & Chapman, E. (2008). Partial knowledge in a tip of the tongue state about two and three word proper names. *Psychonomic Bulletin & Review*, 15, 156–160.

Harley, T. A., & Bown, H. E. (1998). What causes a tip-of-the-tongue state? Evidence for lexical neighbourhood effects in speech production. *British Journal of Psychology*, 89, 151–174.

Hart, J. T. (1965). Memory and the feeling-of-knowing experience. *Journal of Educational Psychology*, 56, 208–216.

(1966). Methodological note on the feeling-of-knowing experiments. *Journal of Educational Psychology*, 57, 347–349.

Heine, M. K., Ober, B. A., & Shenaut, G. K. (1999). Naturally occurring and experimentally induced tip-of-the-tongue experiences in three adult age groups. *Psychology and Aging* 14, 445–457.

James, W. (1893). *The principles of psychology*. New York: Holt.

Jones, G. V. (1989). Back to Woodworth: Role of interlopers in the tip-of-the-tongue phenomenon. *Memory & Cognition*, 17, 69–76.

Koriat, A., & Lieblich, I. (1974). What does a person in a "TOT" state know that a person in a "don't know" state doesn't know? *Memory & Cognition*, 2, 647–655.

Kikyo, H., Ohki, K., & Sekihara, K. (2001). Temporal characterization of memory retrieval processes: An fMRI study of the "tip of the tongue" phenomenon. *European Journal of Neuroscience*, 14, 887–892.

Maril, A., Simons, J. S., Weaver, J. J., & Schacter, D. L. (2005). Graded recall success: An event-related fMRI comparison of tip of the tongue and feeling of knowing. *NeuroImage*, 24, 1130–1138.

Maril, A., Wagner, A. D., & Schacter, D. L. (2001). On the tip of the tongue: An event related fMRI study of semantic retrieval failure and cognitive conflict. *Neuron*, 31, 653–660.

Miozzo, M., & Caramazza, A. (1997). Retrieval of lexical-syntactic features in tip-of-the-tongue states. *Journal of Experimental Psychology: Learning, Memory, & Cognition*, 23, 1410–1423.

Reason, J. T., & Lucus, D. (1984). Using cognitive diaries to investigate naturally occurring memory blocks. In J. Harris & P. E. Morris (Eds.), *Everyday memory, actions, and absent mindedness* (pp. 53–70). London: Academic Press.

Schwartz, B. L. (1998). Illusory tip-of-the-tongue states. *Memory*, 6, 623–642.

(2001). The relation of tip-of-the-tongue states and retrieval time. *Memory & Cognition*, 29, 117–126.

(2002). *Tip-of-the-tongue states: Phenomenology, mechanism, and lexical retrieval*. Mahwah, NJ: Erlbaum Associates.

(2006). Tip-of-the-tongue states as metacognition. *Metacognition and Learning*, 1, 149–158.

Schwartz, B. L. & Metcalfe, J. (2011). Tip-of-the-tongue (TOT) states: Retrieval, behavior, and experience. *Memory & Cognition*, 39, 737–749.

Schwartz, B. L., Travis, D. M., Castro, A. M., & Smith, S. M. (2000). The phenomenology of real and illusory tip-of-the-tongue states. *Memory & Cognition*, 28, 18–27.

Smith, S. M. (1994). Frustrated feelings of imminent recall: On the tip-of-the-tongue. In J. Metcalfe & A. P. Shimamura (Eds.), *Metacognition: Knowing about knowing*. (pp. 27–46) Cambridge, MA: MIT Press.

Vigliocco, G., Antonini, T., & Garrett, M. F. (1997). Grammatical gender is on the tip of Italian tongues. *Psychological Science*, 8, 314–317.

Vigliocco, G., Vinson, D., Martin, R. C., & Garrett, M. F. (1999). Is "count" and "mass" information available when the noun is not? An investigation of tip of the tongue states and anomia. *Journal of Memory and Language*, 40(4).

Warriner, A. B., & Humphreys, K. R. (2008). Learning to fail: Reoccurring tip-of-the tongue states. *Quarterly Journal of Experimental Psychology,* 61, 535–542.

Wellman, H. M. (1977). Tip of the tongue and feeling of knowing experiences: A developmental study of memory monitoring. *Child Development,* 48, 13–21.

Yaniv, I., & Meyer, D. E. (1987). Activation and metacognition of inaccessible stored information: Potential bases for incubation effects in problem solving. *Journal of Experimental Psychology: Learning, Memory, & Cognition,* 13, 187–205.

2

Tip-of-the-Tongue (TOT) States: Mechanisms and Metacognitive Control

BENNETT L. SCHWARTZ AND JANET METCALFE

The tip-of-the-tongue state (TOT) is a conscious feeling that occurs when an item that a person is trying to retrieve is temporarily inaccessible. The TOT includes two components: the underlying cognitive level, consisting of the act of trying to retrieve information from memory, and the metacognitive level, which is the reflection or feeling state based on the cognitive level (Bacon, Schwartz, Paire-Ficout, & Izaute, 2007). The cognitive level refers to the disfluent retrieval, whereas the metacognitive level brings that retrieval attempt to conscious attention. TOTs feel a particular way that distinguishes them from other conscious states, such as those that accompany successful study or that occur when a retrieved answer is thought to be correct.

This conception of the TOT addresses a fundamental concern in the study of human psychology, in particular, how experience, cognition, and behavior are related (e.g., Woodworth, 1931; see Costall, 2006; Tulving, 1989). Introspectionists were interested in the nature of consciousness, but foundered not only on the replicability of their results, but also on introspection's relation to observable behavior (cf. Costall, 2006). TOTs are conscious experiences, but unlike those studied by the early introspectionists, TOTs have a clear behavioral correlate, that is, the retrieval of specific target words (Schwartz & Metcalfe, 2011). It is our thesis that the importance of the TOT phenomenon rests in its status as a case study of human subjective experience and how it causes cognition and behavior.

Correspondence concerning this chapter should be addressed to Bennett L. Schwartz, Department of Psychology, Florida International University, University Park, Miami, Florida, 33199 USA. Phone number: 305-348-4025. E-mail may be sent to Bennett L. Schwartz at bennett.schwartz@fiu.edu or to Janet Metcalfe at jm348@columbia.edu.

TOTs are important across several subfields of cognitive psychology, including memory retrieval theory, language production, and metacognition. From the standpoint of memory retrieval, the study of TOTs has contributed to our understanding of the effects of interference on recall (see Brown, 1991; Kornell & Metcalfe, 2006). From the standpoint of language production, TOTs are used to study stalled word retrieval and to understand the structure of the lexicon (Gollan & Brown, 2006; Harley & Bown, 1998). From the metacognitive view, TOTs are feelings that arise when retrieval founders (Schwartz & Metcalfe, 2011). In this chapter, we will argue that the TOT experience also induces aspects of metacognitive control. TOTs implore us to continue our search to retrieve unrecalled words. The TOTs are like an itch that can only go away when the target word is retrieved. It is the "itch" of the TOTs that causes us to find them problematic, but it is the drive that they give us to continue our search that is likely their cognitive function (Litman, Hutchins, & Russon, 2005).

TOT AS A CASE STUDY OF PHENOMENOLOGY

TOTs provide case studies that can advance the understanding of the nature of phenomenological experience (henceforth, experience) and its relation to cognition and behavior. We present four arguments that recommend TOTs as the "lab rat" of experimental phenomenology.

(1) **Universality**. TOTs are universal experiences across languages and cultures. In a survey of languages, Schwartz (1999) found that nearly 90 percent of those questioned expressed the feeling of temporary inaccessibility using the same tongue metaphor used in English, even though many are unrelated to Indo-European languages (e.g., Cheyenne, Hausa, Vietnamese). Moreover, Brennen, Vikan, and Dybdahl (2007) identified a Mayan language, Q'eqchi', that lacks a specific term for TOTs. Brennen and colleagues tested Q'eqchi' speakers, many of whom had limited skills in Spanish. When the Spanish term (*punta de la lengua*) was explained to them, they reported having *experienced* TOTs many times before in the Q'eqchi' language. When examining general information retrieval in Q'eqchi' speakers, Brennen and colleagues found TOT rates among the Q'eqchi' speakers to be comparable to those among speakers of Western languages. Although Brennen and colleagues (2007) tapped into a population different from the typical college student population, the TOTs the Mayan speakers reported closely resembled those English-speaking college students described.

TOTs are experienced by monolingual and bilingual speakers (e.g., Gollan & Acenas, 2004), and by ASL speakers as "tip-of-the-finger" states rather than TOTs (Thompson, Emmorey, & Gollan, 2005). TOTs are also experienced by synesthetes, who are able to recall synesthetic characteristics of words that they cannot recall (Simner & Ward, 2006). Across developmental trajectories, TOTs are similarly experienced by children (Hanly & Vandenberg, 2010), college-age students (Schwartz, 2006), and older adults (Brown & Nix, 1996; Schwartz & Frazier, 2005). They are also associated with a number of neurological conditions, including Alzheimer's disease, anomic aphasia, and temporal lobe epilepsy (for a review, see Brown, 2012).

(2) **Frequency of experience.** Diary studies have shown that TOTs occur about once a week for younger adults and increase in frequency for older adults (Dahlgren, 1998; Heine, Ober, & Shenaut, 1999; see Brown, 2012).

(3) **Observable in lab.** It is simple to induce TOTs in the laboratory (Brown, 1991, 2012; Smith, 1994). In a half-hour experiment, a researcher can elicit numerous TOTs from a single participant, thereby allowing the researcher to examine the effects of a variety of experimental variables on TOT rates, accuracy of TOTs, and resolution probability.

(4) **Referent in behavior.** Another feature of TOTs that recommends them as case studies of experience is that they are tied to a specific mental referent, namely the retrieval of a particular word. In contrast, other subjective experiences may be harder to induce in the lab or not have a specific referent. Déjà vu is a vague feeling that one has been somewhere before (Brown, 2003). Though Cleary and colleagues (2012) have succeeded at evoking déjà vu experiences in the lab, it is still unclear what would make a déjà vu experience accurate or illusory, as the familiarity that produces them is not tied to a specific target, as it is with TOTs (also see Cleary, Staley, & Klein, Chapter 5, this volume). A TOT has a referent, the target that the participant is trying to retrieve, thus allowing evaluations of accuracy (Brown, 2012).

To summarize, TOTs are an important metacognitive state because of their universality, frequency of the experience in everyday life, ease of observability in the lab, and referent behavior. These characteristics make TOTs good candidates for case study in the scientific evaluation of human phenomenology, in particular the relation between subjective experience, cognition, and behavior. We also claim that TOTs have a causal role in metacognition because they drive people to search deeper for a missing word.

TOT MECHANISMS

TOTs provide us with a marker that an unretrieved word is stored in memory and thus retrievable, acting as metacognitive monitoring judgments.

Like other metacognitive assessments, they signify what we know, do not know, can learn, and cannot learn. This, in turn, can drive us to employ strategies to retrieve the target item. We will argue that TOTs, like most metacognitive judgments, are based on heuristic mechanisms that count retrievable information as a surrogate for access of the unretrieved item. We first review the differences between direct access theories of TOTs and inferential theories of TOTs, and then describe a synthesis of the two views.

THE DIRECT ACCESS VIEW

The first researchers who studied TOTs (Brown & McNeill, 1966; James, 1890/1864; Koriat & Lieblich, 1974) assumed that they were caused by unconscious access to the actual to-be-retrieved target, but that something prevents the retrieval of the target word. The target word has activation sufficient to trigger the TOT, but not to trigger recall (Brown & McNeill, 1966; Perfect & Hanley, 1992). The direct access view still guides research on the phenomenon (Hamberger & Seidel, 2003; Lesk & Womble, 2004). However, newer models postulate multiple processes of retrieval or multiple levels of representation (see Brown, 2012; Gollan & Brown, 2006; Kornell & Metcalfe, 2006). In these views, TOTs occur because some information, usually semantic, is retrieved, but that retrieved information fails to initiate the retrieval of the correct phonological information.

Most contemporary models of TOT focus on the fact that participants are sometimes able to retrieve partial phonological information about the target itself, as well as semantic information related to the target, and that this suggests that the unretrieved item is stored in memory. If it is stored in memory, it logically may be driving the TOT experience. The partial information includes phonological information, such as the starting sound and numbers of syllables (Koriat & Lieblich, 1974), or syntactical information, such as the grammatical gender (Miozzo & Caramazza, 1997). Bilinguals may be able to access the translation equivalent in their other language (Gollan & Acenas, 2004; Gollan & Brown, 2006). Moreover, Hanley and Chapman (2008) showed that participants could remember if performers were known by three names (e.g., Catherine Zeta Jones, Sarah Jessica Parker) or two names (e.g., Gwyneth Paltrow, Cameron Diaz) even when they could not actually recall the names themselves. Finally, Simner and Ward (2006) found that synesthetes could recall the sensory characteristics associated with unretrieved TOT items. That is, if a particular word, such as "incantation," was experienced as green, they could recall the color association even when they could not recall "incantation." Thus participants have access to semantic, syntactic, syllabic, sensory, and partial phonological information about the target when they are in a TOT state.

Lexical access models focus on the difference between retrieval of semantic information, which occurs successfully during all TOTs, and the retrieval of complete phonological information, which is thought to be what fails during the TOT (Gollan & Brown, 2006). According to these models, retrieval occurs in two steps. First, a person retrieves meaning-based information (and perhaps syntactic information). Second, the phonological form is activated. If that semantic information does not activate the appropriate or complete phonological information, a TOT occurs. The two-step view of TOTs leads to two hypotheses. First, TOTs may stem from semantic retrieval without phonological retrieval of items. The participant may recover much semantic and grammatical information about the target, but without retrieving its phonological representation. Second, TOTs are related to increased activation of targets rather than the failure to retrieve them (see Gollan & Brown, 2006).

To review Gollan and Brown's (2006) two-level model, TOTs result when the semantic form or some close approximation is retrieved, but the phonological form is not. As we shall see, this account of TOTs is compatible with the heuristic-metacognitive account, which hypothesizes that retrieved semantic, syntactic, and phonological information combined with other related information converges to inform a metacognitive monitor that retrieval of the word is likely, stimulating the TOT phenomenology.

Nonetheless, data rule out the idea that only partial target activation can cause TOTs (as in Brown and McNeill's, 1966, original model). For example, Cleary (2006) examined the relation of TOTs to the familiarity of the answers. In her experiment, she presented participants with general information questions. Unbeknownst to the participants, they had seen the answers to some of the questions in an earlier "unrelated" task. During the general information task, participants did not have more TOTs for questions whose answers they had seen earlier than for questions whose answers they had not seen earlier. Thus, priming the targets did not increase the likelihood that those items would later be experienced as TOTs. Target priming did increase the likelihood that the person judged that the answer to the unanswered question had been presented earlier. That target priming did not affect TOTs runs counter to the view that target strength alone is the only possible source of TOTs.

Schwartz (2008) found evidence that was inconsistent with the direct access view when looking at interference between TOTs and working memory. General information questions were used to induce TOTs (e.g., "What is the last name of the composer who wrote *Don Giovanni*?). After unsuccessful retrieval of a target, participants were immediately presented with a series of digits and asked to keep those digits in mind (i.e., a digit span task) for half of the trials. For the other half of the trials, a digit span task was not given. For the other half of the trials, there was no concurrent memory load. Participants made TOT judgments for the general information questions that they could not recall and then attempted to recognize the correct answer for those questions. After the participants made the TOT and recognition judgment, they were required to recall the digits. Relative to the control condition, there were fewer TOTs when participants were maintaining a digit load. However, recognition was not altered by the working memory load. Thus, the digit span task lowered TOT rates, but did not affect the memorability of the target, as measured by recognition of the unrecalled items. That is, a factor other than the strength of the target was driving the TOTs.

THE HEURISTIC-METACOGNITIVE ACCOUNT

The heuristic-metacognitive account explains TOTs by focusing on the sources of information that contribute to TOTs (Schwartz & Metcalfe, 2011). When a person is unable to recall a word, metacognitive processes are activated, which inform the person of whether the word is potentially retrievable. The monitor examines the amount of related and partial information recalled, the familiarity of the cue, and even the recent history of retrieving the particular word (Warriner & Humphreys, 2008). That is, it is not sub-threshold activation of the actual word that triggers the TOT, but a host of accessible cues and clues, which may include partial activation or whole activation of a bit of the target, or even the whole target itself, if the person is not sure that the answer is correct (see Figure 2.1). Thus, the heuristic-metacognitive view explains the TOT experience, not the retrieval failure.

Although it is tempting to think of the metacognitive monitor as a kind of homunculus, it is not necessary to do so. In the CHARM model, for example, Metcalfe (1993) proposed a metacognitive monitor to explain feeling-of-knowing judgments that was a simple accumulator of feature matches and mismatches (also see Hazy, Frank, & O'Reilly, 2007). The magnitude of the match mapped directly into the judgments. In the present case, the metacognitive monitor need not be more than an accumulator of retrieved information from all sources, and this produces a TOT response at a certain criterion. When the amount of information accumulated reaches that

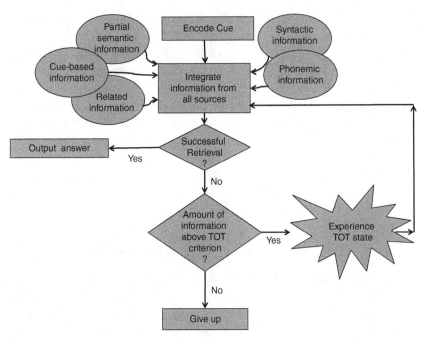

FIGURE 2.1. The heuristic-metacognition monitor weighs evidence associated with the retrieval failure to determine if a TOT is warranted.

predetermined criterion, it triggers a TOT state, which in turn induces attempts to retrieve more information rather than quitting, as is shown in Figure 2.1.

The information that produces the TOT may include both semantic and syntactic retrieved information. Thus, if a person retrieves that an actress uses three names rather than two, this suggests to the metacognitive monitoring system that the person may also possess the actual name, albeit in a currently inaccessible state. Similarly, if a person recalls the first letter of a word, or the hair color of a person, this information may drive one to feel as if one can retrieve the missing name. In Koriat's (1993, 2012) theory, the metacognitive monitor counts the amount of retrieved information (regardless of its correctness) in order to derive a judgment. In Metcalfe's (1993) theory, the familiarity of the cue or question is paramount. In this context, "familiarity" means the ease of processing or fluency of processing the cue terms. If the question is familiar (e.g., "What was your great grandmother's name?"), we are more likely to experience a TOT than if the question is not familiar (e.g., "What is the capital of Kyrgyzstan?"). Like other heuristic judgments, these mechanisms are usually successful because most, but not all, cues and clues are correlated with the actual likelihood of maintaining the TOT target in memory (see Cleary, 2006; Metcalfe, 1993).

In Koriat's (1993, 2012) view, it is the amount of information retrieved, regardless of its correctness, that matters to the metacognitive monitor. Koriat claimed that we have no objective way to determine if our retrieved information is correct. For example, when asked "what is the capital of New Zealand?" many participants may experience a TOT and have partial information, but this TOT may be directed incorrectly at the name "Auckland" rather than "Wellington." So the partial or related information that the person retrieves about Auckland will fuel the TOT, even though this answer is incorrect.

BEHAVIORAL EVIDENCE FOR THE
HEURISTIC-METACOGNITIVE ACCOUNT

Behavioral evidence that supports the heuristic-metacognitive account comes from studies that show that the rate of TOTs can be influenced by factors other than those that affect retrieval. Koriat and Lieblich (1977) found that the cue or question contributed to the number of TOTs people reported when they were unable to recall the target. Participants indicated more TOTs for definitions that were long or redundant (e.g., "nimbus: a circle, or any indication of radiant light, around the head of divinities, saints, sovereigns in pictures, medals, etc.") than for definitions that were shorter and more concise (e.g., "numismatics: the science of coins"). Although better cues may lead to stronger target activation, it is also possible to interpret these results in favor of the heuristic-metacognitive view that the familiarity of cues itself produced the TOTs (see Table 2.1).

Metcalfe, Schwartz, and Joaquim (1993) compared direct access and heuristic-metacognitive theories by evaluating the role of cue familiarity in feeling-of-knowing judgments and TOTs. Participants studied word pairs, such as "captain-carbon." In one condition, both the cue and the target were repeated (A-B, A-B) in a subsequent list. In a second condition, the cue was repeated, but paired with an unrelated target (A-B, A-D). This induces more fluent processing of the cue (A), but should lead to interference in target recall (B). In a third condition, the cue was not repeated but the target was (A-D, C-D). After the study session, participants were given an opportunity to recall the first-list target word, given the cue word. In accordance with results from interference paradigms (e.g., Postman & Underwood, 1973), the recall was lowest in the A-B, A-D condition and highest in the A-B, A-B condition. In one of the experiments, if participants could not recall the target, they made a

TABLE 2.1. *Evidence for the heuristic-metacognition approach to TOTs*

Study	Behavioral or neural	Finding
Koriat (1977)	Behavioral	Longer definitions led to more TOTs
Metcalfe, Schwartz, & Joaquim (1993)	Behavioral	TOTs caused by cue familiarity
Schwartz & Smith (1997)	Behavioral	TOTs caused by related information
Maril and colleagues (2001, 2005)	Neuroimaging	TOTs associated with same areas as executive control
Warriner & Humphreys (2008)	Behavioral	History of retrieval failure led to repeated TOTs
Cleary, Konkel, Nomi, & McCabe (2010)	Behavioral	Items in TOT states more likely judged to have been studied earlier in the experiment

TOT judgment. If direct access to the target caused TOTs, the A-B, A-B condition should produce more TOTs than other conditions because these were the most strongly encoded items. Heuristic-metacognitive theory, which includes cue familiarity, predicts that TOTs would track the repetition of the cue. That is, the A-B, A-B and A-B, A-D conditions should produce an equal number of TOTs because the cue was repeated, and both conditions should produce more TOTs than A-B, C-D. This is exactly what was found, with TOTs highest in the two conditions in which the cue was repeated. In fact, the condition that produced the lowest recall (A-B, A-D) produced the highest number of TOTs, and suggested to Metcalfe et al. (1993) that participants were using cue familiarity as a heuristic to determine TOTs.

Schwartz and Smith (1997) found evidence to support the heuristic-metacognitive view of TOTs using a different paradigm. They asked participants to study the names, pictures, and biographical information (habitat, size, diet) of fictional animal species. For example, the participants saw "Yelkey – Panama," which indicated that the "yelkey" is an animal that lives in Panama. Of the animals for which drawings were provided, half were accompanied by information pertaining to the size and diet of the animal. This led to three encoding conditions; minimum information (just the name-country pair), medium information (name-country pair and line drawing), and maximum information (name-country pair, line drawing, and additional biographical information). At test, participants were given the name of the country (i.e., Panama) and asked what animal came from that country. Recall of the target name (i.e., yelkey) was not significantly different across conditions.

If participants used the amount of related information accessible as a mechanism to determine TOTs, there should have been more TOTs when more related information was available (see Koriat, 1993, 1995), namely in the medium and maximum information conditions. The results showed that, indeed, there were more TOTs in the medium and maximum information conditions (19%) than in the minimum information (11%) condition, supporting Koriat's (1993) view.

Retrieval of information concerning the past success or retrieval of the inaccessible target also influences TOTs. Warriner and Humphreys (2008) examined TOTs at two points, during an initial test and then during a second test 48 hours later. One of their questions was whether participants would experience TOTs for the same items at these two different testing periods, and if being stuck in a TOT for longer, initially, would increase the likelihood of having another TOT on that same word. In the initial test, once a TOT had occurred, the experimenter manipulated the attempted retrieval interval such that some TOT items were allowed 10 seconds to resolve whereas other TOT items (randomly determined) were given 30 seconds to resolve. After the 10- or 30-second retrieval period, participants were shown the correct answer. Warriner and Humphreys then gave a second test to participants 48 hours later. In this second test, participants had equal amounts of time to attempt retrieval. Those items in which more time was spent trying to recover the TOT targets initially (30-second condition) were more likely to lead to another TOT than those in which less time was spent trying to recover the TOT initially (10-second condition). That is, there were more TOTs during the second test for questions in which session 1 TOTs were followed by a 30-second retrieval attempt than for those followed by a 10-second retrieval attempt. We think that these results show that even when the participants had forgotten the semantic information related to the target answer, they may have remembered the event of being in the TOT itself, and this remembrance may have contributed to their feeling of being in a TOT state again. That is, remembering that one was in a TOT state may serve as relevant related information that may drive a TOT the next time around, even if the person is not explicitly aware that the item produced a TOT earlier. Thus, remembering past retrieval failures may serve as another clue that informs the inferential process of TOTs.

Finally, Cleary, Konkel, Nomi, and McCabe (2010) examined TOTs for the names of odors. Odors often elicit feelings of familiarity, but are also difficult to name (Jönsson & Olsson, 2003; see Jönsson and Stevenson, Chapter 14, this volume), making them good stimuli for TOT experiments. In Cleary and colleagues' study, participants were presented with scents and were asked to generate the names of the odors. If the participants could not recall the name, they were asked if they were in a TOT for the name of that odor and if the odor had been presented in an earlier phase of the study. Cleary et al. found that being in a TOT predicted that a participant would indicate that he or she had smelled the odor before, regardless of whether he or she actually had. That is, if a TOT was experienced, an attribution was made that the odor had been studied. Here, too, TOTs are related to attributional processes rather than direct access to the name of the smell, consistent with the heuristic-metacognitive account.

It is noteworthy that in Cleary et al.'s (2010) study, as in others, the monitoring system may produce a spurious TOT if there is sufficient heuristic information, but the actual target is not represented in memory. Under normal circumstances, however, TOTs accurately predict eventual recall as well as recognition (Brown, 2012; Koriat, 2012). Nonetheless, because the experience results from this heuristic process, researchers can induce TOT experiences by increasing the familiarity of the cue or providing non-diagnostic related information.

NEUROIMAGING EVIDENCE FOR THE HEURISTIC-METACOGNITIVE ACCOUNT

Researchers conducted two studies using fMRI support of the heuristic-metacognitive account (see Galdo-Álvarez, Lindín, & Díaz, 2009, for a discussion of TOTs and EEG). The fMRI studies were designed to examine the functional brain regions involved during TOTs, and both implicate areas of the prefrontal lobe. Maril, Wagner, and Schacter (2001) and Maril, Simons, Weaver, and Schacter (2005) presented definitions of words and general information questions ("*Carmen,* composer") and asked participants to retrieve the word that matched them (Bizet). Participants gave one of three responses while in the MRI, indicating that they (1) were recalling the answer, (2) did not know the answer, or (3) were in a TOT for the target. Maril et al. (2005) compared brain activity across these three responses, and areas of the brain uniquely activated during TOTs were mostly in the right prefrontal lobe, including the anterior cingulate, right dorsolateral cortex, and right inferior prefrontal cortex. These areas previously have been associated with a number of monitoring and supervisory functions, including executive control (see Botvinick, 2007; Shimamura, 2008). Thus the neuroimaging studies are consistent with the heuristic-metacognitive views of TOTs, though it is worth noting that they do not specify which cognitive mechanisms are responsible for the increase in TOTs (e.g., partial information retrieval, cue familiarity). Nonetheless, the areas of the brain activated during TOTs support the idea that a TOT is a metacognitive signal.

TOTS AND THE CONTROL OF RETRIEVAL

In metacognition theory, our experiential feelings are flags or markers that inform us that a particular task is possible, that a particular item is memorable, or that a particular word is retrievable. These markers can then alter our behavior through control processes that direct our behavior. Just as the feeling of pain causes us to withdraw our hands from a sharp object, the TOT feeling nags us, compels us, or beckons us to engage in explicit retrieval processes. Indeed, Litman et al. (2005) found that when people experienced TOTs, they also experienced a drive to recall the item themselves rather than "look it up" or have someone tell them the word. Litman argued, as do we, that TOTs induce a sense of curiosity that may be beneficial for recall. TOTs provide us with information into an otherwise opaque retrieval system and signal that further effort is warranted. Thus, from the metacognitive perspective, TOTs are not a marker of failed retrieval but a premonition of and a prod to future successful recall.

A number of studies have demonstrated a relation between TOTs and the control of retrieval. For example, Schwartz (2001) found that participants spent more time trying to resolve an unrecalled target if a TOT had occurred than if no TOT had occurred. In this study, if participants failed to retrieve the answers to general information questions, they were asked if they were experiencing a TOT. More time was spent trying to retrieve items accompanied by TOTs than was spent trying to retrieve "don't know" responses. Given that these data are correlational, it is possible that longer retrieval times are used as a cue to TOTs. But it is also likely that the TOT experience itself drives the longer retrieval attempts, consistent with the view that TOTs serve a control function.

Studies also show that the presence of TOTs interferes with other cognitive tasks. Ryan, Petty, and Wenzlaff (1982) asked participants to retrieve word definitions. If they failed to retrieve the word, they were asked if they were in a TOT, and then immediately engaged in a concurrent number probe task. They were presented with a series of numbers, and were required to indicate every time they saw a particular number. When participants were experiencing a TOT for the word definition, they made more errors on the subsequent number probe task. Similarly, Schwartz (2008) examined dual task performance. Participants were required to maintain a digit span while they did a TOT prospecting task. Schwartz found that working memory performance decreased during TOTs relative to n-TOTs. Moreover, Schwartz found that being in a TOT interfered with one's ability to do the working memory task. Digit span performance decreased significantly when participants were in TOTs for general information questions. These two studies suggest that participants are allocating attention and resources to resolving TOTs, which causes performance on the secondary task to suffer. The studies suggest that TOTs alter the way we attempt retrieval, alerting us to temporary inaccessibility, which allows us to devote more resources to resolving those TOTs.

A GENERAL MODEL OF TOTS: A SYNTHESIS OF TWO THEORIES

Generally, direct access theories and heuristic-metacognitive theories have been seen as competing (but see Schwartz & Metcalfe, 2011). Traditionally, direct access theories postulate that the same events trigger retrieval failure and TOTs (e.g., Brown & McNeill, 1966). Heuristic-metacognitive theories do not focus on retrieval failure, but rather on the mechanisms that produce the experience of a TOT. We propose that models, such as those of Gollan and Brown (2006), speak to the processes underlying people's inability to quickly and efficiently retrieve a desired target item; these models explain retrieval failure. However, this is not enough for a TOT to occur. Sufficient cues must exist that the item is stored in memory to trigger a TOT. The TOT experience, then, is best accounted for by the heuristic-metacognitive account that speaks to the function of a TOT. As frustrating as it may be, a TOT nags us to continue to search for the missing, but likely present, target.

Thus, in the synthesis, a cue is given that starts a retrieval process. For some cues (e.g., What country uses the dollar as its currency?), the item will be retrieved quickly, resulting in immediate successful recall. For other items, retrieval failure will also be quick, but because the participant has no clue whatsoever about the answer (e.g., What country uses the tenge as its currency?). TOTs do not occur for either successful retrieval or confident "don't know" responses (Kazakhstan uses the tenge as its currency). Instead, only when retrieval comes up short after a modest search effort will the monitoring system be engaged. In such cases, if sufficient related and cue information is accessible, a TOT may be triggered (e.g., What country uses the yuan as its currency?). In this case, knowledge that the currency is undervalued or from an Asian country may inform the rememberer that retrieval is imminent. Thus, the TOT is metacognitive, insofar as it is both conscious and reflects the underlying cognitive process by giving a marker that a certain amount of information has accumulated. Furthermore, and perhaps most important, it has motivational consequences of its own. It indicates that access of the target might still be possible, causing the individual to continue to search in the hopes of retrieval success.

CONCLUSIONS

TOTs interest researchers in metacognition (e.g., Schwartz, 2006, memory retrieval (e.g., Kornell & Metcalfe, 2006), and language production (e.g., Biedermann, Ruh, Nichols, & Coltheart, 2008; Warriner & Humphreys, 2008). TOTs are conscious experiences that exist across cultures, languages, and ages (Brennen et al., 2007; Brown & Nix, 1996). Since Brown and McNeill's (1966) study, we have been able to bring TOTs into the lab and study them under controlled experimental conditions. Recent research continues to show the value of TOTs across areas of cognitive science (see Brown, 2012; Schwartz & Metcalfe, 2011).

Progress has been made in coming to a more firm understanding of the underlying mechanisms that contribute to TOTs and to their function. TOTs continue to offer us insights into the nature of cognition – both in terms of the mechanisms of the retrieval process and in the mechanisms that monitor retrieval and motivate renewed efforts to continue searching for the target word. The study of TOTs provides fertile ground for research on the relation of metacognition and the control of behavior. Our synthesis model of TOTs describes an accumulative retrieval process in which the content of the target-related information retrieved may include a variety of domains, but in which a sufficient amount of such information triggers the TOT state. It is not isomorphic to the two-level direct access view of TOTs, in which semantic access is complete but phonological translation breaks down (Gollan & Brown, 2006). In the synthesis, the accumulation of semantic and syntactic information is likely to trigger a TOT. Other information, such as the familiarity of the cue, may also play a role in triggering that nagging uncomfortable feeling that we label a TOT. Moreover, the TOT is a metacognitive experience that accompanies the breakdown in retrieval. It is not the retrieval failure itself. This new synthesis was designed to accommodate both the psycholinguistic and the metacognitive data. More important, the synthesis view highlights the *function* of TOTs in guiding further memory retrieval and lexical access processes. Namely, we propose that the function of TOTs is to alert us to the possibility that an apparent current retrieval failure in fact has the potential for future retrieval success, and it therefore directs us to appropriate continued retrieval efforts. This focus on the function of TOTs may be fruitful in applying the work on TOT states to conditions such as aging or dyslexia or anomia, as well as to more accurately describing the role of TOTs in normal human cognition.

REFERENCES

Bacon, E., Schwartz, B. L., Paire-Ficout, L., & Izaute, M. (2007). Dissociation between the cognitive process and the phenomenological experience of the TOT: Effect of the anxiolytic drug lorazepam on TOT states. *Cognition and Consciousness*, 16, 360–373.

Biedermann, B., Ruh, N., Nickels, L., & Coltheart, M. (2008). Information retrieval in tip of the tongue states: New data and methodological advances. *Journal of Psycholinguistic Research*, 37, 171–198.

Botvinick, M. (2007). Conflict monitoring and decision making: Reconciling two perspectives on anterior cingulate function. *Cognitive, Affective and Behavioral Neuroscience*, 7, 356–366.

Brennen, T., Vikan, R., & Dybdahl, R. (2007). Are tip-of-the-tongue states universal? Evidence from an unwritten language. *Memory*, 15, 167–176.

Brown, A. S. (1991). A review of the tip-of-the-tongue experience. *Psychological Bulletin*, 109, 204–223.

(2003). A review of the déjà vu experience. *Psychological Bulletin*, 129, 394–413.

(2012). *Tip of the tongue state*. Psychology Press.

Brown, A. S., & Nix, L. A. (1996). Age differences in the tip-of-the-tongue experience. *American Journal of Psychology*, 109, 79–91.

Brown, R., & McNeill, D. (1966). The "tip of the tongue" phenomenon. *Journal of Verbal Learning and Behavior*, 5, 325–337.

Cleary, A. M. (2006). Relating familiarity-based recognition and the tip-of-the-tongue phenomenon: Detecting a word's recency in the absence of access to the word. *Memory & Cognition*, 34, 804–816.

Cleary, A. M., Brown, A. S., Sawyer, B. D., Nomi, J. S., Ajoku, A. C., & Ryals, A. J. (2012). Familiarity from the configuration of objects in 3-dimensional space and its relation to déjà vu: A virtual reality investigation. *Consciousness and Cognition*, 21, 969–975.

Cleary, A. M., Konkel, K. E., Nomi, J. S., & McCabe, D. P. (2010). Odor recognition without identification. *Memory & Cognition*, 38, 452–460.

Costall, A. (2006). "Introspectionism" and the mythical origins of scientific psychology. *Consciousness and Cognition*, 15, 634–654.

Dahlgren, D. J. (1998). Impact of knowledge and age on tip-of-the-tongue rates. *Experimental Aging Research*, 24, 139–153.

Galdo-Álvarez, S., Lind í n, M., & Díaz, F. (2009). The effect of age on event-related potentials (ERP) associated with face naming and the tip-of-the-tongue (TOT) state. *Biological Psychology*, 81, 14–23.

Gollan, T. H., & Acenas, L. A. (2004). What is a TOT?: Cognate and translation effects on tip-of-the-tongue states in Spanish-English and Tagalog-English bilinguals. *Journal of Experimental Psychology: Learning, Memory, & Cognition*, 30, 246–269.

Gollan, T. H., & Brown, A. S. (2006). From tip-of-the-tongue (TOT) data to theoretical implications in two steps: When more TOTs means better retrieval. *Journal of Experimental Psychology: General*, 135, 462–483.

Hamberger, M. J., & Seidel, W. T. (2003). Auditory and visual naming tests: Normative and patient data for accuracy, response time, and tip-of-the-tongue. *Journal of International Neuropsychological Society*, 9, 479–489.

Hanley, J. R., & Chapman, E. (2008). Partial knowledge in a tip of the tongue state about two and three word proper names. *Psychonomic Bulletin & Review*, 15, 156–160.

Hanly, S., & Vandenberg, B. (2010). Tip-of-the-tongue and word retrieval deficits in dyslexia. *Journal of Learning Disabilities*, 43, 15–23.

Harley, T. A., & Bown, H. E. (1998). What causes a tip-of-the-tongue state? Evidence for lexical neighbourhood effects in speech production. *British Journal of Psychology*, 89, 151–174.

Hazy, T. E., Frank, M. J., & O'Reilly, R. C. (2007). Toward an executive without a homunculus: Computational models of the prefrontal cortex/basal ganglia system. *Philosophical Transactions of the Royal Society, Series B*, 362, 1601–1613.

Heine, M. K., Ober, B. A., & Shenaut, G. K. (1999). Naturally occurring and experimentally induced tip-of-the-tongue experiences in three adult age groups. *Psychology and Aging*, 14, 445–457.

James, W. (1890). *The principles of psychology*. New York: Holt.

Jönsson, F. U., & Olsson, M. J. (2003). Olfactory metacognition. *Chemical Senses*, 28, 651–658.

Koriat, A. (1993). How do we know that we know? The accessibility account of the feeling of knowing. *Psychological Review*, 100, 609–639.

(1995). Dissociating knowing and the feeling of knowing: Further evidence for the accessibility model. *Journal of Experimental Psychology: General*, 124, 311–333.

(2012). The self-consistency model of subjective confidence. *Psychological Review*, 119, 80–113.

Koriat, A., & Lieblich, I. (1974). What does a person in a "TOT" state know that a person in a "don't know" state doesn't know? *Memory & Cognition*, 2, 647–655.

(1977). A study of memory pointers. *Acta Psychologica*, 41, 151–164.

Kornell, N., & Metcalfe, J. (2006). "Blockers" do not block recall during tip-of-the-tongue states. *Metacognition & Learning*, 1, 248–261.

Lesk, V. E., & Womble, S. P. (2004). Caffeine, priming and tip of the tongue: Evidence for plasticity in the phonological system. *Behavioral Neuroscience*, 118, 453–461.

Litman, J. A., Hutchins, T. L., & Russon, R. K. (2005). Epistemic curiosity, feeling-of-knowing, and exploratory behaviour. *Cognition and Emotion*, 19, 559–582.

Maril, A., Simons, J. S., Weaver, J. J., & Schacter, D. L. (2005). Graded recall success: An event-related fMRI comparison of tip of the tongue and feeling of knowing. *NeuroImage*, 24, 1130–1138.

Maril, A., Wagner, A. D., & Schacter, D. L. (2001). On the tip of the tongue: An event-related fMRI study of semantic retrieval failure and cognitive conflict. *Neuron*, 31, 653–660.

Metcalfe, J. (1993). Novelty monitoring, metacognition, and control in a composite holographic associative recall model: Interpretations for Korsakoff amnesia. *Psychological Review*, 100, 3–22.

Metcalfe, J., Schwartz, B. L., & Joaquim, S. G. (1993). The cue familiarity heuristic in metacognition. *Journal of Experimental Psychology: Learning, Memory, and Cognition*, 19, 851–861.

Miozzo, M., & Caramazza, A. (1997). Retrieval of lexical-syntactic features in tip-of-the-tongue states. *Journal of Experimental Psychology: Learning, Memory, & Cognition*, 23, 1410–1423.

Perfect, T. J., & Hanley, J. R. (1992). The tip-of-the-tongue phenomenon: Do experimenter-presented interlopers have any effect? *Cognition*, 45, 55–75.

Postman, L., & Underwood, B. J. (1973). Critical issues in interference theory. *Memory & Cognition*, 1, 19–40.

Ryan, M. P., Petty, C. R., & Wenzlaff, R. M. (1982). Motivated remembering efforts during tip-of-the-tongue states. *Acta Psychologica*, 51, 137–147.

Schwartz, B. L. (1999). Sparkling at the end of the tongue: The etiology of tip-of-the-tongue phenomenology. *Psychonomic Bulletin and Review*, 6, 379–393.

(2001). The relation of tip-of-the-tongue states and retrieval time. *Memory & Cognition*, 29, 117–126.

(2006). Tip-of-the-tongue states as metacognition. *Metacognition and Learning*, 1, 149–158.

(2008). Working memory load differentially affects tip-of-the-tongue states and feeling-of-knowing judgment. *Memory & Cognition*, 36, 9–19.

Schwartz, B. L., & Frazier, L. D. (2005). Tip-of-the-tongue states and aging: Contrasting psycholinguistic and metacognitive perspectives. *Journal of General Psychology*, 132, 377–391.

Schwartz, B. L., & Metcalfe, J. (2011). Tip-of-the-tongue (TOT) states: Retrieval, behavior, and experience. *Memory & Cognition*, 39, 737–749.

Schwartz, B. L. & Smith, S. M. (1997). The retrieval of related information influences tip-of-the tongue states. *Journal of Memory and Language*, 36, 68–86.

Shimamura, A. P. (2008). A neurocognitive approach to metacognitive monitoring and control. In J. Dunlosky & R. A. Bjork (Eds.), *Handbook of memory and metamemory: Essays in honor of Thomas O. Nelson* (pp. 373–390). New York: Psychology Press.

Simner, J., & Ward, J. (2006). The taste of words on the tip of the tongue. *Nature*, 444, 438–438.

Smith, S. M. (1994). Frustrated feelings of imminent recall: On the tip-of-the-tongue. In J. Metcalfe & A. P. Shimamura (Eds.), *Metacognition: Knowing about knowing* (pp. 27–46). Cambridge, MA: MIT Press.

Thompson, R., Emmorey, K., & Gollan, T. (2005) Tip-of-the-fingers experiences by ASL signers: Insights into the organization of a sign-based lexicon. *Psychological Science*, 16, 856–860.

Tulving, E. (1989). Memory: Performance, knowledge, and experience. *European Journal of Cognitive Psychology*, 1, 3–26.

Warriner, A. B., & Humphreys, K. R. (2008). Learning to fail: Reoccurring tip-of-the-tongue states. *Quarterly Journal of Experimental Psychology*, 61, 535–542.

Woodworth, R. S. (1931). *Contemporary schools of psychology*. London: Methuen & Co.

3

There It Is Again on My Tongue: Tracking Repeat TOTs

ALAN S. BROWN AND KATIE CROFT CADERAO

The tip-of-the-tongue (TOT) state has provided an enduring fascination for researchers, reflected in the geometrically increasing number of publications on the topic that have appeared over the past several decades (Brown, 2012). It is remarkable that such a seemingly simple cognitive error evokes such broad interest to researchers across many disciplines: memory, language, neuropsychology, and philosophy. One important ingredient in this fascination may be that TOTs reflect an essential instability and unreliability in what we would like to believe is our stable and reliable knowledge base. By definition, our TOTs happen with items that we believe to be securely stored in our memory. Word-retrieval processes should be an automatic servant to our information access needs, especially for bits of information that have been easily accessed over and over again. Having a TOT on a well-known word feels like getting an error code from the computer on a routine operation. In this chapter, we will go one step beyond this to address the infinitely more aggravating situation of repeatedly getting that identical error code from our brain, even after we thought that we had fixed the problem.

Historically, TOTs have been examined as isolated incidents, with little consideration of the likelihood that a TOT experience might occur again for that same word. It would naïvely seem that the TOT word should be more readily accessible on the next attempt, especially if we eventually resolved it by retrieving the sought-after word. However, informal observation and anecdotes suggest that a TOT experience can become an irritatingly repeatable feature for certain words. When discussing TOT research with others, many people volunteer reports of getting stuck time and again on certain problematic words. Strangely, this particular difficulty has been addressed in only a few published reports.

The first was a book chapter by Linton (1996), in which she detailed how she tracked her personal retrieval efforts across several decades. She began

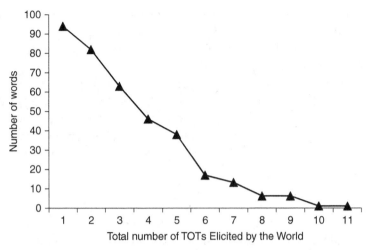

FIGURE 3.1. Number of words eliciting different numbers of TOTs in Linton (1996).

by memorizing a large body of Latin botanical names, with the intent of repeatedly testing herself. Over a nine-year period, Linton performed 3,331 tests on her previously learned corpus of names. More than a third (34%) of these retrieval attempts resulted in a TOT, and these data are summarized in Figure 3.1. The 367 words yielded 1,137 TOTs over these years, and the number of TOTs on each word ranged from 1 to 11. As indicated in Figure 3.1, the vast majority of TOTs do not happen as an isolated incident. More specifically, 92 percent of all TOT experiences occur as one of multiple TOTs on the same word, and this is represented by frequencies 2 through 11 in Figure 3.1. Of the 273 words that elicited repeated TOTs (2+), more than two-thirds (70%) evoked three or more experiences. Looked at another way, more than half (50%) of all TOTs Linton experienced consisted of the third, fourth, or fifth TOT on that same word. In short, it appears that if a word causes a TOT, it is more likely than not to elicit additional TOT experiences.

Linton (1996) conducted supplementary analyses on the 14 words evoking the highest number of repeated TOTs – 8 through 11 occurrences. The likelihood of eventual resolution was considerably lower (27%) for this subset of words than the overall average resolution probability across all words associated with TOTs (47%). Thus, the higher the repeat TOT rate for a word, the lower the likelihood of eventual retrieval on each occasion. During each TOT, Linton also made a personal prediction about whether the TOT would be resolved (correct word retrieved). From the select set of

14 high-TOT words, her resolution prediction accuracy did not differ comparing those TOTs that eventually were resolved (45%) with those that were not (38%). Thus, Linton was unable to reliably differentiate between these two sets of words based on her own predictions.

Summarizing Linton's (1996) findings from her personal experience, repeated TOTs are a common experience, accounting for a large percentage of all of her TOTs. If a TOT happens for a word, another one is highly likely to occur on that same word. Given the reliability of repeated TOTs, understanding them appears to be essential to our complete appreciation of the basic TOT experience. Although Linton provides incredible documentation, her study leaves many questions unanswered. To start with, are these repeat TOTs reliably related to any specific characteristics of the sought-after word? For instance, are these words longer (more letters) than average, or did they require more trials to initially learn, or tend to start with a particular subset of letters? Linton also used a unique set of words – Latin botanical terms. Her goals were scientifically admirable – to establish a high degree of control over the learning and testing of a set of words that were uncontaminated with prior knowledge. But does the phenomenon generalize in the same manner to other categories of words, such as capital cities or desserts?

There is a broader array of questions regarding repeated TOTs that Linton (1996) could not address from her data. Foremost is how commonly the experience happens. How many people are aware of having the experience of repeated TOTs in everyday life? Do repeated TOTs occur with different frequency as we age? If the target word eventually comes to mind (TOT resolved), does this alter the likelihood of having a repeat TOT on the next attempt? That is, do repeated TOTs come in succession for that particular word, or is successful word retrieval occasionally interleaved between repeated TOTs? Perhaps the length of time taken to eventually retrieve the target word influences the probability that it will be repeated.

The first laboratory documentation on repeated TOTs appears in Schwartz (1998), although this phenomenon was not the main focus of his investigation. Subjects attempted to retrieve answers to 80 general information items, and at the end of this session, they were immediately re-presented with the same cues that resulted in TOTs or don't know (DK) responses on the first try. For initial TOTs, the second attempt resulted in 12 percent correct resolutions, 52 percent repeat TOTs, and 36 percent DKs. In comparison, initial DK items yielded 9 percent resolutions on the second try, 7 percent TOTs, and 84 percent remained DKs. The incidence of repeated TOTs found by Schwartz (1998) is much greater than that found by Linton (1996), and there may be several explanations. One is that the TOTs in Schwartz (1998) may have been lingering from the first to the second attempt, in that some residual mental resources may still have been active in the search for the elusive word. The short inter-test interval (15 to 20 minutes) Schwartz (1998) used may make this more a measure of the persistence of the *same* TOT than an indication of a separate, repeated TOT (as in Linton). The rate in Schwartz (1998) may also have been boosted upward by the subjects' recollection that the item elicited a TOT a few minutes before and their desire to respond in a consistent manner. Schwartz (1998) did not re-cue words that were correctly retrieved on the first attempt, but it would have been interesting to see if (and how often) correct retrievals occasionally slip into TOTs.

The second laboratory investigation on this topic was specifically designed to evaluate the probability of repeated TOTs. Warriner and Humphreys (2008) proposed that this was an understudied but important phenomenon, and that a recurrence of a TOT may be related to the nature of the earlier retrieval experience. More specifically, the inability to retrieve a particular word may become a conditioned habit. In their error learning theory of repeated TOTs, a retrieval glitch becomes a reinforced response to a particular word cue. An inability to successfully retrieve the word is incrementally strengthened, and this error response is then set in competition to correct retrieval on the next attempt.

Warriner and Humphreys (2008) used 50 low-frequency words and presented definitional cues for each word on two separate occasions. On Session 1, when subjects were in a TOT or DK state, they were given 10 or 30 seconds (randomly determined) before seeing the correct word. Two days later, the subjects then returned for an identical test over the same 50 words. With respect to the TOT rates in Session 2, Warriner and Humphreys presented probabilities that items representing each of three different retrieval outcomes from Session 1 would lead to a Session 2 TOT: know (K) = 3 percent, DK = 7 percent, and TOT = 23 percent. The DK-to-TOT percentage was identical to what Schwartz (1998) found, but the TOT-to-TOT rate was considerably lower. Also of interest is that some items correctly retrieved on the first attempt turned into TOTs on the second, illustrating the modest instability of our well-learned knowledge base that makes the TOT experience inherently intriguing.

Looking at repeated TOTs in more detail, Warriner and Humphreys (2008) proposed that error learning predicts that a subsequent repeated TOT should be more likely for words in the 30-second condition compared to the 10-second condition. Subjects spend more time experiencing the non-retrieval error in the 30-second condition, so the error habit should become stronger. This is exactly what they found: repeated TOTs occurred for 37 percent of the TOTs that subjects were allowed to ponder for 30 seconds, compared to 25 percent of 10-second TOTs. A second outcome also supported an error learning interpretation. Examining only TOTs that were resolved in Session 1, if the resolution occurred within 10 seconds, the likelihood of a repeated TOT was much lower (8%) than if the resolution took longer than 10 seconds (30%). Again, the longer time spent in the TOT state initially, the stronger the non-retrieval habit, leading to a greater likelihood of experiencing another TOT on the next try. In short, Warriner and Humphreys (2008) demonstrated support for a reasonable account for TOTs that recur: an inappropriate response strengthened during an earlier attempt increases the likelihood that the same response (TOT) will occur on the next try.

It should be emphasized that Warriner and Humphreys (2008) proposed the error learning theory specifically to address the *repetition* of a TOT, rather than its initial cause. There are two well-established theories regarding TOT etiology – the transmission deficit hypothesis (TDH; Burke, MacKay, Worthley, & Wade, 1991) and heuristic-metacognitive theory (Schwartz & Metcalfe, 2011). Although neither theory specifically addresses why a TOT should recur for the same word, we will speculate about what each position may say with regard to repeated TOTs after we present our own investigations in repeated TOTs.

RETROSPECTIVE SURVEY

First, we conducted a survey to determine whether individuals are aware of repeated TOTs in their everyday lives and whether such retrospective assessments differ as a function of age. Participants were alumni of Southern Methodist University recruited using an e-mail solicitation. A total of 1,400 people were originally contacted, with 200 randomly selected from each of seven age decades ranging from the 20s through the 80s. We received 280 responses (57% female), distributed as follows: 20s ($N = 41$), 30s ($N = 41$), 40s ($N = 50$), 50s ($N = 55$), 60s ($N = 62$), 70s ($N = 50$), and 80s ($N = 16$). Respondents were asked two questions: 1) have you ever experienced a repeated TOT on the same word, and if so, 2) what is your estimate of the percentage of all TOTs that are comprised of such repeats? As shown in Figure 3.2, 40 percent of respondents admitted having a repeated TOT. Furthermore, the percentage of respondents increased across age groups, as

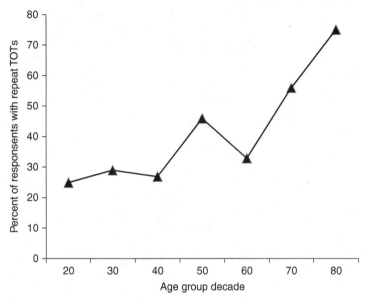

FIGURE 3.2. Percentage of respondents at each age group decade who claim to have experienced repeated TOTs.

reflected in a significant linear trend, $F(1, 350) = 5.19$, $MSe = 0.24$ (an alpha level of .05 is used, unless otherwise noted). Interestingly, the answer to the second question – what percentage of all of your TOTs do you think are repeated? (see Figure 3.3) – showed an age trend in the opposite direction, although the linear trend fell short of significance, $F(1, 134) = 2.99$, $MSe = 3.46$, $p = .086$. The average estimated percentage of repeated TOTs across age group was 12.7 percent.

The central findings of this exploratory survey are that two out of five adults reported that they have experienced repeated TOTs, and that this incidence increases with age. Estimates are that one in eight TOTs are repeats, and these repetitions appear to comprise a progressively smaller percentage of all TOTs experienced as one ages. Although a prospective diary study would make a valuable complement to this retrospective query (cf. Burke et al., 1991), the low frequency of repeated TOTs may make this effort difficult. Although research indicates that this could happen frequently (52%, Schwartz, 1998; 92%, Linton, 1996; 23%, Warriner & Humphreys, 2008), the best prediction from our retrospective data is that a repetition of a TOT may be much rarer. Based on our estimate, we expect perhaps one or two repeated TOTs per month (Brown, 1991), which would make it difficult for a diarist to keep focused on such a task.

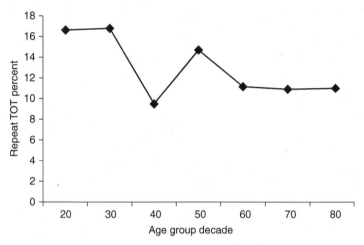

FIGURE 3.3. Percentage of TOTs estimated to be repeated, for respondents at each age group decade.

LAB STUDY

In our laboratory investigation, the primary goal was to replicate Warriner and Humphrey's (2008) finding on repeated TOTs, and we were also interested in how frequently TOTs followed initial K and DK responses. As noted earlier, Warriner and Humphreys tracked how often Session 1 Ks, DKs, and TOTs turned into TOTs, but we wanted to expand the response measurement in several respects. Warriner and Humphreys excluded items associated with an incorrect response on Session 1, for both the TOT and DK categories. This was a reasonable strategy, but it eliminated nearly a third of their responses (32%). We believe that it would be valuable to include these error responses, for several reasons. First, we wanted to know how likely a TOT on Session 2 would follow an incorrect K response (K-negative; declaring that you know the word but providing an incorrect response) or a TOT response (TOT-negative; declaring a TOT but producing an incorrect word, *or* not recognizing the target word presented as the one you were seeking).

According to the error learning theory Warriner and Humphreys (2008) proposed, an error can consist of either an insufficient (omission) or errant response (commission). More specifically, the TOT may occur because the degree of activation passed from the lexical to phonological representation of the word is insufficient to boost it over production threshold (no word comes to mind), or an incorrect word (interloper) is retrieved and then rejected. Excluding trials in which an incorrect word was actually produced (Kn; TOTn) potentially eliminates valuable data. More specifically, overtly thinking about an interloper and then rejecting it may be mentally similar to overtly producing an incorrect response. Another change from Warriner and Humphreys is that we used a finer gradation of DK responses – unfamiliar (UF), vaguely familiar (VF), moderately familiar (MF) – to determine if the likelihood of a Session 2 TOT was related to the initial confidence rating in Session 1. This alteration was intended to explore whether the strength of the feeling of knowing for DK items is predictive of a subsequent TOT. The simple prediction is that a TOT would be more likely following an earlier higher-confidence response (MF) than a lower-confidence (UF) response. Our assumption is that a modest fluctuation in item strength could push an MF to TOT states, but a much larger boost is needed to push a UF or VF item to a TOT.

We used a two-stage design, similar to Warriner and Humphreys (2008) – the same set of words tested twice, two weeks apart. Following Warriner and Humphreys, we performed their same two tests of the error learning theory. One involves resolution probability, in which resolved TOTs should result in fewer repeated TOTs than initially unresolved TOTs. The second uses resolution time, and predicts that short initial TOT resolutions should result in fewer TOT repetitions than longer resolutions. We included a third test of the error learning theory of repeat TOTs by comparing a condition in which the correct response was provided after each trial (feedback) versus a condition in which the correct response was not supplied (no feedback). Error learning should be reduced if the target word is provided after a Session 1 retrieval attempt, as this should strengthen the correct response to better compete with the conditioned strength of the error response. Thus, repeat TOT probability should be lower in the feedback relative to the no feedback condition.

We used two groups of college students selected from the Human Subjects Pool of the Psychology Department at SMU. One group was shown the correct target word after each retrieval attempt, whether successful or not ($N = 16$). This is the same procedure Warriner and Humphreys (2008) used. The other group ($N = 34$) received no feedback after its responses. Targets were 50 low-frequency words chosen from published TOT stimuli sets (Abrams, Trunk, & Margolin, 2007; Alario & Ferrand, 1999; Burke et al., 1991; Snodgrass & Vanderwart, 1980), and included animate object names (e.g., locust), inanimate object names (e.g., hourglass), and verbs (e.g., molt).

Subjects were tested individually in the laboratory and randomly assigned to the feedback or no feedback group. In Session 1, all subjects completed three practice trials followed by 50 experimental retrieval trials. Retrieval trials were presented in a randomized order using Qualtrics online software. Each trial consisted of a short prompt phrase (e.g., "time-measurement device consisting of two transparent bulbs and sand") to cue the target word (hourglass). After seeing the cue, participants selected one of the following response options:

1) **know** (K) (type in the target word on the computer)
2) **tip of the tongue** (TOT): I am certain that I know the word, but cannot think of it right at the moment
3) **moderately familiar** (MF): I have a strong sense of familiarity about the word, but can't recall it
4) **vaguely familiar** (VF): I am somewhat familiar with the word, but can't recall it
5) **unfamiliar** (UF): I do not know the word.

After choosing TOT, participants were allowed 30 seconds to retrieve the target word while the definition remained on the screen. At the end of every trial, the actual target word was displayed for five seconds (feedback group) *or* the next trial was initiated (no feedback group). Feedback group participants indicated on each TOT trial whether the word shown was the one that they were thinking of. Based on previous research (Warriner & Humphreys, 2008), we assumed that the time spent attempting to retrieve a target word during a TOT is directly related to the amount of error learning that takes place. Rather than manipulating this, as in Warriner and Humphreys (2008), by assigning items to 10- or 30-second conditions, we let this vary freely. Thus, the time from the cue presentation to the retrieval of the target word (typing the word) was recorded on the computer on TOT trials.

Figure 3.4 summarizes the percent of words in each response category in Session 1 that became TOTs during Session 2. Aside from the three types of DKs (UF, VF, MF), we separated items given a know (K) response evaluation by the subject in Session 1 into those that turned out to be correct (K-positive) and incorrect (K-negative). We also separated TOTs into three categories. For the no feedback group, a TOT-positive occurred when the correct response was produced, a TOT-unretrieved reflected that the subject gave no response during the 30-second interval allowed, and a TOT-negative indicated that the subject produced an incorrect response. For the feedback group, the definition of the TOT-negative and TOT-unretrieved for Session 1 was slightly modified. A TOT-negative reflected the retrieval of an incorrect word *or* that the feedback word was not the one that the

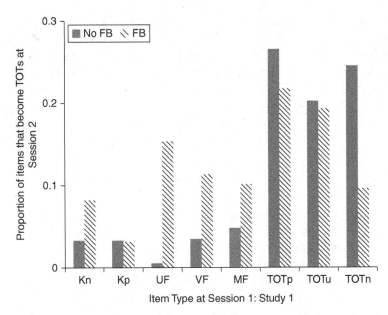

FIGURE 3.4. Proportion of Session 1 items that become TOTs during Session 2, separately for each type of item classification and feedback condition during Session 1 (lab study).

subject was seeking, whereas TOT-unretrieved included trials in which no word was retrieved but in which the target word was identified as the one the subject intended. Prior to examining the specific outcome in more detail, it is worth noting that the correct retrieval success on Session 2 did benefit from Session 1 feedback. More specifically, successful retrieval in the feedback group increased from Session 1 (34%) to Session 2 (54%), whereas there was no change for the no feedback group from Session 1 (37%) to Session 2 (38%).

Over both groups, TOTs occurred on 12.8 percent of Session 1 retrieval attempts. Of these, 2.7 percent were TOT-positive, 6.6 percent were TOT-negative, and 3.5 percent were TOT-unretrieved. Note that TOT-negative responses made during Session 2 were not included in the analyses, and it is standard procedure to exclude them (Brown, 2012; Schwartz, 2002). The reason for including them as a Session 1 category is that they are similar to a K-negative (response is incorrect), but differ in level of expressed certitude about the answer.

Turning to repeat TOTs, 20.4 percent of the Session 1 TOTs elicited a TOT again on Session 2 (see Figure 3.4). Examining overall totals, there was no difference in the percentage of repeated TOTs for the TOT-positive,

TOT-unretrieved, and TOT-negative conditions, $F < 1$. Comparing the feedback and no feedback conditions within each of the TOT item types, the trends were in the direction that error learning theory predicted. More specifically, the feedback group consistently showed a lower percentage of repeated TOTs during Session 2. However, this difference was not statistically significant for either TOT-positive, $t(29) = 0.37$, or TOT-unretrieved, $t(26) = 0.08$, $SE = 0.12$ (see Figure 3.4), but was significant for TOT-negative, $t(39) = 2.40$, $SE = 0.05$. These findings present only modest support for the error learning theory, which predicts that seeing the correct word should strengthen the correct response and lessen the impact of the just-experienced wrong response.

We did two other tests of predictions from error learning. First, TOTs were split into those that were resolved versus unresolved during Session 1. Warriner and Humphreys (2008) discovered that resolved initial TOTs resulted in fewer repeated TOTs (11.5%) compared to those TOTs that were unresolved during the original attempt (29.7%). This finding supported error learning theory, in that a greater amount of time spent in the error state (TOT) should lead to a stronger habit, resulting in a higher likelihood of repeating the TOT on the next occasion. Our outcome, however, was just the opposite. A repeated TOT was more likely following a prior resolution (24.6%) than an unresolved TOT (19.8%). A statistical test of this difference using the 20 (out of 50) subjects who had both resolved and unresolved TOTs yielded a nonsignificant outcome, $t(19) = 0.50$, $SE = 0.09$. In summary, the data trended in the opposite direction from what one would expect based on error learning.

For the final test of error learning theory, we compared TOTs with long versus short resolution times. Using the 40 subjects who had at least two resolved TOTs, short and long TOTs were defined relative to each other on a subject-by-subject basis. When there were an odd number of resolved TOTs, the TOT with the resolution time in the middle was grouped with the closest other TOT time. To illustrate, if a subject experienced three Session 1 TOTs that were resolved in 3, 9, and 12 seconds, the 3-second resolution would be considered "short" and both the 9- and 12-second resolutions would be considered "long" because 9 seconds is closer to 12 seconds. To review, Warriner and Humphreys (2008) predicted that less time spent in a TOT state would result in less error learning and a resultant likelihood of a subsequent TOT. Confirming this, they found that short-resolution TOTs were less likely to result in a repeated TOT (7.8%) compared to long-resolution TOTs (30.0%), supporting the error learning theory. Although we also found that repeated TOTs were less likely following short (20.1%)

versus long (25.7%) TOT resolutions in Session 1, this difference was not statistically significant, t (40) = 1.40, SE = 0.05. As a general summary of our tests of error learning in our lab study, out of five comparisons, four were in the expected direction with respect to the mean difference, but only one was statistically significant. Thus, some support for error learning does exist, but it is relatively weak.

Aside from repeated TOTs, we also examined what percentage of each item type from Session 1 evolved into TOTs on the second retrieval attempt (see Figure 3.4). These analyses were not directly related to error learning theory, but more to a general curiosity about the future fate of various types of retrieval outcomes. For K responses, 4.1 percent slipped into a TOT on the second attempt, and no significant difference appeared between K-negative (4.9%) and K-positive (3.3%), $F < 1$. This finding for K-positive items is nearly identical to Warriner and Humphreys's (2008) finding (3%) at a much shorter retention interval (2 days). Although this percentage of K items turning into subsequent TOTs may be relatively small, it is noteworthy that such slippage is reliable across investigations and apparently unrelated to the test-to-test interval. We also compared the feedback and no feedback groups (Figure 3.4), but found no significant group differences in Session 2 TOT percentages for either K-positive items, t (48) = 0.58, SE = .03, or K-negative items, t (18) = 1.24, SE = .31.

Turning to DK items, both Warriner and Humphreys (2008) and Schwartz (1998) discovered that 7 percent of DKs turned into TOTs on a second try. Our overall finding is similar (5.8%), with no significant difference across DK confidence levels, $F < 1$: UF = 5.0 percent, VF = 5.8 percent, and MF = 6.6 percent. However, an interesting difference emerges when comparing groups. Combined across UF, VF, and MF, the feedback group showed consistently higher Session 2 TOT rates than the no feedback group, F (1,42) = 17.11, MSe = 0.02 (see Figure 3.4). However, when each confidence level was considered separately, this difference remained significant only for UF: UF t (13) = 2.63, SE = 0.15; VF t (16) = 1.77, SE = 0.10; MF t (47) = 1.45, SE = 0.04. It appears that being given feedback boosts the likelihood of responding with a TOT on the subsequent occasion, and that this effect is most pronounced for items in the lowest confidence category (UF). One interpretation of this outcome is that subjects may be more likely to expect that they know the correct item after receiving feedback earlier, pushing them into the TOT evaluation. This interpretation supports the heuristic-metacognitive interpretation of TOTs (Schwartz & Metcalfe, 2011). Alternatively, perhaps as subjects learn new information as a result of the feedback, this leads to a larger number of TOTs than for the no feedback group because word strength has been increased. This other interpretation would be congruent with the TDH (Burke et al., 1991).

To summarize, although the present study did yield a percent of repeat TOTs similar to that found by Warriner and Humphreys (2008), there was weak support for the error learning theory of TOTs. More specifically, there were no significant differences in the likelihood of experiencing another TOT between the feedback and no feedback groups, between initially resolved versus unresolved TOTs, and between short versus long resolution times for initially resolved TOTs.

Present findings related to other TOT theories. Current theoretical models of TOT etiology do not specifically address why a TOT would recur on the same word, mainly because this empirical phenomenon was not identified in such formulations. Nevertheless, we provide the following speculations. The leading TOT model, the transmission deficit hypothesis (TDH) (Burke et al., 1991), proposes that TOTs result when an insufficient amount of activation passes from semantic-to-phonological nodes for a particular word. Such weak semantic-to-phonological connections may result from non-recent word use, infrequent word use, or aging. If a TOT is *not* resolved with the correct word, then one would expect that the next effort may result in a similar outcome. More specifically, if there is no alteration in the semantic-to-phonological connection strength during the TOT experience, then it would seem reasonable to predict that a similar result (i.e., TOT) would occur on the next retrieval attempt for that particular word.

However, experiencing the target word through retrieval or feedback should strengthen these semantic-to-phonological connections, reducing (or perhaps eliminating) the likelihood of a repeated TOT (Rastle & Burke, 1996). That is, if a TOT is resolved or if the correct word is presented to the subject at the end of the TOT trial, this should reduce the probability of a repeated TOT, compared to when a TOT is experienced but unresolved. Our laboratory study did not support this extrapolation from TDH theory, in that there is no reduction in a repeated TOT probability following feedback (versus no feedback). TDH would also suggest that resolving an initial TOT should decrease the likelihood of a repeated TOT, using the same reasoning given earlier. Warriner and Humphreys (2008) did support this prediction, in that TOT repeats were three times more likely following unresolved TOTs than resolved TOTs. However, we found no significant difference in repeated TOTs following resolved versus unresolved initial TOTs. If there is something problematic about the connection between semantic and phonologic nodes, then even a temporary boost from feedback or recent retrieval may not be sufficient to repair the inadequate linkage.

The second general position regarding the etiology of TOTs is heuristic-metacognitive theory (Schwartz & Metcalfe, 2011), which proposes that retrieval of general information related to a word (Schwartz & Smith, 1997), as well as word features (whether correct or not) (Koriat, 1993), can lead to a personal assessment that one is experiencing TOT. This related information can also include one's knowledge of the general category of information, or the familiarity of the cue information provided (Metcalfe, Schwartz, & Joaquim, 1993). In the case of repeated TOTs, recollection of a prior TOT on that particular word may elicit a feeling of being in a TOT state again during a future encounter with that same word (Schwartz & Metcalfe, 2011). This speculation is supported by the higher rate of TOTs that follow a previous TOT, compared to a previous K or DK experience. However, the speculation is predicated on the assumption that TOT experiences are memorable, and this needs empirical verification. There is some evidence that words associated with TOTs are better recalled than non-TOT words immediately afterward (Gardiner, Craik, & Bleasdale, 1973), but no study has examined subjects' memory for having a previous TOT experience.

SUMMARY AND SPECULATION

The experience of having recurring TOTs on the same word has been only occasionally addressed in the prior literature. Linton's (1996) case study revealed that most TOTs (57%) turn into repeated TOTs, but a laboratory study by Warriner and Humphreys (2008) showed a considerably lower rate. More specifically, 24 percent of TOTs are repeated at a second test, two days later. Our online survey indicated that the prevalence of repeated TOTs increases with age, from 25 percent of respondents in their 20s to 75 percent of respondents in their 80s. The survey also revealed that repeated TOTs are estimated to comprise 15 percent of TOTs across all age groups, and that this percentage dropped gradually (but not significantly) with age. Our laboratory investigation with undergraduates revealed that 20 percent of TOTs repeat two weeks later, figures that are in line with Warriner and Humphreys (2008). Also, this finding is comparable to the retrospective estimates of comparable individuals from our survey, in that respondents in their 20s judged 17 percent of their TOTs to be repeated.

Warriner and Humphreys (2008) suggest that error learning underlies repeat TOTs, in that one strengthens the wrong response of non-retrieval during a TOT. Supporting their speculation, the more time spent on the TOT increased the chances of it being repeated, and resolved TOTs were less likely than unresolved TOTs to lead to a subsequent repeated TOT.

Both of these predictions are direct extrapolations from the assumption that the more time one spends processing the error response, the stronger that response will become. The outcome of our laboratory investigation of repeat TOTs failed to yield strong support for the error learning theory based on several different analyses. First, error learning predicts that a repeat TOT is more likely after an unresolved than a resolved TOT because the stronger reinforced habit is having (being stuck in) a TOT, rather than resolving it. However, we found no significant difference between resolved and unresolved TOTs on the likelihood of a subsequent (repeated) TOT. Second, error learning also predicts that receiving feedback should ameliorate the likelihood of a subsequent TOT because the correct habit (target word) is reinforced. However, we found no difference in the likelihood of a repeated TOT after seeing the correct response versus not having this supplied. Finally, the length of an initial TOT experience should make a difference for the error learning theory because a longer TOT should lead to a stronger error habit compared to a shorter TOT. We failed to support this prediction, in that we found no difference in repeated TOT probabilities comparing short versus long initial TOT resolutions. Note, however, that even though statistical support does not exist in our laboratory investigation, the preponderance of the outcomes were in the predicted direction. Thus, one should not write off the error learning theory, as our investigation may simply have lacked sufficient power to detect such differences.

Although the focus of this chapter is on repeated TOTs, a related topic also holds a great deal of fascination – the probability that a known and successfully retrieved word can fall prey to a TOT state at a later time. Although reported once before in passing (Warriner & Humphreys, 2008), this puzzle has received virtually no attention in the literature. Our finding from our laboratory study is that approximately 5 percent of Ks turn into TOTs at a two-week interval, a figure somewhat higher than the 3 percent found in Warriner and Humphreys (2008) at a two-day interval. Although these percentages may not seem impressive, it is striking that 1 in 20 successful retrievals may become subsequently unsuccessful. This finding suggests that retrieval of well-learned material is a probabilistic process. Even though there are reasonable and empirically supported theoretical accounts for TOT experiences, there are none concerning why an ostensibly stable unit of knowledge that is verifiably retrievable on prior occasions may be inaccessible on a future attempt.

The stability of long-term memory for information well stored in long-term memory has been investigated by Bahrick (2000) with respect to high school names/faces (Bahrick, Bahrick, & Wittlinger, 1975), Spanish words

(Bahrick, 1984), and math concepts (Bahrick & Hall, 1991a). These investigations have demonstrated a remarkable retention level for different types of information across 50 years, a phenomenon labeled "permastore." However, Bahrick and Hall (1991b) as well as Berger, Hall, and Bahrick (1999) have found some instability in the knowledge residing in permastore. More specifically, some items of stored information may be less readily accessible at any given time, defined as unrecallable but yet recognizable on a subsequent test. Such items at the fringe of permastore are referred to as *marginal information*. Bahrick and Hall (1991b) note that research on "unstable" knowledge is sparse, and they present experimental procedures on preventative maintenance to shore up this information. We further propose that this marginal knowledge may play a substantial role in TOT experiences, and that this instability is reflected in the repetition of TOT experiences even in the face of corrective feedback (the target word). We also assume that successfully retrieved words that subsequently slip into a TOT also represent marginal knowledge.

Although only a handful of investigations evaluate retrieval success on repeated occasions with material from semantic memory, these also seem to support that random fluctuations occur for well-learned semantic knowledge in permastore (Au et al., 1995; Barresi, Nicholas, Connor, Obler, & Albert, 2000; Connor, Spiro, Obler, & Albert, 2004). These studies have tracked word retrieval performance of older adults (30s through 80s) on the Boston Naming Test. The evaluations were given on three sessions, each separated by several years. Evidence for knowledge instability is reflected in the proportion of retrievals that change from correct to incorrect, or vice versa, across tests. Illustrative of these fluctuations, Barresi and colleagues (2000) discovered that among those subjects in their 50s through 70s, 3 percent of previously correct responses were not successfully retrieved on the following try, and 7 percent of items that were not produced earlier were correctly recalled at the subsequent session. Thus it appears that a small percentage of information in permastore exhibits inconsistencies in access across repeated retrieval attempts, switching into and out of ready access.

We speculate that this relates to the TOT experiences in that subjects have a core platform of knowledge that is reliably accessible under any circumstances, but a small percentage of information that remains unstable at the fringes, fluctuating from recallable to unrecallable across different attempts. These items may be found at either the high or low end of normative frequency of usage (Gollan & Brown, 2006). Furthermore, the lack of a concerted effort to stabilize this information through rehearsal or focused mnemonic techniques (cf. Bahrick & Hall, 1991b; Berger et al., 1999) may doom them to continually drift in and out of TOT status (Linton, 1996). On the other hand, expending additional cognitive energy on such items through focused mnemonic techniques may actually invite additional TOTs by increasing the amount of information required to be accessible. A worthy extension of the present research would be to increase the number of repeated tests (3 to 5) and use longer inter-test intervals to get a better picture of the long-term instability of such fringe items. This would also clarify the pattern of fluctuations for the frequent TOT items in Linton (1996). Do some of these words get stuck in a repeating TOT cycle (linguistic purgatory?), or are correct retrievals interspersed among TOTs in an alternating fashion?

REFERENCES

Abrams, L., Trunk, D. L., & Margolin, S. J. (2007). Resolving tip-of-the-tongue states in young and older adults: The role of phonology. In L. O. Randal (Ed.), *Aging and the elderly: Psychology, sociology, and health* (pp. 1–41). Hauppauge, NY: Nova Science.

Alario, F. X., & Ferrand, L. (1999). A set of 400 pictures standardized for French: Norms for name agreement, image agreement, familiarity, visual complexity, image variability, and age of acquisition. *Behavioral Research Methods, Instruments & Computers, 31*, 531–552.

Au, R., Joung, P., Nicholas, M., Obler, L. K., Kass, R., & Albert, M. L. (1995). Naming ability across the adult life span. *Aging and Cognition, 2*, 300–311.

Bahrick, H. P. (1984). Semantic memory content in permastore: Fifty years of memory for Spanish learned in school. *Journal of Experimental Psychology: General, 113*, 1–29.

(2000). Long-term maintenance of knowledge. In E. Tulving & F. I. M. Craik (Eds.), *The Oxford handbook of memory.* Oxford: Oxford University Press.

Bahrick, H. P., Bahrick, P. O., & Wittlinger, R. P. (1975). Fifty years of memory for names and faces: A cross-sectional approach. *Journal of Experimental Psychology: General, 104*, 54–75.

Bahrick, H. P., & Hall, L. K. (1991a). Lifetime maintenance of high school mathematics content. *Journal of Experimental Psychology: General, 120*, 20–33.

(1991b). Preventative and corrective maintenance of access to knowledge. *Applied Cognitive Psychology, 5*, 1–18.

Barresi, B. A., Nicholas, M., Connor, L. T., Obler, L. K., & Albert, M. L. (2000). Semantic degradation and lexical access in age-related naming failures. *Aging, Neuropsychology, and Cognition, 7*, 169–178.

Berger, S. A., Hall, L. K., & Bahrick, H. P. (1999). Stabilizing access to marginal and submarginal knowledge. *Journal of Experimental Psychology: Applied, 5*, 438–447.

Brown, A. S. (1991). A review of the tip of the tongue phenomenon. *Psychological Bulletin, 109*, 204–223.

(2012). *The tip of the tongue state.* New York: Psychology Press.

Burke, D. M., MacKay, D. G., Worthley, J. S., & Wade, E. (1991). On the tip of the tongue: What causes word finding failures in young and older adults? *Journal of Memory & Language, 30*, 542–579.

Connor, L. T., Spiro, A., Obler, L. K., & Albert, M. L. (2004). Change in object naming ability during adulthood. *Journal of Gerontology: Psychological Sciences, 59B*, P203–P209.

Gardiner, J. M., Craik, F. I. M., & Bleasdale, F. A. (1973). Retrieval difficulty and subsequent recall. *Memory & Cognition, 1*, 213–216.

Gollan, T. H., & Brown, A. S. (2006). From tip-of-the-tongue (TOT) data to theoretical implications: When more TOTs means better retrieval. *Journal of Experimental Psychology: General, 135*, 462–483.

Koriat, A. (1993). How do we know that we know? The accessibility account of the feeling of knowing. *Psychological Review, 100*, 609–639.

Linton, M. (1996). The maintenance of a complex knowledge base after seventeen years. In D. L. Medin (Ed.), *Psychology of learning and motivation: Advances in research and theory* (vol. 35, pp. 127–163). San Diego, CA: Academic Press.

Metcalfe, J., Schwartz, B. L., & Joaquim, S. G. (1993). The cue-familiarity heuristic in metacognition. *Journal of Experimental Psychology: Learning, Memory, and Cognition, 19*, 851–864.

Rastle, K. G., & Burke, D. M. (1996). Priming the tip of the tongue: Effects of prior processing on word retrieval in young and older adults. *Journal of Memory & Language, 35*, 585–605.

Schwartz, B. L. (1998). Illusory tip-of-the-tongue states. *Memory, 6*, 623–642.

(2002). *Tip-of-the-tongue states: Phenomenology, mechanism, and lexical retrieval.* Mahwah, NJ: Erlbaum Associates.

Schwartz, B. L., & Metcalfe, J. (2011). Tip-of-the-tongue (TOT) states: Retrieval, behavior, and experience. *Memory & Cognition, 39*, 737–749.

Schwartz, B. L., & Smith, S. M. (1997). The retrieval of related information influences tip-of-the-tongue states. *Journal of Memory and Language, 36*, 68–86.

Snodgrass, J. G., & Vanderwart, M. (1980). A standardized set of 260 pictures: Norms for name agreement, image agreement, familiarity, and visual complexity. *Journal of Experimental Psychology: Human Learning and Memory, 6*, 174–215.

Warriner, A. B., & Humphreys, K. R. (2008). Learning to fail: Reoccurring tip-of-the-tongue states. *The Quarterly Journal of Experimental Psychology, 61*, 535–542.

4

Retrieval Failures for the Names of Familiar People

J. RICHARD HANLEY

Retrieval failures that occur during attempts to recall the names of familiar people have been the subject of intense scrutiny in the 40 years that
have elapsed since the publication of Yarmey's original investigation in
1973. Whereas Brown and McNeill (1966) had used definitions of words of
relatively low frequency to elicit tip-of-the-tongue (TOT) states, Yarmey
attempted to generate TOTs for familiar names by presenting participants
with photographs of 50 famous people. As with Brown and McNeill, Yarmey's
study provided a detailed record of the structural information about an elusive name that was available to participants when they experienced a TOT.
Moreover, the use of photographs allowed Yarmey to investigate the biographical or "semantic" information about a person that participants could
recall during a TOT, which cannot be assessed when using standard semantic cues such as definitions (Brown & McNeill, 1966).

WHAT CAN BE RECALLED DURING A TOT STATE
FOR A PERSON'S NAME?

When experiencing a positive TOT state (defined as either subsequent
TOT resolution or recognition of the correct name when it was read out),
Yarmey's (1973) participants could provide accurate estimates about the
number of syllables that were in a person's name; 73 percent of estimates
were correct for first names, and 79 percent were correct for last names.
Even more impressive, 68 percent of estimates concerning the identity of

I would like to thank Alan Brown and Andy Young for their helpful comments on an earlier
version of this chapter.
Address for correspondence: Prof. Rick Hanley, Department of Psychology, University of
Essex, Colchester CO4 3SQ, UK. E-mail: rhanley@essex.ac.uk. Telephone 0044 1206–874331.
Fax 0044 1206–873598.

the initial letter of the first name were correct, and 59 percent of estimates of the initial letter of the last name were correct. Yarmey suggested that performance was likely to have been well above chance, particularly in the letter condition.

More recently, Hanley and Chapman (2008) provided further evidence that detailed structural information about a name is often available during a TOT. They asked participants to identify celebrities whose names comprised either three words (e.g., *Catherine Zeta Jones*) or two words (e.g., *Gwyneth Paltrow*). They showed that participants often knew the number of words in a name when they were experiencing an unresolved TOT. That is, participants could reliably report during a TOT that the name *Catherine Zeta Jones* comprised three words whereas *Gwyneth Paltrow* contained only two. This information was unavailable to participants who were not experiencing a TOT when attempting to recall a person's name.

Yarmey (1973) also found that participants could often provide estimates of how recently they had encountered a person whose name was causing a TOT. In a study that examined episodic memory for famous names, Cleary and Specker (2007) subsequently provided confirmation that accurate information about recency can be accessed during a TOT. In phase 1 of their experiment, Cleary and Specker showed participants famous names, and then presented famous faces in phase 2. Half of these faces represented people whose names had been presented in phase 1. Cleary and Specker found that participants who were experiencing a TOT when attempting to identify a face often knew whether the name had been presented in phase 1, even though they were unable to recall it. This information on unrecalled names was not available when participants were not experiencing a TOT state.

Yarmey's (1973) investigation of the semantic information that is available during a positive TOT revealed that participants could accurately report a celebrity's profession on over 90 percent of trials on which recall of occupation was attempted. Participants performed equally well when attempting to recall the location (e.g., television, newspaper, movies, etc.) where they typically encountered the person. When in a TOT state, the person's occupation was generally the information that participants first attempted to recall, followed by their typical location. Consequently, Yarmey suggested that attempts to resolve a TOT may start with a search of possible professions.

Yarmey (1973) did not provide information about whether participants could *consistently* recall accurate semantic information about a person when in a TOT state. Hay, Young, and Ellis (1991) provided a clear-cut answer to this question in an experiment that provided a detailed examination of naming failures during familiar face identification. Hay and colleagues defined naming failures as a participant not recalling a person's name but subsequently recognizing it as belonging to the person at post-test. If participants were able to recall only vague semantic information about a person (e.g., "sportsman"), they invariably stated that the naming failure had occurred because the name and face were not strongly linked in their memory. Naming failures in which participants knew the name and expressed frustration at their failure to recall it, as in a TOT state, were never experienced unless specific semantic information about the person was available (e.g., the party to which a politician belonged). It therefore seems reasonable to conclude from Hay and colleagues' finding that some specific semantic information about a person is always available during a positive TOT experience.

THE BRUCE AND YOUNG MODEL

The finding that semantic information about a person can be retrieved during a TOT was a key piece of evidence that Bruce and Young used to develop their sequential model of person recognition. Bruce and Young argued that a TOT experience is caused by a breakdown between a set of *person identity* nodes that contain semantic information about the person and a lexical store that contains phonological information about the person's name (1986, p. 314). This explanation of TOTs, in which activation of the conceptual representation of the word is successful, but there is insufficient transmission of activation from its semantic to phonological representation, illustrates what Burke, Mackay, Worthley, and Wade (1991) subsequently referred to as *transmission deficit*. According to this hypothesis, information about the structural or phonological features of a name can be accessed during a TOT (Hanley & Chapman, 2008; Yarmey, 1973) because there has been partial activation of the phonological nodes by the semantic system.

In Bruce and Young's (1986) model, there is no direct link between the representation of a familiar face in memory and its phonological representation. One strong line of evidence for this claim is the fact that neither diary studies (Young, Hay, & Ellis, 1985) nor laboratory studies (Hanley & Cowell, 1988; Hay et al., 1991) have revealed situations such as "I know that his name is Dustin Hoffman, but I have no idea what he does or where I know him from." Consequently, Bruce and Young argued that it is always necessary to access semantic information about a person from their face before their name can be recalled.

Bruce and Young's (1986) model received support from the results of an experiment by Brennen, Baguley, Bright, and Bruce (1990), who asked participants to answer general knowledge questions about familiar people:

Who played Basil Fawlty's Spanish waiter Manuel?
Which actor is better known as Captain James T Kirk?

The key issue was whether a photo of a face would help an individual to recall a person's name if they experienced a TOT when attempting to answer one of these questions. Bruce and Young's model would predict that a photo should not resolve a TOT state because a photo contains no information that could help the system at the point of failure: the link between semantic information stored in the person identity nodes and the phonological representation of their name. If, contrary to Bruce and Young (1986), there *is* a direct link between the representation of a familiar person's face and name in memory, then providing a photograph of the face should prove highly effective in resolving TOTs. The results strongly supported Bruce and Young's model. A photo led to the resolution of only 14.5 percent of TOT states, a figure not significantly higher than the percentage of TOTs resolved by simply repeating the question (10.7%). In a subsequent experiment, Brennen and colleagues (1990) reported identical findings when participants were experiencing TOTs for the names of famous landmarks.

It appears that semantic information may constitute an amodal hub that provides the link between modality-specific representations of a person's face, voice, and name (Craigie & Hanley, 1993, 1997). Craigie and Hanley (1993) presented participants with a famous name and asked them to provide information about the celebrity's occupation and visual appearance (e.g., whether they have facial hair). Craigie and Hanley found that it was often possible to recall a person's occupation in response to their name without remembering his or her facial appearance. This appears to represent an approximate visual analog of a TOT state, and brings to mind an incident reported in Young and colleagues' (1985, p. 508) study of person recognition errors when a diarist heard a familiar male voice on the radio and could remember the person's occupation "but could not think what he looked like." Crucially, Craigie and Hanley found that it was extremely rare to recall a person's facial appearance from their name without also recalling their occupation. Once again, evidence for a direct link between representations of faces and names in the person recognition system proved elusive.

RESOLUTION AND PREVENTION OF TOT STATES FOR PEOPLE'S NAMES

Even though photographs did not overcome TOTs for people's names, Brennen and colleagues (1990) found that TOTs could be resolved at above baseline levels by presenting participants with the initials of the name. Presumably, resolution occurred because the initials provided enough additional activation of the phonological representation of the name to allow recall to take place.

Burke, Locantore, Austin, and Chae (2004) showed that the number of TOTs could be significantly reduced and the number of correct responses significantly increased if participants generated a homophone of a person's name prior to recall. Participants were asked to respond to questions such as "the hard stone as of the plum or cherry, which contains the seed is called the p____." Retrieval of the correct answer (pit) reduced TOT probability when the participant subsequently attempted to identify a photo of a celebrity whose name was a homophone of the word for the object (Brad Pitt). Presumably the phonological representation of *Pitt* was primed by retrieval of *pit*, which meant that less activation was required to retrieve *Brad Pitt* in response to his photograph. These findings can be explained in terms of the transmission deficit hypothesis, and also suggest that the phonological representations of proper names may be shared with those of homophonous common names.

THE VOLUME OF TOT STATES FOR PEOPLE'S NAMES

The evidence reviewed so far suggests strong parallels between TOT states for the names of people and TOT states for common object names. Indeed, the sequential model of face naming that Bruce and Young (1986) put forward was functionally identical to the model they proposed for object naming. However, a series of classic diary studies provided a challenge to this account by reporting evidence that attempts to retrieve the names of people elicited disproportionately large numbers of TOTs.

The first study was by Reason and Lucas (1984), who asked their participants to keep records of situations in which TOTs occurred in the course of everyday life. Although Reason and Lucas's diarists recorded retrieval failures for both common and proper names, as many as 77 percent of their reported TOTs were for proper names. Burke and colleagues (1991) conducted a similar study and showed that 58 percent of the TOTs reported by young participants (mean = 19 years) were for proper names compared to 35 percent for abstract words with only 7 percent for object names. For older adults, the proportion of TOTs that were recorded for proper names rose to 69 percent. In Cohen and Faulkner's (1986) diary study, participants were asked to record only proper name TOTs with the intent to compare whether retrieval failures were equally divided across different types of proper names. For all age groups, more than 80 percent of these proper name TOTs occurred for the names of people. Only around 10 percent of TOTs reported by young and mid-age groups were for place names, with even fewer recorded for brand names and book titles. TOTs for the names of people were also by far the most common type of proper name TOT in Burke and colleagues' (1991) diary study. It therefore appears that problems with proper name retrieval are confined to the names of people.

Although the preponderance of TOTs for names of people in these diary studies is very striking, it is also important to demonstrate differences between retrieval failures for names of people and common names under laboratory conditions. If, for example, participants tend to make more attempts to recall difficult proper names in the course of everyday life compared to attempts to recall difficult common names, then more TOTs are likely to be reported even if proper names are as easy to recall as common names.

In one experimental study, Burke and colleagues (1991) found that more TOTs were produced for names of people or places than for names of common objects by older, but not by younger, participants. Rastle and Burke (1996) obtained similar results. However, neither study controlled for the possibility of familiarity differences between the sets of proper and common names, so they may have chosen a relatively difficult set of common objects. Evrard (2002) showed participants a set of pictures of famous people and common objects that were matched for familiarity, and participants of all ages experienced many more TOTs in response to the faces than the objects. Nevertheless, Evrard did not report the number of correct retrievals, so her results do not necessarily reflect a retrieval difficulty for people's names (cf. Schwartz & Frazier, 2005).

These methodological problems were avoided by Hanley (2011a, Experiment 1), who asked participants to name a set of photographs of 40 objects and 40 famous faces. The objects and the faces were matched for familiarity, as were their names. Hanley examined both the number of TOTs and the number of correct retrievals associated with the objects and faces. The TOT rate was significantly higher for the faces (13%) than for the objects (7%). Moreover, the percentage of objects that were correctly named was significantly higher for objects (50%) than for faces (43%) by a similar margin.

It appears reasonable to conclude from the available empirical evidence that attempts to retrieve names of people do genuinely elicit a significantly higher proportion of TOTs than attempts to retrieve common names. Why should this be the case? The Bruce and Young (1986) model provides no obvious reason why people's names should be particularly susceptible to transmission deficits.

PHONOLOGICAL DIFFICULTIES WITH RETRIEVAL OF PEOPLE'S NAMES

A possible answer to this question was provided by Brennen's (1993) "plausible phonology" hypothesis. Brennen claimed that the number of different possible phonological forms is much larger for proper names than for common names because a person's name can comprise virtually any phonotactically legal word or nonword. As a consequence, he argued, it is relatively difficult to generate the correct phonology for a proper name. Brennen's arguments suggest that the phonological neighborhood is likely to be denser for common names than proper names. His viewpoint derives some support from the findings of Harley and Brown (1998), who observed that words from dense phonological neighborhoods were associated with fewer TOTs than words from sparse neighborhoods. It appears that the segments that words share with their phonological neighbors activate each other during word production and reduce the number of TOTs that are experienced. It is therefore possible that a denser phonological neighborhood for common names plays a role in reducing the number of TOTs for common names relative to names of people.

AN EXTRA STAGE OF PROCESSING FOR PEOPLE'S NAMES?

Burke and colleagues (1991), as well as Valentine, Brennen, and Brédart (1996), suggest that there is something unusual about the way proper names (i.e., people) are represented within the cognitive system relative to other kinds of words. To these authors, however, it is the lexical-semantic rather than the phonological features of proper names that makes them particularly vulnerable to retrieval problems.

Valentine and colleagues argued that a proper name is a noun that designates a "*unique* being or thing." This definition includes the names of people (e.g., *Barak Obama*), geographical names (e.g., *Everest*), unique objects (e.g., *Titanic*), individual animals (e.g., *Dumbo*), newspapers (e.g., *The Times*), song titles (e.g., *Summertime*), and single events (e.g., *D-Day*).

A common name, conversely, denotes a set of items that are similar in at least one respect. A day of the week (e.g., *Monday*) or month of the year (e.g., *January*), a brand name (e.g., *Kellogg's*), and an annual event (e.g., *Wimbledon Championships*) were therefore all considered by Valentine and colleagues to be common names rather than proper names. But the difference is not simply that proper names reference a unique being or thing because the term *Queen of England* refers to a specific individual without being a proper name. Following Mill (1843), philosophers such as Kripke (1980) have argued that proper names are *pure referring expressions*. Technically, this term means that proper names have reference but not sense. That is, they pick out an individual (reference) without providing additional information about any of the characteristics that this individual possesses (sense). A proper name is associated with an individual simply because it was assigned to them at birth. Conversely, a common name such as *a door* or *Queen of England* is attributed to an object or person by virtue of the semantic and/or physical features that they possess.

Of course a proper name such as *Carpenter* has meaningful associations such as *works with wood*. But although these associations are crucial when *carpenter* is used as a common name for an occupation, they are irrelevant when *Carpenter* is a person's name. Take, for example, the following epitaph next to an English lawyer's grave:

> *Sir John Strange: Here lies an honest lawyer,*
> *And that is Strange.*

This epitaph is only amusing because the semantic associations of a person's name are not normally taken into consideration when the qualities of the person are being discussed. Consistent with this viewpoint, psychologists such as McWeeny, Young, Hay, and Ellis (1987) and McCluney and Krauter (1997) have argued that such associations are routinely ignored when *Carpenter* is learned as a person's name. McWeeny and colleagues suggest that it would be confusing to believe "Ms Carpenter might really be a carpenter" (1987, p. 148). As the philosopher Coates points out, even the association of a proper name with a feature such as the male gender is not logically secure. "If I call my daughter Archibald, it is hard luck on her, but I have committed no sin against logic or semantics, and it will be her name" (2009, p. 435). Of course these considerations do not apply to names of people in cultures where they *do* have meaning and can change to reflect altered personal circumstances, such as becoming a parent (see Griffin, 2010, for further details).

Valentine and colleagues (1996) argued that there is a direct link between the philosophical literature on proper names and the number of retrieval

failures that names of people elicit. They claimed that it is the senseless-
ness of proper names that makes them vulnerable to TOT experiences.
Consistent with the node structure model of Burke and colleagues (1991),
they suggested that the lexical representation of a common name such as
bush is directly associated in semantic memory with each of the cluster
of features that represent its meaning (e.g., *plant, branches, smaller than a
tree*). Because proper names lack sense, however, the lexical representation
of a proper name such as *George Bush* (Sr.) is not directly linked to any
semantic features (e.g., *U.S. president, Republican Party*). Instead, it only
has links to a single abstract node (the "*proper name phrase*") that serves as
a hidden unit between the semantic feature nodes and the lexical node (for
further details, see Valentine et al., 1996, p. 106; Burke et al., 2004, p. 165).
According to Valentine and colleagues, the lexical node for *George Bush*
(Sr.) is vulnerable to a transmission deficit because it can only be activated
directly by one other node in the production system. Conversely, the lexical
node for a common name such as *bush* is more accessible because it can be
directly activated by any of the semantic features with which it is associated. In summary, Valentine and Burke and their colleagues argue that an
additional level of processing is required to produce proper names, and this
makes them more vulnerable to transmission deficits and retrieval failures
than common names.

ABSENCE OF ALTERNATIVES TO PEOPLE'S NAMES

A different explanation was put forward by Brédart, who argued that "face
naming is difficult because of the simple fact that it requires the retrieval of
one particular label, whereas object naming may allow for the use of syn-
onyms or labels from other relevant levels of categorisation of the object"
(1993, p. 364). A similar view was expressed by Maylor, who argued that "if
a name retrieval failure occurs to an object, it is often possible to substitute a reasonably accurate alternative word or phrase. However, this is not
the case for people's names; hence, proper name retrieval failures are more
noticeable, frustrating, and difficult to circumvent" (1997, p. 213).

Brédart (1993) provided some support for this view by showing that
participants reported fewer retrieval failures when they were allowed to
name actors' faces using either their real name or the name of the character
that they were playing in the cue photograph (e.g., *Harrison Ford/Indiana
Jones*). It might appear that this explanation was contradicted by Bonin,
Perret, Meot, Ferrand, and Mermillod's (2008) finding that faces with low
name agreement were associated with more TOTs than faces with high

name agreement. However Bonin and colleagues' measure of name agreement comprised the sum of the correct name plus all incorrect names that participants produced when attempting naming a particular famous face. This measure does not, therefore, provide a test of Brédart's account.

The results of Hanley's (2011a, Exp. 1) study provided further support for Brédart and Maylor's position because the incorrect responses that participants made to objects were mostly semantically related alternates, whereas incorrect responses to faces were mostly *don't know* responses. If TOTs were not reported for objects because a semantically related alternate was recalled instead, then the number of possible TOTs for common names that were actually recorded would be substantially reduced. Consistent with Brédart's account, differences between TOTs for common and proper names disappeared in Hanley's second experiment in which a set of common names that generated relatively few alternatives was used. One possible explanation for the large number of TOTs that are associated with the recall of names of people, therefore, is that they refer so precisely to the individual they represent that retrieval failures cannot be disguised by the recall of a semantically similar alternative.

AGING AND TOT STATES FOR PROPER NAMES

Is there evidence that the disproportionate number of TOTs associated with retrieval of people's names relative to common names becomes more severe as people get older? Addressing the first part of this question, there is clear evidence that older people produce more TOTs for people's names than younger participants. Maylor (1990) asked participants to name a set of famous faces and found that older adults (mean age = 76 years) produced more TOTs and fewer correct recalls than did younger adults. Nevertheless, the older adults also knew fewer semantic facts about these celebrities, so the additional TOTs could have reflected poor knowledge about the people rather than a specific problem with their names. In a subsequent study, however, James (2006) found that older participants produced more TOTs and fewer correct recalls of names of celebrities than did younger participants, even though they identified an equivalent number of people by occupation. Furthermore, Cross and Burke (2004) found that older adults were more likely to report TOT states and were less likely than younger adults to recall the names of famous people even though the number of "don't know" (DK) responses was equivalent for the younger and older participants.

Participants also tend to experience more TOT states for common names as they get older (e.g., Heine, Ober, & Shenaut, 1999). Is there any evidence that aging disproportionately affects retrieval of names of people? Burke and colleagues' (1991) diary study compared the number of TOTs that were reported by participants classified as young and older. The results showed that the older adults produced more TOTs for both objects and people's names than did younger participants. In Burke and colleagues' subsequent experimental study, however, older people experienced a significantly greater number of TOTs for people's names but no more TOTs for object names or place names than the younger participants. Rastle and Burke (1996) found that the age group difference on the number of TOTs was twice as large for proper names (names of people and places) as for common names. Although Rendell, Castell, and Craik (2005) did not ask participants to indicate TOTs, their older participants recalled the names of significantly fewer people that they claimed to know than did younger participants. There was no corresponding difference for the names of objects even though the objects and names were matched for familiarity.

There appears, therefore, to be strong evidence that older adults experience differentially more retrieval problems than younger adults during attempts to recall people's names. Moreover, although older adults also report more TOTs than younger adults during common name retrieval, the problem appears to be more severe for names of people. There is no evidence of an equivalent problem with the names of places. Some researchers have argued that older adults may experience more TOTs of all kinds because they have increased semantic knowledge and so have more opportunities to experience retrieval failures of this kind (cf. Schwartz & Frazier, 2005). This does not appear to be the case with TOTs for the names of people because, as we have seen, they seem to occur more frequently in older participants even when the familiarity of the test items is matched across age of participant. This conclusion is consistent with Bahrick, Hall, and Baker (2013), who provide evidence that older adults are less able to access their available knowledge of familiar people's names than are younger adults. Crucially, Bahrick and colleagues' analyses revealed no differences as a function of age in this availability/accessibility ratio for other types of vocabulary.

There is also evidence that older individuals with mild cognitive impairment (MCI), in the early prodromal stages of Alzheimer's disease, have particular problems in producing proper names. Ahmed, Arnold, Thompson, Graham, and Hodges (2008) showed that individuals with MCI were worse at recalling the names of famous people, buildings, and landmarks than the names of common objects. Juncos-Rabadán, Rodriguez, Facal, Cuba, and Pereiro (2011) showed that these problems with the retrieval of people's names were associated with significantly more TOTs in individuals with

MCI than in a group of age-matched controls. In contrast, there was no evidence of any corresponding differences in the ease with which the MCI and control groups could access semantic information about famous people. The increased number of TOTs appears, therefore, to reflect a deficit in MCI in the retrieval of phonological information from the semantic representations of familiar people.

Might age-related retrieval difficulties reflect atrophy in areas of the brain that are involved in retrieval of people's names? Using voxel-based morphometry, a technique used to assess brain volume, Shafto, Burke, Stamatkakis, Tam, and Tyler (2007) found a strong relationship between the number of TOTs that participants experienced when attempting to name pictures of famous people and atrophy of the insula in the left hemisphere. Moreover, there was a strong negative correlation between brain volume in this area and number of TOTs even when the effects of aging were partialed out. Important, PET studies (Tranel, 2009) with normal participants have shown maximal activation in Brodmann area 38 in the left temporal pole during retrieval of people's names, and this area is known to be strongly interconnected with the insula. There is also evidence that surgical removal of the uncinate fasciculus in patients with temporal gliomas leads to problems in proper name retrieval (Papagno et al., 2011). Intriguingly, the uncinate fasciculus has close connections with both the temporal pole and insula. If these areas form a circuit that is disproportionately involved in recalling names of people, then associated atrophy of these areas in older adults might explain why they experience more TOTs for names of people.

Unfortunately, however, Tranel's (2009) suggestion that areas of the left temporal pole are *selectively* involved in the retrieval of names of people and other proper names such as landmarks is not particularly convincing at the present time. For example, evidence from lesion studies in aphasia indicates that the left temporal pole also plays an important role in activating lexical representations during object naming (Schwartz et al., 2009). In Papagno and colleagues' (2011) study, removal of the uncinate fasciculus appeared to have a significant detrimental effect on both object and face naming. It is possible that similar areas of the brain would have been implicated in Shafto and colleagues' (2007) study if participants had been asked to report TOTs for pictures of objects.

A plausible alternative explanation arises from the suggestion that there are separate semantic systems for objects and people (e.g., Gentileschi, Sperber, & Spinnler, 2001; Kay & Hanley, 1999; Miceli et al., 2000). There is considerable neuropsychological evidence (cf. Hanley, 2011b) that patients with semantic deficits associated with right anterior temporal lobe lesions tend to experience more problems in retrieving semantic information about people than about objects, whereas patients with left temporal lobe damage are more likely to experience such problems for objects than for people. Consistent with this claim, Ross, McCoy, Wolk, Coslett, and Olson (2010) found that transcranial stimulation of the right anterior temporal lobes in neurologically normal adults below 40 years of age significantly improved the accuracy of the naming of famous people, but not landmarks. In contrast, stimulation of the left anterior temporal lobes had no effect. According to Semenza (2006), proper name anomia in stroke patients occurs as a consequence of a lesion that disconnects the semantic system for people from representations of names in the left hemisphere. If the connections between the right anterior temporal lobes and the left temporal pole are particularly vulnerable to age-related atrophy, then it would follow that older people might experience more retrieval failures for the names of familiar people than for the names of objects. One way of investigating this possibility would be to examine the effect that transcranial stimulation of the right anterior temporal lobes might have on recall of people's names in an older population. In conclusion, though, it must be acknowledged that the precise reason older adults experience a disproportionate number of TOTs for names of people remains an open question.

FREQUENCY AND TOT STATES FOR PROPER NAMES

In Cohen and Faulkner's (1986) diary study, 71 percent of TOTs occurred for names that were considered well known. In Reason and Lucas's (1984) diary study, 74 percent of names associated with TOTs were considered "very" or "moderately" familiar. The mean familiarity rating of proper names associated with TOTs in Burke and colleagues' (1991) study was 3.4 (on a 7-point scale) by young participants and 4.8 for older participants.

A simple explanation of these findings is that unless a person is at least moderately familiar to us, we may not know their name and so cannot experience a genuine TOT when attempting to identify them. Cohen (1990) suggested, instead, that there might be *a reverse frequency* effect in proper name retrieval such that more TOTs are experienced for well-known than less familiar names. Cohen attempted to explain reverse frequency in terms of the *fan effect*. According to the fan effect, an association with multiple units within a semantic network increases competition among these units. Because more facts will be stored about more familiar people, it should become more difficult to recall any one of these facts, such as their name.

Consequently, Cohen argued, there are likely to be more TOTs for the names of highly familiar people.

As Harley and Bown's (1998) participants reported more TOTs for object names of low than high familiarity, such an outcome would be extremely striking. In fact, a number of findings cast doubt on Cohen's suggestion. First, Burke and colleagues' (1991) diary study suggested that names that had not been used frequently or for a long time were more likely to elicit TOTs than more familiar names. Second, participants in experimental studies by Brédart (1996) and by Bonin and colleagues (2008) reported more TOTs for names of lower than higher familiarity. Finally, using calculations devised by Gollan and Brown (2006) that make it possible to examine the number of TOTs in relation to the number of correct retrievals, Hanley and Chapman (2008) showed that low familiarity names were more susceptible to phonological retrieval failure than names of higher familiarity. Although highly familiar names are sometimes associated with TOTs, there is therefore no convincing evidence of a reverse frequency effect for retrieval failures for the names of people.

Further evidence about the role of familiarity in preventing retrieval failures for names of people emerges from research on TOTs that bilinguals experience. The opposite pattern of performance from that seen in older adults can be observed in bilingual adults. Relative to monolinguals, bilinguals experience *more* TOTs for the names of objects (Roberts, Garcia, Desrochers, & Hernandez, 2002) but *fewer* TOTs for the names of people (Gollan, Bonanni, & Montoya, 2005). Gollan and colleagues (2005) argue that bilinguals experience more TOT states and recall fewer names of pictured objects than monolinguals because they have less practice than monolinguals in recalling the name of an object in any one language, resulting from objects often being represented by a different word in different languages. Gollan and colleagues suggested that these differences disappear for the recall of proper names because the same proper name is almost always used to refer to a particular person in different languages. Bilinguals will therefore have just as much experience as monolinguals retrieving the name of *Bill Clinton* because he has the same name in English as in most other languages.

OTHER VARIABLES THAT INFLUENCE THE NUMBER OF TOTS FOR PEOPLE'S NAMES

Bonin and colleagues (2008) asked participants to name a set of photographs of 110 famous faces and noted the number of TOTs that each face elicited. They asked different sets of participants to rate the names of the celebrities in terms of age of acquisition (AoA) and subjective frequency. Participants also rated the faces for distinctiveness and for the quality of the likeness of the photograph. As noted earlier, they also measured the number of different names (correct plus incorrect) each face elicited. All of these dimensions were significantly correlated with the number of reported TOTs. Unfortunately, these variables were all inter-correlated, so it is difficult to know how many of them play an important causal role in eliciting TOTs.

Bonin and colleagues (2008) also found a significant correlation between the number of phonemes in a word and the number of reported TOTs. Interesting, phoneme length correlated with none of the other variables apart from number of different names, so it appears that longer names may well cause more retrieval failures than shorter names. Hanley and Chapman's (2008) results were consistent with this conclusion. They asked participants to retrieve the names of celebrities whose names comprised either three words (e.g., *Catherine Zeta Jones*) or two words (e.g., *Gwyneth Paltrow*). They found that names of celebrities that contain three words were associated with more TOTs than names of celebrities that contain two words. If TOT states reflect problems with the phonological retrieval of people's names, then it is not surprising that phonological representations that contain more units or more phonemes would be the source of a greater number of retrieval failures.

BLOCKING AS A CAUSE OF TOTS

An alternative to the transmission deficit account of the etiology of TOTs is the blocking hypothesis. Blocking is said to occur when retrieval of a target word is suppressed by activation of a competitor, sometimes called an interloper. As Brown (2012) points out, the blocking hypothesis has a long tradition of support within experimental psychology. Colorful examples of situations in which interlopers are retrieved have been provided by Cohen and Faulkner (1986) and Reason and Lucas (1984). For example, one of Cohen and Faulkner's diarists retrieved a number of phonological neighbors (Keller, Klemperer, Kellet, Kendler) of the name that they were trying to retrieve (Kepler).

However, there is very little research to indicate that blocking is a reliable cause of TOTs for the names of people. Cross and Burke (2004) prompted their participants to generate the name of a fictional character, such as *Eliza Doolittle* from *My Fair Lady*. They then investigated whether recall of this name would block retrieval of the name of an actress who is well known for playing *Eliza Doolittle* (Audrey Hepburn). In fact, Cross and Burke's results indicated that this manipulation had no effect on the number of TOTs and actually reduced the number of incorrect retrievals. As appears to be the case with TOTs in general (e.g., Kornell & Metcalfe, 2006), there is no clear evidence that interlopers are a cause rather than a consequence of the retrieval problems that accompany a TOT experience.

FAMILIAR-ONLY STATES

A different type of metacognitive state that occurs when a familiar face cannot be identified is known as a *familiar-only state*. Young and colleagues (1985) asked 22 participants to keep a diary of all the problems that they had encountered in person recognition over an eight-week period. Approximately a quarter of the 922 incidents occurred when someone was felt to be familiar but no further information about the person could be recalled. In other words, the face rang a bell, but the participant was unable to place the person. This is quite different from what participants experience during a TOT state because, as we have seen, semantic information about the person can be readily accessed during a TOT. Just more than half of the people who had elicited the familiar-only experiences were subsequently identified by Young and colleagues' diarists. It turned out that the people concerned were often of relatively low familiarity and were seen in a context in which they were not usually encountered. For example, "I was at the theatre when I saw someone in the audience I thought I knew. I didn't know who she was till I saw her with her sister and parents who I know better" (Young et al., 1985, p. 506).

Familiar-only experiences are also observed in laboratory studies of the errors that participants experience when attempting to identify photos of famous faces (Hanley & Cowell, 1988; Hay et al., 1991). Hay and colleagues' participants attributed their failure to place the person to a variety of causes. Either the exposure in the experiment was too brief (39%), the photo was a bad likeness (29%), there was no link in their memory between the face and additional information about the person (13%), context was missing in the photograph (11%), or the person had not been encountered recently (8%). Interestingly, "no link" was the only attribution participants used to explain a retrieval failure for the name of a familiar face when able to recall semantic information about the person. There were no claims that name retrieval failures of this kind were related to missing context, bad likenesses, or brief exposures.

Hanley and Cowell (1988) and Young and colleagues (1985) argued that familiar-only states reflect a breakdown in the connection between face recognition units that represent the visual features of familiar faces and the person-identity nodes that store semantic information about familiar people. Familiar-only states, therefore, occur earlier in the recognition system than the transmission deficit between the semantic system and the phonological representation of the name that is the putative cause of a TOT. Hanley and Cowell showed that presenting a participant with a retrieval cue that contained semantic information about the person was particularly useful in resolving a familiar-only state and allowing successful recall of the person's name. Conversely, consistent with the results of Brennen and colleagues (1990), when participants had already recalled detailed information about a familiar face, as in a TOT state, it was the person's initials that resolved the most name retrieval failures.

Nevertheless, familiar-only experiences occur relatively rarely during attempts to recognize the faces of familiar people. Hay and colleagues estimated that in 94 percent of trials where a famous face was found familiar, the participant successfully recalled semantic information about the person. As Hay and colleagues put it, once a face has been recognized, "the system is extremely efficient in accessing semantic information" (1991, p. 779) about the person. When famous voices are presented instead of faces, however, significantly more familiar-only experiences are reported (Hanley, Smith, & Hadfield, 1997). Not surprisingly, voice identification was much more difficult than face identification, so the larger number of familiar-only responses may be an automatic consequence of the lower hit rate in the voice condition. Even when voices are judged to be of very high familiarity, however, there are still more familiar-only responses to voices than faces. Moreover, Hanley and Damjanovic (2009) and Brédart, Barsics, and Hanley (2009) showed that, as long as a voice cannot be identified on the basis of the content of the message, similar results are obtained even when hit rates are equated in the face and voice conditions by blurring the faces. It appears that semantic information is particularly difficult to retrieve from familiar voices relative to familiar faces.

There is no evidence of such modality effects on the number of TOTs that are experienced with faces and voices. Hanley and Damjanovic (2009) showed that as long as semantic information was successfully recalled about a familiar person, the correct name could be recalled equally often in the face and voice conditions. Presumably, the modality effect on the number of familiar-only responses arises because there are weaker connections between the semantic system and the recognition units for voices than between the semantic system and the face recognition units. Conversely, there are no modality effects associated with TOT experiences because

TOTs reflect a retrieval problem that occurs after the voice and face recognition systems have converged into a single person recognition system.

In conclusion, several striking differences exist between familiar-only states and TOT experiences. Unlike TOTs, familiar-only experiences are more likely to occur when a person is encountered out of context and are more common with voices than faces. In addition, different types of retrieval cues are effective in resolving familiar-only experiences (semantic information about the person) compared to resolving TOT states (initials of the person concerned). It therefore appears that familiar-only experiences represent a qualitatively different metacognitive state from TOT experiences.

FEELINGS OF KNOWING FOR THE NAMES OF FACES

Feeling-of-knowing (FOK) experiences (Hart, 1965) are metacognitive states in which an individual can indicate that they would be able to recognize the answer to a question or recognize the name of an object or face even though they are currently unable to recall it. A feeling of knowing differs from a TOT state in that in an FOK there is no requirement that the elusive name feels as if it is about to be recalled.

Relatively little research has looked specifically at FOK experiences for the names of people. An exception is a study by Hosey, Peynircioglu, and Rabinovitz (2009) in which participants were asked to give FOK ratings when they were unable to recall the names of either pre-experimentally familiar or unfamiliar faces. Hosey and colleagues also asked their participants to indicate whether they attributed their positive FOK ratings to a feeling of familiarity with the face or to the recall of a piece of information about the face. Results showed that FOK ratings were equally predictive of correct recognition regardless of whether participants could or could not retrieve a piece of information about the person. Nevertheless, participants were more likely to give a higher FOK rating when they were basing their decision on retrieval of a fact about the person rather than on a feeling of familiarity. This finding suggests that FOKs are probably not based entirely on the strength of the feeling of familiarity.

On the basis of this study, it would appear that feelings of knowing are likely to arise when a participant is experiencing either a TOT or a familiar-only experience for a person they have recognized. However, Hosey and colleagues did not ask participants to report TOT experiences, nor did they report whether it was possible to have a familiar-only experience without having an FOK. Consequently, the relationship between familiar-only responses, TOTs, and FOKs for familiar names requires further investigation.

According to dual-process accounts (e.g., Mandler, 1980), recognition memory in list-learning tasks can occur on the basis of either *familiarity* or *retrieval* (now more commonly referred to as *recollection*). According to Mandler, recognition on the basis of familiarity involves making a decision according to the strength of the feeling of familiarity that the word arouses independent of the context in which it appears. Recollection that a word in a recognition test was recently presented requires the ability to retrieve some episodic detail associated with the original encounter with the word when it appeared as part of the to-be-remembered list. Following Gardiner (1988), participants in recognition memory experiments are sometimes asked to indicate whether recognition occurred on the basis of recollection (referred to as a *remember response*) or familiarity (referred to as a *know response*).

Experiments of this kind often use familiar-only experiences as examples of know responses in the instructions to participants. Perhaps this is because Mandler (1980) used the example of a familiar-only experience to explain what he meant by familiarity without retrieval. He described a situation in which an individual might encounter his or her butcher on the bus and at first fail to retrieve information about who the butcher was despite feeling sure that this was a person he or she had seen before.

Unfortunately, the analogy between know responses and familiar-only experiences is misleading. In a recognition memory experiment, a participant is never expected to make a response on the basis that the item feels familiar, as in a familiar-only experience. Generally, all of the words in a recognition memory test are familiar to the participant, and a "know" decision is presumably made on the basis that the word feels more familiar than had it not been presented at encoding. Furthermore, many situations in which it is possible to retrieve information about a familiar person such as their name and where they are typically encountered are also examples of "know" responses. This is because a "remember" response would require retrieval of episodic information about the person concerned. This point has been made clearly by Westmacott and Moscovitch (2003), Damjanovic and Hanley (2007), and Barsics and Brédart (2011), who all showed that even when we can fully identify a famous person, we are often unable to recall from our autobiographical memory a specific episode in which that person appears.

INFERENTIAL V DIRECT ACCESS ACCOUNTS OF TOT STATES

Following the inclination of many other researchers who are interested in person recognition, this chapter has adopted the *direct access* account of TOT states. That is, identification errors such as TOTs and familiar-only experiences are interpreted as reflecting breakdowns at specific processing stages within a cognitive model. Indeed, errors such as TOTs have been used as a major source of evidence in the development of theories of face and person identification, such as the models put forward by Bruce and Young (1986) and Burke and colleagues (1991).

Nevertheless, it must be acknowledged that the direct access approach to the etiology of TOTs is not universally accepted (e.g., Schwartz & Metcalfe, 2011). Some researchers instead adopt an alternative perspective known as the *inferential* account, where TOTs do not necessarily reflect a transmission deficit in which there is insufficient activation of the phonological representation of a word to allow recall. From this perspective, TOTs do not provide a window through which we can gain insight into the underlying cognitive mechanisms involved in word production. Instead, a TOT for a familiar person may arise as a simple consequence of recalling information about that individual, whether correct or incorrect, but being unable to recall their name. The subjective experience associated with a TOT may spur further retrieval attempts for the elusive name.

Evidence taken as support for the inferential view is that participants sometimes report illusory TOTs, defined as a TOT state for an item that does not exist, such as an invented object or fictitious person (e.g., Schwartz, Travis, Castro, & Smith, 2000). According to the inferential view, a transmission deficit cannot be operating here because the participant logically cannot have either a phonological or semantic representation of a nonexistent word. Consistent with the direct access view, however, Hay and colleagues (1991) showed that retrieval of semantic information about a person whose name cannot be recalled does not necessarily lead to the experience of a name retrieval block. Retrieval failures only occurred when the participant subsequently indicated that they knew the person's name.

As Brown (2012) has argued, the evidence seems to be stronger for the direct access rather than the inferential approach to TOTs. The success of models of person recognition that have adopted a direct access approach to retrieval errors for the names of people (cf. Bruce & Young, 1986) is certainly consistent with Brown's conclusion. However, the existence of illusory TOTs means that it would be incautious to assume that all TOTs for people's names reflect a transmission deficit. It seems highly likely that, for example, some reported TOTs for people's names are instead the result of demand characteristics, strong feelings of knowing or familiar-only states.

CONCLUSION

In conclusion, a large body of research can be readily explained in terms of the transmission deficit hypothesis whereby TOTs for people's names occur because there is insufficient activation of phonological nodes to allow recall to take place (Bruce & Young, 1986; Burke et al., 1991). Familiar-only responses appear to reflect a problem earlier in the processing system, in which semantic nodes are not activated sufficiently strongly to allow biographical information about a person to be retrieved. There is also clear evidence that TOT experiences are more likely to occur for the names of people than for the names of objects and that these problems become increasingly severe in old age. There is, however, no evidence that other types of proper names, such as geographical locations, are associated with the same volume of TOTs as names of people, although relatively little work on proper name retrieval has looked at anything other than recall of people's names.

There is currently no universally accepted explanation of exactly why there are so many retrieval failures for people's names. According to some theorists, there is something unusual about the phonological (Brennen, 1993) or lexical representations of proper names (Burke et al., 1991; Valentine et al., 1996) that makes them particularly susceptible to transmission deficits. There is, however, no independent empirical evidence to support that these claims. A plausible alternative is that people's names refer so precisely to the individual they represent that TOTs cannot be side-stepped by the recall of a semantically similar alternative (Brédart, 1993; Hanley, 2011a; Maylor, 1997). But even if this account is true, it does not provide an explanation of why retrieval problems for people's names are so much greater in old age.

REFERENCES

Ahmed, S., Arnold, R., Thompson, S. A., Graham, K. S., & Hodges J. R. (2008). Naming of objects, faces and buildings in mild cognitive impairment. *Cortex*, 44, 746–752.
Bahrick, H. P., Hall, L. K., & Baker, M. K. (2013). *Life-span maintenance of knowledge* (essays in cognitive psychology). Hove, UK: Psychology Press.

Barsics, C., & Brédart, S. (2011). Recalling episodic information about personally known faces and voices. *Consciousness & Cognition, 20,* 303–308.

Bonin, P., Perret, C., Meot, A., Ferrand, L., & Mermillod, M. (2008). Psycholinguistic norms and face naming times for photographs of celebrities in French. *Behavior Research Methods, 40,* 137–146.

Brédart, S. (1993). Retrieval failures in face naming. *Memory, 1,* 351–366.

Brédart, S., Barsics, C., & Hanley, R. (2009). Recalling semantic information about personally known faces and voices. *European Journal of Cognitive Psychology, 21,* 1013–1021.

Brennen, T (1993). The difficulty with recalling people's names: The plausible phonology hypothesis. *Memory, 1,* 409–431.

Brennen, T., Baguley, T., Bright, J., & Bruce, V. (1990). Resolving semantically induced tip-of-the-tongue states for proper nouns. *Memory and Cognition, 18,* 339–347.

Brown, A. S. (2011). *The tip of the tongue state.* Hove, UK: Psychology Press.

Brown, R., & McNeill, D. (1966). The "tip of the tongue" phenomenon. *Journal of Verbal Learning and Verbal Behaviour, 5,* 325–337.

Bruce, V., & Young, A. W. (1986). Understanding face recognition. *British Journal of Psychology, 77,* 305–327.

Burke, D., Locantore, J. K., Austin, A., & Chae, B. (2004). Cherry pit primes Brad Pitt: Homophone priming effects on young and older adults' production of proper names. *Psychological Science, 15,* 164–170.

Burke, D., Mackay, D. G., Worthley, J. S., & Wade, E. (1991). On the tip-of-the-tongue: What causes word-finding failures by young and older adults? *Journal of Memory & Language, 30,* 542–579.

Cleary, A. M., & Specker, L. E. (2007). Recognition without face identification. *Memory & Cognition, 35,* 1610–1619.

Coates, R. (2009). A strictly Millian approach to the definition of the proper name. *Mind & Language, 24,* 433–434.

Cohen, G. (1990). Why is it difficult to put names to faces? *British Journal of Psychology, 81,* 287–297.

Cohen, G., & Faulkner, D. (1986). Memory for proper names: Age differences in retrieval. *British Journal of Developmental Psychology, 4,* 187–197.

Craigie, M., & Hanley, J. R. (1993). Access to visual information from a name is contingent on access to identity specific semantic information. *Memory, 1,* 367–391.

(1997). Putting faces to names. *British Journal of Psychology, 88,* 157–171.

Cross, E., & Burke, D. M. (2004). Do alternative names block young and older adults' retrieval of proper names? *Brain & Language, 89,* 174–181.

Damjanovic, L., & Hanley, J. R. (2007). Recalling episodic and semantic information about famous faces and voices. *Memory & Cognition, 35,* 1205–1210.

Evrard, M. (2002). Aging and lexical access to common and proper names in picture naming. *Brain and Language, 81,* 174–179.

Gardiner, J. M. (1988). Functional aspects of recollective experience. *Memory & Cognition, 16,* 309–313.

Gentileschi, V., Sperber, S., & Spinnler, H. (2001). Crossmodal agnosia for familiar people as a consequence of right infero-polar temporal atrophy. *Cognitive Neuropsychology, 18,* 439–463.

Gollan, T. H., & Brown, A. S. (2006). From tip-of-the-tongue (TOT) data to theoretical implications in two steps: When more TOTs means better retrieval. *Journal of Experimental Psychology: General*, 135, 462–483.

Gollan, T. H., Bonanni, M. P., & Montoya, R. I. (2005). Proper names get stuck on bilingual and monolingual speakers' tip of the tongue equally often. *Neuropsychology*, 19, 278–287.

Griffin, Z. M. (2010). Retrieving personal names, referring expressions, and terms of address. *The Psychology of Learning and Motivation*, 53, 345–387.

Hanley, J. R. (2011a). Why are people's names associated with so many phonological retrieval failures? *Psychonomic Bulletin & Review*, 18, 612–617.

(2011b). An appreciation of Bruce and Young's (1986) serial stage model of face naming after 25 years. *British Journal of Psychology*, 102, 915–930.

Hanley, J. R., & Chapman, E. (2008). Partial knowledge in a tip of the tongue state about two and three word proper names. *Psychonomic Bulletin & Review*, 15, 156–160.

Hanley, J. R., & Cowell, E. (1988). The effects of different types of retrieval cues on the recall of names of famous faces. *Memory & Cognition*, 16, 545–555.

Hanley, J. R., & Damjanovic, L. (2009). It is more difficult to retrieve a familiar person's name and occupation from their voice than from their blurred face. *Memory*, 17, 830–839.

Hanley, J. R., Smith, T., & Hadfield, J. (1998). I recognise you but I can't place you: An investigation of familiar-only experiences during tests of voice and face recognition. *The Quarterly Journal of Experimental Psychology*, 51A, 179–195.

Harley, T. A., & Bown, H. E. (1998). What causes a tip-of-the-tongue state? Evidence for lexical neighbourhood effects in speech production. *British Journal of Psychology*, 89, 151–174.

Hart, J. T. (1965). Memory and the feeling-of-knowing experience. *Journal of Educational Psychology*, 56, 208–216.

Hay, D. C., Young, A. W., & Ellis, A. W. (1991). Routes through the face recognition system. *Quarterly Journal of Experimental Psychology*, 43A, 761–791.

Heine, M. K., Ober, B. A., & Shenaut, G. K. (1999). Naturally occurring and experimenter induced tip-of-the-tongue experiences in three adult age groups. *Psychology and Aging*, 14, 445–457.

Hosey, L. A., Peynircioglu, Z. F., & Rabinovitz, B. E. (2009). Feeling of knowing for names in response to faces. *Acta Psychologia*, 130, 214–224.

James, L. E. (2006). Specific effects of aging on proper name retrieval: Now you see them, now you don't. *Journals of Gerontology Series: B-Psychological Sciences and Social Sciences*, 61, 180–183.

Juncos-Rabadán, O., Rodriguez, N., Facal, D., Cuba, J., & Pereiro, A. X. (2011) Tip-of-the-tongue for proper names in mild cognitive impairment: Semantic or post-semantic impairments? *Journal of Neurolinguistic Research*, 24, 636–651.

Kay, J., & Hanley, J. R. (1999). Person-specific knowledge and knowledge of biological categories. *Cognitive Neuropsychology*, 16, 171–180.

Kornell, N. & Metcalfe, J. (2006). "Blockers" do not block recall during tip-of-the-tongue states. *Metacognition and Learning*, 1, 248–261.

Kripke, S. (1980). *Naming and necessity*. Oxford: Blackwell.

McWeeny, K. H., Young, A. W., Hay, D. C., & Ellis, A. W. (1987). Putting names to faces. *British Journal of Psychology, 78,* 143–149.

McCluney, M. M., & Krauter, E. E. (1997). Mr Barber or a barber: Remembering names and occupations. *Psychological Reports, 81,* 847–863.

Mandler, G. (1980). Recognizing: The judgment of prior occurrence. *Psychological Review, 87,* 252–271.

Maylor, E. A. (1990). Age, blocking and the tip of the tongue state. *British Journal of Psychology, 81,* 123–134.

(1997). Proper name retrieval in old age: Converging evidence against disproportionate impairment. *Aging, Neuropsychology, and Cognition, 4,* 211–226.

Miceli, G., Capasso, R., Daniele, A., Esposito, T., Magarelli, M., & Tomaiuolo, F. (2000). Selective deficit for people's names following left temporal damage. *Cognitive Neuropsychology, 17,* 489–516.

Mill, J. S. (1843). *A system of logic.* London: Longmans.

Papagno, C., Miracapillo, C., Casarotti, A., Romero Lauro, L. J., Castellano, A., Falini, A., Casaceli, G., Fava, E., & Bello, L. (2011). What is the role of the uncinate fasciculus? Surgical removal and proper name retrieval. *Brain, 134,* 405–414.

Rastle, K. G., & Burke, D. M. (1996). Priming the tip of the tongue: Effects of prior processing on word retrieval in young and older adults. *Journal of Memory and Language, 35,* 586–605.

Reason, J. T., & Lucas, D. (1984). Using cognitive diaries to investigate naturally occurring memory blocks. In J. Harris & P. E. Morris (Eds.), *Everyday memory, actions and absentmindedness* (pp. 53–70). London: Academic Press.

Rendell, P. G., Castel, A. D., & Craik, F. I. M. (2005). Memory for proper names in old age: A disproportionate impairment. *Quarterly Journal of Experimental Psychology, 58A,* 54–71.

Roberts, P. M., Garcia, L. J., Desrochers, A., & Hernandez, D. (2002). English performance of proficient bilingual adults on the Boston Naming Test. *Aphasiology, 16,* 635–645.

Ross, L. A., McCoy, D., Wolk, D. A., Coslett, H. B., & Olson, I. R. (2010). Improved proper name recall by electrical stimulation of the anterior temporal lobes. *Neuropsychologia, 48,* 3671–3674.

Schwartz, B. L., & Frazier, J. D. (2005). Tip-of-the-tongue states and aging: Contrasting psycholinguistic and metacognitive perspectives. *The Journal of General Psychology, 132,* 377–391.

Schwartz, B. L., & Metcalfe, J. D. (2011). Tip-of-the-tongue states: retrieval behavior and experience. *Memory and Cognition, 39,* 737–749.

Schwartz, B. L., Travis, D. M., Castro, A. M., & Smith, S. M. (2000). The phenomenology of real and illusory tip-of-the-tongue states. *Memory and Cognition, 28,* 18–27.

Schwartz, M. F., Kimberg, D. Y., Walker, G. M., Faseyitan, O., Brecher, A., Dell, G. S., & Coslett, H. B. (2009). Anterior temporal involvement in semantic word retrieval: voxel-based lesion-symptom mapping evidence from aphasia. *Brain, 132,* 3411–3427.

Semenza, C. (2006). Retrieval pathways for common and proper names. *Cortex, 42,* 884–891.

Shafto, M. A., Burke, D. M., Stamatkakis, E. A., Tam, P. P., & Tyler, L. K. (2007) On the Tip-of-the-tongue: Neural correlates of increased word-finding failures in normal aging. *Journal of Cognitive Neuroscience*, 19, 2060–2070.

Tranel, D. (2009). The left temporal pole is important for retrieving words for unique concrete entities. *Aphasiology*, 23, 867–884.

Valentine, T., Brennen, T., & Brédart, S. (1996). *The cognitive psychology of proper names*. London: Routledge.

Westmacott, R., & Moscovitch, M. (2003). The contribution of autobiographical significance to semantic memory. *Memory & Cognition*, 31, 761–774.

Yarmey, A. D. (1973). I recognize your face but I don't remember your name: Further evidence on the tip-of-the-tongue phenomenon. *Memory & Cognition*, 1, 287–290.

Young, A. W., Hay, D. C., & Ellis, A. W. (1985). The faces that launched a thousand slips: everyday difficulties and errors in recognizing people. *British Journal of Psychology*, 76, 495–523.

5

The Effect of Tip-of-the-Tongue States on Other Cognitive Judgments

ANNE M. CLEARY, SHELLY R. STALEY, AND
KIMBERLY R. KLEIN

Since the publication of Brown and McNeill's (1966) seminal article on the topic, tip-of-the-tongue (TOT) states have been the focus of many empirical studies. In recent years, the heuristic-metacognitive approach has become an important theoretical approach to explaining the TOT phenomenon (see Schwartz, 2002, or Schwartz & Metcalfe, 2011, for a review). According to this account, TOTs can result from an inference or attribution based on the information available at the time that the target word fails to come to mind. For example, people may infer that the target word is in memory based on the availability of other related information (e.g., Schwartz & Smith, 1997), or they may attribute the fluency or familiarity of the question or cue itself to the likelihood that the target word is in memory (e.g., Metcalfe, Schwartz, & Joaquim, 1993). The present chapter focuses on a TOT attribution effect of a different sort: the effect of TOT states themselves on other reported cognitive phenomena.

THE ASSOCIATION BETWEEN TOT STATES AND RECOGNITION MEMORY JUDGMENTS

An association between reported TOT states and recognition judgments was discovered by Cleary (2006), who showed that participants thought it more likely that an inaccessible target answer to a general knowledge question was studied on an earlier list if experiencing a TOT state than if not experiencing a TOT state. With a subset of stimuli from Nelson and Narens's (1980) norms, participants first studied a list of words that each served as an answer (e.g., TOTO, INSOMNIA) to a general knowledge question presented later (e.g., "What is the name of Dorothy's dog in *The Wizard of Oz*?" and "What is the name of an inability to sleep?"). On the later general knowledge question test, answers to half of the general

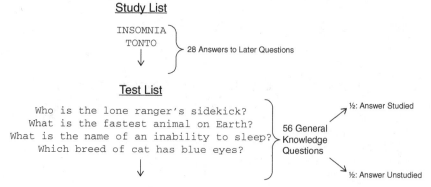

FIGURE 5.1. A diagram of the general experimental procedure used by Cleary (2006). Two study test blocks, each containing 28 answers followed by 56 general knowledge questions, were used.

knowledge questions had appeared at study and half had not. (The general procedure is illustrated in Figures 5.1 and 5.2.)

For each question presented on the test (e.g., "What is the name of the inability to sleep?"), participants were first prompted to provide the answer. Then, regardless of whether they could do so, they were prompted to rate the likelihood that the answer had appeared at study using a scale of 0 (definitely not studied) to 10 (definitely studied). Because the primary interest was in those questions for which the answer could not be identified, if the answer was not correctly identified on the first attempt, participants were given a second chance to answer the question and were encouraged to guess. In Experiment 1, it was shown that among those questions whose answers went unidentified by participants, higher recognition ratings were given to those whose answers had appeared at study than to those whose answers had not. This ability to discriminate studied from unstudied answers when the answers could not be identified is a variation of the recognition without identification (RWI) effect (e.g., Cleary & Greene, 2000, 2001, 2004, 2005). In short, participants could detect, to some degree, whether an inaccessible target answer was presented earlier in the experiment, which is a form of recognition memory.

Cleary (2006) explored whether this form of recognition memory is related to the TOT phenomenon. In Experiment 2, participants were additionally prompted to indicate if they were experiencing a TOT state for all unretrieved answers (see Figure 5.2). It was found that, for unanswered questions, participants gave higher retrospective recognition ratings when experiencing a TOT state than when not. In short, the TOT state appeared

What kind of poison did Socrates take at his execution?

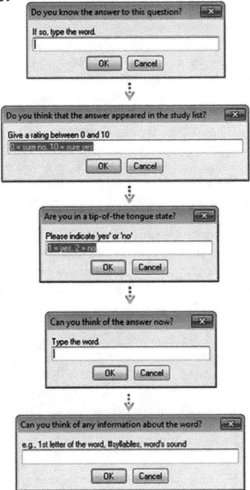

FIGURE 5.2. A diagram of the sequence of prompts that occurred with each general knowledge question presented in Cleary (2006), Experiment 3.

to impart upon participants a greater sense of an answer having appeared recently. At first glance, this may seem consistent with the idea that the RWI for inaccessible target answers may be synonymous with TOT states. However, some aspects of the results are inconsistent with this idea. First, the RWI effect itself is not dependent on the presence of a TOT state; the effect still occurs among questions that did not elicit TOT states. Second, even among inaccessible non-studied targets, ratings were higher when TOT states occurred compared to when they did not; thus, the tendency to give higher recognition ratings when in a TOT state did not depend on having studied the targets in question. Finally, studying a target answer did not increase the probability of a TOT state later in response to a question for which that target was the answer; thus, TOT states later on should not have been diagnostic of a target's study status.

Cleary (2006) further examined if the association between reported TOT states and recognition ratings in the RWI paradigm (as well as the RWI effect itself) might be driven by access to partial information about the inaccessible target. Research has suggested that people may sometimes have access to partial target information, such as the first letter of the inaccessible target word, when experiencing TOT states (e.g., Brown, 1991). This raises the possibility that the higher recognition ratings given during TOT states than during non-TOT states is due to access to partial target information. Perhaps participants are not attributing the TOT state to study status, per se, but rather are attributing the partial access that typically drives the report of the TOT experience to the study status of the target.

However, Experiment 3 of Cleary's (2006) study showed that the association between reported TOT states and recognition ratings occurred whether partial information was available or not. More specifically, as illustrated in Figure 5.2, participants typed in any accessible partial information about the unretrievable target answer (e.g., first letter of the word, number of syllables, similar sounding word), and when these instances of correct partial identification of target information were removed from the data, higher recognition ratings were still given during TOT states than during non-TOT states. This suggests that it is not merely access to partial information about the target that drives the association between TOT states and recognition ratings.

Of course, TOT states can be brought on by other types of situations besides general knowledge questions; for instance, one can experience a TOT state for someone's name in response to seeing the person's face (e.g., Schwartz, 2002). Other studies have extended the pattern of higher recognition ratings during TOT than during non-TOT states with a wider range of stimuli. For instance, the pattern has been shown when partial target information cannot be accessed for celebrity faces (Cleary & Specker, 2007), famous scenes (Cleary & Reyes, 2009), and odors (Cleary, Konkel, Nomi, & McCabe, 2010).

More specifically, Cleary and Specker (2007, Experiment 2) extended the association between reported TOT states and recognition ratings to pictures of celebrities who could not be identified. Participants viewed names of celebrities (e.g., Jennifer Aniston, Bruce Willis) at study, then later received pictures of celebrities' faces for cues at test. Half of the celebrities shown at test had had their names presented at study; half had not. For each face presented at test, participants were first asked to identify the person by typing in his or her name. Then, regardless of whether the participant could identify the celebrity, the participant rated the likelihood that the celebrity's name was studied (0 = definitely not studied; 10 = definitely studied). Participants were additionally prompted to indicate the presence or absence of a TOT state for the celebrity's name that could not be retrieved. Participants gave higher recognition ratings when reporting a TOT state than when reporting a non-TOT state. Thus, participants thought it more likely that an unidentified celebrity's name was studied when in a TOT state, even when instances of partial identification were removed. In short, the pattern shown by Cleary (2006) with general knowledge questions was extended to celebrity photos.

Cleary and Reyes (2009) extended the findings of Cleary and Specker (2007) to pictures of famous scenes and landmarks. Participants studied names of famous scenes and landmarks (e.g., Falling Water, Taj Mahal) and were later tested with pictures of famous scenes and landmarks, half of which had had their names presented at study and half of which had not. For each scene presented at test, participants were first asked to identify the scene by providing its name. Then they rated the likelihood that the scene's name was studied (0 = definitely not studied; 10 = definitely studied). They were also prompted to indicate the presence or absence of a TOT state for the scene's name and to provide any partial information about the name that came to mind. As in Cleary and Specker's study with celebrities, among scenes that went unidentified, participants gave higher recognition ratings when in a TOT state than when not, even when instances of correct partial identification of the target name were removed.

Finally, Cleary and colleagues (2010) examined the TOT ratings pattern with odors that could not be identified. Participants studied either odors plus names (e.g., smell of strawberry along with its name; smell of lilac along with its name) or just odor names (e.g., just the word *strawberry* or *lilac*) and were then tested on odors alone, half of which had appeared on the study list as either just a name or as a name plus the odor, and half of which were new. Participants attempted to identify each odor or any partial information about the odor's name, rated the likelihood that it (or its name) had been studied, and indicated whether they were in a TOT state for the odor's name. As with celebrity faces (Cleary & Specker, 2007) and famous scenes (Cleary & Reyes, 2009), odors that could not be identified showed the same association between recognition ratings and reported TOT states: participants rated it more likely that an unidentified odor or its name was studied when in a TOT state than when not.

THE ASSOCIATION BETWEEN TOT STATES AND RECOGNITION RATINGS FOR UNIDENTIFIED TARGETS: ARE TOTS AND RECOGNITION WITHOUT IDENTIFICATION (RWI) THE SAME PHENOMENON?

One potential explanation for the association between reported TOT states and RWI judgments is that TOT states and recognition judgments for inaccessible targets share the same underlying basis. Put differently, perhaps the RWI effect is essentially a manifestation of the TOT phenomenon itself. Several lines of evidence suggest, however, that this is not the case; the RWI phenomenon appears to be distinct from the TOT phenomenon.

First, if TOT and RWI are the same, then one would expect to see the proportion of reported TOT states increase with study status. That is, when a target was studied, there should be a higher probability of subsequent TOT states than when the target was unstudied. That is not what is found, however. In fact, the opposite pattern is often found – a decreased probability of reporting a TOT state among unidentified but studied targets (e.g., Cleary, 2006, Experiment 2; Cleary & Reyes, 2009). This pattern can be explained in terms of the transmission deficit model of TOT experiences (e.g., Rastle & Burke, 1996) by assuming that answers that were presented at study were primed in memory and thus were more accessible at test than they otherwise would have been. In other words, because primed targets are more accessible from being primed, target answers that would have otherwise led to a TOT experience are now retrieved. Thus, targets in the non-studied condition are actually more likely to lead to TOT experiences than targets in the studied condition.

Second, if RWI and TOT were the same phenomenon, RWI should not appear in non-TOT states; that is, the TOT state should be necessary for the detection of an inaccessible word's recent appearance on a study list. Although larger RWI effects have sometimes been reported for TOT than for non-TOT states (e.g., Cleary, 2006, Experiment 2; Cleary & Specker, 2007, Experiment 2), the RWI effect is usually found in non-TOT states, and this effect is often of the same magnitude as during TOT states (e.g., Cleary, 2006, Experiment 3; Cleary et al., 2010).

Third, if RWI and the TOT were the same phenomenon, then the pattern of higher recognition ratings during TOT than during non-TOT states should disappear in situations where the RWI effect is not found. That is, manipulations that diminish RWI should also reduce the higher ratings when in a TOT state than when not. However, as discussed later in this chapter, the pattern of higher recognition ratings during TOT than during non-TOT states emerges regardless of whether the RWI effect itself occurs.

THE ASSOCIATION BETWEEN TOT STATES AND RECOGNITION RATINGS FOR UNIDENTIFIED TARGETS WHEN RECOGNITION WITHOUT IDENTIFICATION (RWI) DOES NOT OCCUR

One case in point is recognition ratings to unidentified odors. Cleary and colleagues (2010) presented participants with either labeled odors (e.g., lavender, strawberry, lilac, cedar) at study or just the labels without the odors themselves. In the label-with-odor condition, the odors were blank scratch-and-sniff stickers fastened to note cards. Participants scratched and smelled the odor while noting its label, trying to remember that odor and its identity for a later memory test. In the label-only condition, just the labels (e.g., "lavender" or "strawberry") were presented on the cards without the corresponding odors, and participants tried to remember each name for a later memory test. All participants received the same test, consisting of unlabeled odors presented on note cards. Participants scratched and sniffed the test odor, then attempted to identify the odor by writing its name on the test card. Regardless of whether the odor could be identified, participants rated the likelihood that the odor or its name was studied (0 = definitely not studied; 10 = definitely studied). Finally, participants indicated whether they were experiencing a TOT state for those odor names that could not be retrieved.

This study helped to determine some of the boundary conditions of the RWI effect itself. While RWI occurred when both odors and their labels were presented at study, it did not occur when only odor labels were shown at study. Specifically, when odors plus labels had been presented at study, participants could subsequently discriminate between unidentified test odors that had, and had not, been studied. More specifically, they gave higher recognition ratings to test odors that had been studied than those that had not. However, when only the odor labels had been studied, participants showed no such discrimination, with ratings roughly equivalent in both studied and unstudied conditions. This finding suggested that RWI for odors was driven largely by perceptual information. However, in contrast, the pattern of higher recognition ratings during TOT states than during non-TOT states occurred even when only odor names were studied and only actual odors were presented at test, suggesting that the higher recognition ratings when in a TOT than in a non-TOT state was *not* driven by perceptual information. In fact, participants gave higher ratings when in a TOT state than when not regardless of whether RWI occurred. In short, higher recognition ratings when in a TOT state are not dependent on the presence of RWI; this pattern appears to be driven by a different mechanism.

Other data from our laboratory also support this idea. In a study carried out by visiting summer program student Toniea Harrison (Harrison & Cleary, 2008), participants viewed celebrity names at study (e.g., Oprah Winfrey, Bill Clinton) and then listened to voice clips of celebrities. Half of the voice clips were from celebrities whose names had been studied and half were from celebrities whose names had not been studied. For each voice clip presented at test, participants were first prompted to identify the celebrity from the voice, then rate the likelihood that that celebrity's name had appeared at study, and finally indicate whether they were in a TOT state for that celebrity's name. As with odors, no RWI effect was found for celebrity names from their voices at test. That is, when celebrities could not be identified by voice, participants could not discriminate between those whose names were and were not studied. However, similar to the outcome with the unidentified odors (Cleary et al., 2010), participants gave a higher likelihood rating that a celebrity's name was studied when in a TOT state for that person's name than when not. This represents another instance in which there is an association between recognition ratings and TOT states when RWI does not occur.

In a music variation of the celebrity voice study, another visiting summer program student to our lab (Nova Jaramillo) had given participants names of well-known television shows and cartoons (e.g., *The Addams Family, Looney Tunes, The Jetsons*) at study, then later tested participants on their ability to identify television programs from their theme songs. In each of four study test blocks, participants studied 15 television program names and then received a test list of 30 theme song clips. For each theme song test clip, participants first attempted to identify the television program from which the theme song came (or any partial information about that program). Then, regardless of whether participants could identify the TV program, they rated the likelihood that the program name was presented at study (o = definitely not presented; 10 = definitely presented). Then, they were prompted to indicate if they were in a TOT state for the name of the TV program.

The primary interest was in theme songs whose corresponding TV programs could not be identified. No RWI effect was found, with ratings roughly equivalent for unidentified theme songs whose names were studied and those whose names were not. Similar to studies with odors (Cleary et al., 2010) and celebrity voices (Harrison & Cleary, 2008), this is another demonstration of boundary conditions for the RWI effect; not all types of referents lead to RWI of having studied those names. However, also like the findings of Cleary and colleagues (2010) and Harrison and Cleary (2008), despite no RWI effect, participants exhibited a tendency to give higher recognition ratings when in a TOT state than when not, suggesting that this outcome is not dependent on the RWI effect.

Taken together, these findings suggest that although RWI does not occur across all types of inaccessible names from their referents, the tendency to give higher recognition ratings when in a TOT than in a non-TOT state may generalize across most types of inaccessible names from their referents. Specifically, RWI occurs with celebrity names from their faces (Cleary & Specker, 2007) and with famous scene names from their scene pictures (Cleary & Reyes, 2009), but not with odor names from their odors (Cleary et al., 2010), celebrity names from their voices (Harrison & Cleary, 2008), or TV program names from their theme songs (Jaramillo & Cleary, 2006). Yet, in all of these cases, the tendency to give higher ratings when in a TOT than in a non-TOT state is consistently found.

Regarding why RWI is not consistently found across all forms of referents and their names, Cleary and colleagues (2010) speculate that it may be that some referents are more strongly tied to their names in semantic memory than others, and that a strong bond is needed for RWI to occur. However, no obvious differences appear in name recall across the studies. Though odor name identification in the unstudied condition of Cleary and colleagues (2010) was indeed quite low (.04 in one condition and .05 in the other), this was not the case in other studies that failed to show an RWI effect. For instance, name identification from celebrity faces in the unstudied condition of Cleary and Specker's (2007) study (where an RWI effect was found) was .15 in Experiment 1 and .09 in Experiment 2; when celebrity voices were used instead of faces in Harrison and Cleary's (2008) study (where an RWI effect was not found), the probability of name recall from voices in the unstudied condition was .17, which is not even numerically lower than the recall rates in the unstudied condition of Cleary and Specker (where an RWI effect was found). Likewise, in the case of identifying TV shows or movies from their theme songs, where no RWI effect was shown, identification in the unstudied condition occurred at a rate of .27, which is higher than the rates from Cleary and Specker (2007), and comparable to the rates demonstrated by Cleary and Reyes (2009), who showed RWI with famous scenes and landmarks (.22 in Experiment 1, and .30 and .28 in the two conditions of Experiment 2).

An alternative theoretical approach that may fare better is the idea that the degree of feature overlap between the test cue and an item or items in memory (e.g., Ryals & Cleary, 2012) is what matters to the RWI effect, where a high degree of feature match between the test cue and items in memory leads to a stronger familiarity signal than a low degree of feature match. In short, RWI may be brought on by familiarity detection that results from a feature-matching process, such as that described in global matching models (e.g., Clark & Gronlund, 1996) and by Ryals and Cleary (2012). Recent evidence from our lab using semantic feature production norms to manipulate semantic feature overlap from study to test suggests that semantic features can participate in the feature-matching process to produce familiarity detection with a test cue when target retrieval fails (Cleary, Ryals, & Wagner, 2014; see Cleary, 2014, for a review). Given that prior evidence has suggested that the same semantic feature production norms can account for a large degree of variance in processing pictures of objects (Chang, Mitchell, & Just, 2011), it is feasible that RWI that occurs for names from their pictorial referents may be due to semantic feature overlap. Perhaps there is a high degree of semantic feature overlap between celebrity faces and their names, and between pictures of famous landmarks and their names, but there is not a high degree of semantic feature overlap between celebrity voices and their names, or between TV show theme songs and their show names, or between odors and their names. Future research may investigate this possible explanation for this particular boundary condition of the RWI effect.

Whatever the reason for the existence of this boundary condition with RWI, the tendency to give higher recognition ratings when in a TOT state than when not does not have this boundary condition. It still occurs in situations where either the link in semantic memory between the referent and the name may not be strong enough to lead to RWI, or the degree of feature overlap between the test item and its corresponding studied information is not high enough to lead to RWI. Thus, the inclination to give higher recognition ratings when in a TOT state appears to be driven by factors different from those that drive the RWI effect.

TOT STATES AS SOURCES OF ATTRIBUTION IN MAKING RECOGNITION JUDGMENTS

Rather than being driven by the same mechanisms as RWI, the association between TOT states and recognition ratings is likely the result of an attribution of TOT states themselves to the likelihood that a currently inaccessible target item was studied. Specifically, participants appear to use the presence of a TOT state to infer that the item in question was presented on the study list. Regardless of whether RWI is present, participants can make this TOT attribution in any recognition testing situation in which the target items themselves are inaccessible. The fact that participants attribute TOT states to the likely study status of an inaccessible word is interesting given that TOTs are not diagnostic of a word's study status: TOT states are actually equally or even *less* likely for studied targets compared to unstudied targets. Thus, a TOT state should not indicate an increased likelihood that an inaccessible target was studied. The question of why participants may make this attribution is discussed later in this chapter.

DO THE HIGHER RECOGNITION RATINGS FOR UNIDENTIFIED TARGETS DURING TOT STATES PERSIST WHEN THE RECOGNITION WITHOUT IDENTIFICATION (RWI) EFFECT IS REVERSED?

Thus far, three studies have been described in which the RWI effect was not present for unidentified targets, yet the TOT ratings pattern (i.e., higher recognition ratings during TOT than during non-TOT states) was. These studies suggest that participants use TOTs as a source of attribution in making recognition decisions. Even more compelling would be showing that the TOT ratings pattern persists even when the ratings pattern that is characteristic of RWI is reversed. Nomi and Cleary (2012) recently reported such a reversal. They compared ratings of the likelihood that a currently inaccessible target would be recognized later (Feeling of Knowing, or FOK, judgment) to ratings of the likelihood that the currently inaccessible target was studied on an earlier list.

In a between-subjects design, participants were randomly assigned to either the standard RWI or the FOK task. In a modification of the design used by Cleary and Reyes (2009), participants studied the names of famous scenes and landmarks (e.g., Taj Mahal, Falling Water), then were tested on pictures of famous scenes and landmarks, half of which had had their names presented at study and half of which had not. For each scene presented at test, participants first attempted to identify the scene by typing in its name. Then, regardless of whether the scene could be identified, participants gave a rating.

Participants in the RWI condition rated the likelihood that the target name was studied (0 = definitely not studied; 10 = definitely studied), whereas participants in the FOK condition rated the likelihood that they would recognize the target name if presented later in the experiment (0 = definitely will not recognize it later; 10 = definitely will recognize it later). Participants were also prompted to provide partial information for unretrieved targets, and items associated with correctly identified partial information were removed from the subsequent analyses.

Across three different experiments using this design, the ratings pattern consistently reversed in the FOK condition compared to the pattern shown in the standard RWI condition. More specifically, in the standard RWI condition, ratings for unidentified scenes were significantly higher when names were studied compared to those not studied. However, in the FOK condition the opposite pattern occurred. Ratings were significantly *lower* for unidentified scenes whose names were studied than for those whose names were not studied. Thus, by simply having participants rate the likelihood that a currently inaccessible target will be recognized later rather than the likelihood that the currently inaccessible target was studied recently, the usual old-new discrimination pattern that is found in standard RWI paradigms can be reversed.

The Current Experiment

Of particular interest in the present study is whether the higher recognition ratings when in a TOT state than when not would extend to the situation where the old-new discrimination pattern that is found in the usual RWI paradigm is reversed. That is, if participants are asked to rate the likelihood that they would later recognize the currently inaccessible target, will they still give higher recognition ratings when in a TOT state than when not? Nomi and Cleary's (2012) method was used, but using general knowledge questions and their answers rather than famous scenes and their names. As in Cleary (2006), participants were asked on each trial to indicate the presence or absence of a TOT state for the target answer.

Method
Participants. Sixty-nine Colorado State University students participated in exchange for credit in a psychology course. They were randomly assigned to

either the RWI condition or the feeling-of-knowing (FOK) condition. One participant in the RWI condition was excluded for not finishing the experiment, leaving 34 participants in the RWI and 34 in the FOK condition.

Materials. To compare the RWI and FOK conditions, it was critical that participants not know the nature of the rating until the time of the test. Otherwise, any differences could be due to differences in encoding strategies as opposed to the information used in making the rating itself. Therefore, only one study test block could be used, and because prior research has suggested that RWI effects may be diminished when longer lists are used (e.g., Cleary & Greene, 2000), we used fewer items than in previous studies such as Cleary (2006). Therefore, participants studied one list of 40 items and were tested with one list of 80 items; these were a subset of 80 questions and target answers selected from the Nelson and Narens (1980) norms. For each participant, 40 of the target answers appeared in a study list that preceded the 80-question test list. Which answers were studied versus non-studied was counterbalanced across participants.

Procedure. The procedure was similar to that used by Cleary (2006, Experiment 3; see Figures 5.1 and 5.2). Participants were instructed that they would be presented with a list of words on the computer screen and that following the list, they would be asked a series of questions, and that instructions regarding the questions would be provided after the list of words. The study list of 40 words appeared individually on the computer screen for one second each with an interstimulus interval of one second.

Following the study list, participants in both conditions were told that they would receive a set of general knowledge questions to answer. For each question, they should attempt to answer the question by typing the answer (then press Enter), and if they could not think of the answer to simply press Enter.

Participants in the RWI condition were instructed similarly to Cleary (2006; see Figure 5.2). Regardless of whether they could successfully answer the question, they should rate the likelihood that the answer had appeared on the earlier list that they had viewed (0 = answer was definitely NOT studied; 10 = answer was definitely studied).

Participants in the FOK condition were instead told that regardless of whether they could successfully answer the question, they should rate the likelihood that they would recognize the answer if they were to see it later (0 = answer would definitely NOT be recognized later; 10 = answer would DEFINITELY be recognized later).

Following the rating response, participants in both conditions were prompted for partial information about unretrieved targets, such as the first letter, what the word sounds like, and the number of syllables in the word. After the prompt for partial information, participants in both conditions indicated the presence or absence of a TOT state. Following from prior research (Cleary, 2006; Schwartz, 2001), a tip-of-the-tongue state was defined as: "You feel as if it is possible that you could recall the target answer, and that you feel as if its recall is imminent. It's as if the answer is on the 'tip of your tongue,' about to be recalled, but you simply cannot think of the word at the moment." After indicating whether a TOT state was occurring, participants in both conditions were provided a second chance at identifying the answer and encouraged to guess.

Results

The primary interest was in ratings given to questions whose answers went unidentified, and in how these varied across study status (target studied vs. unstudied), TOT status (TOT vs. non-TOT state), and rating condition (RWI vs. FOK). Some participants were not included in the analyses because they did not have at least two TOTs in a given TOT state category (unidentified studied target; unidentified non-studied target). In the RWI condition, 10 participants were lost because of having fewer than two items in a category. In the FOK condition, 17 participants were lost because of having fewer than two items in a category. These adjustments left a total of 24 participants in the RWI condition and 17 participants in the FOK condition for comparison to one another.

A 2 x 2 x 2 Study status (target studied vs. unstudied) x TOT status (TOT vs. non-TOT) x Rating Condition (RWI vs. FOK) mixed ANOVA was performed on ratings given to questions whose target answers were not identified. The mean ratings and their standard deviations across conditions are reported in Table 5.1. A significant main effect of TOT status was found, $F(1, 39) = 165.00$, $MSE = 2.13$, $p < .001$, reflecting that participants gave higher ratings when in a TOT state than when in a non-TOT state. Furthermore, there was no three-way Study-status x TOT-status x Rating Condition interaction ($F < 1.0$), nor was there a two-way Study-status x TOT-status interaction ($F < 1.0$). Thus, regardless of the rating type, participants gave higher ratings when experiencing a TOT state than when not. In other words, participants thought it more likely that an unidentified target was a) studied earlier and b) would be recognized later, if in a TOT state than if not.

A significant two-way TOT status x Rating Condition interaction was found, $F(1, 39) = 34.13$, $MSE = 2.13$, $p < .001$, reflecting a larger tendency to give higher ratings when in a TOT state in the FOK condition than when in a TOT state in the RWI condition. This is interesting because it suggests

TABLE 5.1. *Ratings given to unidentified targets in the RWI and FOK conditions*

	RWI				RWI			
	Target Studied		Target Unstudied		Target Studied		Target Unstudied	
TOT-Status	M	SD	M	SD	M	SD	M	SD
TOT State	**5.18**	*2.33*	**4.62**	*2.29*	**7.14**	*1.85*	**7.49**	*1.81*
Non-TOT State	**3.43**	*1.45*	**3.14**	*1.40*	**2.76**	*1.46*	**3.22**	*1.60*

that participants consider TOTs to be even more diagnostic in the FOK than in the RWI condition.

While there was no main effect of Study status, $F < 1.0$, this was due to a Study status x Rating Condition crossover interaction similar to that found by Nomi and Cleary (2012), whereby the usual RWI pattern (i.e., higher ratings for unidentified studied than unidentified unstudied targets) was reversed in the FOK condition (i.e., lower ratings for unidentified studied than for unidentified unstudied targets), $F(1, 39) = 4.80$, $MSE = 1.42$, $p < .05$. This extends the reversal of the usual RWI pattern that was first shown by Nomi and Cleary with FOK judgments for unidentified scene names to unidentified answers to general knowledge questions.

Finally, there was a main effect of Rating Condition, $F(1, 39) = 5.19$, $MSE = 8.59$, $p < .05$, reflecting higher ratings overall in the FOK than the RWI condition; this was carried largely by the tendency to give higher ratings when in a TOT state in the FOK compared to when in a TOT state in the RWI condition.

Discussion

This experiment suggests that the tendency to give higher recognition ratings when in a TOT state than when not in a TOT state occurs even when the rating is regarding the likelihood of future recognition of the currently inaccessible target. This is especially interesting given that the usual ratings pattern characteristic of the RWI effect reverses in this situation, yet the tendency to give higher ratings when in a TOT state is stronger. This even further supports the claim that the tendency to give higher ratings when in a TOT state than when not has a different basis than the RWI effect, and suggests that participants use the TOT state as a source of attribution in assessing past and future likelihoods regarding currently inaccessible items.

WHAT DRIVES THE TENDENCY TO GIVE HIGHER
RECOGNITION RATINGS DURING TOT STATES?

TOT States as Sources of Attribution in Making other Types of Judgments.
Given that the tendency to give higher recognition ratings when in a TOT
state than when not is dissociable from RWI, what then drives this tendency? In all likelihood, participants attribute the presence of a TOT state
to other likelihoods regarding the inaccessible target. The attribution goes
something like this: If a TOT state is present, participants infer from this
that the currently inaccessible target a) was more likely to have been studied and b) will be more likely to be recognized if seen later, than when not
in a TOT state. Support for this idea is evident in the finding by Cleary
and Reyes (2009) that the tendency to give higher recognition ratings in
TOT than in non-TOT states is greater when the prompt to indicate TOT
state status precedes the recognition rating than when it follows the rating.
Specifically, Cleary and Reyes (2009) examined the effects of making the
TOT state judgment before versus after giving the recognition rating (see
Figure 5.2 for an example of making the TOT state judgment *after* giving
the rating). The tendency to give higher recognition ratings when in a TOT
state than when not was greater when the prompt to indicate the presence
versus the absence of a TOT state came *before* the rating compared to when
it came after the rating. This finding suggests that participants may be using
the state itself as a basis for giving ratings.

In short, participants appear to be viewing TOT states as diagnostic of
whether an inaccessible target was presented recently, and whether an inaccessible target will be recognized if seen later on. This is interesting, given
that TOT states are not diagnostic of whether a target actually was presented recently. In studies of RWI, the probability of a reported TOT state
has never been increased when the target was studied relative to when it
was not studied, and often it has actually been decreased (e.g., Cleary, 2006;
Cleary & Reyes, 2009; Cleary & Specker, 2007; Cleary et al., 2010).

Why are TOT States Assumed to be Diagnostic Sources of Information?
So, if TOT states are not necessarily diagnostic with respect to retrieval
decisions, why then do participants treat them as if they are? One possibility is that, although TOT states themselves have a different underlying
basis than RWI or FOK judgments, the subjective feeling of the TOT state
is similar to the subjective feeling of familiarity. A subjective sense of familiarity with a test cue or item is thought to drive many RWI decisions (e.g.,
Nomi & Cleary, 2012), as well as many FOK decisions (e.g., Koriat & Levy-
Sadot, 2001; Metcalfe et al., 1993). If the subjective feeling of being in a TOT

state is similar enough to the subjective feeling of familiarity to be confused with it, this could explain why participants would attribute the TOT state itself to the likelihood that an inaccessible item was studied earlier or will be recognized later.

In support of this idea, Cleary and Reyes (2009) compared reports of TOT and non-TOT states with reports of déjà vu and non-déjà vu states. They found a similar attribution pattern for ratings given during TOT versus non-TOT states as for ratings given during déjà vu versus non-déjà vu states. Given other evidence that suggests that participants equate déjà vu with feelings of familiarity (Cleary, Ryals, & Nomi, 2009), the findings of Cleary and Reyes suggest that it is highly probable that participants attribute TOT states to the likely study status of an inaccessible target simply because the feeling is similar to the familiarity feeling that often *is* diagnostic of the study status of an item. Furthermore, given also that cue familiarity has been shown to be one of the factors used in making FOK judgments (e.g., Koriat & Levy-Sadot, 2001; Metcalfe et al., 1993), it is possible that participants attribute TOT states to the likelihood of later recognition simply because the feeling is similar to the type of familiarity feeling that often *is* used in FOK judgments.

SUMMARY AND CONCLUSIONS

Taken together, the full pattern of findings discussed in this chapter suggests that TOT states are being used as information from which to make attributions. Most researchers focus on the attributions used to infer the presence of a TOT (see Schwartz, 2002, for a review), but the findings discussed in this chapter suggest that the reverse may also be possible: people may use TOTs to make inferences about other cognitive states or likelihoods. This increases the importance of discovering the basis of TOT states, as whatever drives TOTs is also used as the basis of other decisions, such as the likelihood of study status, or that an item will be later recognized.

FUTURE DIRECTIONS

The present chapter discusses many instances in which TOT states are used to make attributions about other cognitive phenomena, such as the study status of a currently inaccessible item in memory, and the likelihood of later recognition of a currently inaccessible item. Other work has also hinted at the possibility that TOT states influence other cognitive judgments. For example, Schwartz (2011) found that the likelihood of a reported TOT is diminished on trials immediately following a reported TOT state. Thus, the presence of a TOT state on one trial can influence judgments of TOT states on subsequent trials.

One potential avenue for future work is whether TOT states are used to make judgments of learning (JOLs). Would participants judge their learning of something to be better when in a TOT state than when not in a TOT state? If predicting how much study time they will need to relearn the inaccessible target word, will participants judge that to be less time when in a TOT state than when not? In a related arena of decision making, the availability heuristic suggests that participants attribute the accessibility or availability of information to its probability or frequency of occurrence in the world (e.g., Tversky & Kahneman, 1973, 1974). When participants are unable to access a current piece of information, are they similarly inclined to attribute the presence of a TOT state to the frequency or probability of its occurrence in the world? Numerous heuristics and biases are used in making decisions (e.g., see Gilovich, Griffin, & Kahneman, 2002, for an overview), and TOT states (and possibly other subjective cognitive states as well) may serve as yet another source of heuristics and biases that people use. Therefore, future research should aim to understand not only the basis of such subjective states as TOT states, but how they are used for making decisions.

REFERENCES

Brown, A. S. (1991). A review of the tip-of-the-tongue experience. *Psychological Bulletin, 109*, 204–223.

Brown, R., & McNeill, D. (1966). The "tip of the tongue" phenomenon. *Journal of Verbal Learning and Verbal Behavior, 5*, 325–337.

Chang, K. K., Mitchell, T., & Just, M. A. (2011). Quantitative modeling of the neural representation of objects: How semantic feature norms can account for fMRI activation. *Neuroimage, 56*, 716–727.

Clark, S. E., & Gronlund, S. D. (1996). Global matching models of recognition memory: How the models match the data. *Psychonomic Bulletin & Review, 3*, 37–60.

Cleary, A. M. (2006). Relating familiarity-based recognition and the tip-of-the-tongue phenomenon: Detecting a word's recency in the absence of access to the word. *Memory & Cognition, 34*, 804–816.

(2014). The sense of recognition during retrieval failure: Implications for the nature of memory traces. In B. H. Ross's *Psychology of Learning and Motivation, Volume 60*. Elsevier.

Cleary, A. M., & Greene, R. L. (2000). Recognition without identification. *Journal of Experimental Psychology: Learning, Memory, and Cognition, 26*, 1063–1069.

(2001). Memory for unidentified items: Evidence for the use of letter information in familiarity processes. *Memory & Cognition, 29*, 540–545.

(2004). True and false memory in the absence of perceptual identification. *Memory, 12,* 231–236.

(2005). Recognition without perceptual identification: A measure of familiarity? *Quarterly Journal of Experimental Psychology, 58A,* 1143–1152.

Cleary, A. M., Konkel, K. E., Nomi, J. N., & McCabe, D. P. (2010). Odor recognition without identification. *Memory & Cognition, 38,* 452–460.

Cleary, A. M., & Reyes, N. L. (2009). Scene recognition without identification. *Acta Psychologia,* 131, 53–62.

Cleary, A. M., Ryals, A. J., & Nomi, J. (2009). Can déjà vu result from similarity to a prior experience? Support for the similarity hypothesis of déjà vu. *Psychonomic Bulletin & Review,* 16, 1082–1088.

Cleary, A. M., Ryals, A. J., & Wagner, S. R. (2014). Semantic recognition without cued recall: Semantic feature matching as a basis for recognition of semantic cues when recall fails. Manuscript submitted for publication.

Cleary, A. M., & Specker, L. E. (2007). Recognition without face identification. *Memory & Cognition,* 35, 1610–1619.

Gilovich, T., Griffin, D., & Kahneman, D. (2002). *Heuristics and biases: The psychology of intuitive judgment.* Cambridge University Press.

Harrison, T., & Cleary, A. M. (2008, April). *Getting an Earful.* Poster presented at the Annual Meeting of the Rocky Mountain Psychological Association. Boise, ID.

Jaramillo, N., & Cleary, A. M. (2006, August). *Song Recognition with TOT Experiences.* Poster presented at the Annual REU Banquet for the Summer Program on Mind and Brain at Colorado State University.

Koriat, A., & Levy-Sadot, R. (2001). The combined contributions of the cue-familiarity and accessibility heuristics to feelings of knowing. *Journal of Experimental Psychology: Learning, Memory, and Cognition,* 27, 34–53.

Metcalfe, J., Schwartz, B. L., & Joaquim, S. G. (1993). The cue-familiarity heuristic in metacognition. *Journal of Experimental Psychology, Learning, Memory, and Cognition,* 19, 851–861.

Nelson, T. O., & Narens, L. (1980). Norms of 300 general-information questions: Accuracy of recall, latency of recall, and feeling-of-knowing ratings. *Journal of Verbal Learning and Verbal Behavior,* 19, 338–368.

Nomi, J. S., & Cleary, A. M. (2012). Judgments for inaccessible targets: Comparing recognition without identification and the feeling of knowing. *Memory & Cognition.*

Rastle, K. G., & Burke, D. M. (1996). Priming the tip of the tongue: Effects of prior processing on word retrieval in young and older adults. *Journal of Memory and Language,* 35, 586–605.

Ryals, A. J., & Cleary, A. M. (2012). The recognition without cued recall phenomenon: Support for a feature-matching theory over a partial recollection account. *Journal of Memory and Language,* 66, 747–762.

Schwartz, B. L. (2001). The relation of tip-of-the-tongue states and retrieval time. *Memory & Cognition,* 29, 117–126.

(2002). *Tip-of-the-tongue states: Phenomenology, mechanism, and lexical retrieval.* Mahwah, NJ: Lawrence Erlbaum Associates.

(2011). The effect of being in a tip-of-the-tongue state on subsequent items. *Memory & Cognition, 39,* 245–250.

Schwartz, B. L., & Metcalfe, J. (2011). Tip-of-the-tongue (TOT) states: Retrieval, behavior and experience. *Memory & Cognition, 39,* 737–749.

Schwartz, B. L., & Smith, S. (1997). The retrieval of related information influences tip-of-the-tongue states. *Journal of Memory and Language, 36,* 68–86.

Tversky, A., & Kahneman, D. (1973). Availability: A heuristic for judging frequency and probability. *Cognitive Psychology, 5,* 207–232.

(1974). Judgment under uncertainty: Heuristics and biases. *Science, 185,* 1124–1131.

6

Why the Journey to a Word Takes You No Closer

TREVOR A. HARLEY AND SIOBHAN B. G. MACANDREW

INTRODUCTION

What is a tip-of-the-tongue state (TOT)? People appear to know instinctively when they have TOTs, but as psychologists we nevertheless need a formal definition. A TOT is characterized by a *delay* in retrieving the word we are intending to say, a sense of *imminence*, sometimes called loosely *feeling of knowing* (FOK) the word, and a feeling of *effort* of active search for the target. What's more, in experimental settings where we induce TOTs using tasks such as responding to definitions, the word the person in the TOT state is searching for must be the target the experimenter has in mind. If this correspondence is verifiable – for example, by the participant eventually retrieving the word (*resolution*), the TOT is said to be *objective*. We might also accept a weaker criterion of objectivity if the participant recognizes that the experiment-supplied target was indeed the word for which they were searching. All other TOTs that are not verifiable in any way are called *subjective*.

It is possible to take these three dimensions – delay, imminence, and effort – and use them to construct a three-dimensional lexical retrieval space (see Figure 6.1). Indeed, such a conceptualization is more generally useful because all types of normal and pathological disfluency fall within this space. Normal, near-instantaneous lexical retrieval lies at the origin. Aging, normal disfluencies, and pathological retrieval can all be described as vectors that shift retrieval from the origin to some other point in this space (see Figure 6.1). Effortful recall in the form of active search is a particularly interesting aspect of TOT, meaning that in TOTs, lexical retrieval is

Please send any correspondence to Professor Trevor Harley at t.a.harley@dundee.ac.uk. We would like to thank all our participants for their time in taking part in our research.

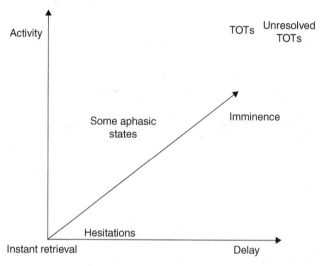

FIGURE 6.1. A 3-D space for lexical retrieval.

not as usual almost completely automatic, but instead involves what Harley, Jessiman, and MacAndrew (2011) call *deliberative language processing* – involving executive processing and placing a load on working memory (see Schwartz & Metcalfe, Chapter 2, this volume, for a discussion of similar issues from a metacognitive perspective).

The Disfluency Space

It is worth taking a little time to consider how lexical access difficulties in general can be represented in Figure 6.1. Note that as this is a continuous 3-D space, there is no logical reason that discontinuities should appear in this space, so our definition of what constitutes a TOT, for example, might quite legitimately be a little fuzzy. With instant retrieval at the origin, non-pathological transient lexical access difficulties (e.g., caused by hesitations before low-frequency items) map on to a shift along the *Delay* axis. The greater the hesitation before a word, the further the movement along the axis. Sometimes we sense we are effortfully searching for the word during this delay, so such occurrences lie in the *Delay-Effort* plane. Aphasic anomia, characterized by effortful search and delay but often with no sense of *Imminence* of recall, lie in the plane defined by *Effort* and *Delay*. In all cases, unsuccessful recall reflects *Delay* equal to a point infinitely far along the *Delay* axis. Note that we have probably all experienced TOTs in which resolution can occur several days after the initial difficulty, so meaningful points on the *Delay* axis can fall a very long way away! TOTs of all sorts are particularly interesting theoretically because they are unique in that they occupy the furthermost sector of the space from the origin along all dimensions, stretching out to infinity, and involve translation from the origin along the *Imminence*, *Delay*, and *Effort* axes.

What Is the Origin of TOTs?

In this section, we briefly review models of what causes TOTs. We do not attempt a comprehensive review of the literature (see Brown, 1991, 2012), but instead aim to draw out relevant findings for our general argument that TOTs reflect a particular sort of lexical-access failure that can be placed within the context we have described.

A Simple Model of Why TOTs Happen

The simplest model of a TOT is that we know we know a word but we cannot retrieve it immediately. But what is the "word" that we cannot retrieve? In the simplest possible account, a word is a phonological form. We know that we have activated a semantic representation corresponding to a phonological form in our lexicon, but we cannot retrieve that form. Of course, as Brown and McNeill (1966) observed, access to phonological forms is not all or nothing; sometimes we have partial access to the phonological form in the form of, for example, knowing the number of syllables in the word, or being able to access the initial sound.

A MORE COMPLEX MODEL

What is wrong with this simple model? It assumes an immediate mapping from semantics to phonology. Now virtually all researchers in the area accept some form of a two-stage model of lexical access in speech production in which semantic and phonological representations of words are mediated by an intermediate level of abstract lexical representations called *lemmas* that are syntactically and semantically specified but that are prior to any phonological information. In the two-stage account, a TOT happens when we access the lemma but cannot access all of the associated phonological form (Levelt, 1989).

How do we know that we have accessed the lemma? Evidence comes from TOT studies in languages such as Italian that have the syntactic property of gender, in which people in the TOT state know the gender of the word upon which they are stuck (Vigliocco, Antonini, & Garrett, 1997). There is some debate about whether syntactic features can be uniquely and universally accessed in TOT states: Miozzo and Caramazza (1997) found that although gender can be retrieved in TOTs in Italian speakers, it was far from perfect, as seems also to be the case in Hebrew (Gollan & Silverberg, 2001). One interpretation of this result, and that preferred by Miozzo and Caramazza, is that syntactic features are not necessarily specified at the lemma level (and see Biedermann, Ruh, Nickels, & Coltheart, 2007, for further research on the same topic).

Although there might be some debate about the exact locus of syntactic (and frequency) effects, the great preponderance of the evidence from neuroimaging, speech errors, picture-word interference studies, and modeling (the need for hidden units to mediate between semantic and phonological units so that all arbitrary mappings can be learned) points to some kind of intermediate lexical representation between universal abstract semantic representations and specific phonological representations (see, for example, Dell, 1986; Harley & MacAndrew, 2001; Indefrey & Levelt, 2004; Levelt, Roelofs, & Meyer, 1999).

Note these models do not explain *why* the phonological form is relatively inaccessible. To explain this inaccessibility we must turn to two very different accounts.

The Blocking Hypothesis

One early idea focused on the words that are sometimes generated when we are in a TOT state. These words are called *interlopers*, and are usually related to the target phonologically, semantically, or both. One possibility is that TOTs are caused by interference from similar but more accessible words; that is, the interlopers retrieved in a TOT state played an active role in causing it. This idea became known as the *Blocking hypothesis* (Jones, 1989; Jones & Langford, 1987). A number of problems soon emerged with this proposal, suggesting that the results of these initial experiments were unfortunate artifacts of the methodology and materials used (Meyer & Bock, 1992; Perfect & Hanley, 1992). Indeed, subsequent research showed that, on the contrary, phonological interlopers might actually play a *positive* role in resolving the TOT (Kornell & Metcalfe, 2006). Two studies in particular showed that TOTs are more likely on words that occupy a sparse phonological space with few neighbors (Harley & Bown, 1998; James & Burke, 2000).

The Transmission Deficit Model

Scholars now generally accept that interlopers play no role in causing TOTs. The leading model of TOT is currently the *transmission deficit* (TD) hypothesis, originally proposed by Burke, MacKay, Worthley, and Wade in 1991. In this model, TOTs happen when the connections between the lexical and phonological units have become weakened for some reason, such as infrequent use or aging. See Gollan and Brown (2006) for an update of this model.

The TD model provides a very useful framework for understanding TOTs, and can account for a wide range of findings. We can retrieve partial information about a word because the phonological form is not a unitary whole, but comprises syllables and, at a lower level, phonemes, and some of these sub-word units might be active enough to be retrieved correctly. Interlopers (or *persistent alternates* as Burke and colleagues call them) come to mind when alternative target words are activated above threshold by top-down or bottom-up processing or by both. Note that one thing the TD model cannot readily explain is the order in which interlopers are produced.

Feeling of Knowing (FOK)

Failed or partial retrieval is only one aspect of a TOT, however; by definition a TOT also involves a feeling of knowing (FOK) that a person knows the word, a feeling we have placed along the *Imminence* axis of lexical retrieval space. This FOK introduces a metacognitive aspect to the state that distinguishes it from being merely unable to retrieve a word. Note that the sense of imminence of recall lies on a continuum, from being certain that we do not know the word (note that we might be wrong and do indeed know it, but it is the *feeling* of knowing that matters), to complete certainty that we know the word (and again we might be wrong and do not in fact know the target). Note that being certain you do not know a word can only happen in a laboratory setting or in response to a question; such situations cannot arise in spontaneous speech. Surprisingly little is known about how we make this judgment, but see Schwartz and Metcalfe (2011 or Chapter 2, this volume) for an excellent analysis of some of the metacognitive processes that might be involved. Not all researchers make an FOK a necessary part of the definition of a TOT, instead expanding the definition to include all types of delayed recall (see Schwartz, 2006, for a review). Schwartz goes further and defines a TOT as a metacognitive rather than a cognitive state, in which the feeling of temporary inaccessibility is an essential part of the TOT state, and argues that TOTs and FOKs are similar but can be distinguished by neuroimaging and behavioral manipulations. We are using FOK in a looser sense than Schwartz, and see no conflict in our 3-D classification of lexical access failures and his account. We agree that TOTs involve more than delayed lexical access and partial recall, and must involve some metacognitive or FOK component.

WHAT MAKES A TOT STATE MORE LIKELY?

We can learn much about what causes TOTs by examining the factors of the circumstances in which they occur. Are TOTs more likely on some words than others?

Frequency

There is a widespread assumption that TOTs are more likely on less common words. Indeed, many researchers have utilized this assumption in constructing their materials, as did Brown and McNeill in their original 1966 experiment, which, although talking of TOTs as a failure to retrieve familiar words, used definitions of items with a very low frequency of between just one and four per million words.

A few studies have manipulated word frequency as a main variable and have uniformly found that TOTs are indeed more common on low-frequency words (e.g., Harley & Bown, 1998; MacAndrew, Harley, & Jessiman, in preparation). In a diary study, Burke and colleagues (1991) found that TOTs were more common on very low-frequency words. Such a result is consistent with the two-stage model with TOTs reflecting difficulties in retrieving phonological forms *if* we believe the data showing that frequency effects lie at the phonological form level (Jescheniak & Levelt, 1994). There is even an effect of syllable frequency, with TOTs being more common on words with a low-frequency initial syllable, at least for older adults (Farrell & Abrams, 2011).

We should ask what frequency measures in operational terms. We agree with Burke and colleagues that frequency reflects ease of access, with lower frequency words being generally more difficult to access.

Phonological Neighborhood

TOTs are also more likely on words with sparse phonological neighbors, though the precise ways in which sparseness has its effect are unclear (Harley

& Bown, 1998). A sparse phonological neighborhood is one in which there are few or no words that sound similar to a particular word (e.g., "rhythm"), while a dense phonological neighborhood is one in which there are many phonologically similar words (e.g., "cat," "bat," "mat," "cot," "kit"). Indeed, processing phonologically related words increases correct recall when in a TOT state (James & Burke, 2000).

Why does a sparse phonological neighborhood, independent of frequency, increase the likelihood of TOTs? There are two, nonexclusive possibilities: unusual phonological patterns might be less accessible, or similar phonological forms might support each other if they are interconnected by facilitatory connections. Given that in most production architectures within-level connections need to be inhibitory (to ensure that the winner takes all), we favor the former possibility: unusual phonological forms are more difficult to access. This idea is supported by the priming experiments (James & Burke, 2000) that show that temporary activation of infrequent lexical-phonological connections subsequently makes them more accessible.

Semantic Variables

Surprisingly little is known about the semantic properties of words on which TOTs are more likely to occur. Koriat and Lieblich (1977) explored the characteristics of the definitions used in the laboratory-induction paradigm, and identified two dimensions of importance: the effectiveness of the definition in identifying the target, and the likelihood that the definition induces an FOK. These are characteristics of the experimental definitions of the target words, rather than properties of the words themselves, so do not help with our question. MacAndrew and colleagues (submitted) found an interaction between imageability and frequency such that TOTs were particularly likely on less frequent, less imageable words. This finding is problematic for any model of TOT origin that locates the retrieval difficulty solely at the level of retrieving phonological forms. Instead, we argue that a number of factors can lead to the temporary inaccessibility of the phonological form, including weakened activation from semantic units. Following Hinton and Shallice (1991), we argue that imageability reflects the "semantic richness" of a word, with a larger number of semantic units being activated with more imageable words. A larger number of active semantic units in a word's semantic representation means that with more imageable words more activation flows to the lexical units. The finding that frequency and imageability are interactive rather than additive points to some factor that amplifies their joint effect (e.g., feedback between levels in the two-stage model). Furthermore, we seem to be able to learn to have recurrent TOTs such that we "learn to fail" to process particular words (Warriner & Humphreys, 2008).

We have seen that there is no evidence for phonological blocking; what about semantic blocking, in which semantic cues are presented around the same time as the definition? Again, scholars have conducted little research on this topic. Jones and Langford (1987) found no effect of semantic cueing on the likelihood of a TOT occurring, whereas Meyer and Bock (1992) found a small facilitatory effect of presenting semantically related words at the time of recall. We think that the role of semantics has been neglected in the study of TOTs. An interesting recent study (Higgins & Johnson, 2013) shows that "lost thoughts," ideas that were the focus of attention only a moment ago, happen at least in part because of implicit semantic interference. Hence although there is no phonological blocking, we argue that there might well be semantic blocking in some TOTs, an idea we are currently investigating further experimentally.

Of course, the modification of weakened semantic-lexical connections to the general theory is still entirely compatible with the general transmission deficit model, and indeed perhaps a prediction of it.

Proper Names

TOTs are reportedly more common for proper names (Burke et al., 1991; Rastle & Burke, 1996). There are of course, in principle, several confounds here: proper names tend to be low frequency and also often occupy sparse phonological neighborhoods. It is possible to control for these effects (e.g., by using names that are also common words – for example, *butcher* and Butcher), but there nevertheless seems to be something special about proper names (Brédart, Brennen, & Valentine, 1995). In addition, many proper names (e.g., Harley) have no independent meaning. We propose that this lack of semanticity makes them behave like low-imageability words. The same should be true for quiz-like "facts," such as the names of movies or books.

Aging

Does aging increase the number of TOTs in everyday speech? Considerable evidence suggests that it does, and that aging has its effect by weakening the connection strengths within the production network (Burke & Shafto,

2004; Burke et al., 1991). However, it seems that the increase in TOT rate of occurrence is not uniform across all words; instead, the TOT rate depends on the difficulty of the target word, so that there is an increase in the rate only for more difficult targets (Gollan & Brown, 2006). The increase in TOT rates with aging has been linked with age-related changes to the brain, particularly the prefrontal cortex (Galdo-Álvarez, Lindín, & Díaz, 2009).

Naturalistic Versus Experimental Settings

Finally we should remember that there are two types of TOT, naturally occurring and experimentally induced, and there is no reason to assume that they will be similar in every respect. Certainly there are aspects of experimentally induced TOTs that are usually irrelevant to natural ones, such as the length or accuracy of the definition (Koriat & Lieblich, 1977).

JOURNEY TO A WORD

In our research, we have examined the "journey to a word" in TOT states in younger adults, typically aging individuals, and people with Parkinson's disease, using items controlled for imageability and frequency (MacAndrew et al., submitted). First, we found that TOTs were more common when responding to definitions of low-imageability, low-frequency words. We have already commented on our finding regarding target imageability.

We also examined the sequence of persistent alternates participants generated in TOT states as they strove to retrieve the target. One striking finding is the lack of any clear pattern in these journeys; they are not like the *conduit d'approche* states of patients with conduction aphasia (Goodglass & Kaplan, 1983). There is no pattern of approach to the target, with interlopers gradually converging to the targets in terms of frequency or imageability. Instead at first sight, an item's persistent alternates appear to be output in a random fashion. Indeed, it is misleading to call them "persistent" alternates because often an alternate might be produced only once. Furthermore, not all words that people produce might reflect automatic activation of words in the way that alternates do; we observed in the study described later in this chapter that people top-down generate words that help them in their search: *signpost words.*

Note that the very existence of semantic alternates needs some explanation. According to the standard model of TOT origins, TOTs happen when we access the lemma but can get no further. We get phonological alternates because of partial activation of the target phonological form and feedback connections from the phonological units to the lemmas, leading to the activation of phonological neighbors. But according to the standard TD model, we know the correct semantic representation of the target item, and must have activated it to get to the right lemma. So why do we get semantic interlopers at all? Our suggestion is that semantic and phonological alternates might have different origins. Phonological alternates arise automatically from partial activation of phonological forms, whereas semantic alternates arise from more metacognitive processing, such as is shown by the phenomenon of spontaneous cuing in the TOT state. At present, though, this suggestion is highly speculative.

A STUDY INTO THE JOURNEY TO A WORD

Our study (MacAndrew et al., submitted) involved testing 47 participants in total, comprising 15 younger adults (YA; mean age 26, range 20–35), 15 typically aging adults (TAA; mean age 66, range 59–76), and 17 people with moderate Parkinson's disease (PPD; mean age 67, range 56–72).

We included a PPD group because our previous research has shown that people with Parkinson's disease have a particular sort of problem with language: as a result of damage to the fronto-striate loop, they are impaired at what we call deliberative language, the processes that involve controlling and manipulating language itself. Therefore they should have particular difficulty with search processes, as are likely to be involved in tip-of-the-tongue states (Harley et al., 2011; Harley, Oliver, Jessiman, & MacAndrew, 2013).

We used a total of 80 definitions.

In total, we received 3,760 responses. Responses can be divided into the following categories:

1. The correct word was produced almost immediately.
2. The correct word was produced after a very short delay.
3. A null response in which the participant could not offer a word.
4. The first response was incorrect (i.e., the participant produced a non-target word that was not a valid response to the definition), and the participant did not subsequently finally retrieve the target.
5. The first response was incorrect, but the participant subsequently did retrieve the target.
6. The immediate production was of an alternative legitimate word (i.e., a word that almost fit the definition but was not the target that we as experimenters had in mind), and the participant did not subsequently finally retrieve the target.

7. The immediate production was of an alternative legitimate word (i.e., a word that almost fit the definition but was not the target that we as experimenters had in mind), but the participant subsequently did retrieve the target.
8. The participant reported that they knew the word but were *not* in a TOT state. We called this category *Knowing Searches* (KS states; see Harley, Jessiman, MacAndrew, & Astell, 2008).
9. The participant reported that they knew the word but *were* in a TOT state.

We used a very strict definition of TOT state; the participant had to report that they had a TOT experience, incorporating a sense of imminence of recall, and also they ultimately correctly output the target word. Note that this a stricter definition of a TOT than the traditionally used notion of an objective TOT because we restricted TOTs to those responses in which participants said they were in a TOT before they retrieved the word. That is, we excluded those responses in which the participant output the target prior to reporting a TOT state after knowledge of the target or claimed a TOT post hoc, and also those responses in which the speaker delayed responding and said they knew the target word and were actively searching for it, but that it lacked a metacognitive component.

To achieve closure for participants on unsuccessful responses, we also offered hints; however, we excluded these responses from analysis for obvious reasons.

For this chapter, we analyzed in detail categories 6 (knowing searches) and 7 (TOTs). In conditions where the participants knew the word but could not immediately retrieve it, we told the participants to say anything they could about the target, particularly "anything on their mind." Hence, in each of these two key conditions the participants always produced at least one non-target response on the way to the target word. Out of 3,760 total responses, the category 6 and 7 responses were distributed as shown in Table 6.1.

Both KS (knowing states) and TOT states lie to the further end of the continuum of delay in producing the target word. Both KS and TOT states are associated with a feeling of imminence; participants have a belief that they will be able to retrieve the word soon. They are also actively engaged in both searching and processing. KSs and TOTs are distinguished purely in terms of their phenomenology; people in TOTs say they are in a peculiar TOT state that is like "being on the brink of a sneeze" (Brown & McNeil, 1966), whereas people in KSs know that they know the word, are delayed in

TABLE 6.1. *Distribution of "Knowing Search" (KS) and "Tip-of-the-Tongue" (TOT) states across all three groups (Younger Adult; Typically Aging Adult; Adult with Parkinson's Disease) when participants produced up to three signpost words (see below). A total of 1,122 responses fell into these two response categories across all three groups*

Group	Knowing Search	TOTs
YA	142	7
TAA	305	21
PPD	612	35

retrieving it, and are actively searching for it, but do not have that sneeze-like feeling.

Several researchers have identified neural correlates of the FOK of being in a TOT state (e.g., Kikyo & Ohki, 2002; Maril, Wagner, & Schachter, 2001; Shafto, Burke, Stamatakis, Tam, & Tyler, 2007). However, all these studies have confounded KSs and TOTs because both possess an FOK. In our characterization, TOTs are a particular and peculiar phenomenological state qualitatively distinct from KSs. To our knowledge, the only researcher to have explored this phenomenological aspect of TOTs is Schwartz (e.g., Schwartz, 2006; Schwartz & Metcalfe, 2011; Schwartz, Travis, Castro, & Smith, 2000).

Note that overall true TOTs, accompanied by a phenomenological state, make up a small proportion of what many others would classify as TOTs: just 5.6 percent of the total KS + TOT are true TOTs, making up just 1.7 percent of all possible responses in our data. Such a figure is more in line with our intuitions about the rate of TOTs in everyday life than found in many experiments, even given the focus on low-frequency words.

A Lexical Journey

What happens in KS and TOT states when people are searching for words? We asked our participants to output all words that came to mind while they were in a KS or TOT search state. As we noted previously, we call these words *signpost* words because they are guides to the target and think of them as occupying slots en route to the target. Remember that, according to our strict definition of KSs and TOTs, participants must retrieve the target word correctly eventually – the journey's end. Across all trials the number of signpost words output for each target varied between one (by definition) and a maximum of six. The great majority of participants produced three or

TABLE 6.2. *Phonological relationship between signpost words and targets. For this analysis we used just the items from Table 6.1 for which we also had frequency and imageability data (hence the reduced N)*

Group	KSs	TOTs
YA		
Slot 1	16/102 = 15.7%	1/2 = 50%
Slot 2	5/36 = 13.9%	0/0
Slot 3	0/5 = 0	0/0
TAA		
Slot 1	15/187 = 8.0%	1/16 = 7.3%
Slot 2	5/84 = 6.0%	0/2 = 0
Slot 3	3/28 = 10.7%	0/0
PPD		
Slot 1	17/170 = 10.0%	8/13 = 61.5%
Slot 2	6/53 = 11.3%	0/0
Slot 3	4/16 = 25.0%	0/0

fewer signpost words in a KS/TOT state (1,122 as earlier, out of a grand total of 1,173 total KS/TOT), so in the first instance we analyzed just these three or fewer signposts.

We examined the relationship between the target and the signpost words. Among the data we analyzed, of particular interest here is the possible semantic and phonological relationship between targets and each successive signpost. The results are summarized in Tables 6.2 and 6.3.

We used a very simple definition of phonological relationship: whether the target and signpost word shared the same initial consonant. We know that this is a very conservative estimate of a phonological relationship, and that the chance probability of a word being related to another in this fashion has an upper bound of around $p = 0.10$ (Harley, 1984).

There is no obvious pattern here, although we can make a few useful observations. First, people in TOTs don't tend to produce many signposts (or alternates) other than their first guess. They very clearly say what first comes to mind, hesitate, and then eventually get the target right without saying anything else. People in KS states, however, do say much more. Hence, although we provided a phenomenological definition of the KS-TOT distinction, there is clearly a behavioral correlate in the number of filled slots.

Second, given the very small N for TOTs, we cannot say much about phonological convergence on the target other than that the first word that comes to mind might be related to the target. The number is far too small for the YA.

TABLE 6.3. *Semantic relationship between signpost words and targets, using the same items as in Table 6.2. Right-hand figures are percentages*

Group	KSs		TOTS	
	Semantic		Semantic	
	Formal	Associate	Formal	Associate
YA				
Slot 1	65/102 = 63.7	36/102 = 35.3	1/2 = 50.0	1/2 = 50.0
Slot 2	21/36 = 58.3	14/36 = 38.9	-	-
Slot 3	1/5 = 20.0	3/5 = 60.0	-	-
TAA				
Slot 1	87/187 = 46.5	92/187 = 49.2	3/16 = 18.8	11/16 = 68.8
Slot 2	36/84 = 42.9	46/84 = 54.8	0/2 = 0	2/2 = 100
Slot 3	7/28 = 25.0	21/28 = 75.0	-	-
PPD				
Slot 1	88/170 = 51.8	77/170 = 45.3	3/13 = 23.1	8/13 = 61.5
Slot 2	21/53 = 39.6	27/53 = 47.2	-	-
Slot 3	6/16 = 37.5	8/16 = 50.0	-	-

The people with PD show a higher rate of phonological similarity for the first word that comes to mind compared with the target relative to the TA adults.

We find a broadly similar pattern for the KS trials. The YAs show phonological similarity between the alternates and the targets for all slots, the TAAs show very little, and the people with PD a considerable amount. Only the PPD group shows any sign of convergence – that is, their alternates getting closer to the target.

Now we turn to semantic convergence (Table 6.3). We divided the semantic relationship into alternate as none, formal semantic (e.g., category coordinate, subordinate, or superordinate, e.g., chair-sofa, chair-furniture), or semantic associate (e.g., dog-bark). We used two raters to make these judgments.

Again, the number of TOTs is too small to conclude anything much. However, it is obvious that the KS alternates are clearly semantically related to the targets across all groups and all slots. However, they show no sign whatsoever of semantic convergence; if the alternates were getting semantically closer to the targets with time, we would expect the proportion of formally semantically related alternates to increase with slot position. Instead, if anything, we are finding formal semantic divergence, replaced by more loosely related semantic associates. Bear in mind that these are words the speaker ultimately correctly recalls: the pattern we have found, then, is that as they search memory they appear to be getting further away in semantic space before correctly retrieving the word. Hence the title of our chapter: in TOT-like states the journey to the target word is taking us no closer. Nevertheless, people often start off in the right semantic ballpark.

DOUBLE-ATTRACTOR NETWORKS

How can we explain these results? In particular, how do we explain the findings that suggest that semantic factors play such an important role in generating and spontaneously resolving TOTs, given that TOTs are thought to be a failure of retrieval at the lemma level? Why does imageability have an effect, and why do we get semantic alternates?

We want to argue that TOTs can involve two types of difficulty rather than just one: the first is the traditional difficulty with retrieving the phonological form given that we have accessed the lemma, but we think that TOTs also sometimes happen because of difficulty with accessing the lemma itself from the semantic level. We have found that frequency and imageability interact in generating TOTs, and that for any single target word we might produce both semantic and phonological alternates. Therefore, for any target word there might be difficulty with accessing *either* the lemma (which of course will result in difficulty with accessing phonological forms) *or* accessing phonological forms given successful access of the lemma.

At this point, it is useful to think in more detail about lexicalization, the process of accessing words in speech production. We think that it is useful to introduce the concept of an *attractor* into our discussion. Attractors have been used to account for phenomena in the arena of language understanding (e.g., deep dyslexic reading errors; see Hinton & Shallice, 1991), but we believe they are also a useful way of thinking about speech production. An attractor is a point in some multidimensional space to which initial values are attracted. A simple three-dimensional analogy is that if you drop a tennis ball on the side of a large basin, it will soon roll to the bottom of the basin; in this case, the bottom of the basin is an attractor. Talking in terms of attractors has many advantages; finding the right attractor fits well with the process of search, we do not need to talk in terms of lexical units as discrete entities but rather as patterns of activation across lexical space (or phonological forms and phonological sense), and it makes sense to talk about the relative closeness of attractors in the multidimensional space characterized by the appropriate features.

In this framework, lexical access in production is a two-stage process, which involves moving from semantic features to lexical attractors, and then from lexical attractors to phonological attractors. We therefore conceptualize language production for single words in terms of a *double-attractor network*. We can make errors (e.g., because of random noise, because of weak connections caused by aging or lack of use) at either stage of the process. We need feedback links between the units over which a pattern of activation comprises phonological forms and the levels of lexical units, and in turn semantic units, to be able to account for phenomena such as mixed errors in speech production (Dell, 1986; Harley, 1984, Harley & MacAndrew, 2001).

Speaking a word consists of activation spreading from the semantic level to the lexical level, where the appropriate lexical attractor then starts transmitting activation to the phonological level. Semantic whole-word substitutions occur if activation leads to the wrong lexical attractor; phonological whole-word substitutions occur if activation leads to the wrong lexical attractor.

In general, TOTs happen because of difficulty with activating the appropriate attractor because the connections between levels are weakened in some way (see Burke et al., 1991). If retrieval is ultimately successful (in normal speech or a resolved TOT), then the person maps correctly from the appropriate lexical attractor to the correct phonological representation, or in our terms, phonological attractor. In unresolved TOTs the situation is different. If the speaker generates phonological alternates, they are in the correct region of phonological space but are caught by nearby attractors. If they generate partial phonological information, they are retrieving features of phonological space. If, however, they generate semantic alternates, they are partially successful in mapping from semantic to lexical space, but not wholly so, and are getting caught in nearby semantic attractors. We sometimes persist with incorrect items (hence the name, persistent alternates), a state corresponding to getting stuck in an incorrect basin of attraction. We call this double attractor network the TOTAL (for tip-of-the tongue and aging in language) model.

Search in TOT States

In general, though, in TOTs, access does not converge on the right semantic or phonological attractor; instead, the journey appears to be largely random. Contrast this with *conduite d'approche* in conduction aphasia in which patients output a string of words or word fragments in which convergence on the target does sometimes occur, and in which clearly the patient is trying to approximate the target word (Goodglass & Kaplan, 1983). Why should we find this difference in convergence?

The presence of sequential dependencies between items generated can be described in terms of a Markov process. Although *conduite d'approche* might be a Markov process, as might semantic and phonological fluency tasks, with dependencies between items generated, our data do not look like this pattern: alternates are generally unrelated to those generated immediately prior. Indeed, the shift from formal semantic relationships to semantic associates suggests that in a TOT-like state the person has exhausted searching the neighborhood of the target lexical attractor basin and broadens the search. This type of search is known as a Levy flight: searching a particular area and then moving on to a totally different area (rather like birds feeding, where they probe one area quite thoroughly before flying off to start searching a different one). Aspects of searching through alternates resemble other tasks that involve search through semantic space; these can be described formally in terms of foraging models (Hills, Jones, & Todd, 2012), including Levy flights. Such a foraging pattern could explain why Kornell and Metcalfe (2006) found increased TOT resolution after a delay. On the occasions in which the participant is successful in escaping from the TOT, we attribute success to there being sufficient noisy jitter in the semantic-lexical stage for the speaker to find an appropriate lexical attractor.

However, we think two kinds of search are going on in TOT-like states. The first is an automatic process of lexical access in which words are automatically activated by the trickling down of activation from the conceptual level. In this type of search, words "pop" into mind. The second is a more attentional, controlled search through the semantic and phonological spaces generated by the partial activation of semantic and phonological features. In this type of search, the person generates items and examines them before accepting or rejecting them. The partial activation of features enables us to know that there are possible candidates among which we could continue searching. We have elsewhere described a distinction between automatic and deliberative processing (Harley et al., 2011), and think these different types of search are manifestations of this distinction. We think that search in true TOT-states corresponds to the first, automatic type of search, while search in KS-states corresponds to the second, deliberative type of search. Remember that both states are distinguished by different phenomenologies and behavioral criteria.

One curious and important finding is that in these resolved TOT-like states the speaker appears to be running out of steam, getting further away from the target before suddenly getting it right. What is happening here? The process is very similar to *incubation* in problem solving. We can only speculate that while the person has been engaged in either type of search, sufficient activation must have trickled down to the target item to enable it to reach some threshold meaning that it becomes accessible to consciousness.

The Phenomenology of Being in a TOT State

Finally, we would like to make an additional note on the phenomenological aspect of TOT states. TOT resolution is a *catastrophe*: it is the sudden coming of a word into consciousness. A catastrophe is a phase transition: it is a sudden change in state, here from inaccessible to accessible, or unconscious to conscious. TOTs are interesting from a phenomenological perspective because they illustrate that although consciousness might be all or none, there are a variety of states leading to it associated with self-appraised FOK or imminence of recall. FOK in TOTs probably reflects the involvement of the same sorts of mechanisms as in knowing that you've forgotten something, or a déjà vu state (see Cleary, Staley, & Klein, Chapter 5, this volume). TOTs are therefore unique in serving as a powerful weapon in understanding both lexical access and consciousness.

CONCLUSION

We have placed TOTs within a context of retrieval difficulties in speech production. We have also argued that current models of the origin of TOTs, such as the transmission deficit model, are only three-quarters right; TOTs arise whenever there is difficulty accessing phonological forms, not just because the links between the lexical units and phonological forms are weak, but also because the links between the semantic units and lexical forms may be weak. We have described speech production in terms of a double-attractor network. We also stress the place of TOTs as a unique tool in understanding the relation between language and consciousness. We have examined the way alternates come to mind in TOT-like states, and have shown that although they often bear phonological and especially semantic similarities with the targets, they do not sequentially converge upon them. We have distinguished between "knowing search" TOT-like states and true TOT states, arguing that these can be distinguished both phenomenologically and behaviorally, and also that they involve different kinds of search. We have introduced a double-attractor network we have called TOTAL (tip-of-the-tongue and aging and language) in which TOTs can arise as a result of failure of access at the semantic or lexical stages, and related these different failures to different types of search. We can relate the findings to the search space shown in Figure 6.1: active searches obviously involve states further along the activity dimension, but less so along the imminence dimension, while failures at the lexical level are likely to be associated with increased imminence of recall.

REFERENCES

Biedermann, B., Ruh, N., Nickels, L., & Coltheart, M. (2007). Information retrieval in tip of the tongue states: New data and methodological advances. *Journal of Psycholinguistic Research*, 37, 171–198.

Brédart, S., Brennen, T., & Valentine, T. (1995). *The cognitive psychology of proper names*. London: Routledge.

Brown, A. S. (1991). A review of the tip-of-the-tongue experience. *Psychological Bulletin*, 109, 204–223.

(2012). *The tip of the tongue state*. Hove: Psychology Press.

Brown, R., & McNeill, D. (1966). The "tip of the tongue" phenomenon. *Journal of Verbal Learning and Verbal Behavior*, 5, 325–337.

Burke, D. M., MacKay, D. G., Worthley, J. S., & Wade, E. (1991). On the tip of the tongue: What causes word finding failures in young and older adults? *Journal of Memory and Language*, 30, 542–579.

Burke, D. M., & Shafto, M. A. (2004). Aging and language production. *Current Directions in Psychological Science*, 13, 21–24.

Dell, G. S. (1986). A spreading-activation theory of retrieval in sentence production. *Psychological Review*, 93, 283–321.

Farrell, M. T., & Abrams, L. (2011). Tip-of-the-tongue states reveal age differences in the syllable frequency effect. *Journal of Experimental Psychology: Learning, Memory and Cognition*, 37, 277–285.

Galdo-Álvarez, S., Lindín, M., & Díaz, F. (2009). Age-related prefrontal over-recruitment in semantic memory retrieval: Evidence from successful face naming and the tip-of-the-tongue state. *Biological Psychology*, 82, 89–96.

Gollan, T. H., & Brown, A. S. (2006). From tip-of-the-tongue (TOT) data to theoretical implications in two steps: When more TOTs means better retrieval. *Journal of Experimental Psychology: General*, 135, 462–483.

Gollan, T. H., & Silverberg, N. B. (2001). Tip-of-the-tongue states in Hebrew-English bilinguals. *Bilingualism: Language and Cognition*, 4, 63–83.

Goodglass, H., & Kaplan, E. (1983). *The assessment of aphasia and related disorders*. Philadelphia, PA: Lea & Febiger.

Harley, T. A. (1984). A critique of top-down independent levels models of speech production: Evidence from non-plan-internal speech errors. *Cognitive Science*, 8, 191–219.

Harley, T. A., & Bown, H. (1998). What causes tip-of-the-tongue states? *British Journal of Psychology*, 89, 151–174.

Harley, T. A., Jessiman, L. J., & MacAndrew, S. B. G. (2011). Decline and fall: A biological, developmental and psycholinguistic account of deliberative language processing and ageing. *Aphasiology*, 25, 123–153.

Harley, T. A., Jessiman, L. J., MacAndrew, S. B. G., & Astell, A. J. (2008). I don't know what I know: Evidence of preserved semantic knowledge but impaired meta-linguistic knowledge in adults with probable Alzheimer's disease. *Aphasiology*, 22, 321–335.

Harley, T. A., & MacAndrew, S. B. G. (2001). Constraints upon word substitution speech errors. *Journal of Psycholinguistic Research*, 30, 395–418.

Harley, T. A., Oliver, T. M., Jessiman, L. J., & MacAndrew, S. B. G. (2013). Ageing makes us dyslexic. *Aphasiology*, 27, 490–505.

Higgins, J. A., & Johnson, M. K. (2013). Lost thoughts: Implicit semantic interference impairs reflective access to currently active information. *Journal of Experimental Psychology: General*, 142, 6–11.

Hills, T. T., Jones, M. N., & Todd, P. M. (2012). Optimal foraging in semantic memory. *Psychological Review*, 119, 431–440.

Hinton, G. E., & Shallice, T. (1991). Lesioning an attractor network: Investigations of acquired dyslexia. *Psychological Review*, 98, 74–95.

Indefrey, P., & Levelt, W. J. M. (2004). The spatial and temporal signatures of word production components. *Cognition*, 92, 101–144.

James, L. E., & Burke, D. M. (2000). Phonological priming effects on word retrieval and tip-of-the-tongue experiences in young and old adults. *Journal of Experimental Psychology: Learning, Memory and Cognition*, 26, 1378–1391.

Jescheniak, J. D., & Levelt, W. J. M. (1994). Word frequency effects in speech production: Retrieval of syntactic information and of phonological form. *Journal of Experimental Psychology: Learning, Memory and Cognition*, 20, 824–843.

Jones, G. V. (1989). Back to Woodworth: Role of interlopers in the tip-of-the-tongue phenomenon. *Memory & Cognition*, 17, 69–76.

Jones, G. V., & Langford, S. (1987). Phonological blocking in the tip of the tongue state. *Cognition*, 26, 115–122.

Kikyo, H., & Ohki, K. (2002). Neural correlates for feeling-of-knowing: An fMRI parametric analysis. *Neuron*, 36, 177–186.

Koriat, A., & Lieblich, I. (1977). A study of memory pointers. *Acta Psychologica*, 41, 151–164.

Kornell, N., & Metcalfe, J. (2006). "Blockers" do not block recall during tip-of-the-tongue states. *Metacognition Learning*, 1, 248–261.

Levelt, W. J. M. (1989). *Speaking: From intention to articulation*. Cambridge: MA: MIT Press.

Levelt, W. J. M., Roelofs, A., & Meyer, A. S. (1999). A theory of lexical access in speech production. *Behavioral and Brain Sciences*, 22, 1–38.

MacAndrew, S. B. G., Harley, T. A., & Jessiman, L. J. (in preparation). *Lexical navigation in normal and pathological aging: "I know how to get there, I just don't know where it is."*

Maril, A., Wagner, A. D., & Schachter, D. L. (2001). On the tip of the tongue: An event-related fMRI study of semantic retrieval failure and cognitive conflict. *Neuron*, 31, 653–660.

Meyer, A. S., & Bock, K. (1992). The tip-of-the-tongue phenomenon: Blocking or partial activation? *Memory & Cognition*, 20, 715–726.

Miozzo, M., & Caramazza, A. (1997). Retrieval of lexical-syntactic features in tip-of-the-tongue states. *Journal of Experimental Psychology: Learning, Memory and Cognition*, 23, 1410–1423.

Perfect, T. J., & Hanley, J. R. (1992). The tip-of-the-tongue phenomenon: Do experimenter-presented interlopers have any effect? *Cognition, 45,* 55–75.

Rastle, K. G., & Burke, D. M. (1996). Priming the tip of the tongue: Effects of prior processing on word retrieval in young and older adults. *Journal of Memory and Language, 35,* 586–605.

Schwartz, B. L. (2002). The strategic control of retrieval during tip-of-the-tongue states. *Korean Journal of Thinking and Problem-Solving, 12,* 27–38.

(2006). Tip-of-the-tongue states as metacognition. *Metacognition Learning, 1,* 149–158.

Schwartz, B. L., & Metcalfe, J. (2011). Tip-of-the-tongue (TOT) states: Retrieval, behavior, and experience. *Memory and Cognition, 39*(5), 737–749.

Schwartz, B. L., Travis, D. M., Castro, A. M., & Smith, S. M. (2000). The phenomenology of real and illusory tip-of-the-tongue states. *Memory and Cognition, 28,* 18–27.

Shafto, M., Burke, D., Stamatakis, E., Tam, P., & Tyler, L. (2007). On the tip-of-the-tongue: Neural correlates of increased word-finding failures in normal aging. *Journal of Cognitive Neuroscience, 19,* 2060–2070.

Vigliocco, G., Antonini, T., & Garrett, M. D. (1997). Grammatical gender is on the tip of Italian tongues. *Psychological Science, 8,* 314–317.

Warriner, A. B., & Humphreys, K. R. (2008). Learning to fail: Reoccurring tip-of-the-tongue states. *Quarterly Journal of Experimental Psychology, 61,* 535–542.

7

Tip-of-the-Tongue in Mild Cognitive Impairment (MCI)

ONÉSIMO JUNCOS-RABADÁN, DAVID FACAL, AND
ARTURO X. PEREIRO

The tip-of-the-tongue phenomenon (TOT) constitutes one of the most frequently self-acknowledged types of memory failure among elderly people, especially as regards recall of proper nouns. Research has found that difficulty with retrieving people's names is common in the early stages of Alzheimer's disease (AD) and is predictive of progression to AD in individuals with probable dementia. However, the nature of personal name deficits in MCI, which represents one of the earliest clinical features of AD, remains to be fully investigated. This chapter addresses two important issues: a) the deterioration in the ability to recall people's names in MCI, in relation to impaired lexical access and/or breakdown in the structure of semantic knowledge, and b) the study of the TOT phenomenon for proper nouns, as a lexical measure that can be used in epidemiological studies to detect MCI. We present a review of the literature concerning these issues, along with data obtained in our current research.

THE CONCEPT OF MCI

The concept of mild cognitive impairment (MCI) was first proposed by Flicker and colleagues (Flicker, Ferris, & Reisberg, 1991). Petersen and colleagues (Petersen, 2004; Petersen et al., 1999, 2001) employed MCI as a diagnostic entity for characterizing individuals who suffer from cognitive

This work was financially supported by the Spanish Directorate General for Science and Technology under Projects SEJ2007–67964-CO2–01, PSI2010–22224-C03–01 and by Xunta Galicia Government under Project 10 PXIB 211070 PR.
Corresponding author: Onésimo Juncos-Rabadán, Department of Developmental and Educational Psychology, University of Santiago de Compostela, Campus Sur, 15782 Santiago de Compostela, Spain. Phone: +34 881813908. Fax: +34 881813900. E-mail: onesimo.juncos@usc.es.

impairment that is not severe enough to constitute dementia. Petersen and colleagues (1999) proposed the following diagnostic criteria for MCI: complaints of defective memory and abnormal memory functioning for age on testing, with normal general cognitive functioning and conserved ability to perform activities of daily living. MCI initially referred to memory deficits and the absence of functional impairment, but recent research has found that other cognitive domains and everyday functioning may be affected (Ritchie & Ritchie, 2012). Although somewhat controversial, the term MCI is generally used to refer to a clinical construct that may imply development of Alzheimer's disease (AD) or of another form of dementia in the future, or it may imply stability or, less commonly, improvement in clinical symptoms (Petersen, 2009; Petersen et al., 2001).

There is general consensus regarding the criteria used to diagnose MCI and the classification of MCI into two main broad types, amnestic and non-amnestic, depending on whether the memory is deteriorated or not. There is also general agreement regarding the possible etiologies of MCI, which may be degenerative, vascular, psychiatric, traumatic, or metabolic (Petersen, 2003, 2004; Winblad, Palmer, Kivipelto, Jelic, & Fratiglioni, 2004). The following general criteria are used in diagnosing MCI: (i) evidence of concern about a change in cognition, preferably corroborated by an informant, (ii) lower performance in one or more cognitive domains that is greater than would be expected for the patient's age and educational background, (iii) functional activities mainly preserved or minimally impaired, and (iv) nonfulfillment of diagnostic criteria for dementia (Albert et al., 2011). The two main types of MCI may be differentiated into four subtypes (single domain amnestic, multiple domain amnestic, single domain non-amnestic, and multiple domain non-amnestic), depending on whether the impairment affects one or more cognitive domains. The single domain amnestic (sda-MCI) and multiple domain amnestic MCI (mda-MCI) subtypes are most likely to progress to AD and probably represent prodromal or pre-clinical forms of AD (Dubois & Albert, 2004; Dubois et al., 2007; Petersen et al., 2004; Petersen & Morris, 2005; Ritchie & Ritchie, 2012). The National Institute on Aging-Alzheimer's Association workgroup on diagnostic guidelines for Alzheimer's disease recently proposed use of the term "mild cognitive impairment (MCI) due to AD" to refer to amnestic subtypes as preclinical forms of AD (Albert et al., 2011). Diagnostic criteria for amnestic subtypes of MCI include impairment of episodic memory (i.e., the ability to learn and retain new information). Although no particular tests or thresholds have been specified for fulfillment of this criterion, scores on cognitive tests of 1.5 SDs below age norms have been suggested (Albert et al., 2011;

Petersen, 2004), and several memory tests, such as free recall, cued recall, and delayed recall tests, have been recommended for differentiating MCI from other memory deficits that predominate in depression, such as frontotemporal dementia, vascular dementia, and even normal aging (Dubois & Albert, 2004; Gauthier et al., 2006).

Multiple domain non-amnestic (mdna-MCI) and single domain non-amnestic (sdna-MCI) subtypes are defined, following the criteria proposed by Petersen and colleagues (2009) and Gauthier and colleagues (2006), by the presence of impairment in one or several cognitive domains such as language, attention, praxis, and executive function, although performance on episodic memory tests (short-term and long-term recall) is well preserved. Although amnestic MCI is most closely associated with Alzheimer's dementia, non-amnestic MCI is more heterogeneous in its associations, which include vascular dementia, frontotemporal dementia, and dementia with Lewy bodies (Ritchie & Ritchie, 2012).

TIP-OF-THE-TONGUE (TOT) FOR PROPER NAMES

To have a word on the tip of one's tongue is the experience of the "failure to recall a word of which one has knowledge" when one wishes to recall, accompanied by the feeling that recall is imminent and accompanied by a feeling of knowing (Brown, 2012; Brown & McNeill, 1966, p. 325). Such tip-of-the-tongue events (TOTs) constitute one of the most frequently self-acknowledged types of memory failure among elderly people (especially as regards recall of proper nouns) and appear to increase in frequency with age. This self-acknowledgment represents the metacognitive level, which is the reflection on the cognitive level, that is, the attempt to retrieve a missing item from memory (Schwartz & Metcalfe, 2011). The actual failure of recall is the focus of our work, taking into account that the metacognitive aspect of TOT is also an important issue in the TOT research (Schwartz, 2006).

Researchers have presented compelling arguments and empirical evidence in support of the thesis that in lexical access there is a moment at which a semantically specified lexical representation has been accessed, but not its phonological content. This thesis is accepted by theorists who subscribe to discrete- versus interactive-stage models of lexical access and by those who assume componential versus holistic views of word meaning (Caramazza & Miozzo, 1997, p. 329). Serial and connectionist models of language production have coincided in attributing TOTs to failure in phonological activation following successful activation of the semantic representation of the target word (Caramazza & Miozzo, 1997; Dell, Schwartz,

Martin, & Gagnon, 1997; Levelt, Roelofs, & Meyer, 1999; MacKay, 1987; MacKay & Burke, 1990). All of these models entail at least two processing stages in which meaning-based representations are activated before form-based representations (Rapp & Goldrick, 2006). The most relevant hypothesis regarding the causes of phonological failure considers that TOTs occur when phonological activation of a semantically activated word fails to reach the necessary threshold owing to faulty transmission of the priming signal. Correct transmission is facilitated by frequent and recent use, which makes a word more familiar, and transmission degradation occurs as we age (Burke, MacKay, Worthley, & Wade, 1991). The current TOT literature provides the strongest support for the transmission deficit model (for a review, see Brown, 2012, pp. 160–169).

Experimental studies on TOTs in normal aging show that increased failure in access to the phonological representation of words, especially proper names, is associated with aging, whereas semantic representations and access are relatively well preserved in aging (Cross & Burke, 2004; Facal-Mayo, Juncos-Rabadán, Álvarez, Pereiro-Rozas, & Díaz, 2006; Gollan & Brown, 2006; James, 2006; Juncos-Rabadán, Facal, Rodriguez, & Pereiro, 2010).

Lexical access of person names, according to several models (Burke et al., 1991; Valentine, Brennen, & Brédart, 1996), involves a particular process that requires specific activation of the conceptual or semantic knowledge about that person, followed by an additional lexical-level representation of the name itself and its phonological representation. Proper names are purely referential; they pick out individuals rather than categorizing them as exemplars as object names do. This one-to-one relationship is often cited as a reason that personal names are more difficult to produce than object names (for a review, see Griffin, 2010). Proper names are particularly vulnerable to TOTs because (to use the example given in Burke et al., 1991, p. 571), correct naming of someone called John Baker requires activation of the conceptual level node for that person, followed by additional lexical-level representation of the name Baker itself, which is shared by other people named Baker. It is the additional one-to-one connections, between John Baker (proper noun phrase) and Baker (family proper name), and then from Baker to the phonology, that make proper names vulnerable to transmission deficits. This one-to-one connection via the proper noun phrase has been shown from experiments that demonstrated it is possible to remember if celebrities were known by three names (e.g., Catherine Zeta Jones) rather than two (Cameron Diaz), even when it is impossible to recall the names themselves (Hanley & Chapman, 2008). In contrast, the lexical representation of common nouns is directly connected to multiple semantic nodes. The lexical node for "baker" is connected to an extended and diffuse network of nodes in the semantic systems and provides wealthy information about this profession, whereas the lexical node John Baker (proper noun phrase) has no semantic connections independent of those for a particular person.

TOTs for personal names have been recently studied with the event-related potential (ERP) technique. Studies by Díaz, Lindín, Galdo-Álvarez, Facal, and Juncos-Rabadán (2007) have shown that the smaller amplitude ERPs in TOT events than in correct responses (over the 550–750 ms interval, which includes the late P3 component) may represent correlates of the TOT state. This may reflect lower activation of the lexical route from semantic representations through the proper name phrase to the phonological representations, which would explain the difficulty in naming. Buján, Galdo-Álvarez, Lindín, and Díaz (2012) have found similar ERP correlates of recognition and access to semantic and lexical information for TOTs and correct responses, but they have also observed that a delayed onset of the response selection occurs in TOT in relation to correct naming, which suggests insufficient activation of phonological information (see Díaz, Lindín, Galdo-Álvarez, & Buján, Chapter 10, this volume).

Several studies have investigated the neural correlates of lexical access to proper names, and these findings appear to indicate a role for the left temporal pole as a mediational structure that is engaged by structures that support conceptual and semantic knowledge (high-order sensory cortices in both hemispheres) and that drives the process of phonological representation in vocalization (supported by left perisylvian language areas) (Damasio & Damasio, 1994; Damasio, Grabowski, Tranel, Hichwa, & Damasio, 1996; Grabowski et al., 2001). As a multimodal association cortex, the temporal pole is also reciprocally connected to the entorhinal cortex and hippocampus (Arnold, Hy man, & Van Hoesen, 1994), which are affected by vascular and neurodegenerative processes in AD and MCI.

Behavioral and brain-related studies of TOT need to resolve certain methodological problems (see for a review Brown, 2012). One of the most important problems involved in the TOT paradigm of memory failures in lexical accessing concerns the measures that may be used to evaluate semantic and phonological access. Gollan and Brown (2006) proposed two main measures that represent success in the semantic and phonological processes involved in TOT events. Semantic access was estimated by a proportional measure that represents successful access to the semantic representations of the names and indicates success in the processing stage during which meaning-based representations are activated. Juncos-Rabadán and colleagues (2010) calculated semantic access with the equation [(Correct responses + positive TOTs)/Total presented names], which is adapted from the original formula proposed by Gollan and Brown (2006), and which represents the proportion of responses that involve successful semantic access in the total number of items. Positive TOTs are TOT events in which the word on the tip of the subject's tongue is indeed the correct word, whereas negative TOTs are those in which the word on the tip of the tongue is not the target word. Phonological access or success in phonological access was calculated as [Correct responses/(Correct responses + positive TOTs)], which is a modified version of the measure proposed by Gollan and Brown (2006) and represents the proportion of successful semantic retrievals in which form retrieval is also successful and indicates success in the processing stage during which form-based representations are activated.

RETRIEVING PEOPLE'S NAMES IN MCI

Several researchers have found that difficulty with retrieving people's names is common in the early stages of AD and is highly predictive of progress to AD in individuals with probable dementia (Ahmed, Arnold, Thompson, Graham, & Hodges, 2008; De Jager & Budge, 2005; Semenza, Borgo, Mondini, Pasini, & Sgaramella, 2003; Thompson, Graham, Patterson, Sahakian, & Hodges, 2002). However, the nature of personal name deficits in AD and MCI remains to be fully investigated. Access to semantic knowledge about famous people is particularly vulnerable in patients in the early stages of AD (Ahmed et al., 2008; Beeson, Holland, & Murray, 1997; Estevez-Gonzalez et al., 2004; Greene & Hodges, 1996). However, studies of patients with MCI are scarce and not conclusive. Estevez-Gonzalez and colleagues (2004) found that patients with MCI who developed probable AD within at least two years had more problems associated with access to semantic knowledge than did MCI patients who did not develop AD, although the authors did not find any differences between the latter group (possibly sufferers of amnestic MCI) and control subjects. In a comparison of the performance of a naming task (with 30 photographs of famous people) by a group of 15 patients with amnestic MCI and a group of healthy control subjects, Joubert and colleagues (2010) found that the amnestic MCI (aMCI) patients performed less well than the control group as regards naming famous faces and their semantic knowledge about the famous people. These authors proposed that naming deficits in MCI are associated with underlying semantic deficit for famous people. Considering the results shown by the authors (Joubert et al., 2010; figure 1, p. 982), we can see that the percentage of correct responses for naming in aMCI was 49.8 compared with 75.7 for semantic knowledge, which indicates that performance on semantic knowledge was better than performance on accessing the corresponding names. Moreover, on examining the overall number of occurrences at the single item level (Joubert et al., 2010, Table 2A, p. 982), we can see that the number was 90 when naming and semantic knowledge were correct, 212 when naming and semantic knowledge were incorrect, 14 when naming was correct but semantic knowledge was incorrect, and 134 when naming was incorrect but semantic knowledge was correct. As the authors stated, there were more naming deficits (subject was unable to provide the full name of the presented famous face) than correct responses, and these were associated with incorrect semantic knowledge in 47 percent (212/450) of the instances. However, naming deficits or unsuccessful naming was associated with success in semantic knowledge (correct semantic knowledge) in 30 percent (134/450) of the instances, indicating that naming deficits were never produced by semantic breakdown. In a comparison of the performance of several tasks evaluating naming and semantic knowledge of famous people by an amnestic MCI group (13 people) and a control group (14 people), Clague, Graham, Thompson, and Hodges (2011) found that the amnestic MCI group performed less well (as measured by correct responses) than controls on verbal fluency in people's names, naming people from pictures and several tasks of personal knowledge. These authors also indicated that combined tasks regarding personal knowledge were sensitive to severe impairment of general cognitive ability as measured by MMSE. Their results provide evidence about the deterioration in naming people in amnestic MCI, although the sensitivity of the battery of tests is questionable because of the small size of the MCI group and because the analyses did not provide sensitive enough measures to discriminate amnestic MCI patients from normal controls.

Although the aforementioned studies provide some evidence for a decrease in semantic knowledge in subjects suffering from amnestic MCI, the question of whether impaired naming of people in MCI reflects problems associated with lexical access or a breakdown in the structure of semantic knowledge has not been adequately addressed. The study by Joubert and colleagues (2010) demonstrated that amnestic MCI patients were often (around 30% of the trials) not able to access the correct name, even though they knew the corresponding person and their responses about semantic knowledge were correct. The consistency between incorrect semantic knowledge and incorrect naming found by the authors in 47 percent of the instances only indicates that when patients did not know the person very well, they did not access the correct name; however, this does not explain the most important phenomenon, that is, the difficulty with finding the name when the corresponding semantic knowledge is correctly accessed. We think that the previously explained theoretical and experimental paradigm of TOT may be useful for studying this phenomenon. However, to date few studies have directly investigated TOTs for famous people's names in MCI.

TOT FOR FAMOUS PEOPLE'S NAMES IN MCI: SEMANTIC OR POST-SEMANTIC IMPAIRMENT

Although recent studies have shown that both semantic knowledge and naming of famous people are impaired in amnestic MCI patients (Ahmed et al., 2008; Clague et al., 2011; Joubert et al., 2008, 2010), it is not clear whether the impairment in naming people reflects problems associated with semantic knowledge and access (access to meaning-based representations) or a breakdown in lexical-phonological access (access to form-based representations). To address this question, we review the literature on TOT in MCI and AD, and we present data and conclusions from our own research on production of the TOT phenomenon by MCI patients in naming famous people.

In a study exploring TOT production for common nouns in AD patients, Astell and Harley (1996) found that AD patients produced fewer correct responses and more don't know and TOT responses than controls (46%–80%; 14%–0.5%; and 12%–5.5% respectively), and they suggested that AD increases the weakness of semantic-to-lexical connections that Burke and colleagues proposed (1991), and that AD contributes to the loss of semantic knowledge. In an interesting study of TOT for proper names in patients with mild and moderate AD, Beeson and colleagues (1997) found that all patients had difficulties with providing correct semantic information as well as in recognizing the first letter and correct shape of the proper names. However, the semantic access (provision of correct semantic information) was fairly good in the mild AD group (75%) and lower (42%) in the moderate AD group. Recognition of the first letter (7% and 9% for mild and moderate AD group respectively) and correct shapes (3% and 10% respectively) was equally deteriorated in both groups, indicating similar levels of disturbance in phonological access.

Delazer, Semenza, Reiner, Hofer, and Benke (2003) compared how successful a group of AD patients, a group of amnestic MCI patients, and healthy controls were in naming famous people from photographs. These authors found that the AD group identified fewer items correctly than the amnestic MCI or control groups, with no significant differences between the latter two groups. The AD group provided significantly less semantic information and produced a higher proportion of TOTs than the MCI and control groups (although the absolute number of TOTs did not differ significantly between groups). There was no difference between the MCI group and controls regarding semantic and phonological access, but the control group retrieved names more frequently than the MCI group when a phonological cue (first letter of name) was provided. The number of errors (wrong names) was significantly lower in the MCI group than in the AD and control groups. Delazer and colleagues (2003) concluded that AD patients suffer from lexical deficits (i.e., problems in accessing the phonological representation of the name) in addition to semantic deficits. In TOT responses, AD patients recognized famous faces, claimed to know the name but temporarily not to retrieve it. They were able to deliver specific semantic information to the person and finally to name him/her with a cue or to recognize the name in a multiple choice task. The amnestic MCI group did not differ from controls in either semantic or phonological access, which suggested no impairment in semantic or post-semantic processes. The only significant difference between MCI and controls was in free recall and verbal recognition memory; the authors affirmed that this memory deficit did not extend to proper name retrieval.

A study by our research group, in which multiple domain amnestic MCI and healthy control groups were compared, showed that the MCI patients produced more TOTs and fewer correct answers than controls during a naming task involving 60 photographs of famous people (Juncos-Rabadán, Pereiro, & Rodríguez, 2009; Rodríguez, Juncos-Rabadán, & Facal, 2008), indicating that impairment in phonological accessing of proper names occurs in multiple domain amnestic MCI.

Considering that amnestic MCI is the type of MCI that is most likely to progress to AD and represents a cognitive state between normal aging and AD (Albert et al., 2011), we hypothesized that amnestic MCI may have different effects on the two main processes involved in naming famous people: access to semantic knowledge and lexical access. Semantic knowledge of the persons, including access to semantic representations such as face, profession, and main aspects of their life and personality, is relatively well preserved in normal aging (Juncos-Rabadán et al., 2010), but deteriorates in AD (Ahmed et al., 2008; Beeson et al., 1997; Estevez-Gonzalez et al., 2004; Greene & Hodges, 1996). Phonological access to the lexical unit that constitutes the proper name (usually first name and family name) is impaired in normal aging (Burke et al., 1991; Evrard, 2002; Facal-Mayo et al., 2006; James, 2006; Juncos-Rabadán et al., 2010; Maylor, 1990; Rastle & Burke, 1996; Rendell, Castel, & Craik, 2005), probably because of a deficit in transmission of activation from semantic representations through proper name phrase to phonological representations (Burke et al., 1991). Our general hypothesis was that in amnestic MCI, semantic access might be preserved or only slightly impaired, but that phonological access must be significantly deteriorated relative to that in normal aging. Amnestic MCI would represent a step between normal aging and AD with respect to retrieval of personal names, and the main important characteristics in this respect would be greater difficulty with accessing lexical-phonological representations than in normal aging, and an initial difficulty with accessing semantic representations, which is already evident in AD.

In our first study (Juncos-Rabadán, Rodríguez, Facal, Cuba, & Pereiro, 2011), we investigated whether difficulties with retrieving the names of famous people in amnestic MCI patients were related to general semantic knowledge, the particular semantic knowledge of the persons, the semantic access to the names, or the phonological access to the names. We used a TOT experimental paradigm consisting of a famous person naming task (photographs of 50 famous people), in which several processes were differentiated: (1) the feeling of knowing that participants have about the name of the famous person, as a feeling that they will able to recognize that name, independently of whether it was recalled or not (Schwartz, 2002); (2) the actual knowledge that participants have about the name; (3) the semantic knowledge that they have about profession and several details about the person's life; (4) the semantic access to the proper name, which is represented, according the aforementioned formula [(Correct responses + positive TOTs)/Total presented names], by names for which semantic representation is successfully accessed, even though the phonological representation is not retrieved; and (5) the phonological access to the proper name, which is represented by names for which phonological representation is not retrieved, even though the semantic representation is successfully accessed, and calculated by the other aforementioned formula [Correct responses/(Correct responses + positive TOTs)]. We controlled the associations between the described processes and familiarity of the target names. Familiarity is an important factor in name retrieval and depends on frequency and recency of use (Burke et al., 1991; Hanley & Chapman, 2008), but had not been controlled for in previous studies (Delazer et al., 2003; Estevez-Gonzalez et al., 2004; Joubert et al., 2010). General semantic information, represented by the level of vocabulary, has been shown to be involved in semantic access but not in phonological access (Juncos-Rabadán et al., 2010), and was measured by the Wechsler vocabulary test.

Amnestic MCI is mainly defined by impairment in episodic memory (i.e., the ability to learn and retain new information). This is assessed in the

California Verbal Learning Test, which tests both immediate and delayed recall. Therefore, it was important to investigate whether deficits in immediate and delayed recall verbal memory extend to proper name retrieval in order to have more data to test the hypothesis by Delazer and colleagues (2003) that stated that this memory deficit did not influence proper name retrieval. For these purposes, we compared four groups that represented a continuum with respect to memory impairment: a multiple domain amnestic MCI (mda-MCI) group composed of 35 individuals with memory impairment, together with impairment in other cognitive domains such as attention, praxis, and executive functions, and a decrease in general cognitive functioning measured by the MMSE; a single domain amnestic MCI (sda-MCI) group consisting of 23 individuals with impairment only in memory but with normal general cognitive functioning; a control group including 38 healthy individuals with high subjective memory complaints (hmc-Control), but with no objective memory or other cognitive deficits; and another control group comprising 34 healthy individuals with a low level of subjective memory complaints (lmc-Control), but with normal memory and cognitive functioning. All participants were more than 50 years old, and all groups were matched according to age and level of education. Amnestic MCI patients fulfilled the criteria outlined by Petersen and colleagues (Petersen, 2004; Winblad et al., 2004) and Dubois and colleagues (Dubois & Albert, 2004; Gauthier et al. 2006).

The results indicated that semantic knowledge of the 50 target names was not impaired in either of the two amnestic MCI groups, who obtained similar scores as the control groups not only for subjective knowledge represented by the feeling of knowing (Koriat, 2000) and familiarity that participants had about the names and people, but also for objective knowledge about the famous people (Figure 7.1).

The scores for the proportional measure of success in semantic access obtained by individuals with amnestic MCI indicated no impairment as regards accessing semantic representations of very familiar famous people. The main process affected in naming famous people, which was significantly impaired only in the individuals with multiple domain amnestic MCI, was phonological access (Figure 7.2), although the scores obtained by the single domain amnestic MCI group were lower than those obtained by the control groups.

We found that the TOT events provided evidence that impairment of naming famous people in amnestic MCI reflects a breakdown in phonological access, but does not reflect problems associated with semantic knowledge and access when familiarity or knowledge of the famous people (depending

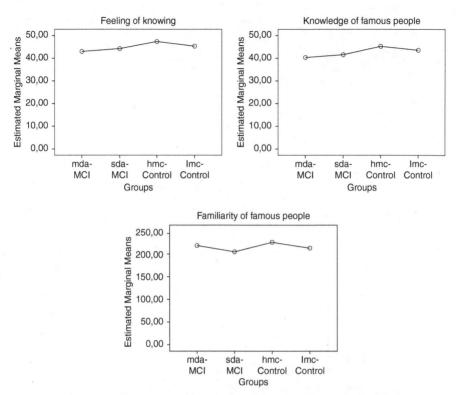

FIGURE 7.1. Profiles of knowledge variables, with estimated marginal means (up to the maximum possible scoring) for multiple domain amnestic MCI (mda-MCI), single domain amnestic MCI (sda-MCI), normal healthy controls with a high level of subjective memory complaints (hmc-Control), and normal healthy controls with a low level of subjective memory complaints (lmc-Control).

on their recency and frequency of use) was controlled for. The breakdown in phonological access may also explain why the amnestic MCI patients studied by Joubert and colleagues (2010) were sometimes (30% of times) unable to access the names, even though they possessed accurate semantic knowledge about the corresponding people. General semantic knowledge measured by vocabulary tests was not a significant covariate for phonological access. The level of vocabulary representing crystallized verbal abilities is not an important variable explaining phonological access to proper names. Impairment of phonological access to lexical representation of proper names was maintained in multiple domain amnestic MCI, independently of the level of vocabulary of individuals, owing to the particular structure of proper names (Juncos-Rabadán et al., 2010; Laver & Burke, 1993).

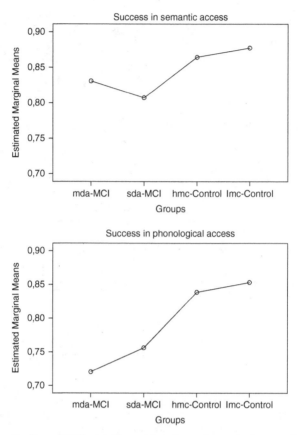

FIGURE 7.2. Profiles of TOT variables, with estimated marginal means (percentage) for multiple domain amnestic MCI (mda-MCI), single domain amnestic MCI (sda-MCI), normal healthy controls with a high level of subjective memory complaints (hmc-Control), and normal healthy controls with a low level of subjective memory complaints (lmc-Control).

Taking into account that phonological access was only significantly impaired in the multiple domain MCI group, we considered the role of verbal memory (immediate and delayed recall) in this impairment. Results from multivariate regression analyses performed on all groups showed that success in phonological access was best predicted by age, which explained 14 percent of the variance, and then by general cognitive functioning, measured by the MMSE, which added 17 percent to the variance explained only by age, and then by memory, which added 5 percent to the variance explained by age and general cognitive functioning together. We provisionally suggested that impairment in phonological access (the main impairment in the naming processes in amnestic MCI) may be mainly due to aging and general cognitive deterioration and only secondarily due to impairment in verbal memory.

THE ROLE OF EPISODIC MEMORY IN IMPAIRMENT IN NAMING PEOPLE IN MCI

To investigate the influence of verbal memory on the impairment in phonological access in MCI, we carried out a second study on TOTs for proper names (Juncos-Rabadán, Facal, Lojo-Seoane & Pereiro, 2013a). We compared performance on the same TOT task used in the previous study among a multiple domain amnestic MCI group (32 participants), a multiple domain non-amnestic MCI group (28 participants), and a normal control group (65 participants). The multiple domain amnestic MCI (mda-MCI) group displayed impairment in short and delayed verbal episodic memory, together with impairment in other cognitive domains such as attention, praxis, and executive functions, and decreased general cognitive functioning, measured by the MMSE. The multiple domain non-amnestic MCI (mdna-MCI) was characterized by normal functioning in short and delayed verbal episodic memory, impairment in several cognitive domains such as attention, praxis and mainly executive functions, and a decrease in general cognitive functioning. The results showed that amnestic and non-amnestic MCI patients did not differ from controls in the subjective (feeling of knowing, familiarity of the famous people) or objective semantic knowledge about the people (Figure 7.3), or in success in semantic access, whereas the performance of both was significantly poorer than that of the controls in the success in phonological access (Figure 7.4). Amnestic and non-amnestic MCI showed the same pattern of impairment as regards phonological access to the names of famous people.

To test the influence of verbal episodic memory on semantic and phonological access, we performed multivariate regression analyses, with age, familiarity, general cognitive functioning (measured by MMSE), short and long delay free recall (measured by the California Verbal Learning Test), and executive function (measured by the CAMCOG-R; Roth, Huppert, Mountjoy, & Tym, 1999) as independent variables or predictors. Semantic access was only significantly predicted by age and familiarity, which explained 44 percent of the variance. Cognitive status, represented jointly by general cognitive functioning, verbal episodic memory, and executive functions, did not explain the success in semantic access. Phonological access was significantly predicted by general cognitive functioning and

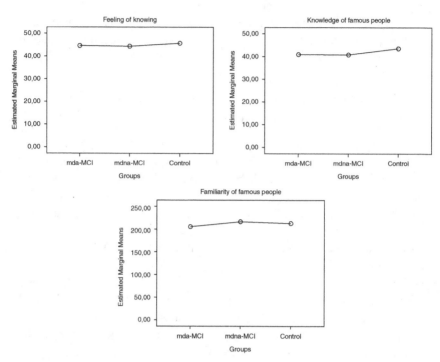

FIGURE 7.3. Profiles of knowledge variables, with estimated marginal means (up to the maximum scores possible) for multiple domain amnestic MCI (mda-MCI), multiple domain non-amnestic MCI (mdna-MCI), and normal healthy controls.

executive functions, which explained 33 percent of the variance, but not by verbal episodic memory.

From this study, we concluded that amnestic and non-amnestic MCI did not display any disturbances in semantic knowledge and semantic access to very familiar famous names and that phonological access was the most impaired process, mainly because of deterioration of general cognitive functioning, particularly of the executive functions. Impairment of verbal episodic memory, which was represented by short and long delay recall deficits, was not related to phonological access. These conclusions were partly consistent with the hypothesis maintained by Semenza and colleagues (2003), that is, that in amnestic MCI, deficits in free and cued verbal recall do not extend to proper name recall.

Impairment in general cognitive functioning and in executive functions represents a decrease in cognitive resources and greater difficulty in controlling these resources, and may be responsible for impaired access to the phonological representations of famous names once the semantic

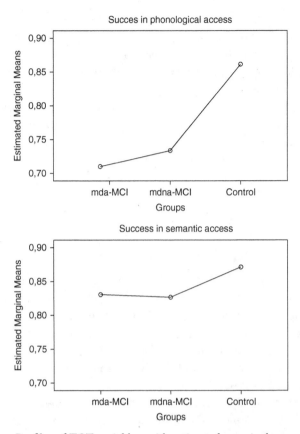

FIGURE 7.4. Profiles of TOT variables, with estimated marginal means (percentage) for multiple domain amnestic MCI (mda-MCI), multiple domain non-amnestic MCI (mdna-MCI), and normal healthy controls.

representations have been successfully accessed. A recent study by our research team (Facal, Juncos-Rabadán, Rodríguez, & Pereiro, 2012) investigated the relations between TOT production and processing speed in normal aging. We found a negative effect of age on TOT mediated by processing speed, which may reveal the action of some cognitive control mechanisms. If TOT is considered as a failure of automatic transmission processes involved in activation from semantic to phonological representations, and if it is assumed that other controlled processes may be involved in modulation of the lexical system in response to demands of TOT events, the relationship between slowed processing and TOTs can be interpreted in the sense that slowing in older adults may reflect the use of controlled compensatory mechanisms.

We interpret these findings in light of the transmission deficit hypothesis (Burke et al., 1991), by considering that along with age, multiple domain MCI (amnestic or non-amnestic) weakens connections to phonological representations, makes the production of TOTs in naming person names more likely, and reduces the production of correct names. Individuals suffering from single domain amnestic MCI did not differ from the controls in phonological access, suggesting that only multiple domain amnestic and non-amnestic MCI produces a deficit in naming of people in photographs, and involves a greater deficit in transmission of the activation from semantic to phonological representations than that produced by age in normal control groups.

DOES TIP-OF-THE-TONGUE FOR FAMOUS NAMES INDICATE MCI?

Individuals diagnosed with MCI constitute a high-risk population for the development of dementia and are thus of major clinical interest with regard to a reliable early diagnosis of the disease. Cognitive evaluation of MCI includes, as Albert and colleagues (2011) have pointed out, the assessment of language as one important cognitive domain that may be impaired. In this section, we discuss the utility of TOT for famous people as a measure for an early diagnosis of MCI, taking into account that other linguistic processes have to be assessed in the current neuropsychological evaluation.

Although there is increasing evidence that naming people may be compromised in MCI, which supports the inclusion of a famous people naming task in the neuropsychological screening of MCI patients (Joubert et al., 2010), only the study by Brouillette and colleagues (2011) has directly investigated the utility of famous people naming tasks in discriminating MCI from normal controls. Brouillette and colleagues (2011) proposed their Memory for Names test (Mem4Names test), which comprises photographs of 72 famous people that patients have to name, to distinguish MCI from healthy subjects. These authors reported that the test displayed good sensitivity (68.3%) and specificity (68.6%) (cut-score of 49) for classifying healthy controls and MCI participants (including amnestic and non-amnestic), with an AUC (area under curve ROC) value of 0.75 (95% CI: 0.66–0.84). This overall value for correct classification was similar to that other researchers obtained with verbal fluency tests. *Verbal fluency* is typically defined as the ability to produce words under specific constraints (categories or letters) and within a fixed time interval (Lezak, 2004), and it is the core of the most widely used lexical task for detecting MCI (Taler &

Phillips, 2009). Two of the most recent studies concerning the classification value of verbal fluency for detecting MCI reported an AUC between 0.87 to discriminate an unspecified group of MCI with animal category fluency (Cunje, Molloy, Standish, & Lewis, 2007) and of 70.4 and 61.7 (respectively for fruits and animals) to discriminate control subjects and MCI patients that included multiple domain, amnestic single domain, and non-amnestic single domain subtypes (Radanovic et al., 2009).

Our research team (Juncos-Rabadán, Facal, Lojo-Seoane, & Pereiro, 2013b) recently investigated the potential utility of a famous people's naming task in discriminating between amnestic MCI patients and normal controls. However, unlike previous studies, we incorporated TOT measures. In the study, 32 participants with multiple domain amnestic MCI, 52 with single domain amnestic MCI, and 106 normal controls performed the same TOT task as described before. A multivariate logistic regression model that included feeling of knowing, semantic knowledge of the person, success in semantic access, and success in phonological access (all significant factors in univariate analysis) was used to assess the predictive value of the TOT measures to discriminate between normal controls and amnestic MCI patients. Only phonological access (OR=5.13; 95% CI=2.64–10.00) remained significantly associated with amnestic MCI. The model correctly classified 70 percent of controls (specificity) and 71.6 percent of amnestic MCI patients (sensitivity); the AUC value (ROC analysis) was 0.74 (95% CI=0.67–0.81) and accounted for 23.5 percent of the variance.

Another multivariate logistic regression model included 21 multiple domain non-amnestic MCI patients in the analysis. Among the TOT measures (feeling of knowing, semantic knowledge of the person, success in semantic access, and success in phonological access), which were significant factors in univariate analysis, only success in phonological access (OR=5.85; 95% CI=3.08–11.13) remained significantly associated with MCI. The model correctly classified 68.2 percent of controls (specificity) and 74.5 percent of aMCI patients (sensitivity); the AUC value (ROC analysis) was 0.76 (95% CI=0.69–0.82) and accounted for 26.7 percent of the variance.

To compare the value of the TOT variables with that of the verbal fluency to differentiate amnestic MCI from controls, univariate regression analysis was applied, with the verbal fluency scores (animals) as the dependent variable. This analysis revealed that the incidence of amnestic MCI increased significantly when the verbal fluency decreased (OR=4.52; 95% CI=1.51–6.68). Verbal fluency correctly classified 55.2 percent of controls (specificity) and 78.6 percent of aMCI patients (sensitivity); the AUC value was 0.66 (95% CI=0.59–0.74), and accounted for 15.4 percent of the variance. Similarly, when amnestic and non-amnestic MCI types were analyzed together, verbal fluency differentiated MCI patients from controls (OR=4.49; 95% CI=2.44–8.27), and also correctly classified 54.1 percent of controls (specificity) and 79.2 percent of aMCI patients (sensitivity); the AUC value was 0.66 (95% CI=0.59–0.74), and it accounted for 15.2 percent of the variance.

The results of the latter studies showed that TOT measures for proper names are sensitive to differences between amnestic MCI patients and healthy controls and between MCI (amnestic and non-amnestic) and healthy controls. The sensitivity (71.6%), specificity (70%), and AUC value (0.74) of the measures for classifying amnestic MCI patients from normal controls and for discriminating MCI (amnestic and non-amnestic) from normal controls (sensitivity 74.5%, specificity 68.2 %, and AUC 0.76) were adequate and slightly higher than those obtained by Brouillette and colleagues (2011) with the Memory for Names test and similar to those reported by Cunje and colleagues (2007) and Radanovic and colleagues (2009) with respect to verbal fluency tests (animals). The proportion of variance explained was between 25 percent and 26.7 percent, which is high considering that only the TOT variables were entered in the models. We concluded that TOTs for proper names may be sensitive indicators, able to distinguish multiple domain amnestic and non-amnestic MCI patients from healthy controls, especially with a variable that represents lexical and phonological access.

CONCLUSIONS OF THE RESEARCH ON TOTS IN MCI

We can conclude that the difficulty MCI subjects experienced in recalling names of people may be explained by failures in phonological access, which also occurs in the early stages of AD (Ahmed et al., 2008; De Jager & Budge, 2005; Semenza et al., 2003; Thompson et al., 2002). In other words, in multiple domain MCI, activation of the form-based representations rather than the meaning-based representations appears to be impaired in naming people. In previous studies (Juncos-Rabadán et al., 2011), we suggested that deterioration in naming is a continuous process between normal aging and AD. The process begins with difficulties in phonological access in normal aging, as reflected by an increase in the incidence of TOTs, and progresses to deterioration in semantic access in AD. As a cognitive state between normal aging and AD, MCI exhibits an increase in phonological difficulties relative to normal aging, but without (at least not to a significant degree) the semantic deterioration that implies AD. It appears that MCI mainly affects

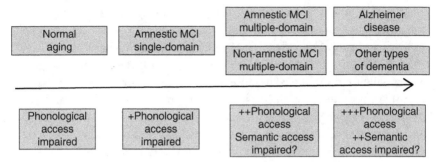

FIGURE 7.5. Representation of the deterioration in naming of famous people as a continuum from normal aging to Alzheimer's disease and other types of dementia, via different types of amnestic and non-amnestic Mild Cognitive Impairment.

transmission of activation from semantic representations through proper name phrases to phonological representations, and that it increases the difficulty in recalling names observed in normal aging.

Considering the results from all our TOT studies on MCI, we are now reformulating our general hypothesis about the deterioration of famous people naming between normal aging and AD as a continuum (Figure 7.5), in which meaning-based representations and form-based representations are differentially impaired. In normal aging, the TOT phenomenon increases and the main process that deteriorates is the activation of the lexical and phonological representation of proper names, whereas activation of the semantic representation is well preserved. MCI represents a deterioration of cognitive functioning in one or more domains relative to normal aging. If the deterioration mainly affects memory, as in single domain amnestic MCI, impairment of lexical-phonological access increases, although not sufficiently to be differentiated from normal aging. If the deterioration affects several cognitive domains, including executive function and memory (as in the case of multiple domain amnestic MCI), or including executive function but not memory (as in multiple domain non-amnestic MCI), the difficulty with accessing the lexical and phonological representations increases, and consequently the difficulty with retrieving names also increases. Semantic knowledge may be compromised in multiple domain amnestic and non-amnestic MCI; however, when the famous people are very familiar, as in our studies, this knowledge is quite well preserved. The progression of amnestic MCI to AD and of non-amnestic MCI to other types of dementia, such as vascular dementia or dementia with Lewy bodies, presumably involves progressive deterioration of the access to lexical-phonological and semantic representation of names.

We are currently investigating TOTs for famous people naming in subjects with single domain non-amnestic MCI, especially when the executive function is the most impaired domain, but as yet we do not have enough data to enable us to reach any conclusions. We expect that lexical-phonological access will be compromised because of difficulties in controlling processing resources. Further research is also necessary to investigate the boundaries between normal aging and MCI, and between the different MCI subtypes and different types of dementia. Longitudinal and conversion studies represent a challenge for understanding the deterioration processes concerning meaning-based representation and access and form-based representations and access to personal names.

Impairment of multiple domain MCI for phonological access in recalling personal names is consistent with previous findings that appear to indicate the role of the left temporal pole as a mediational structure that is engaged by those structures that guide the implementation of the process of phonological representation in vocalization (supported by left temporal perisylvian language areas) (Damasio & Damasio, 1994; Damasio et al., 1996; Grabowski et al., 2001; Shafto, Burke, Stamatakis, Tam, & Tyler, 2007). As a multimodal association cortex, the temporal pole is also reciprocally associated with the entorhinal cortex and hippocampus, which are affected in multiple domain MCI. As deterioration of executive functioning is related to increased difficulties in access to the lexical and phonological representations of personal names in MCI patients, further research on the involvement of the left prefrontal cortex at the level of the inferior frontal gyrus in such access is necessary. This area has been associated with the control mechanisms that interact with semantic representations and retrieval of semantic knowledge (Jefferies & Lambon Ralph, 2006; Joubert et al., 2010). Further studies on psycho-physiological correlates of TOT for personal names in MCI, such as those being carried out by Díaz and colleagues, should provide a better understanding of the brain correlates of personal names impairment in MCI (see Díaz, Lindín, Galdo-Álvarez, & Buján, Chapter 10, this volume).

TOTs for famous people's names may discriminate multiple domain MCI patients from healthy controls by use of a measure that represents phonological access. TOT-based tasks may be used in combination with other lexical tasks, such as verbal fluency tasks, to detect MCI in people with subjective cognitive complaints. Indeed, correct classification of MCI with naming tests, or with a complex battery of instruments, represents an important neuropsychological challenge.

WHAT DOES MCI TELL US ABOUT THE NATURE OF TOT?

At the beginning of part 2 of this chapter, we pointed out that our current research is focused on the cognitive level of TOT, that is, on the failure to recall a word of which one has knowledge, but we also recognized that the metacognitive level involved in experiencing TOT is also a important research issue. Unfortunately, this metacognitive level is not yet addressed in the MCI research. Nevertheless, we will start this section with a speculation about what MCI may tell us about the metacognitive level of TOT for personal names. TOT for personal names constitutes one of the most frequently self-acknowledged types of memory failure among elderly people and increases in frequency among individuals suffering from MCI. This self-acknowledgment of increased difficulties with naming persons represents one of the first signs of alert for the individuals themselves, for their families, and for clinicians about a possible cognitive deterioration process. Individuals are conscious that something wrong is happening with their memory capacities because they have subjective conviction that they actually know the name and the person at the same time that they are unable to produce it. MCI represents an increase in the dissociation between the subjective knowledge of the person and his or her name and the objective inability to retrieve the corresponding item from memory that Koriat (2000) highlighted in characterizing TOT. The data presented in different parts of this chapter are evidences of this increased dissociation in MCI patients with respect to healthy controls. MCI patients did not differ from healthy controls in their feeling of knowing and familiarity, but they exhibited significantly more difficulties in accessing the corresponding names than healthy controls. One might also speculate on other subjective aspects of TOT in MCI that is its function in guiding and alerting and directing patients to increase retrieval effort and cognitive resources (Schwartz & Metcalfe, 2011). The subjective need of more efforts and cognitive resources is present in MCI patients who usually ask for learning strategies and methods to improve their memory. Further research is needed on the objective increase of cognitive resources when MCI patients experience TOT and on the subjective knowledge that patients have about their efforts in resolving TOT.

With respect to the objective inability to retrieve the names of people, our data on TOT in MCI are new empirical evidence in support of the dual-stage models of lexical access that coincide in attributing TOTs to failure in phonological activation following successful activation of the semantic representation of the target word (Burke et al., 1991; Caramazza & Miozzo,

1997; Dell, Schwartz, Martin, & Gagnon, 1997; Levelt et al., 1999), particularly in support of the dual-stage models of lexical access to personal names (Burke et al., 1991; Valentine, Brennen, & Brédart, 1996). We interpret our data in light of the transmission deficit hypothesis (Burke et al., 1991) by considering that, along with age, MCI maintains a sufficient level of activation of the semantic nodes to characterize a famous and familiar person but weakens connections to the phonological representations via the proper name phrase, makes the production of TOTs in naming person names more likely, and reduces the production of correct names. The one-to-one relationship between semantic nodes and phonological representations via the proper name phrase may explain why retrieval of personal names is more impaired than retrieval of object names, adjectives, or words for professions such as "singer" or "princess" that MCI patients can easily retrieve for giving semantic information about the famous faces. The words "singer" or "princess" are connected to an extended network of nodes in the semantic systems and provide wealthy information about these professions that makes their phonological representations easier to find than those corresponding to the proper names "Julio Iglesias" or "Cristina de Borbón." Semantic activation is maintained such as is shown from our data on semantic knowledge of the famous people in TOTs and from data by Joubert and colleagues (2010) indicating that the MCI patients were unable to access the names, even though they possessed accurate semantic knowledge about the corresponding people. Nevertheless, this presence of semantic activation in TOT states doesn't mean absence of semantic deficits in MCI patients who performed less well than controls in other semantic tasks such as Clague and colleagues (2011) showed. A similar interpretation may be made in light of other dual-stage models of lexical access such as that proposed by Caramazza and Miozzo (1997), by considering that MCI reduces the amount of activation from the target lexical node to its phonological segments and it is insufficient for their selection.

MCI produces a deficit in naming people from photographs and involves a greater deficit in transmission of the activation, or a reduction of the activation itself, from semantic to phonological representations than that produced by age in normal control groups, possibly because of a reduction in cognitive resources and executive functions that are particularly required for lexical selection and phonological encoding of personal names. Recently, Belke and Meyer (2007), assuming the classical two-step model proposed by Levelt and colleagues (1999), proposed modifications on the processing flow suggesting that lexical selection and phonological encoding are not automatic (e.g., Levelt, 1989), but they require cognitive capacity. From their study on object naming in healthy aging, they suggested that lexical retrieval processes might be more capacity-demanding for older than for young speakers. The reductions of cognitive resources in MCI may contribute to the documented increasing of phonological accessing in naming persons. However, further studies are required to test the specific role of cognitive resources, particularly executive functions, on TOT events, and new studies should compare multiple domain MCI patients and single domain MCI patients with specific deficits in executive functions.

REFERENCES

Ahmed, S., Arnold, R., Thompson, S. A., Graham, K. S., & Hodges, J. R. (2008). Naming of objects, faces and buildings in mild cognitive impairment. *Cortex*, 44, 746–752.

Albert, M. S., DeKosky, S. T., Dickson, D., Dubois, B., Feldman. H. H., Fox, N. C., ... Phelps, C. H. (2011). The diagnosis of mild cognitive impairment due to Alzheimer's disease: Recommendations from the National Institute on Aging-Alzheimer's Association workgroups on diagnostic guidelines for Alzheimer's disease. *Alzheimer's & Dementia*, 7, 270–279.

Arnold, S. E., Hyman, B. T., & Van Hoesen, G. W. (1994). Neuropathologic changes of the temporal pole in Alzheimer's disease and Pick's disease. *Archives of Neurology*, 51, 145–150.

Astell, A. J., & Harley, T. A. (1996). Tip-of-the-tongue states and lexical access in dementia. *Brain & Language*, 54, 196–215.

Beeson, P. M., Holland, A. L., & Murray, L. L. (1997). Naming famous people: An examination of tip-of-the-tongue phenomena in aphasia and Alzheimer's disease. *Aphasiology*, 11, 323–336.

Belke, E., & Meyer, A. S. (2007). Single and multiple object naming in healthy ageing. *Language and Cognitive Processes*, 22, 1178–1211.

Brouillette, R. M., Martin, C. K., Correa, J. B., Davis, A. B., Han, H., Johnson, W. D., Foil, H. C., Hymel, A., & Keller, J. N. (2011). Memory for names test provides a useful confrontational naming task for aging and continuum of dementia. *Journal of Alzheimer's Disease*, 23, 665–671.

Brown, A. S. (2012). *The tip of the tongue state*. New York: Psychology Press.

Brown, R., & McNeill, D. (1966). The "tip of the tongue" phenomenon. *Journal of Verbal Learning and Verbal Behaviour*, 5, 325–337.

Buján, A., Galdo-Álvarez, S., Lindín, M., & Díaz, F. (2012) An event-related potentials study of face naming: Evidence of phonological retrieval deficit in the tip-of-the-tongue state. *Psychophysiology*, 49, 980–990.

Burke, D. M., MacKay, D. G., Worthley, J. S., & Wade, E. (1991). On the tip of the tongue: What causes word finding failures in young and older adults? *Journal of Memory and Language*, 30, 542–579.

Caramazza, A., & Miozzo, M. (1997). The relation between syntactic and phonological knowledge in lexical access: Evidence from the "tip-of-the-tongue" phenomenon. *Cognition*, 64, 309–343.

Clague, F., Graham, K. S., Thompson, S. A., & Hodges, J. R. (2011). Is knowledge of famous people compromised in mild cognitive impairment? *Cognitive and Behavioral Neurology*, 24, 124–134.

Cross, E.-S., & Burke, D. M. (2004). Do alternative names block young and older adults' retrieval of proper names? *Brain and Language*, 89, 174–181.

Cunje, A., Molloy, W., Standish, T. I., & Lewis, D. L. (2007). Alternate forms of logical memory and verbal fluency tasks for repeated testing in early cognitive changes. *International Psychogeriatrics*, 19, 65–75.

Damasio, A. R., & Damasio, H. (1994). Cortical systems for retrieval of concrete knowledge: The convergence zone framework. In C. Koch & J. L. Davis (Eds.), *Large-scale neuronal theories of the brain* (pp. 62–74). Cambridge, MA: MIT Press.

Damasio, H., Grabowski, T. J., Tranel, D., Hichwa, R. D., & Damasio, A. R. (1996). A neural basis for lexical retrieval. *Nature*, 380, 499–505.

De Jager, C. A., & Budge, M. M. (2005). Stability and predictability of the classification of mild cognitive impairment as assessed by episodic memory test performance over time. *Neurocase*, 11, 72–79.

Delazer, M., Semenza, C., Reiner, M., Hofer, R., & Benke, T. (2003) Anomia for people names in DAT – evidence for semantic and post-semantic impairments. *Neuropsychologia*, 41, 1593–1598.

Dell, G. S., Schwartz, M. F., Martin, N., Saffran, E. M., & Gagnon, D. A. (1997). Lexical access in aphasic and non-aphasic speakers. *Psychological Review*, 104, 801–838.

Díaz, F., Lindín, M., Galdo-Álvarez, S., Facal, D., & Juncos-Rabadán, O. (2007). An event-related potentials study of face identification and naming: The tip-of-the-tongue state. *Psychophysiology*, 44, 50–68.

Dubois, B., & Albert, M. L. (2004). Amnestic MCI or prodromal Alzheimer's disease? *Lancet Neurology*, 3, 246–248.

Dubois, B., Feldman, H. H., Jacova, C., DeKosky, S. T., Barberger-Gateau, P., Cummings, J., ... Scheltens, Ph. (2007). Research criteria for the diagnosis of Alzheimer's disease: Revising the NINCDS–ADRDA criteria. *Lancet Neurology*, 6, 246–248.

Estevez-Gonzalez, A., Garcia-Sanchez, C., Boltes, A., Otermin, P., Pascual-Sedano, B., Gironell, A., & Kulisevsky, J. (2004). Semantic knowledge of famous people in mild cognitive impairment and progression to Alzheimer's disease. *Dementia and Geriatric Cognitive Disorders*, 17, 188–195.

Evrard, M. (2002). Ageing and lexical access to common and proper names in picture naming. *Brain and Language*, 81, 174–179.

Facal, D., Juncos-Rabadán, O., Rodriguez, M. S., & Pereiro, A. X. (2013). Tip-of-the-tongue in aging: Influence of vocabulary, working memory and processing speed. *Aging Clinical & Experimental Research*, 24, 647–659.

Facal-Mayo, D., Juncos-Rabadán, O., Álvarez, M., Pereiro-Rozas, A. X., & Díaz, F. (2006). Efectos del envejecimiento en el acceso al léxico. El fenómeno de la punta de la lengua en los nombres propios (Effects of aging on lexical access: The tip-of-the-tongue phenomenon in proper names). *Revista de Neurologia*, 43, 719–723.

Flicker, Ch., Ferris, St. H., & Reisberg, B. (1991). Mild cognitive impairment in the elderly: Predictors of dementia. *Neurology,* 41, 1006–1009.

Gauthier, S., Reisberg, B., Zaudig, M., Petersen, R. C., Ritchie, K., Broich, K., ... Winblad, B. (2006). Mild cognitive impairment. *Lancet,* 367, 1262–1270.

Gollan, T. H., & Brown, A. S. (2006). From tip-of-the-tongue (TOT) data to theoretical implications in two steps: When more TOTs means better retrieval. *Journal of Experimental Psychology: General,* 135, 462–483.

Grabowski, T. J., Damasio, H., Tranel, D., Boles-Ponto, L., Hichwa, R. D., & Damasio, A. R. (2001). A role for left temporal pole in the retrieval of words for unique entities. *Human Brain Mapping,* 13, 199–212.

Greene, J. D. W., & Hodges, J. R. (1996). Identification of famous names and famous faces in early Alzheimer's disease: Relationship to anterograde episodic and general semantic memory. *Brain,* 119, 111–128.

Griffin, Z. M. (2010). Retrieving personal names, referring expressions, and terms of address. In B. H. Ross (Ed.), *The psychology of learning and motivation,* Vol. 53 (pp. 345–287). Burlington, VT: Academic Press.

Hanley, J. R., & Chapman, E. (2008). Partial knowledge in a tip-of-the-tongue state about two- and three-words proper names. *Psychonomic Bulletin & Review,* 15, 156–160.

James, L. E. (2006). Specific effects of aging on proper name retrieval: Now you see them, now you don't. *Journal of Gerontology: Psychological Sciences,* 61B, P181–P183.

Jefferies, E., & Lambon Ralph, M. A. (2006). Semantic impairment in stroke aphasia versus semantic dementia: A case-series comparison. *Brain,* 129, 2132–2147.

Joubert, S., Brambati, S. M., Ansado, J., Barbeau, E. J., Felician, O., Didic, M., ... Kergoat, M. J. (2010). The cognitive and neural expression of semantic memory impairment in mild cognitive impairment and early Alzheimer's disease. *Neuropsychologia,* 48, 978–988.

Joubert, S., Felician, O., Barbeau, E. J., Didic, M., Poncet, M., & Ceccaldi, M. (2008). Patterns of semantic memory impairment in mild cognitive impairment. *Behavioural Neurology,* 19, (1–2), 35–40.

Juncos-Rabadán, O., Facal, D., Lojo-Seoane, C., & Pereiro, A. X. (2013a). Tip-of-the-tongue for famous people names in non amnestic MCI. *Journal of Neurolinguistics,* **26,** 409–420.

(2013b). Does tip-of-the-tongue for proper names discriminate amnestic mild cognitive impairment? *International Psychogeriatrics,* 24, 627–634.

Juncos-Rabadán, O., Facal, D., Rodríguez, M. S., & Pereiro, A. X. (2010). Lexical knowledge and lexical retrieval in aging: Insights from a tip-of-the-tongue (TOT) study. *Language and Cognitive Processes,* 25, 1301–1334.

Juncos-Rabadán, O., Pereiro, A. X., & Rodríguez, N. (2009). Lexical access in MCI: A study on the tip-of-the-tongue events. *Alzheimer's and Dementia,* 5(4), Supplement 1, P376.

Juncos-Rabadán, O., Rodríguez, N., Facal, D., Cuba, J., & Pereiro, A. X. (2011). Tip-of-the-tongue for proper names in mild cognitive impairment: Semantic or post-semantic impairments? *Journal of Neurolinguistics,* 24, 636–651.

Koriat, A. (2000). The feeling of knowing: Some metatheoretical implications for consciousness and control. *Consciousness and Cognition,* 9, 149–171.

Laver, G. D., & Burke, D. M. (1993). Why do semantic priming effects increase in old age? A meta-analysis. *Psychology and Aging,* 8, 34–43.

Levelt, W. J. M. (1989). *Speaking: From intention to articulation.* Cambridge, MA: MIT Press.

Levelt, W. J. M., Roelofs, A., & Meyer, A. S. (1999). A theory of lexical access in speech production. *Behavioral and Brain Sciences,* 22, 1–75.

Lezak, M. D. (2004). *Neuropsychological Assessment, 4th edn.* New York: Oxford University Press.

MacKay, D. G. (1987). *The organization of perception and action: A theory for language and other cognitive skills.* New York: Springer-Verlag.

MacKay, D. G., & Burke, D. (1990). Cognition and aging: A theory of new learning and the use of old connections. In T. M. Hess (Ed.), *Aging and cognition: Knowledge organization and utilization* (pp. 213–263). Amsterdam, N. Holland: Elsevier.

Maylor, E. A. (1990). Recognizing and naming faces: Aging, memory retrieval, and the tip of the tongue state. *Journal of Gerontology: Psychological Sciences,* 45(6), P215–P226.

Petersen, R. C. (2003). Conceptual overview. In R. C. Petersen & J. C. Morris (Eds.), *Mild cognitive impairment* (pp. 1–14).New York: Oxford University Press.

　(2004). Mild cognitive impairment as a diagnostic entity. *Journal of Internal Medicine,* 256, 183–194.

　(2009). Mild cognitive impairment. Ten years later. *Archives of Neurology,* 66, 1447–1455.

Petersen, R. C., Ivnik, R. J., Boeve, B. F., Knopman, D. S., Smith, G. E., & Tangalos, E. G. (2004).Outcome of clinical subtypes of mild cognitive impairment. *Neurology* (abstract), 62, A29S.

Petersen, R. C., & Morris, J. C. (2005). Mild cognitive impairment as a clinical entity and treatment target. *Archives of Neurology,* 62, 1160–1163.

Petersen, R. C., Smith, G. E., Waring, S. C., Ivnik, R. J., Tangalos, E., & Kokmen, E. (1999). Mild cognitive impairment. *Archives of Neurology,* 56, 303–308.

Petersen, R. C., Stevens, J. C., Ganguli, M., Tangalos, E. G., Cummings, J. L., & DeKosky, S. T. (2001). Practice parameter: Early detection of dementia: mild cognitive impairment (an evidence-based review). Report of the quality standards subcommittee of the American Academy of Neurology. *Neurology,* 56, 1133–1142.

Radanovic, M., Satler-Diniz, B., Mirandez, R., da Silva, T. M., Kneese-Flacks, M., Yassuda, M., & Forlenza, O. V. (2009). Verbal fluency in the detection of mild cognitive impairment and Alzheimer's disease among Brazilian Portuguese speakers: The influence of education. *International Psychogeriatrics,* 21, 1081–1087.

Rapp, B., & Goldrick, M. (2006). Speaking words: Contributions of cognitive neuropsychological research. *Cognitive Neuropsychology,* 23, 39–73.

Rastle, K. J., & Burke, D. (1996). Priming the tip of the tongue effects of prior processing on word retrieval in young and older adults. *Journal of Memory and Language,* 35, 586–605.

Reid, L. M., & MacLullich, A. M. J. (2006). Subjective memory complaints and cognitive impairment in older people. *Dementia and Geriatric Cognitive Disorders,* 22(5–6), 471–485.

Rendell, P. G., Castel, A. D., & Craik, F. I. M. (2005). Memory for proper names in old age: A disproportionate impairment? *Quarterly Journal of Experimental Psychology,* 58A, 54–71.

Ritchie, K., & Ritchie, C. W. (2012). Mild cognitive impairment (MCI) twenty years on. *International Psychogeriatrics,* 24, 1–5.

Rodríguez, N., Juncos-Rabadán, O., & Facal, D. (2008). El fenómeno de la punta de la lengua en el Deterioro Cognitivo Leve. Un estudio piloto (The phenomenon of the tip of the tongue in mild cognitive impairment: A pilot study). *Revista de Logopedia, Foniatría y Audiología,* 28, 22–27.

Roth, M., Huppert, F. A., Mountjoy, C. Q., & Tym, E. (1999). *CAMDEX-R. The Cambridge Examination for Mental Disorders of the Elderly-Revised.* Cambridge: Cambridge University Press.

Shafto, M. A., Burke, D. M., Stamatakis, M. A., Tam, Ph. P., & Tyler, L. K. (2007). On the tip-of-the-tongue: Neural correlates of increased word-finding failures in normal aging. *Journal of Cognitive Neuroscience,* 19, 2060–2070.

Schwartz, B. L. (2002). *Tip-of-the-tongue states: Phenomenology, mechanism, and lexical retrieval.* Mahwah, NJ: Erlbaum.

(2006). Tip-of-the-tongue states as metacognition. *Metacognition and Learning,* 1, 149–158.

Schwartz, B. L., & Metcalfe, J. (2011). Tip-of-the-tongue (TOT) states: Retrieval, behavior, and experience. *Memory and Cognition,* 39, 737–749.

Semenza, C., Mondini, S., Borgo, F., Pasini, M., & Sgaramella, M. T. (2003). Proper names in patients with early Alzheimer's disease. *Neurocase,* 9, 63–69.

Taler, V., & Phillips, N. A. (2009). Language performance in Alzheimer's disease and mild cognitive impairment: A comparative review. *Journal of Clinical and Experimental Neuropsychology,* 30, 501–556.

Thompson, S. A., Graham, K. S., Patterson, K., Sahakian, B. J., & Hodges, J. R. (2002). Is knowledge of famous people disproportionately impaired in patients with early and questionable Alzheimer's disease? *Neuropsychology,* 16, 344–358.

Valentine, T., Brennen, T., & Brédart, S. (1996). *The cognitive psychology of proper names.* London, Routledge.

Winblad B., Palmer, K., Kivipelto, M., Jelic, V., & Fratiglioni L. (2004). Mild Cognitive Impairment: Beyond controversies, towards a consensus. *Journal of Internal Medicine,* 256, 181–182.

8

Metamemory and Parkinson's Disease

JUSTIN D. OH-LEE AND HAJIME OTANI

Parkinson's disease (PD) is one of the most common movement disorders, affecting 1 percent to 5 percent of the population older than 60 years (Farrer, 2006). It is a progressive neurodegenerative disorder with primary motor symptoms including resting tremor (shaking), rigidity (stiffness), bradykinesia (slowness), and impaired postural reflexes (dysbalance) (Lang & Lozano, 1998). The hallmark of PD pathophysiology is a selective loss of dopaminergic neurons in the substantia nigra pars compacta in the midbrain (Greenfield & Bosanquet, 1953). The gradual degeneration of nigro-striatal projections leads to a progressive loss of the neurotransmitter dopamine in the striatum, which is the major input structure to the basal ganglia. When the loss of dopamine exceeds 50 percent to 80 percent, parkinsonian symptoms become clinically evident (Ehringer & Hornykiewicz, 1960; Hornykiewicz, 1963).

Although PD is often categorized as a movement disorder with well-defined motor symptomatology, non-motor symptoms have become more widely recognized. The non-motor symptoms, particularly cognitive and behavioral dysfunction, are not only common, but occur across all stages of the disease and may dramatically affect the quality of patients' life as well as that of their caregivers (Herlofson & Larsen, 2002). The cognitive symptoms are sometimes present before the onset of the motor symptoms or emerge with disease progression, dementia being among the most common in the advanced stages of the disease (Chaudhuri, Healy, & Schapira, 2006). The cognitive symptoms occur in up to 88 percent of PD patients and affect neuropsychiatric, sleep, autonomic, and sensory domains (Shulman, Taback, Bean, & Weiner, 2001). A comprehensive look at PD pathogenesis and disease management, therefore, should include cognitive as well as motor symptomology (Chaudhuri, Yates, & Martinez-Martin, 2005). However, because cognitive functioning is not always apparent, and because it encompasses a wide variety of behavioral and mental functions, it is more difficult to diagnose and manage than motor symptoms.

With respect to the types of cognitive deficits, PD patients show deficits in learning, memory, and attentional processes (Grahn, Parkinson, & Owen, 2009) that resemble deficits that occur in other clinical populations with basal ganglia and frontal lobe dysfunction, such as patients with Huntington's disease (Hinton et al., 2007), Tourette's disorder (Mink, 2006), attention-deficit/hyperactivity disorder (Mehler-Wex, Riederer, & Gerlach, 2006), and other related diseases. In PD, dopaminergic denervation results in cognitive and behavioral symptoms affiliated with dysfunction in the prefrontal cortex (PFC), which is a critical neurological substrate of executive function (Fuente-Fernández, 2012). In preclinical PD, the dopaminergic denervation is thought to occur first in the frontostriatal cognitive loop, comprised of dorsal striatum and dorsolateral PFC, and is associated with the genesis of a host of PFC-related dysfunctions throughout the course of the disease, including deficits in working memory (Giovannoni, O'Sullivan, Turner, Manson, & Lees, 2000), sensorimotor integration (Almeida & Lebold, 2010), decision making (Lou, Kearns, Oken, Sexton, & Nutt, 2001; Schifitto et al., 2008), and set shifting (Fellows & Farah, 2005; Lewis, Dove, Bobbins, Barker, & Owen, 2004). Much less damaged frontostriatal limbic loop, comprised of ventral striatum and ventral PFC, has also been associated with an array of non-motor clinical features including apathy, depression, anxiety, fatigue, pain, and dementia (Fuente-Fernández, 2012; Grahn, Parkinson, & Owen, 2008). However, it should be noted that certain types of PFC-mediated cognitive processes are not as severely impaired in PD patients as was once purported (Emre, 2003; Ivory, Knight, Longmore, & Caradoc-Davies, 1999; McKinlay, Dalrymple-Alford, Grace, & Roger, 2009; McPherson & Cummings, 2009; Press, Mechanic, Tarsy, & Manoach, 2002; York & Alvarez, 2008). Nevertheless, given that PFC functions appear central to the decision-making process, more comprehensive understanding of PFC-mediated cognitive processes that are unimpaired in PD would promote the development of more effective cognitive/behavioral training strategies that can be used to improve patients' memory, learning, and quality of life.

An additional way to assess prefrontal function in patients with PD is through a metamemory task. *Metamemory* is a term used to describe monitoring and control of one's own memory (Janowsky, Shimamura, & Squire, 1989; Nelson & Narens, 1994). One widely investigated dimension of metamemory is the change in metamemory monitoring as one's memory functioning declines (e.g., Ghetti, Lyons, Lazzarin, & Cornoldi, 2008;

Perrotin, Belleville, & Isingrini, 2007). The rationale behind these investigations is that metamemory is not an epiphenomenon, but instead plays an important executive role in normal functioning of one's memory (Koriat, Levy-Sadot, Edry, & de Marcas, 2003; Son & Schwartz, 2002; Souchay, Isingrini, & Gil, 2006). Metamemory strategies may, therefore, play an important role in regulating one's own learning and memory, and training in the use of such metamemory strategies may yield broad cognitive benefits in improving memory functioning to complete daily tasks in patients with PD as well as other related disorders.

To date, research investigating metamemory functioning among PD patients has examined self-awareness ratings, global predictions, global postdictions, retrospective confidence judgments (RCJ), feelings of knowing (FOK), and the tip-of-the-tongue (TOT) phenomenon (Baran, Tekcan, Gürvit, & Boduroglu, 2009; Ivory et al., 1999; Koerts et al., 2011; Oh-Lee, Szymkowicz, Smith, & Otani, 2012; Sitek, Soltan, Wieczorek, Robowski, & Sławek, 2011; Smith, Souchay, & Moulin, 2011; Souchay et al., 2006; Yu, Wu, Tai, Lin, & Hua, 2010). Self-awareness ratings are the subjective ratings of questionnaire items designed to probe whether PD patients have awareness of memory difficulties (mnestic awareness), whereas other measures consist of online measures of metamemory because these are the judgments that are made while performing encoding and retrieval of information. A global prediction is one's prediction regarding how much of the studied materials one would be able to recall or recognize before one has retrieved the materials. In contrast, global postdictions are the judgments that are made after completing a retrieval test about how much of the studied materials one could recall or recognize. An RCJ is different from a global postdiction in that an RCJ is a confidence rating made on each retrieved item regarding whether the retrieved answer is correct. An FOK is the belief that a piece of information that cannot currently be recalled is still in memory and can be identified correctly if one sees it at a later point in time (Hart, 1965). A TOT is similar to an FOK in that it is a frustrating experience of being aware of having the knowledge of a piece of information but being unable to retrieve the information on demand. However, unlike an FOK, a TOT is accompanied by an intense feeling that the sought-after information will pop into one's mind at any moment (Brown, 2012; Brown & McNeill, 2004; Schwartz, 2002a). Although research on metamemory functioning among PD patients is still at an emerging stage, the number of studies has increased in recent years. We, therefore, determined that it is timely to summarize these studies to provide coherence in the literature as well as the directions for future studies. Although the number of studies remains limited, the goals of this chapter will be to provide an overview of the current findings across different memory types (episodic and semantic), retrieval types (recall and recognition), and metamemory judgment types (e.g., FOK, TOT, RCJ), as well as to offer speculations regarding neural substrates underlying these measures in normal individuals as well as in PD patients.

MEMORY AND PD

Researchers have used a wide variety of memory measures to pinpoint which memory type is impaired among PD patients. However, memory deficits are often subtle, particularly at the early stage of the disease, and although the evidence is clear that PD patients suffer from memory impairments, finding exactly which type of memory is impaired is rather difficult.

Ivory and colleagues (1999) reported that among 29 studies that investigated a variety of memory functions among PD patients, 20 studies showed impairments by PD patients. In their own study, Ivory and colleagues used a range of tests to examine PD patients' memory functions. First, direct and indirect tests were examined with free recall as the direct test and word completion as the indirect test. Further, the free recall test was administered with an incidental learning instruction. Second, verbal learning and memory was examined using the Rey Auditory Verbal Learning Test (RAVLT), which consisted of five study-test (free recall) trials of a list of 15 words, followed by a study-test trial of another list of 15 words (interference list), and then recall of the original 15 words. Third, remote memory was tested with general knowledge questions about 70 famous people from the 1930s, 1950s, 1970s, and 1980s. PD patients showed impairments, relative to the control participants, on incidental free recall (direct test), whereas PD patients did not show impairments on word completion (indirect test). Further, no difference appeared between PD patients and the control participants on any measures of RAVLT, indicating that PD patients did not show impairments in free recall when the test was administered with an intentional learning instruction. Remote memory showed that recall was steady across the decades for PD patients, whereas recall was higher during the earlier decades than the recent decades for the control participants. Ivory and colleagues concluded that memory impairments among these patients were modest. However, the finding that these patients showed impairments in incidental free recall was consistent with the notion that PD patients are vulnerable when they do not receive explicit instructions or external cues because without these, they must rely on internally generated strategies or cues.

The notion that PD patients need support from the external cues gave rise to the retrieval deficit hypothesis (see Higginson, Wheelock, Carroll, & Sigvardt, 2005), which asserts that encoding and storage processes are not impaired among PD patients, and that their memory problems stem from deficits in retrieval processes. However, this hypothesis has been challenged by the finding that recognition is also impaired among PD patients. For instance, Brønnick, Alves, Aarsland, Tysnes, and Larsen (2011) tested a large group of drug-naïve, newly diagnosed PD patients, based on the argument that past studies did not have sufficient statistical power to show the difference in recognition between PD patients, particularly drug-free patients, and control participants. Their sample included 201 PD patients who had never received medication for PD as well as 201 control participants who were free of PD. Verbal learning and memory were tested by the California Verbal Learning Test-2, which consisted of (1) immediate free recall, (2) free recall with short and long delay, (3) free recall of an interference list, (4) cued recall, and (5) recognition. PD patients had lower performance than the control participants on all three measures of free recall: immediate, short delay, and long delay. Further, the learning curve (computed based on five study-test trials) was steeper for the control participants than for PD patients, indicating that PD patients showed impairments in encoding. More importantly, PD patients showed lower cued recall and recognition than the control participants. The retention measure (difference between short and long delay free recall), intrusions, and repetition did not show a group difference. Finally, the executive function measures indicated that PD patients showed lower category clustering and category fluency scores. These results are consistent with the notion that PD patients show impairments in both encoding and retrieval, rejecting the retrieval deficit hypothesis. This conclusion is also supported by the results of memory tests from the studies that will be reviewed in the next metamemory section.

METAMEMORY AND PD

Although a variety of measures exist to assess metamemory, early research on metamemory with PD patients focused on two measures, FOK and RCJ. Pannu and Kaszniak (2005) published a comprehensive review of the early literature on metamemory among neurological populations, summarizing evidence of *anosognosia*, or the lack of self-awareness of neurological and cognitive impairments across nine different neurological conditions: (1) Korsakoff's and amnesia, (2) focal frontal lobe patients, (3) multiple sclerosis, (4) traumatic brain injury, (5) temporal lobe epilepsy, (6) Alzheimer's disease (AD), (7) Parkinson's disease, (8) Huntington's disease, and (9) HIV patients. Obviously, the literature on any patient group is conflicting, showing both positive (impairments) and negative (no impairments) results, because of a variety of factors influencing the outcome. Alzheimer's disease is a case in point. Among the 10 measures reported by eight different studies (Bäckman & Lipinska, 1993; Duke, 2001; Moulin, James, Perfect, & Jones, 2003; Moulin, Perfect, & Jones, 2000a, 2000b; Pappas et al., 1992; Schacter, McLachlan, Moscovitch, & Tulving, 1986; Souchay, Isingrini, & Gil, 2002), five showed impaired awareness by AD patients relative to control participants (Duke, 2001; Moulin et al., 2000b; Pappas et al., 1992; Schacter et al., 1986; Souchay et al., 2002).[1] In contrast, for PD patients, all three measures (two measures with FOK and one measure with RCJ) reported by three studies (Coulter, 1989; Dellapietra, 1995; Ivory et al., 1999) showed that self-awareness was not impaired among PD patients. Pannu and Kaszniak speculated that the lack of metamemory impairments may be based on the fact that not all PD patients show deficits in frontal lobe function, which is assumed to be linked to metamemory functions. Further, unlike Alzheimer's and some other neurological conditions, the damages caused by PD are subcortical in nature, and consequently, the metamemory measures, such as FOK and RCJ, may not be sensitive to the type of deficits these damages create.

Regardless of the reason for the results, Pannu and Kaszniak (2005) left an impression that metamemory is not impaired among PD patients. However, since their review, scholars have published a number of additional studies, and it is clear that the results are not as straightforward as it appeared. Table 8.1 shows the summary of the studies that investigated metamemory among PD patients, including those Pannu and Kaszniak reported. As shown, among 24 measures reported by 14 studies, 9 showed metamemory impairments, whereas 14 did not. Although the results seem hopelessly inconsistent, when the type of metamemory measures as well as the type of memory is considered, a clearer picture emerges.

Metamemory questionnaire. Seven studies used metamemory questionnaires to investigate mnestic awareness among PD patients. These studies did not show obvious impairments in metamemory function among PD patients, even though it is difficult to interpret whether impairments are present or absent when the ratings are similar between PD patients and control participants because these patients do not always show memory deficits.

Hopp (1999) used 17 items from the Metamemory in Adulthood questionnaire as well as one item ("How would you rate your memory in terms

TABLE 8.1 *Summary of metamemory functions among PD patients across studies*

Study	Measure	Instrument	Memory	Results	Impairment
Coulter (1989)	FOK	General Knowledge Questions	Semantic	PD = Control	No
Dellapietra (1995)	FOK	General Knowledge Questions	Semantic	PD = Control	No
Hopp (1999)	Global Prediction	California Verbal Learning Test (Recall)	Episodic	PD < Control	Yes
	Global Prediction	California Verbal Learning Test (Recognition)	Episodic	PD = Control	No
	Global Postdiction	California Verbal Learning Test (Recall)	Episodic	PD = Control	No
	Global Postdiction	California Verbal Learning Test (Recognition)	Episodic	PD = Control	No
	Mnestic Awareness	Capacity Subscale of Metamemory in Adulthood and one item from Memory Functioning Questionnaire	Self-awareness	PD = Control	Yes
Matison et al. (1982)	TOT	Boston Naming Test	Semantic	PD < Norm (PD showing partial knowledge indicative of TOT-like state)	Yes
Ivory et al. (1999)	RCJ	General Knowledge Questions	Semantic	PD = Control	No
	Mnestic Awareness	16-item questionnaire	Self-awareness	PD = Control	No
Johnson et al. (2005)	Mnestic Awareness	Metamemory in Adulthood	Self-awareness	PD < Control (Strategy use indicative of mnestic awareness)	No
Souchay et al. (2006)	FOK	Paired-associates	Episodic	PD < Control	Yes

Study	Measure	Instrument	Memory	Results	Impairment
	Global Prediction	Paired-associates	Episodic	PD = Control	Yes
Baran et al. (2009)	FOK	Paired-associates	Episodic	PD = o Control > o	Yes
Smith, Souchay, et al. (2009)	FOK	Paired-associates	Episodic	PD = o (SPT) PD = o (Read) Control > o (SPT) Control = o (Read)	Yes
Yu et al. (2010)	FOK	Paired-associates	Episodic	PD (ARD) = o PD (TD) > o Control > o	Yes
Sitek et al. (2011)	Mnestic Awareness	Self-Rating Scale of Memory Functions	Self-awareness	Positive correlation between PD and control on Item 5 regarding TOT experience	No
Koerts et al. (2011)	Mnestic Awareness	Disexecutive Questionnaire	Self-awareness	PD = Control.	No
Smith et al. (2011)	Global Prediction	Event-based prospective memory task	Prospective	PD = Control	No
	Global Postdiction	Event-based prospective memory task	Prospective	PD = Control	No
	Global Prediction	Time-based prospective memory task	Prospective	PD < Control	Yes
	Global Postdiction	Time-based prospective memory task	Prospective	PD = Control	No
	Mnestic Awareness	Prospective and Retrospective Memory Questionnaire	Prospective and Retrospective	PD = Control	Yes/No
Oh-Lee et al. (2012)	TOT	General Knowledge Questions	Semantic	PD = Control	No

Note: PD = Parkinson's disease; FOK = Feeling of Knowing; RCJ = Retrospective Confidence Judgment; TOT = Tip-of-the-tongue; SPT = Subject Performed Task.

of the kinds of problems you have?") from the Memory Functioning Questionnaire. The results showed no group difference between PD patients and both the old-young and the old-old control participants. The similar ratings between PD patients and the control participants may indicate that PD patients lacked self-awareness of memory problems because these PD patients also showed lower free recall than the control participants. Further, as shown later in this chapter, global predictions were less accurate for PD patients than for the control participants. Taken together, these results provide evidence that metamemory functions were impaired among PD patients. However, the correlations between the scores of the metamemory questionnaire and the global predictions as well as the postdictions were low, indicating that the questionnaire was not assessing the same construct as other (more online) metamemory measures. In contrast, the Metamovement questionnaire, which assessed participants' awareness of difficulties with movements in daily lives, showed intact self-awareness by PD patients.

Ivory and colleagues (1999) used a 16-item questionnaire, which measured three memory aspects: (1) remote memory, (2) recent memory, and (3) attention. The test revealed no difference between PD patients and the control participants in terms of the overall ratings, the rank order of the rated items, and the effect size. The similar ratings between PD patients and the control participants may indicate that PD patients had impairments in mnestic awareness. However, the memory deficits these patients showed were modest (lower performance in incidental free recall than the control participants), and therefore the ratings might reflect the fact that for the most part, these patients did not experience memory difficulties. Further, the effect size on Item 12 ("My ability to follow what people are saying is") showed the largest difference between PD patients and the control patients, indicating that these PD patients showed some awareness of memory difficulties.

Johnson, Pollard, Vernon, Tomes, and Jog (2005) used the Metamemory in Adulthood questionnaire to examine several dimensions of metamemory; however, the difference between PD patients and the control participants was found only on strategy such that PD patients reported reduced use of memory strategies than the control participants, particularly the use of external memory aid. Although it is unclear whether these patients actually had memory impairments, the fact that PD patients reported lower strategy use indicates that these patients had awareness of memory difficulties.

Sitek and colleagues (2011) used the Self-Rating Scale of Memory Functions to investigate the discrepancy between PD patients and their matched control participants (referred to as proxies) regarding the PD patients' memory functions. The questionnaire consisted of 18 items; however, for the purpose of the present chapter, the most important item was Item 5: "Tendency for a past memory to be 'on the tip of one's tongue,' but not available is." The results showed that among the 18 items, only 6 items showed significant patient-proxy correlations; however, the correlation was significant on Item 5, indicating that both PD patients and their proxies were aware of the patients' metamemory functions.

Koerts and colleagues (2011) used the Dysexecutive Questionnaire to determine whether PD patients had awareness of difficulties they have with executive functions in daily lives, such as inhibiting automatic responses, retrieving information from declarative memory, planning, monitoring, and so forth. This questionnaire consisted of 20 items with three subscales, (1) behavioral-emotional self-regulation, (2) metacognition, and (3) executive cognition, and asked how often one had observed each symptom of dysexecutive syndrome. PD patients reported a higher frequency of problems associated with executive function in daily living than the control participants, indicating that these patients had awareness of their problems. Although the metacognition subscale did not show a difference between PD patients and the control participants, there was a clear trend showing a higher frequency of the problems for PD patients than for the control participants. Further, when the patients' relatives rated the difficulties these patients were experiencing, the relatives' ratings were similar to the patients' ratings, indicating that these PD patients had good self-awareness of the memory difficulties in their daily lives.

Smith and colleagues (2011) used the Prospective Memory Questionnaire in conjunction with a laboratory prospective memory task described later in this chapter. Prospective memory is different from retrospective memory in that the former memory pertains to remembering future actions rather than remembering past experience. This questionnaire consisted of eight questions that represented the prospective memory component (e.g., "Do you forget to tell someone something you had meant to mention a few minutes ago?") and the retrospective memory component (e.g., Do you forget what you watched on TV the previous day?"), asking participants to rate the frequency of occurrence for each item. There was no difference between PD patients and the control participants, indicating that PD patients had little awareness of their past memory failures. However, it is also possible that not remembering past memory failures is an indication of poor memory (i.e., difficulty remembering past memory failures) rather than lack of self-awareness. Further, across the groups, the prospective memory component was correlated with performance on the laboratory prospective memory task, indicating that both PD patients and the control participants showed awareness of their prospective memory ability.

In summary, the studies using metamemory questionnaires did not show particular impairments in metamemory function among PD patients. However, there was weak evidence of impairments that may warrant further investigation.

Global predictions, global postdictions, and retrospective confidence judgments (RCJ). Three studies used global predictions, one study used global postdictions, and two studies used RCJ to examine whether PD patients showed impairments in metamemory. The results were mixed for global predictions, whereas global postdictions and RCJ did not show metamemory impairments.

Hopp (1999) administered the California Verbal Learning Test to a group of PD patients, a group of young-old participants, and a group of old-old participants. There were three memory tests: (1) immediate free recall, (2) delayed free recall, and (3) recognition. Before each trial, participants were asked to predict the number of items they would be able to recall or recognize. Further, following each trial, participants were asked to make a postdiction as to how many items they were able to correctly recall or recognize. PD patients showed lower prediction accuracy than both the young-old and old-old control participants on both immediate and delayed free recall. However, on recognition, prediction accuracy was similar between PD patients and both the young-old and old-old control participants. These results are consistent with the notion that prediction accuracy depends on task difficulty, reminiscent of the retrieval deficit hypothesis. In contrast to prediction accuracy, postdiction accuracy did not show a difference between PD patients and both the young-old and old-old control participants for all three memory tests. These results indicated that PD patients did not show metamemory impairments when they made judgments after the target items were already recalled or recognized.

Souchay and colleagues (2006) used a 20-item paired-associates task and asked participants to make a global prediction as to how many target items they would be able to recall before they studied the items. The results showed that prediction accuracy was not different between PD patients and the control participants.

Smith and colleagues (2011) used both global predictions and postdictions to assess self-awareness of event-based and time-based prospective memory. In a typical prospective memory experiment, participants are asked to perform an ongoing task, such as rating the pleasantness of the stimulus words, with a prospective memory instruction to perform a specific action at a specific moment. In an event-based task, participants are asked to perform the action when a specific target event is presented, whereas in a time-based task, participants are asked to perform the action at a specific time. During Smith and colleagues' study, participants were also instructed to make both predictions and postdictions, estimating the success rate. The results showed that for the event-based task, the prediction accuracy was similar between PD patients and the control participants, whereas for the time-based task, the prediction accuracy was lower for PD patients than for the control participants. However, the postdiction accuracy was similar between PD patients and the control participants regardless of whether the task was event-based or time-based, indicating that predictions are different from postdictions.

Ivory and colleagues (1999) investigated RCJ by presenting participants with general knowledge questions from the Nelson and Narens (1980) norms. Participants were asked to recognize the correct responses, and after completing the recognition test, they were asked to provide a confidence rating to each response. The results showed that the RCJ accuracy was similar between PD patients and the control participants.

In summary, the results were consistent across studies on global postdictions and RCJ; no difference was found between PD patients and the control participants. In contrast, the results on global predictions were mixed, with PD patients showing lower prediction accuracy than the control participants on some measures and similar accuracy to the control participants on other measures. It is possible that the prediction accuracy is related to task difficulty, because PD patients showed lower accuracy than the control participants on free recall (Hopp, 1999) and time-based prospective memory (Smith et al., 2011) tasks, which are assumed to require self-initiated processing (Craik, 1986). In contrast, cued-recall, recognition, and event-based prospective memory tasks did not show metamemory impairments because responses are initiated by highly familiar cues.

Feeling-of-knowing (FOK) judgments. Six studies that compared PD patients and the control participants using FOK judgments produced mixed results. Two studies (Coulter, 1989; Dellapietra, 1995) reported that FOK accuracy was similar between PD patients and the control participants, whereas four studies (Baran et al., 2009; Smith, Souchay, & Conway, 2010; Souchay et al., 2006; Yu et al., 2010) reported that FOK accuracy was lower for PD patients than for the control participants. It is clear that the difference is based on whether FOK was tested using a semantic or an episodic memory paradigm, with the former paradigm showing intact metamemory functions and the latter paradigm showing impaired metamemory functions. Both paradigms use a recall-judgment-recognition (RJR) procedure created by Hart (1965) in which participants are asked to recall target items and then make FOK judgments. After making the judgments, a recognition test is administered to examine FOK accuracy, and a measure, such as Goodman-Kruskal Gamma, is used to determine the degree of association between FOK and recognition. The only difference between the semantic and episodic memory paradigm is that in the former paradigm, participants are tested on recall of the answers to general knowledge questions, whereas in the later paradigm, participants are asked to learn a list of paired-associates items first and then to take a cued recall test.

Using the semantic FOK paradigm, Coulter (1989) and Dellapietra (1995) showed that FOK accuracy was similar between PD patients and the control participants. Coulter compared FOK judgments for semantic knowledge in PD patients with or without depression against age-matched control participants and found no difference across groups, whereas Dellapietra investigated metamemory and awareness of motor abilities and also found that PD patients performed similarly to control participants on an FOK metamemory task. In contrast, when the episodic FOK paradigm was used, PD patients showed lower accuracy than the control participants (Baran et al., 2009; Smith et al., 2010; Souchay et al., 2006; Yu et al., 2010), along with lower cued recall and recognition.

In summary, the literature based on FOK judgments indicates that PD patients show impaired FOK accuracy when FOK is based on episodic memory, whereas PD patients do not show impaired FOK accuracy when FOK is based on semantic memory. The difference can be explained based on the dual theory of FOK (Koriat, Nussinson, Bless, & Shaked, 2008). According to Koriat and his colleagues, FOK judgments are inferences based on information (information-based or IB) as well as experience (experience-based or EB). When FOK is based on the former process (IB), one would make judgments based on explicitly retrieved information regarding the target information, such as the domain of the question, how much expertise one has in the domain, and whether one had an experience of retrieving the information. In contrast, the latter process (EB) is based on largely implicit processes of accessing mnemonic cues, such as the familiarity of the cues or the questions, the ease and the amount of accessing partial information associated with the target information, and feelings of imminent retrieval of the target information (or tip-of-the-tongue state). Regardless of whether PD patients relied on IB or EB to make FOK judgments, relevant information (IB) as well as mnemonic cues (EB) are more available in semantic memory than in episodic memory. Further, in episodic memory, lower FOK accuracy was also accompanied by lower recall by PD patients than the control participants. Based on these results, it is reasonable to assume that PD patients were making FOK judgments based on less relevant information (IB) and fewer mnemonic cues (EB) when an episodic paradigm was used. As such, it is possible that the lower FOK accuracy simply reflected impairments in memory in general rather than impairments in metamemory per se.

Tip-of-the-tongue (TOT) phenomenon. Only two studies have examined the TOT phenomenon among PD patients. Matison, Mayeux, Rosen, and Fahn (1982) presented PD patients with a series of neurological tests: (1) WAIS vocabulary, (2) Boston Naming Test (picture naming), (3) Controlled Word Association, (4) Category Naming, and (5) Sentence Repetition. PD patients showed deficits (compared to the norms based on the healthy normative sample) in word finding in the Boston Naming Test and in Category Naming, as well as in articulation in Sentence Repetition. Further, Matison and colleagues reported that PD patients were experiencing a state analogous to a TOT state because their performance on the Boston Naming Test increased when they received phonetic or semantic cues. The fact that these cues helped was interpreted as evidence that these PD patients had partial knowledge of the words, just like when a person is experiencing a TOT phenomenon. Unfortunately, Matison and colleagues did not ask the participants whether they were in a TOT state or examine the accuracy of the TOT experience.

Oh-Lee and colleagues (2012) investigated TOT among PD patients using general knowledge questions in an RJR procedure. Participants were asked to either (1) answer the question, (2) give a "don't know" response, or (3) indicate that they were in a TOT state, enabling the researchers to examine frequency, accuracy, and strength of TOT. The results showed no difference between PD patients and the older adult control participants on all these measures. However, both PD patients and the older adult control participants showed higher TOT frequency, accuracy, and strength than the college student control participants. These results indicated that TOT was not impaired among PD patients.

In summary, PD patients experience a TOT state that is as frequent, accurate, and strong as age-matched control participants. However, note that when general knowledge questions were used, no difference was found between PD patients and the control participants on FOK judgments (Coulter, 1989; Dellapietra, 1995). Accordingly, it is possible that PD patients show lower TOT accuracy, as well as frequency and strength, than control participants when an episodic paradigm (e.g., a paired-associates list) is used.

METAMEMORY AND EXECUTIVE FUNCTIONS

Pannu and Kaszniak (2005) concluded that frontal lobe functions are linked to metamemory functions, which, in turn, implies that executive functions are involved in metamemory functions. In support of this hypothesis, among the 22 measures of executive functions reported by the studies reviewed in the previous section, 15 showed deficits by PD patients. Further, some studies reported significant correlations between executive function measures and metamemory measures even though others did not. For instance, Hopp (1999) showed that when the composite scores of verbal fluency and the California Card Sorting Test were used as covariates, the group difference between PD patients and the control participants was no longer significant on global prediction accuracy, indicating that the difference in executive functions was responsible for the group difference in this metamemory measure.

In Matison and colleagues (1982), PD patients showed deficits in the Boston Naming Test, the controlled word association test, and the category naming test. Further, a correlation was found between the severity of PD symptoms and the Boston Naming Test with semantic cues. Because a TOT-like state was found with the Boston Naming Test, it is reasonable to assume that the TOT-like state was associated with the deficits in executive function. Baran and colleagues (2009) reported a significant correlation between FOK accuracy and the category score, as well as the perseveration errors of the Wisconsin Card Sorting Task (WCST) for the control participants but not for PD patients. Further, the regression analysis using the composite scores of fluency tests as well as the scores of WCST indicated that the fluency scores showed a marginally significant contribution to one measure of FOK accuracy for PD patients, whereas the WCST score showed a significant contribution to one measure of FOK accuracy and a marginal contribution to another measure of FOK accuracy for the control participants.

Lastly, Yu and colleagues (2010) showed that the category score of the Modified Card Sorting Test was correlated with FOK accuracy for a subgroup of PD patients. In summary, these results showed that executive functions have some involvement in metamemory functions; however, the extent of involvement is still not clear because not all measures of executive function showed an association with the measures of metamemory functions.

METAMEMORY AND NEUROIMAGING

Neuroimaging studies have indicated that brain activities differ during TOT and other metamemory judgments such as FOK and RCJ. Activity in the right prefrontal cortex (PFC), particularly the right inferior PFC, appears to be uniquely associated with semantic TOT judgments (Maril, Simmons, Weaver, & Schacter, 2005; Maril, Wagner, & Schacter, 2001), whereas the same prefrontal regions, particularly on the left hemisphere, including the left ventral PFC, dorsolateral PFC, and ACC, are associated with FOK judgments (Maril, Simons, Mitchell, Schwartz, & Schacter, 2003). These left brain regions have been implicated in mediating the following metamemory processes during unsuccessful retrieval when only partial target information is available: the subjective experience of knowing, post-retrieval monitoring, and conflict monitoring, corresponds to v PFC, dl PFC, and ACC, respectively (Maril et al., 2003). In addition, it appears that FOK and RCJ metamemory judgment tasks, compared to non-metamemory tasks, may be linked to the selective activation of the medial PFC and the parietal cortex (Chua, Schacter, & Sperling, 2009a; Maril et al., 2003). The parietal lobe activity has been suggested to reflect the integration of internal representation of sought-after information during a metamemory judgment as well as during a recognition confidence judgment process (Chua et al., 2009a, 2009b; Maril et al., 2005).

Given that PD patients have frontal, but not parietal, lobe dysfunction (Fuente-Fernández, 2012), it is not surprising that PD patients show impairments in frontal lobe-mediated metamemory judgments, including episodic FOK (Souchay et al., 2006), but not in parietal lobe-mediated RCJ metamemory tasks (Chua et al., 2009a; Ivory et al., 1999). What is surprising, however, is the observation that certain types of TOT metamemory judgments, particularly semantic, are not compromised in PD patients (Oh-Lee et al., 2012). The activities in the right inferior PFC (ri PFC) have been postulated to be involved in mediating reconfiguration and re-representation of currently accessible input during metamemory trials in which enough partial information in the cue warrants a continuation of search (Maril et al., 2001; Maril et al., 2005; Reggev, Zuckerman, & Maril, 2011). Recent studies suggest that the involvement of ri PFC may be required when initiating and terminating the search, in part, by incorporating visual and spatial information when trying to resolve metamemory experience (Maril et al., 2005; Reggev et al., 2011). In PD patients, the hypofunction in the inferior PFC, regardless of the left or right, has been linked to an array of deficits including impairments in inhibition of response, reversal go/no-go learning tasks, and task shifting – a well-known executive and working memory process (Aron, Robbins, & Poldrack, 2004; Reggev et al., 2011) – as well as in apathy (Benoit & Robert, 2011; Reijnders et al., 2010), dementia (Ochudło, Opala, Jasińska-Myga, Siuda, & Nowak, 2003), and risk aversion (Christopoulos, Tobler, Bossaerts, Dolan, & Schultz, 2009; Knoch et al., 2006). Given that semantic TOT judgments appear to draw on this particular brain region (Maril et al., 2001; Maril et al., 2005; Reggev et al., 2011), the observation that TOT judgments are uncompromised is counterintuitive because the inferior PFC, as well as surrounding regions such as ACC and dl PFC, is damaged in PD patients (Fuente-Fernández, 2012; Lewis, Shine, Duffy, Halliday, & Naismith, 2012).

However, there are several plausible explanations for this observation. A possible explanation is that the TOT tasks requiring retrieval of semantic (i.e., knowledge or facts) information in PD patients may differ from the typical TOT state in young participants without PD; it may represent a TOT state that is not accompanied by the typical frontal lobe-mediated processes of persistent searching and monitoring for the inaccessible target information. This may resemble a similar TOT state, previously described in elderly participants as "drawing a blank" (Burk, Mackay, Worthley, & Wade, 1991; Cohen & Falkner, 1986; Maril et al., 2001) or participants experiencing "Blank in the Mind" (Touroutoglou & Efklides, 2010), that is not accompanied by the ri PFC-mediated search process during TOT tasks. The semantic TOT trials in PD patients, and perhaps in older participants, therefore, could be considered as trials in which the low familiarity value of the cue, when the target information does not come to mind, does not favor a continuous search and monitoring processes, resulting in a null outcome. This idea is consistent with the postulation that semantic TOT tasks may not involve the ri PFC brain region and also in agreement with the recent data demonstrating that semantic TOT judgments (Oh-Lee et al., 2012) as well as semantic FOK judgments (Coulter, 1989; Dellapietra, 1995) are not impaired in these patients. It is also possible that partially retrieved semantic knowledge from reconfigured and re-represented target information, again drawing on the ri PFC, may even be detrimental by interfering with the retrieval process because such information resembles, and may compete with, the sought-after information. This speculation raises the possibility that TOT accuracy could improve in the absence of conflicting input originating from the frontal lobe during TOT tasks.

It is interesting to note that other neuropsychological patients with frontal lobe lesions demonstrate similar patterns as PD patients, namely, uncompromised metamemory abilities when semantic materials are used, but impaired abilities when episodic memory is used (Reggev et al., 2011; Souchay et al., 2006). In summary, uncompromised semantic TOT metamemory judgments among the PD patients (Oh-Lee et al., 2012) may represent an atypical TOT experience not necessitating ri PFC and other surrounding frontal regions, including ACC and dorsolateral PFC (Maril et al., 2001; Maril et al., 2005), to resolve these retrieval failures in TOT state.

Another possibility is that, in PD, the ventromedial PFC, of which the medial orbitofrontal cortex and inferior PFC constitute the lowermost part, may not be as damaged as other brain regions (Fuente-Fernández, 2012; Kish, Shannak, & Hornykiewicz, 1988), making it possible to favor the ri PFC-mediated search process during TOT tasks. In keeping with this possibility, PD patients off medication have been reported to perform much better in the ventral PFC-mediated tasks, such as go/no-go reversal learning tasks, than in those tasks involving the dorsal PFC (Cools, 2006; Cools, Lewis, Clark, Barker, & Robbins, 2007; Cools, Miyakawa, Sheridan, & D' Esposito, 2010; Swainson et al., 2000). This postulation is consistent with the observation that participants with mild frontal impairment showed compromised FOK but relatively normal TOT (Widner, Otani, & Winkelman, 2005). Another interesting observation is that in early PD, the PFC areas, in general, showed hyperactivation and enhanced connectivity, for example, between inferior PFC and dl PFC as well as between inferior PFC and ventral striatum (Fuente-Fernández, 2012), conceivably reflecting either the compensatory or drug-induced neural plasticity. Accordingly, one cannot disregard the possibility that the uncompromised TOT performance of PD patients might have resulted from a long-term antiparkinsonian drug-induced effect, a possibility that should be investigated further.

In summary, patients afflicted with PD may integrate TOT experiences in a different manner, and some aspects of TOT metamemory judgments are less vulnerable to PD than others. TOT represents a state of temporary failure to access information stored in memory on the verge of recovery. In parallel with neuropsychological studies, the currently available neuroimaging studies provide evidence that TOT experiences are different from other metamemory states (e.g., FOK and RCJ) in their underlying cognitive and neural processes. In terms of neural correlates that are common with other metamemory experiences (e.g., FOK and RCJ), the TOT state appears to be linked to brain regions implicated in internal representation of the target item as well as in a subjective feeling of knowing, namely, the parietal lobe and the ventral PFC (Chua et al., 2009a; Maril et al., 2005). However, uniquely linked to the TOT state appears to be the right PFC, particularly the right inferior PFC, whose brain function has been posited to be related to reconfiguration or re-representation of partially available target information, perhaps contributing to the decision either to continue or terminate the search (Maril et al., 2001; Maril et al., 2005; Reggev et al., 2011). Although this and surrounding PFC brain regions, including ACC and dl PFC (Maril et al., 2005), appear to be integral neural correlates of the TOT state compared to FOK, surprisingly, PD patients with damages in this brain region showed no deficits compared to age-matched control participants in all of the TOT measurements: frequency, strength, and accuracy (Oh-Lee et al., 2012). Although this inconsistency may be attributable to effects associated with compensatory, antiparkinsonian drugs, or memory type (semantic versus episodic) domain, it certainly raises the possibility that right inferior PFC, and surrounding frontal regions purported to be uniquely linked to the TOT state, may be neither necessary nor sufficient for successful TOT experience. Conceivably, in the absence of potential interference from the frontal lobe-mediated search effort during the TOT state, access to the sought-after information in the parietal, temporal, and association cortex is not only possible, but perhaps is also more advantageous in producing favorable TOT performance.

THEORETICAL ISSUES, METHODOLOGICAL ISSUES, AND FUTURE DIRECTIONS

Several theoretical and methodological issues need to be considered before moving forward with research in this area. First, metamemory is not a unitary concept, and, therefore, a variety of measures have been developed to assess metamemory at various stages of memory function. So far, metamemory research with PD patients examined mnestic awareness, global predictions, global postdictions, RCJ, FOK, and TOT; however, these are not the complete inventory of metamemory measures. Conspicuously absent is the judgment-of-learning (JOL) measure, which is the measure of whether a particular item is learned well enough such that one would be able to retrieve this item later when tested. This measure is important because if one feels that an item has been committed to memory already, one would not put any more effort in encoding this item. In fact, studies have shown that JOL is causally related to studying time; participants declined to restudy items when they felt they were confident that they learned the item, even when the confidence was illusory (Finn, 2008; Metcalfe & Finn, 2008; Thiede, Anderson, & Therriault, 2003). It is possible that JOL is impaired among PD patients; studies have shown that patients with frontal lobe damages (particularly right-anterior damage) show impairment in global JOL (Vilkki, Servo, & Surma-aho, 1998). If JOL is impaired among PD patients, then the treatment can focus on how to compensate for the inaccurate JOL.

The second, and a related issue, is that it is important to link the deficits in metamemory measures to specific deficits in memory functions to develop effective treatments. That is, based on the review, it is clear that FOK accuracy is lower among PD patients than control participants when an episodic memory paradigm is used. However, it is not clear what this means in terms of how this particular deficit is related to memory performance. Does this mean that PD patients are unable to implement effective search strategies when they search their memories for the target information? Or is the low FOK accuracy simply another symptom of poor memory, and, therefore, improving their memory would make the deficits in FOK disappear? The critical question is whether the treatment should include training in how to implement effective metamemory strategies. The answer appears to be yes according to the study conducted by Schwartz (2002b), which examined whether finding an answer (resolution) is more likely when participants had control over how to resolve the TOT state. In one condition, participants decided whether they would continue the search for the answer, delay answering the question, or look up the answer immediately, whereas in another condition, participants did not have control over selecting these resolution strategies. The results showed that the resolution rate was higher in the former condition than the latter, and that the resolution rate was even higher when participants in the former condition were in the TOT state. These results indicate that TOT can be a metamemory tool that one can use to enhance memory. That is, instead of dismissing TOT as another symptom of poor memory, one may use it as a signal to implement a search strategy that would result in successful retrieval of the sought-after answer.

The third issue is the underlying mechanisms of metamemory measures and what these mechanisms indicate about the nature of the deficits PD patients are experiencing. For instance, it is not clear whether FOK and TOT are based on different mechanisms. It has been assumed that TOT is simply a strong FOK judgment (e.g., Koriat & Levy-Sadot, 2001; Shimamura & Squire, 1986); however, there are indications that these two measures are qualitatively different. For instance, Widner and colleagues (2005) found that the PFC functioning is differentially involved in TOT and FOK. They assessed PFC functioning based on the amount of perseveration errors participants made on WCST. When these participants were grouped into low- and high-error groups, participants who showed deficient PFC functioning (high-error group) reported fewer FOK judgments as well as less accurate FOK judgments than those who showed intact PFC functioning (low-error group). In contrast, the frequency and the accuracy of TOT experience was not related to PFC functioning. Further, the strength of TOT was not any higher than the strength of FOK, indicating that TOT is not simply a strong case of FOK.

Schwartz (2008) found that working memory load had different effects on TOT and FOK, such that an increase in working memory load decreased the frequency of TOT judgments but had the opposite effect (Experiment 1) or no impact (Experiment 2) on the frequency of FOK judgments. If these two phenomena are based on the same mechanism, manipulating one variable, such as working memory load, should not affect these measures differently. Note that the results Schwartz reported appear to contradict the results Widner and colleagues (2005) presented because PFC has shown to be involved in working memory functioning (Grahn et al., 2009; Leh, Petrides, & Strafella, 2010) and therefore, according to Widner and colleagues, working memory load should have affected FOK rather than TOT. However, the apparent contradiction can be resolved when the nature of the task used to manipulate the working memory load is considered. Participants in Schwartz's experiments were asked to hold digits in mind while answering general knowledge questions. It is possible that the articulatory nature of holding digits in mind interfered with TOT judgments because TOT experience is also articulatory in nature (e.g., having a partial knowledge such as the answer starts with a letter C for Canberra). The reason for the difference needs further investigation; however, Schwartz's results supported the notion that TOT and FOK are based on different mechanisms. Further, neuroimaging studies revealed differences in neural substrates underlying TOT and FOK, indicating that different areas of the brain, albeit there are overlaps, are activated during each of these metamemory judgment tasks.

The fourth issue is that the PD patient group is diverse, and, therefore, a caution needs to be exercised in terms of selecting participants and generalizing the results. PD is not a homogenous diagnostic category, and, consequently, a finer distinction may be necessary. For instance, Yu and colleagues (2010) compared two subgroups of PD patients, one exhibiting tremor-dominant symptom and the other exhibiting akinetic and rigidity dominant symptom, using an episodic paradigm of FOK. The results showed that impairments in FOK accuracy were found only for the latter group.

Other factors also make this patient group diverse. For instance, it has been shown that depression is commonly associated with PD (estimated to be approximately 40%, Farabaugh et al., 2009); however, Varanese, Perfetti, Ghilardi, and Di Rocco (2011) reported that apathy, rather than depression, is the main culprit of inefficient cognition among PD patients. In this study, the researchers compared PD patients with and without apathy on a variety of neuropsychological tests. Of 20 measures, 9 measures, including recall and recognition, showed lower performance by PD patients with apathy than PD patients without apathy. In contrast, depression did not predict cognitive performance; when PD patients without apathy were separated into two groups based on the depression scores, no differences were found on any measures.

However, the most important factor to consider is whether PD patients are on or off medication to suppress PD symptoms (i.e., antiparkinsonian medication), primarily dopaminergic (DA) agonists. Despite inconsistent and mixed reports on the effects of DA drugs on cognitive and motor functions, (Meck & Beson, 2002; Press et al., 2002), administration of DA agonist has been found to cause alterations in working memory performance (Beato et al., 2008; Farid et al., 2009). For example, during a timing task, DA drugs can produce clock speed shifts to an earlier time (a leftward shift) relative to the time of feedback (MacDonald & Meck, 2006; Meck, 2006; Pope, Praamstra, & Wing, 2006). Although PD patients should have been off medication during experimental sessions, an influence of dopaminergic medication, especially those with a long half-life such as levodopa, cannot be excluded. For instance, in the study by Oh-Lee and colleagues (2012), during a metronome-timing task, PD patients displayed similar effects with a greater proportion of clapping responses occurring earlier relative to the cue (~16% greater leftward shift), than did age-matched adults (80% and 69% early responses by PD and elderly, respectively, unpublished results). We, therefore, could not rule out the possibility that the absence of TOT deficits of PD patients might have resulted, at least in part, from a drug-induced effect.

Finally, another important consideration is the history of the disease. Early stage PD has been associated with more prominent damage in the motor and cognitive loop (projecting to supplementary cortex and dl PFC, respectively) than in the limbic loop, which projects to the ventral PFC (Cools, 2006; Cools et al., 2007; Cools et al., 2010; Fuente-Fernández, 2012; Kish et al., 1988; Swainson et al., 2000). Because the ventral PFC brain regions have been posited to play an important role in mediating the metamemory processes associated with subjective experience of knowing as well as search monitoring during unsuccessful retrieval, it is possible that PD patients at early stage may show increased activities in these brain regions during metamemory tasks when compared to PD patients in advanced stage. In addition to ventral PFC degeneration, other neurotransmitters (e.g., cholinergic) and pathological events (e.g., Lewy bodies and amyloid deposits) appear to be involved in PD dementia in advanced stages of the disease (Edison et al., 2008; Hilker et al., 2005). Additional model refinements may be needed, including a better definition of stages of PD and better tools to distinguish between dorsal and ventral PFC-mediated metamemory attributes, both in judgment and control domain. Such effort may prove fruitful in providing a systematic way to assess cognitive and metamemory processes, thereby helping clinicians find effective and novel ways to manage non-motor symptoms of PD patients at all stages of the disease.

CONCLUSION

PD pathology results in a host of executive deficits, such as planning, attention set shifting, and working memory, largely due to strong and reciprocal impairments between the frontal cortex and the striatum known as the frontostriatal pathway. PD is associated with a large number of non-motor clinical features ranging from apathy, depression, anxiety, fatigue, pain, and dementia. Given the critical role metamemory plays in normal executive functioning of one's memory and learning, modern research has turned to metamemory research in patients with PD.

Based on current data, the emerging picture is that although varied types of metamemory judgments (FOK, TOT, RCJ, etc.) may share common neuropsychological and neural attributes, each may also possess distinct substrates. For example, the metamemory underlying the TOT state, while sharing common neural substrates with other metamemory forms (e.g., the parietal lobe activation), appears to be qualitatively different from other metamemory judgments, in both the neuropsychological and neuroanatomical domain. Right inferior PFC and surrounding frontal regions, in particular, appear to be uniquely associated with semantic TOT compared to other types of metamemory judgments as well as compared to non-metamemory tasks. Interestingly, semantic TOT, as well as RCJ and certain subtypes of FOK, appear to be intact among PD patients, raising the possibility that these metamemory processes may occur relatively independent of the frontal lobe contribution.

Collectively, current data suggest that PD patients may integrate and organize metamemory experiences in a different manner, and that certain aspects of metamemory functions, TOT judgments in particular, are less vulnerable to deficits stemming from PD neural dysfunctions. Perhaps, PFC contributions may not be as important as once thought in some form of metamemory experiences, including semantic TOT, semantic FOK, and RCJ. Further investigation into this issue is critical to better understand the mechanisms of the human metamemory system.

Taken together, the present chapter highlights the utility of TOT research in PD patients not only in metamemory research, but also in providing further insight into potential neural and neuropsychological mechanisms by which metamemory contributes to the regulation of one's memory and learning. Furthermore, better understanding of neuropsychological and neural underpinnings of metamemory in Parkinsonism may prove useful in finding more effective and novel ways to incorporate metamemory training, both in judgment and control, to improve memory in PD patients as well as to advance their quality of life.

NOTES

1. Although Pannu and Kaszniak (2005) listed 11 measures from nine studies, there was one redundant entry.

REFERENCES

Almeida, Q. J., & Lebold, C. A. (2010). Freezing of gait in Parkinson's disease: A perceptual cause for a motor impairment? *Journal of Neurology, Neurosurgery and Psychiatry,* 81, 513–518.

Aron, A. R., Robbins, T. W., & Poldrack, R. A. (2004). Inhibition and the right inferior frontal cortex. *Trends in Cognitive Sciences,* 8, 170–177.

Bäckman, L., & Lipinska, B. (1993). Monitoring of general knowledge: Evidence for preservation in early Alzheimer's disease. *Neuropsychologia,*31, 335–345.

Baran, B., Tekcan, A. İ., Gürvit, H., & Boduroglu, A. (2009). Episodic memory and metamemory in Parkinson's disease patients. *Neuropsychology,* 23, 736–745.

Beato, R., Levy, R., Pillon, B., Vidal, C., du Montcel, S. T., Deweer, B., Bonnet, A. M., Houeto, J. L., Dubois, B., & Cardoso, F. (2008). Working memory in Parkinson's disease patients: Clinical features and response to levodopa. *Arquivos de Neuro-Psiquiatria,* 66, 147–151.

Benoit, M., & Robert, P. H. (2011). Imaging correlates of apathy and depression in Parkinson's disease. *The Journal of Neuroscience,* 310, 58–60.

Brønnick, K., Alves, G., Aarsland, D., Tysnes, O., & Larsen, J. P. (2011). Verbal memory in drug-naive, newly diagnosed Parkinson's disease: The retrieval deficit hypothesis revisited. *Neuropsychology,* 25, 114–124.

Brown, A. S. (2012). *The tip of the tongue state.* New York: Psychology Press.

Brown, R., & McNeill, D. (2004). The "tip of the tongue" phenomenon. In D. A. Barlota & E. J. Marsh (Eds.), *Cognitive Psychology: Key Readings* (pp. 418–430). New York: Psychology Press.

Burke, D. M., Mackay, D. G., Worthley J. S., & Wade, E. (1991). On the tip of the tongue: What causes word finding failures in young and older adults? _Journal of Memory and Language_, 30, 542–579.

Chaudhuri, K. R., Healy, D. G., & Schapira, A. H. V. (2006). Non-motor symptoms of Parkinson's disease: Diagnosis and management. _Lancet Neurology_, 5, 235–245.

Chaudhuri, K. R., Yates, L., & Martinez-Martin, P. (2005). The non-motor symptom complex of Parkinson's disease: A comprehensive assessment is essential. _Current Neurology and Neuroscience Reports_, 5, 275–283.

Christopoulos, G. I., Tobler, P. N., Bossaerts, P., Dolan, R. J., & Schultz, W. (2009). Neural correlates of value, risk, and risk aversion contributing to decision making under risk. _The Journal of Neuroscience_, 29, 12574–12583.

Chua, E. F., Schacter, D. L., & Sperling, R. A. (2009a). Neural correlates of metamemory: A comparison of feeling-of-knowing and retrospective confidence judgments. _Journal of Cognitive Neuroscience_, 21, 1751–1765.

(2009b). Neural basis for recognition confidence in younger and older adults. _Psychology and Aging_, 24, 139–153.

Cohen, G., & Faulkner, D. (1986). Memory for proper names: Age differences in retrieval. _British Journal of Developmental Psychology_, 4, 187–197.

Cools, R. (2006). Dopaminergic modulation of cognitive function-implications for L-DOPA treatment in Parkinson's disease. _Neuroscience and Biobehavioral Reviews_, 30, 1–23.

Cools, R., Lewis, S. J., Clark, L., Barker, R. A., & Robbins, T. W. (2007). L-DOPA disrupts activity in the nucleus accumbens during reversal learning in Parkinson's disease. _Neuropsychopharmacology_, 32, 180–189.

Cools, R., Miyakawa, A., Sheridan, M., & D'Esposito, M. (2010). Enhanced frontal function in Parkinson's disease. _Brain_, 133, 225–233.

Coulter, L. (1989). The feeling-of-knowing in depressed and non-depressed patients with Parkinson's disease. _Journal of Clinical Experimental Neuropsychology_, 11, 91 (abstract).

Craik, F. I. M. (1986). A functional account of age differences in memory. In F. Klix & H. Hagendorf (Eds.), _Human memory and cognitive capabilities: Mechanisms and performances_ (pp. 409–422). Amsterdam: Elsevier.

Dellapietra, L. A. (1995). Metamemory in Parkinson's disease. _Dissertation Abstracts International: Section B: The Sciences and Engineering_.

Duke, L. M. (2001). Underawareness of deficit in Alzheimer's disease: Convergent validation of metamemory tasks and the relationship to risky behavior. _Dissertation Abstracts International: Section B: The Sciences and Engineering_.

Edison, P., Rowe, C. C., Rinne, J. O., Ng, S., Ahmed, I., Kemppainen, N., Villemagne, V. L., O'Keefe, G., Någren, K., Chaudhury, K. R., Masters, C. L., & Brooks, D. J. (2008). Amyloid load in Parkinson's disease dementia and Lewy body dementia measured with [11C]PIB positron emission tomography. _Journal of Neurology, Neurosurgery and Psychiatry_, 79, 1331–1338.

Ehringer, H., & Hornykiewicz, O. (1960). Verteilung von Noradrenalin und Dopamin (3-Hydroxytyramin) im Gehirn des Menschen und ihr Verhalten bei Erkrankungen des extrapyramidalen Systems. *Klinische Wochenschrift*, 38, 1236–1239.

Emre, M. (2003). Dementia associated with Parkinson's disease. *The Lancet Neurology*, 2, 229–237.

Farabaugh, A. H., Locascio, J. J., Yap, L., Weintraub, D., McDonald, W. M., Agoston, M., Alpert, J. E., Growdon, J., & Fava, M. (2009). Pattern of depressive symptoms in Parkinson's disease. *Psychosomatics*, 50, 448–454.

Farid, K., Sibon, I., Guehl, D., Cuny, E., Burbaud, P., & Allard, M. (2009). Brain dopaminergic modulation associated with executive function in Parkinson's disease. *Movement Disorders*, 24, 1962–1969.

Farrer, M. J. (2006). Genetics of Parkinson disease: Paradigm shifts and future prospects. *Nature Reviews: Genetics*, 7, 306–318.

Fellows, L. K., & Farah, M. J. (2005). Different underlying impairments in decision-making following ventromedial and dorsolateral frontal lobe damage in humans. *Cerebral Cortex*, 15, 58–63.

Finn, B. (2008). Framing effects on metacognitive monitoring and control. *Memory & Cognition*, 36, 813–821.

Fuente-Fernández, R. D. L. (2012). Frontostriatal cognitive staging in Parkinson's disease. *Parkinson's Disease*, 2012, 1–8.

Ghetti, S., Lyons, K. E., Lazzarin, F., & Cornoldi, C. (2008). The development of metamemory monitoring during retrieval: The case of memory strength and memory absence. *Journal of Experimental Child Psychology*, 99, 157–181.

Giovannoni, G., O'Sullivan, J. D., Turner, K., Manson, A. J., & Lees, A. J. L. (2000). Hedonistic homeostatic dysregulation in patients with Parkinson's disease on dopamine replacement therapies. *Journal of Neurology Neurosurgery and Psychiatry*, 68, 423–428.

Grahn, J. A., Parkinson, J. A., & Owen, A. M. (2008). The cognitive functions of the caudate nucleus. *Progress in Neurobiology*, 86, 141–155.

(2009). The role of the basal ganglia in learning and memory: Neuropsychological studies. *Behavioural Brain Research*, 199, 53–60.

Greenfield, J. G., & Bosanquet, F. D. (1953). The brain stem lesions in parkinsonism. *Journal of Neurology Neurosurgery and Psychiatry*, 16, 213–226.

Hart, J. T. (1965). Memory and the feeling-of-knowing experience. *Journal of Educational Psychology*, 56, 208–216.

Herlofson, K., & Larsen, J. P. (2002). Measuring fatigue in patients with Parkinson's disease: The Fatigue Severity Scale. *European Journal of Neurology*, 9, 595–600.

Higginson, C. I., Wheelock, V. L., Carroll, K. E., & Sigvardt, K. A. (2005). Recognition memory in Parkinson's disease with and without dementia: Evidence inconsistent with the retrieval deficit hypothesis. *Journal of Clinical and Experimental Neuropsychology*, 27, 516–528.

Hilker, R., Thomas, A. V., Klein, J. C., Weisenbach, S., Kalbe, E., Burghaus, L, Jacobs, A. H., Herholz, K., & Heiss, W. D. (2005). Dementia in Parkinson disease: Functional imaging of cholinergic and dopaminergic pathways. *Neurology*, 65, 1716–1722.

Hinton, S. C., Paulsen, J. S., Hoffmann, R. G., Reynolds, N. C., Zimbelman, J. L., & Rao, S. M. (2007). Motor timing variability increases in preclinical Huntington's disease patients as estimated onset of motor symptoms approaches. *Journal of the International Neuropsychological Society, 13,* 539–543.

Hopp, G. A. (1999). *A comparison of performance on measures of executive function and metacognition in normal aging and Parkinson's disease. Dissertation Abstracts International: Section B: The Sciences and Engineering.*

Hornykiewicz, O. (1963). Die Topische Lokalisation und das Verhalten von Noradrenalin und Dopamin in der substantia nigra des normalen und Parkinsonkranken Menschen. *Wien Klin. Wochenschr, 75,* 309–312.

Ivory, S. J., Knight, R. G., Longmore, B. E., & Caradoc-Davies, T. (1999). Verbal memory in non-demented patients with idiopathic Parkinson's disease. *Neuropsychologia, 37,* 817–828.

Janowsky, J. S., Shimamura, A. P., & Squire, L. R. (1989). Memory and metamemory: Comparisons between patients with frontal lobe lesions and amnesic patients. *Psychobiology, 17,* 3–11.

Johnson, A. M., Pollard, C. C., Vernon, P. A., Tomes, J. L., & Jog, M. S. (2005). Memory perception and strategy use in Parkinson's disease. *Parkinsonism & Related Disorders, 11,* 111–115.

Kish, S. J., Shannak, K., & Hornykiewicz, O. (1988). Uneven pattern of dopamine loss in the striatum of patients with idiopathic Parkinson's disease. *The New England Journal of Medicine, 318,* 876–880.

Knoch, D., Gianotti, L. R. R., Pascual-Leone, A., Treyer, V., Regard, M., Hohmann, M., & Brugger, P. (2006). Disruption of right prefrontal cortex by low-frequency repetitive transcranial magnetic stimulation induces risk-taking behavior. *The Journal of Neuroscience, 26,* 6469–6472.

Koerts, J., Tucha, L., Leenders, K. L., Van Beilen, M., Brouwer, W. H., & Tucha, O. (2011). Subjective and objective assessment of executive functions in Parkinson's disease. *Journal of the Neurological Sciences, 310,* 172–175.

Koriat, A., & Levy-Sadot, R. (2001). The combined contributions of the cue-familiarity and accessibility heuristics to feelings of knowing. *Journal of Experimental Psychology: Learning, Memory, and Cognition, 27,* 34–53.

Koriat, A., Levy-Sadot, R., Edry, E., & de Marcas, S. (2003). What do we know about what we cannot remember? Accessing the semantic attributes of words that cannot be recalled. *Journal of Experimental Psychology: Learning, Memory, and Cognition, 29,* 1095–1105.

Koriat, A., Nussinson, R., Bless, H., & Shaked, N. (2008). Information-based and experience-based metacognitive judgments: Evidence from subjective confidence. In J. Dunlosky & R. A. Bjork (Eds.), *Handbook of metamemory and memory* (pp. 117–135). New York: Psychology Press.

Lang, A. E., & Lozano, A. M. (1998). Parkinson's disease. *New England Journal of Medicine, 339,* 1044–1053.

Leh, S. E., Petrides, M., & Strafella, A. P. (2010). The neural circuitry of executive functions in healthy subjects and Parkinson's disease. *Neuropsychopharmacology, 35,* 70–85.

Lewis, S. J., Dove, A., Bobbins, T. W., Barker, R. A., & Owen, A. M. (2004). Striatal contributions to working memory: A functional magnetic resonance imaging study in humans. *European Journal of Neuroscience, 19,* 755–760.

Lewis, S. J. G., Shine, J. M., Duffy, S., Halliday, G., & Naismith, S. L. (2012). Anterior cingulate integrity: Executive and neuropsychiatric features in Parkinson's disease. *Movement Disorders, 27,* 1262–1267.

Lou, J. S., Kearns, G., Oken, B., Sexton G., & Nutt, J. (2001). Exacerbated physical fatigue and mental fatigue in Parkinson's disease. *Movement Disorders, 16,* 190–196.

MacDonald, C. J., & Meck, W. H. (2006). Interaction of raclopride and preparatory interval effects on simple reaction time performance. *Behavioural Brain Research, 175,* 62–74.

Maril, A., Simons, J. S., Mitchell, J. P., Schwartz, B. L., & Schacter, D. L. (2003). Feeling-of-knowing in episodic memory: An event-related fMRI study. *NeuroImage, 18,* 827–836.

Maril, A., Simons, J. S., Weaver, J. J., & Schacter, D. L. (2005). Graded recall success: An event-related fMRI comparison of tip of the tongue and feeling of knowing. *NeuroImage, 24,* 1130–1138.

Maril, A., Wagner, A. D., & Schacter, D. L. (2001). On the tip of the tongue: An event-related fMRI study of semantic retrieval failure and cognitive conflict, *Neuron, 31,* 653–660.

Matison, R., Mayeux, R., Rosen, J., & Fahn S. (1982). "Tip-of-the-tongue" phenomenon in Parkinson disease. *Neurology, 32,* 567–570.

McKinlay, A., Dalrymple-Alford, J. C., Grace, R. C., & Roger, D. (2009). The effect of attentional set-shifting, working memory, and processing speed on pragmatic language functioning in Parkinson's disease. *European Journal of Cognitive Psychology, 21,* 330–346.

McPherson, S., & Cummings, J. (2009). Neuropsychological aspects of Parkinson's disease and Parkinsonism. In I. Grant & K. Adams (Eds.), *Neuropsychological assessment of neuropsychiatric and neuromedical disorders* (pp. 199–222). New York: Oxford University Press.

Meck, W. H. (2006). Frontal cortex lesions eliminate the clock speed effect of dopaminergic drugs on interval timing. *Brain Research, 1108,* 157–167.

Meck, W. H., & Benson, A. M. (2002). Dissecting the brain's internal clock: How frontal-striatal circuitry keeps time and shifts attention. *Brain and Cognition, 48,* 195–211.

Mehler-Wex, C., Riederer, P., & Gerlach, M. (2006). Dopaminergic dysbalance in distinct basal ganglia neurocircuits: Implications for the pathophysiology of Parkinson's disease, schizophrenia and attention deficit hyperactivity disorder. *Neurotoxicity Research, 10,* 167–179.

Metcalfe, J., & Finn, B. (2008). Evidence that judgments of learning are causally related to study choice. *Psychonomic Bulletin & Review, 15,* 174–179.

Mink, J. W. (2006). Neurobiology of the basal ganglia and Tourette syndrome: Basal ganglia circuits and thalamocortical outputs. In J. T. Walkup, J. W. Mink, & P. J. Hollenbeck (Eds.), *Advances in Neurology,* Vol 99: Tourette Syndrome. Hagerstown, MD: Wolters Klewer Health.

Moulin, C. J. A., James, N., Perfect, T. J., & Jones, R. W. (2003). Knowing what you cannot recognise: Further evidence for intact metacognition in Alzheimer's disease. *Aging, Neuropsychology, and Cognition*, 10, 74–81.

Moulin, C. J. A., Perfect, T. J., & Jones, R. W. (2000a). Evidence for intact memory in Alzheimer's disease: Metamemory sensitivity at encoding. *Neuropsychologia*, 38, 1242–1250.

(2000b). Global predictions of memory in Alzheimer's disease: Evidence for preserved metamemory monitoring. *Aging, Neuropsychology, and Cognition*, 7, 230–244.

Nelson, T. O., & Narens, L. (1980). Norms of 300 general-information questions: Accuracy of recall, latency of recall, and feeling-of-knowing ratings. *Journal of Verbal Learning & Verbal Behavior*, 19, 338–368.

(1994). The role of metacognition in problem solving. In J. Metcalfe & A. Shiminura (Eds.), *Metacognition* (pp. 207–226). Cambridge, MA: MIT Press.

Ochudło, S., Opala, G., Jasińska-Myga, B., Siuda, J., & Nowak, S. (2003). [Inferior frontal region hypoperfusion in Parkinson disease with dementia], *Neurologia i neurochirurgia polska*, 37 (Suppl. 5), 133–144.

Oh-Lee, J. D., Szymkowicz, S. M., Smith, S. L., & Otani, H. (2012). Metacognitive performance, the tip-of-tongue experience, is not disrupted in parkinsonian patients. *Parkinson's Disease*, 2012, 1–12.

Pannu, J. K., & Kaszniak, A. W. (2005). Metamemory experiments in neurological populations: A review. *Neuropsychology Review*, 15, 105–130.

Pappas, B. A., Sunderland, T., Weingartner, H. M., Vitiello, B., Martinson, H., & Putnam, K. (1992). Alzheimer's disease and feeling-of-knowing for knowledge and episodic memory. *Journal of Gerontology*, 47, 159–164.

Perrotin, A., Belleville, S., & Isingrini, M. (2007). Metamemory monitoring in mild cognitive impairment: Evidence of a less accurate episodic feeling-of-knowing. *Neuropsychologia*, 45, 2811–2826.

Pope, P. A., Praamstra, P., & Wing, A. M. (2006). Force and time control in the production of rhythmic movement sequences in Parkinson's disease. *European Journal of Neuroscience*, 23, 1643–1650.

Press, D. Z., Mechanic, D. J., Tarsy, D., & Manoach, D. S. (2002). Cognitive slowing in Parkinson's disease resolves after practice. *Journal of Neurology, Neurosurgery & Psychiatry*, 73, 524–528.

Reggev, N., Zuckerman, M., & Maril, A. (2011). Are all judgments created equal? An fMRI study of semantic and episodic metamemory predictions. *Neuropsychologia*, 49, 1332–1343.

Reijnders, J. S., Scholtissen, B., Weber, W. E., Aalten, P., Verhey, F. R., & Leentjens, A. F. (2010). Neuroanatomical correlates of apathy in Parkinson's disease: A magnetic resonance imaging study using voxel-based morphometry. *Movement Disorders*, 25, 2318–2325.

Schacter, D. L., McLachlan, D., Moscovitch, M., & Tulving, E. (1986). Monitoring and recall performance by memory-disordered patients. *Journal of Clinical and Experimental Neuropsychology*, 8, 130 (abstract).

Schifitto, G., Friedman, J. H., Oakes, D., Shulman, L., Comella, C. L., Marek, K., & Fahn, S. (2008). Fatigue in levodopa-naïve subjects with Parkinson disease. *Neurology, 71*, 481–485.

Schwartz, B. L. (2002a). *Tip-of-the-tongue states: Phenomenology, mechanism, and lexical retrieval*. Mahwah, NJ: Lawrence Erlbaum.

(2002b). The strategic control of retrieval during tip-of-the-tongue states. *Korean Journal of Thinking & Problem Solving, 12*, 27–37.

(2008). Working memory load differentially affects tip-of-the-tongue states and feeling-of-knowing judgments. *Memory & Cognition, 36*, 9–19.

Shimamura, A. P., & Squire, L. R. (1986). Memory and metamemory: A study of the feeling-of-knowing phenomenon in amnesiac patients. *Journal of Experimental Psychology: Learning, Memory, & Cognition, 12*, 452–460.

Shulman, L. M., Taback, R. L., Bean, J., & Weiner, W. J. (2001). Comorbidity of the nonmotor symptoms of Parkinson's disease. *Journal of the Movement Disorder Society, 16*, 507–510.

Sitek, E. J., Sołtan, W., Wieczorek, D., Robowski, P., & Sławek, J. (2011). Self-awareness of memory function in Parkinson's disease in relation to mood and symptom severity. *Aging & Mental Health, 15*, 150–156.

Smith, S. J., Souchay, C., & Conway, M. A. (2010). Improving metamemory in ageing and Parkinson's disease. *Age Ageing, 39*, 116–119.

Smith, S. J., Souchay, C., & Moulin, C. J. A. (2011). Metamemory and prospective memory in Parkinson's disease. *Neuropsychology, 25*, 734–740.

Son, L. K., & Schwartz, B. L. (2002). The relation between metacognitive monitoring and control. In T. J. Perfect & B. L. Schwartz (Eds.), *Applied metacognition* (pp. 15–38). Cambridge University Press.

Souchay, C., Isingrini, M., & Gil, R. (2002). Alzheimer's disease and feeling-of-knowing in episodic memory. *Neuropsychologia, 40*, 2386–2396.

(2006). Metamemory monitoring and Parkinson's disease. *Journal of Clinical and Experimental Neuropsychology, 28*, 618–630.

Swainson, R., Rogers, R. D., Sahakian, B. J., Summers, B. A., Polkey, C. E., & Robbins, T.W. (2000). Probabilistic learning and reversal deficits in patients with Parkinson's disease or frontal or temporal lobe lesions: Possible adverse effects of dopaminergic medication. *Neuropsychologia, 38*, 596–612.

Thiede, K. W., Anderson, M. C. M., & Therriault, D. (2003). Accuracy of metacognitive monitoring affects learning of texts. *Journal of Educational Psychology, 95*, 66–73.

Touroutoglou, A., & Efklides, A. (2010). Cognitive interruption as an object of metacognitive monitoring: Feeling of difficulty and surprise. In A. Efklides & P. Misailidi (Eds.), *Trends and prospects in metacognition research* (pp. 171–208). New York: Springer Science + Business Media.

Varanese, S., Perfetti, B., Ghilardi, M. F., & Di Rocco, A. (2011). Apathy, but not depression, reflects inefficient cognitive strategies in Parkinson's disease. *PLoS ONE, 6*(3), 1–12.

Vilkki, J., Servo, A., & Surma-aho, O. (1998). Word list learning and prediction of recall after frontal lobe lesions. *Neuropsychology, 12*, 268–277.

Widner, R. L., Otani, H., & Winkelman, S. E. (2005). Tip-of-the-tongue experiences are not merely strong feeling-of-knowing experiences. *Journal of General Psychology, 132,* 392–407.

York, M. K., & Alvarez, J. K. (2008). Cognitive impairments associated with Parkinson's disease. In M. Trail, E. Protas, & E. Lai (Eds.), *Neurorehabilitation in Parkinson's disease: An evidence based treatment model* (pp. 71–100). Thorofare, NJ: Slack Incorporated.

Yu, R. L., Wu, R. M., Tai, C. H., Lin, C. H., & Hua, M. S. (2010). Feeling-of-knowing in episodic memory in patients with Parkinson's disease with various motor symptoms. *Movement Disorders, 25,* 1034–1039.

9

The Psychopharmacological Approach to Metamemory and the TOT Phenomenon

MARIE IZAUTE AND ELISABETH BACON

INTRODUCTION

Conventional studies in cognitive psychology involve healthy participants and highlight fundamental notions common to all. Other studies recruit individuals suffering from traumatic or organic memory pathologies. However, the study of clinical populations is likely problematic because the nature and extent of the brain lesion may vary from one individual to the next. It is useful, therefore, to think of what happens to cognition when a particular system is not working or off-line. In our work, we have examined amnesia-inducing drugs, which may be considered tools that reveal functional principles of normal cognitive processing (Danion, 1994). Research on the cognitive effects of benzodiazepines (BZ) in healthy participants usually involves administering acute doses, with testing occurring close to theoretical peak plasma concentration of drugs. The fact that lorazepam, a benzodiazepine widely prescribed for its anxiolytic, hypnotic, and anti-epileptic properties, induces transient amnesia after a single administration is well known (Allen, Curran, & Lader, 1993; Bishop & Curran, 1998; Curran, Gardiner, Java, & Allen, 1993). A considerable body of research was devoted to the effects of lorazepam on memory (Danion, 1994; Danion et al., 1992; Danion, Zimmermann, Willard-Schroeder, Grangé, & Singer, 1989; File, Sharma, & Schaffer, 1992; Legrand et al., 1995; Pompeia et al., 2000; Vidailhet, Kazès, Danion, Kauffmann-Muller, & Grangé, 1996; Weingartner et al., 1993; for review, see Buffet-Jerrott & Stewart, 2002; Curran, 1991, 1999, 2000; Beracochea, 2006; Stewart, 2005). Few studies,

This work was supported by a grant from *Cognitique* (N° COG 53B) "Impairments and recovery of cognitive functions" from the Ministry of Research, by INSERM, Strasbourg University, Strasbourg University Hospital, CNRS, and Clermont University.

however, have concentrated on the effects of lorazepam on metamemory (Mintzer & Griffiths, 2005).

The study of metamemory permits an experimental approach to the disorders of consciousness related to memory processes. More specifically, *metamemory* refers to the subjective awareness of one's memory capacity and the control of the related cognitive behavior. Metamemory can be thought of as a regulatory system that influences both memory encoding and retrieval. Previous metamemory studies conducted with normal participants have confirmed that two processes, monitoring and control, influence memory performance (Koriat & Goldsmith, 1996b; Nelson & Narens, 1990). *Monitoring* refers to the participant's subjective evaluation of her or his cognitive system and is expressed in the form of metamemory judgments such as feeling of knowing (FOK) or confidence level (CL) at the time of retrieval. FOK is a metamemory judgment expressed at the time of retrieval. When people fail to retrieve a target answer, they can at least say whether they have the feeling of knowing (or not knowing) the missing response, that is, that they can recognize the target answer when they see or hear it, despite their failure to recall it. When people produce an answer, they can produce a confidence level (CL) judgment as to the likelihood that the answer is correct. Subjects' CL judgments may be based on the strength of the link between the question and the answer (Metcalfe & Shimamura, 1994). The *control of memory* refers to strategy use, allocation of study time, the decision to produce an answer or to abstain, the choice to continue the memory search or to spend more time searching for the known information, and so forth.

The aim of this chapter is to examine more completely the lorazepam effect on metamemory from short-term to semantic memory. The present chapter is organized as follows. First, short-term memory and metamemory monitoring in lorazepam is discussed with particular emphasis on the implication of the sedation effect on FOK monitoring. We contrast this effect with the claim that the lorazepam impairment in episodic memory is independent of the benzodiazepine-induced sedative effects. In the second part, we report that the lorazepam-treated participants exhibited both memory and metamemory impairments in long-term retrieval. We first present results about impairment of lorazepam-treated participants in their control sensitivity on semantic memory. Then, empirical findings from one TOT study will be presented suggesting that lorazepam-induced amnesia permits researchers to dissociate the two TOT components: the cognitive level and the metacognitive level. Finally, in the last part of this chapter, the interconnections and contradictions between empirical findings in various studies are discussed.

Short-Term Memory and Metamemory

Typically, lorazepam is not considered to have an effect on short-term memory (for review, see Curran, 1991, 1999). However, assessments of the effects of lorazepam are not always consistent. Some authors argue that lorazepam has no effect on short-term memory (Brown, Lewis, Brown, Horn, & Bowes, 1982; Duka, Redemann, & Voet, 1995; Ferrara et al., 1999; Fluck et al., 1998; Kumar, Mac, Gabrielli, & Goodwin, 1987; Mac, Kumar, & Goodwin, 1985; Mallick, Kirby, Martin, Philp, & Hennessy, 1993; Matthews, Kirkby, & Martin, 2002), whereas others claim that lorazepam induces a deficit in short-term memory (Patat et al., 1995). Mintzer and Griffiths (2003) observed an impairment of working memory under the effect of lorazepam, as did Duka and colleagues (1995). Although working memory was impaired in both cases, the latter authors observed that immediate recall remained unaffected. Nevertheless, Izaute and Bacon (2006) reported a study specifically designed to examine the effect of lorazepam in a task requiring short-term retention. Both memory and metamemory hypothesis were evaluated.

According to the accessibility model proposed by Koriat (1993, 1995, 1997), FOK may be related to the products of the retrieval process itself. When we search our memories for a desired target, a variety of incomplete details come to mind, including fragments of the target, semantic attributes, and episodic information pertaining to the target. The main assumption concerning the basis of FOK judgments embodied in this model is that "the cues for FOK reside in the products of the retrieval process itself" (Koriat, 1993). The accessibility hypothesis Koriat developed suggests that a large amount of information is activated early in the search process, that is, before the target has been fully retrieved and even when the target is not retrieved. The model states that the tendency to produce a high or low FOK depends on the overall amount of partial information elicited by the question.

In his 1993 publication, Koriat proposed an experimental paradigm that makes it possible to control the partial information corresponding to a given target answer and to relate the accessibility of partial information to the rating and the accuracy of the FOK. To test this, the participants had to learn nonsense letter strings. Each individual letter constituted an item of partial information contributing to the target answer, which consisted of the entire string of letters itself. In the various experiments presented by Koriat (1993), the recall step occurred after a retention interval that ranged from 15 to 25 seconds, in other words, within a period usually thought to involve short-term memory. Using this paradigm, Koriat observed that the number of letters recalled was a good predictor of future recognition performance and of the participants' FOK ratings. Following Koriat, Izaute and Bacon (2006) showed that for memory, lorazepam participants can memorize four-letter nonsense strings (tetragrams). They are able to recall partial and complete tetragrams. The learning of tetragrams has the advantage of providing a simple measure of the amount of correct and incorrect partial information retained while minimizing the possible contribution of pre-experimental variables. This paradigm allowed Izaute and Bacon to examine both short-term memory and FOK in participants under the influence of lorazepam.

It is important to distinguish between two properties of memory, namely, its production (the number of items retrieved) and its validity (the proportion of correct items among the items retrieved) (see Koriat & Goldsmith, 1994, 1996a). In Izaute and Bacon, the production was the number of letters, and the validity was the correctness of the letters. Regardless of whether recall was complete or incomplete, there was no difference in production in the lorazepam group compared to the placebo group. However, validity was worse in the lorazepam group. The lower memory recall accuracy measured in the lorazepam group was not due to a difference in the basic learning ability of the two experimental groups because their base rates, evaluated before drug intake, were the same. Rather, the lorazepam induced a deficit in metamemory monitoring, leading to the production of more incorrect items.

On monitoring judgments, their results indicate that the FOK estimates increased, both for the placebo and lorazepam participants, with the amount of partial information retrieved, irrespective of the accuracy of this information. Consequently, Koriat's accessibility hypothesis (Koriat, 1993, 1995, 1997; Koriat, Levy-Sadot, Edry, & Marcas, 2003) seems valid even under the effect of an amnesic drug such as lorazepam, and this aspect of the relationship between memory retrieval and monitoring ratings seems to be preserved by the drug. However, the overall FOK estimates were lower in the lorazepam group than in the placebo group, suggesting that the lorazepam participants had some awareness of their deficit.

According to the accessibility model, FOK may be determined by multiple factors (Koriat & Levy-Sadot, 1999). Healthy participants predict their memory performance from cues such as familiarity with the general topic (Costermans, Lories, & Ansay, 1992), or the perceived difficulty of an item, or the ease with which an item is retrieved (Kelley & Lindsay, 1993; Koriat, 1993; Mazzoni & Nelson, 1995). More interesting, Koriat points out the fact that the ease of access, in other words the latency associated with the recall of an answer, could be one of the cues for FOK ratings. In fact, in their study, Izaute and Bacon (2006) observed that the response latency for recalled responses was higher under the effect of lorazepam. In addition, because of its sedative effect, the drug might have delayed access to the mnesic store, making it slower to access information in working memory. The fact that a significant correlation existed between sedation (subjective state assessed by a visual analog scale) and the FOK estimates, both in the placebo and in the lorazepam participants, seems to support such an explanation. Lower FOK estimates could then be expected because the patients under lorazepam were more sedated than the placebo participants. Because of lorazepam's sedative effect on short-term memory, lorazepam participants may have slower access to the products of retrieval and, consequently, lower FOK.

Memory and Metamemory in Long-Term Memory

Episodic Memory and Metamemory
Experimental results showed that episodic memory is specifically impaired when participants are under the influence of lorazepam (Blin et al., 2001; Curran, 1991, 1999; Duka et al., 1996; File et al., 1992; Fluck et al., 1998; Green, McElhom, & King, 1996; Lobo & Greene, 1997; Mattila, Vanakoski, Kalska, & Seppala, 1998; Mintzer, Frey, Yingling, & Griffiths, 1997; Mintzer & Griffiths, 1999; Patat et al., 1995, 2001; Rush, Armstrong, Ali, & Pazzaglia, 1998; Rush & Griffiths, 1996). Research also suggests that this impairment is independent of the benzodiazepine-induced sedative effects (Huron, Giersch, & Danion, 2002; Mintzer & Griffiths, 2003), because there were no correlations with sedation measures.

Bacon and colleagues (1998) conducted a detailed study of the effects of lorazepam on episodic memory and metamemory, the first such study to address metamemory. Their results revealed that in a sentence completion task assessing episodic memory, the lorazepam-treated participants exhibited both memory and metamemory impairments during both recall and recognition. The task assessing episodic memory consisted of completion of sentences. First, the subject was presented with the sentences. After the learning session, the sentences were presented again with the last word missing. Then, the subjects had to rate their confidence (CL) when they produced an answer or their feeling of knowing (FOK) when they did not remember the answer. After completion of the recall task, the sentences that the subjects had failed to answer were again presented for a recognition task with a choice of five alternatives.

In the study, Bacon and colleagues (1998) demonstrated that lorazepam impairs metamemory processes related to episodic memory. Participants who had received the lorazepam dose exhibited metamemory impairments in the recall phase of the task: their confidence ratings accuracy, as measured by G coefficients,[1] was significantly lower than that of the placebo-treated subjects. The gamma correlation was impaired under the effect of lorazepam in a task assessing episodic memory. This impairment is probably the result of a lorazepam-induced lowering of the strength of the link between the question and the answer. The finding that lorazepam impairs metamemory for episodic memory is consistent with the demonstration that subjects treated with triazolam, another benzodiazepine, were as certain as placebo-treated subjects that they could successfully recall words learned under the influence of the drug, when their recall was in fact impaired (Weingartner et al., 1993).

Semantic Illusion and Strategic Regulation

The lorazepam participants are more susceptible to a common semantic illusion known as *the Moses Illusion* (Izaute, Paire-Ficout, & Bacon, 2004). In the first study on this illusion, Erickson and Mattson (1981) revealed a puzzling phenomenon. They asked participants to answer a set of questions, four of which contained semantic anomalies such as "How many animals of each kind did Moses take on the ark?" Most of them responded "two," even though, when it was brought to their attention, they knew that Noah, not Moses, took the animals on the ark. This illusion, known as the Moses illusion, has proven quite robust and can be generalized across other materials and conditions (see Brédart & Docquier, 1989; Brédart & Modolo, 1988; Hannon & Daneman, 2001; Kamas, Reder, & Ayers, 1996; Reder & Kusbit, 1991; Van Oostendorp & Kok, 1990; Van Oostendorp & de Mul, 1990). Reder and her colleagues argue that the failure to detect distortions results from an imperfect or incomplete memory match process, known as the *partial match process* (Kamas et al., 1996; Reder & Cleeremans, 1990; Reder & Kusbit, 1991) or the *partial processing process* (Hannon & Daneman, 2001). In our study, the aim of the Moses illusion study was to test the partial matching hypothesis with participants who were under the effect of benzodiazepine. As lorazepam-treated participants display a strategic-regulation impairment (Massin-Krauss, Bacon, & Danion, 2002), the authors expected a different response bias and a higher rate of Moses illusions in the lorazepam group than in the placebo group.

First, Izaute and colleagues' (2004) results showed that the lorazepam participants produced more Moses illusions than placebo participants. It is as if the drug affected the setting of the detection threshold. We thought this was related to Shafto and MacKay's model of semantic activation. They wrote that "participants detect semantic anomalies when they become aware of novel information that conflicts with simultaneously activated information in semantic memory" (Shafto & McKay, 2000, p. 378). This novelty decision could be interpreted as a threshold for the detection and the production of an answer that remains intact following loraze-pam administration. The lorazepam participants were less sensitive to the conflict between the terms in the query and the terms stored in semantic memory. These data are in agreement with previous results, which have shown that lorazepam and benzodiazepines generally produce robust anticonflict effects (Harvey, 1980; Kleven & Koek, 1999; Vanover, Robledo, Huber, & Carter, 1999). Second, for lorazepam participants, the tendency to say that a question is "wrong" was lower for both an illusion and a filler question. When participants had taken lorazepam, they shifted their bias toward calling a question distorted. The bias observed in the lora-zepam participants was more conservative and significantly lower than in the placebo group. This result allows us to discuss another hypoth-esis according to which the drug might have impaired what Kamas and colleagues (1996) call the strategic control of the semantic store, which is based on nonparametric measures of sensitivity. This interpretation is in accordance with Massin-Krauss and colleagues' (2002) work. Indeed, these authors have suggested that the control mechanism operates as a threshold for the monitoring output. They found that lorazepam-treated participants were impaired in their control sensitivity. Indeed, the lora-zepam participants were accurate in their judgments, but were not able to strictly adhere to these judgments in deciding whether to volunteer or withhold the answers.

In conclusion, lorazepam does not radically disturb semantic processes. Instead, the Moses illusion paradigm reveals subtle and highly specific impairments that may often remain unnoticed in daily life situations. The studies of the long-term effects of benzodiazepines on cognitive functions suggest that a significant impairment remains in comparison to controls or normative data (Curran et al., 1994; Gorenstein, Bernik, Pompéia, & Marcourakis, 1995; Tata, Rollings, Collins, Pickering, & Jacobson, 1994). Subsequently, these specific semantic impairments may be highly prejudi-cial for the normal conduct of daily living activities by chronic users of benzodiazepines. However, researchers observed some degree of improve-ment in cognitive function of long-term benzodiazepine users following withdrawal (Barker, Greenwood, Jackson, & Crowe, 2004).

Retrieval of Semantic Information and Metamemory

In this section, we concentrate on whether benzodiazepines affect retrieval in semantic memory. The retrieval of semantic knowledge is generally considered to remain intact following lorazepam administration. Curran (1991, 1999) argued that benzodiazepines do not alter semantic memory. These conclusions were primarily drawn on the basis of unimpaired performances in verbal fluency tasks in which participants were required to provide in a fixed time the largest possible number of items belonging to a given semantic category (Curran, 1991; File et al., 1992; Fluck et al., 1998; Vermeeren et al., 1995). Allen and colleagues (1993) and Green and colleagues (1996) found that lorazepam did not affect the accuracy of semantic retrieval. Verbal fluency, word stem completion, and conceptual priming have been shown to be unaffected by the drug, although lorazepam often lengthens the time required to complete the task. Nevertheless, in the second experiment by Bishop and Curran (1998), which used general information questions, the slight decrease of performance in the lorazepam participants, albeit not significant with a set of 32 general information questions, may have been associated with a deficit in processing semantic knowledge. Moreover, Vermeeren and colleagues (1995) reported that lorazepam participants made more errors than placebo participants in a sentence verification task. The observations Vermeeren and collaborators made of an impaired performance provide an additional argument for an imperfect treatment of the information supplied within the sentences by participants performing under the effect of lorazepam.

Bacon and colleagues (1998) conducted a detailed metamemory study of the effects of lorazepam on semantic memory and metamemory. Participants answered a set of 120 general information questions of various difficulties (e.g., "In which town is Karl Marx buried?"). We found that the drug impairs semantic memory performance not by decreasing the accessibility to information, but by disturbing participants' production of the answers, as the lorazepam-treated participants provided as many recall answers as the placebo participants in the free recall part of the semantic task, but they produced a greater amount of incorrect recalls.

Bacon and colleagues' (1998) demonstration of a performance deficit in the task of assessing semantic memory in the lorazepam-treated subjects was unexpected, but the deficit was observed in both recall and recognition tasks. The profile of the lorazepam groups' performance, characterized by a preserved number of answers in the recall task and a low proportion of correct answers in the recall and recognition tasks, indicates that the drug impairs performance not by decreasing accessibility to information, but by disturbing subjects' ability to distinguish between correct and incorrect information, therefore creating a metamemory effect.

In a subsequent study, Bacon and colleagues (2002) showed that lorazepam-treated participants respond more often than placebo participants to unanswerable questions. In this study, most of the unanswerable questions were selected from Schwartz's illusory TOT studies (Schwartz, 1998; Schwartz, Travis, Castro, & Smith, 2000). For example, when asked "What is the name of the only kind of living reptile that flies?" some of the lorazepam participants responded "a bat" (3 times) or "an iguana" (once). Lorazepam-treated participants produced more errors than controls, and they failed to detect the anomaly between the question and their answer. This distortion is similar to the processing of the semantic illusion.

WHAT ABOUT MONITORING?

Following Koriat (1993) and Metcalfe (1993), we assert that monitoring is based on inferential processes. Inferential processes may be related to general properties of the questions such as familiarity with the general topic of the item (e.g., I know little about Australia) (Costermans et al., 1992) or the retrieval of pertinent information (e.g., remembering particular events surrounding information acquisition) (Koriat 1994; Metcalfe, Schwartz, & Joaquim, 1993; Reder & Ritter, 1992). According to the model developed by Koriat (1995), inferential processes may also be related to the products of the retrieval process itself. Within the accessibility perspective (Koriat 1993, 1995), the main hypothesis concerning the basis of FOK judgments is that participants rely on a variety of contextual cues activated during the memory search (Koriat 1993, 1995, 1997).

Bacon and colleagues (1998) and Massin-Krauss and colleagues (2002) asked their participants to rate their retrospective confidence level (CL) that the answer they had provided was correct. Both studies observed that participants under lorazepam selectively overestimated their CL judgments for their incorrect recalls compared to the CL judgments of placebo participants. Participants under lorazepam could have been "influenced by the effects of past experiences" (Melzack, Coderre, Katz, & Vaccarino, 2001, p. 157). They could have given to the transitory incorrect recall the high confidence that they would have usually attributed to the correct answer that is momentarily not available because of the effect of the drug. Their behavioral output when rating their confidence would still rely on the past inputs and on the "memory of prior events." This supports the general idea of ghost memories; the participants were basing their judgments on how their memory usually works, not how it works under lorazepam. However, they were still able to discriminate between correct and incorrect answers, as their confidence remained higher for correct than for incorrect answers. At the same time, the accuracy of their CL estimations as well as the predictive accuracy of their FOK estimations regarding future recognition performance (i.e., their G correlations; Nelson, 1984) did not differ from those of the participants who received a placebo. The preservation of monitoring accuracy while under the effect of lorazepam suggests that the drug spares some of the monitoring abilities.

This impaired recall performance may suggest that lorazepam affects the control processes. The drug may perhaps induce a disinhibitory state that leads participants to produce answers that they might otherwise have kept to themselves. Massin-Krauss and colleagues (2002) examined the effects of lorazepam on the processes involved in the strategic regulation of memory accuracy (Koriat & Goldsmith, 1996b). They showed that not all the extra commission errors produced under the effect of lorazepam in a semantic task can be the result of a criterion shift (a lowering of the response criterion setting, that is, the confidence threshold for volunteering an answer).

We have shown that lorazepam creates a reversible semantic memory impairment. We therefore asked why lorazepam participants provide incorrect recall answers. Furthermore, under what circumstances is the memory of healthy participants temporarily impaired in such a way that they are induced to provide an incorrect answer when they actually know the correct answer?

SEMANTIC MEMORY AND TOTS

Vermeeren and colleagues (1995) reported that lorazepam-treated participants made more errors than did placebo participants. In addition, File and colleagues (1992) showed that the benzodiazepine midazolam impaired word completion performance. They observed that participants who had received the benzodiazepine generated more low-frequency exemplars than common words when retrieving categorical information from memory. This may reflect the fact that the "ordinary" high-frequency answers were temporarily inaccessible, and that the participant had to call on more uncommon words to complete the task. In another type of semantic memory task assessing the answers to general knowledge questions (e.g., what is the color of emerald?), Bacon and her colleagues observed that participants under the effect of lorazepam produced as many recall answers as did the participants who were receiving a placebo, but that the proportion of incorrect answers was higher (commission errors) (Bacon et al., 1998; Izaute et al., 2004; Massin-Krauss et al., 2002).

Healthy people experience ordinary memory failures at some time or other (Schacter, 1999). We have all had the subjective experience of knowing that the retrieval of one piece of information can be the first step in the retrieval of all the information for which we are searching. The fact that we have found an item of information suggests to us that we are closer to complete retrieval. It is possible to view tip-of-the-tongue states (TOTs) as temporary and reversible amnesic episodes (Bacon, Schwartz, Paire-Ficout, & Izaute, 2007; Brown, 2012). TOTs have recently gained importance in a number of areas within the field of cognitive psychology (e.g., Choi & Smith, 2005; Gollan & Acenas, 2004; Hamberger & Seidel, 2003; Lesk & Womble, 2004; Maril, Simons, Mitchell, Schwartz, & Schacter, 2003; Maril, Simons, Weaver, & Schacter, 2005). As Schwartz and Metcalfe (2011) suggested, the TOT entails two components: the cognitive level, the state in which a target word is not retrieved (e.g., Burke, MacKay, Worthley, & Wade, 1991; Miozzo & Caramazza, 1997; Vigliocco, Antonini, & Garrett, 1997); and the metacognitive level, the feeling that we will retrieve the target word (strong and frustrating feeling that a particular target word is about to be retrieved, for example, Brown & McNeill, 1966; Schwartz et al., 2000).

TOTs tend to be accurate as they predict recognition and recall (see Schwartz, 2002a). Moreover, diary studies show that 89–95 percent of missing words are subsequently retrieved by the participant in real-world TOTs (Burke et al., 1991; Ecke, 1997; Schwartz, 2002b; for a review, see Brown, 1991, 2012; Schwartz, 2002a). Diary studies and laboratory tasks also show that 50–70 percent of TOTs are accompanied by persistent alternates, also known as blockers and interlopers (Burke et al., 1991; Reason & Lucas, 1984). Burke and colleagues found that nearly 90 percent of the persistent alternates were from the same syntactic category as the missing word. Although these alternates are recognized as incorrect, the participants are unable to retrieve the correct target. Laboratory studies reveal higher rates of both resolution and persistent alternates among TOTs than n-TOTs (Smith, 1994).

Because in all previous studies, lorazepam participants produce more commission errors than placebo-treated participants, this pharmacological tool should provide us with an insight into the TOT phenomenon. In the next experiment, we investigated this point using the experimental procedure based on Schwartz and colleagues (2000). For a complete description, see Bacon and colleagues (2007) and Bacon (2010).

Participants

The participants consisted of 30 healthy students (mean age: 22.6 years). They were pseudo-randomly assigned to one of two parallel groups: a placebo group (n = 15) and a lorazepam group (n = 15) using a procedure that took account of their general knowledge as evaluated by the Information and Vocabulary subtests of the Wechsler Adult Intelligence Scale Revised (WAIS-R, Wechsler, 1987). The two groups did not differ significantly in their pre-drug general knowledge evaluated by the Information (13.1 for the placebo group and 12.8 for the lorazepam group), t (28) = .61, ns and Vocabulary subtests (12.3 and 12.7, respectively), t (28) = .87, ns.

Materials

The stimuli for the experiment consisted of 100 general knowledge questions. The correct answer was always a single word or a proper name. During the recognition task, the participants were offered five possible answers, including the correct one. Twenty unanswerable questions were also presented, most of them taken from Schwartz and colleagues (2000) (e.g., For which country is the jaque the monetary unit?). These questions sounded plausible, but did not have a correct answer (e.g., There is no country with a monetary unit called the jaque).

Procedure

The drug capsule was given orally to each participant at 7:30 AM using a double-blind procedure. The experimental session started at 9:00 AM, 90 minutes after the intake of the drug. Each participant was tested individually in the presence of an experimenter, and the session lasted approximately 1–1.5 hours. The participants were told that they would be asked to answer a series of general knowledge questions, some of which would be easy and some more difficult. The participants were given an explanation of what the term "tip-of-the-tongue" means.

Instructions were provided to avoid the risk that task-demand characteristics might produce TOTs (Widner et al., 1996). The participants were asked to give the answer aloud or to say "I don't know." If the participants produced an omission or a commission error, they were asked if they were in a TOT state and then made an FOK judgment. Finally, the participants completed a recognition test for the answerable questions.

Results

In the recall task, the mean proportion of total answers (correct answers plus commission errors) did not differ significantly between the two groups t (28) = .2, p = .86, ns. However, the proportion of correct answers was significantly lower in the lorazepam participants, t (28) = 2.3, p < .05. Consequently, the lorazepam participants produced a higher proportion of commission errors than did the placebo participants, t (28) = 2.3, p < .05. The lorazepam participants did not produce significantly more answers (3.4) than the placebo participants (2.5) for the unanswerable or illusory questions t (28) = 1.2 p = .26. No difference appeared between the two groups in the recognition test.

Distribution of Tip-of-the-Tongue States across Errors and Groups
Omission TOTs are TOTs not preceded by an answer, whereas commission TOTs are TOTs that occur only after the participant realizes that he or she has produced an incorrect answer.

Overall, the placebo participants reported 166 TOTs, 117 of them omission TOTs and 49 of them commission TOTs. The lorazepam participants reported 184 TOTS, with 108 omission TOTs and 76 commission TOTs. The individual proportions of TOTs were similar in the two groups, and there was no difference between the proportions of TOTs produced after an omission error t (27) = .26, p = .80, ns (respectively, .33 and .32). And there was no significant difference between the proportion of TOTs produced after a commission error in the placebo and lorazepam groups t (25) = .18, p = .86, ns (respectively, .24 and .23). It is likely that the participants with lorazepam exhibited a larger number of commission TOTs because they produced a greater number of commission errors.

TOTs were significantly more common in the case of omission errors than after commission errors in the placebo participants t (13) = 2.35, p < .05. This was not observed for the lorazepam participants who provided only marginally more omission than commission TOTs t (12) = 2.0, p = .07.

Correct Recognition of TOT Targets
Bacon (2010) examined whether TOTs were accurate predictors of recognition and whether lorazepam had a specific effect on the efficiency of TOT recognition. Recognition should be higher after a TOT than after an n-TOT. In the placebo group, the recognition of TOT targets was significantly better than after n-TOTs, t (13) = 8.3, p < .01. In the lorazepam group, the correct recognition of the TOT targets was only marginally better than

that of n-TOTs, t (13) = 2.1, p = .054. These data are also reflected in the correlations, discussed later in this chapter. The difference in the ability to resolve TOTs between the placebo (83.1) and lorazepam (73.2) groups was not significant t (27) = 1.3, p = .19, ns. Resolution of the TOT state (the ability to recognize the correct answer eventually) was unimpaired.

Feeling-of-Knowing Judgment
In the case of the answerable questions, the mean FOK judgments did not differ between the placebo and the lorazepam participants (50.2 and 51.7, respectively), t (28) = .26, p = .80, ns.

For the unanswerable questions, the mean FOK was significantly higher in the lorazepam (26.4) than in the placebo participants (15.2), t (28) = 2.8, p < .01. We also wondered if TOT or n-TOT questions elicited different FOK ratings. The mean FOKs were significantly higher after a TOT than after an n-TOT F (1, 27) = 158.6, MSE = 123000.3, p < .0001. There was no difference between the placebo and lorazepam groups F (1, 28) = .004, MSE = 2.2, p = .95. However, the TOT x group interaction was significant: F (1, 27) = 11.5, MSE = 894.1, p < .01, and the difference in FOK ratings between the placebo and lorazepam groups was significant for TOT and n-TOT (for TOTs F (1, 27) = 6.1, MSE = 476.2, p < .05; n-TOTs, F (1, 27) = 5.3, MSE = 418.1, p < .05). To summarize, the main effect of lorazepam on FOK ratings was an overestimation for unanswerable questions and a loss of sensitivity in the relative rating of the future probability of recall of TOT and n-TOT responses.

Gamma Correlations
We computed three gamma correlations. Three gamma correlations were calculated for each participant: we first computed the correlation between FOK and recognition performance, then that between TOT and recognition, and, finally, between TOT and FOK. For all participants, these gamma correlations were higher than zero, suggesting a relation between either the FOK rating or the TOT rating and the answer in the recognition test, and a relation between the two metamemory judgments themselves. The results revealed no reliable difference between the lorazepam group and the placebo group for the G between metamemory judgments and memory. However, the predictive value of TOTs on FOK estimation was significantly higher in the placebo group (.86 against .67 in the lorazepam group), t (27) = 2.3, p < .05. The lorazepam participants therefore suffered from an impairment of the relationship between the two forms of monitoring knowledge.

Discussion

In our experiments, participants who received lorazepam provided the same number of total recall answers. However, the lorazepam participants produced more incorrect recall responses, that is, commission errors, than the participants who received the placebo. This lower semantic memory performance was not due to a difference in the basic knowledge of the two experimental groups; their base rates were similar. Moreover, recognition ability was preserved given that recognition performance did not differ between the placebo or lorazepam treated-groups. Overall, in the TOT experiment, the lorazepam group experienced a greater number of commission TOTs. However, the lorazepam participants did not produce higher individual rates of commission TOTs than the placebo participants. They experienced more commission TOTs because they made more commission errors. Moreover, the accuracy of these TOT states as predictors of recognition was equivalent.

As Bacon (2010) suggested, the lorazepam experiments provide a model to examine the dissociation between the cognitive TOT (i.e., the failure of the process to retrieve a known word) and the metacognitive TOT states (i.e., the strong feeling that a particular word is on the verge of being retrieved). Participants under the effect of lorazepam experienced more cognitive TOTs than did the control participants. The impaired recall performance under lorazepam implies that the participant knows the correct target but that this target is temporarily inaccessible. In addition, persistent alternates may come to mind, but unlike what occurs in the case of normal participants experiencing a TOT state, the cognitive aspect of the situation would not be accompanied by the metacognitive TOT. Because there is no metacognitive TOT occurring alongside the retrieval failure, the persistent alternates are produced as answers and end up being recorded as commission errors. This seemed to be confirmed insofar as lorazepam participants, overall, experienced more commission TOT states, and their recognition ability was preserved. When lorazepam participants experience a commission TOT, they do not feel the metacognitive TOT, that is, the anxiety and the conflict associated with a TOT. Because lorazepam is an anxiolytic drug with well-known anticonflict effects that alleviates emotions (Harvey, 1980; Kleven & Koek, 1999; Vanover et al., 1999), it is possible that it blocks out the surprise and conflict that are potentially a part of any TOT (see Brown, 2012; Schwartz & Bacon, 2008). When under the effect of lorazepam, people are more likely not to be aware of the emotional conflict between the persistent alternate and missing correct answer. Consequently, they are also more likely to report the persistent alternate with greater frequency. However, when it is brought to their attention that they are wrong, the state of retrieval failure becomes identifiable, triggering the metacognitive TOT state. The anxiolytic and anti-conflict effect of benzodiazepines seems to play a part in the occurrence of these specific memory blocks. The use of lorazepam allowed us to further our understanding of the possible mechanisms of the TOT.

CONCLUSION

The studies described here showed specific impairment in the control processes during retrieval of information in memory. When people fail to retrieve the information that they are looking for, they may neverthe-less still be able to retrieve certain information related to the desired but currently inaccessible target. Indeed, it was shown that metamemory pro-cesses monitor and control various memory and behavior-related aspects of information processing. First on the recently learned material, the lora-zepam participants present an impairment on the total and partial recall and on FOK ratings. Because of lorazepam's sedative effect, the drug might have delayed access to the episodic store. Lorazepam participants may have impaired access to memory representations and, consequently, lower FOK. On long-term memory, lorazepam-treated subjects exhibited an impaired CL accuracy compared to placebo-treated subjects, and their FOK accu-racy was at chance for episodic memory. In semantic memory, participants under lorazepam remained able to correctly set the response criteria, but they provided significantly more answers that should have been withheld according to their response criterion than placebo participants (Massin-Krauss et al., 2002). In the same vein, the lorazepam participants produced more Moses illusions than placebo participants. It is as if the drug affected the setting of the detection threshold. The lorazepam participants were less sensitive to the conflict between the terms in the query and the terms stored in semantic memory. For the TOT, as a retrieval attempt, the lora-zepam participants produced slightly more commission TOTs. The lora-zepam induced a dissociation between the cognitive and metacognitive components of the TOT experience. As with the Moses illusion, lorazepam participants inflated the accessibility of contaminating cues that cannot be discarded (or discounted).

NOTES

1. In studies investigating metamemory, the experiments are typically based on the calculation of the correspondence between the accuracy of an answer and

its metamemory rating (Nelson & Narens, 1990). The rationale and methods for using these indexes were reviewed by Nelson (1984). It has been suggested that a nonparametric measure of association, the gamma correlation, provides a good summary index of FOK performance. The gamma index is a measure of association developed by Goodman and Kruskal (1954) that allows researchers to compare the correct predictions to the incorrect predictions. This index ranges from -1 to +1, with large positive values corresponding to a strong association between memory performance and metamemory judgments, whereas negative values show an inverse relationship.

REFERENCES

Allen, D., Curran, H. V., & Lader, M. (1993). The effects of single doses of CL 284, 846, lorazepam, and placebo on psychomotor and memory function in normal male volunteers. *Eur J Clin Pharmacol*, 45, 313–320.

Bacon E. (2010). Further insight into cognitive and metacognitive processes of Tip Of the Tongue state with an amnesic drug as cognitive tool. In Eckflides A. & Misailidi P. (Eds.), *Trends and Prospects in Metacognition Research* (pp. 81–104). New York: Springer.

Bacon, E., Danion, J. M., Kauffman-Muller, F., Schelstraete, M. A., Bruant, A., Sellal, F., & Grange, D. (1998). Confidence level and feeling of knowing for episodic and semantic memory: An investigation of lorazepam effects on metamemory. *Psychopharmacology*, 138, 318–325.

Bacon, E., Paire-Ficout, L., & Izaute, M. (2002). Dissociation between the subjective experience and the cognitive process: The effects of the anxiolytic drug lorazepam on TOT states. *Abstr Psychon Soc*, 7, 24.

Bacon, E., Schwartz, B., Paire-Ficout, M., & Izaute, M. (2007). Dissociation between the cognitive process and the phenomenological experience of TOT: Effect of the anxiolytic drug lorazepam on TOT states. *Conscious Cognition*, 16, 360–373.

Barker, M. J., Greenwood, K. M., Jackson, M., & Crowe, S. F. (2004). Persistence of cognitive effects after withdrawal from long-term benzodiazepine use: A meta-analysis. *Archives of Clinical Neuropsychology*, 19, 437–454.

Beracochea, D. (2006) Anterograde and retrograde effects of benzodiazepines on memory. *The Scientific World Journal* 6, 1460–1465.

Bishop, K., & Curran, V. (1998). An investigation of the effects of benzodiazepine receptor ligands and of scopolamine on conceptual priming. *Psychopharmacology*, 140, 345–353.

Blin, O., Simon, N., Jouve, E., Habib, M., Gayraud, D., Durand, A., Brugerolle, B., & Pisano, P. (2001). Pharmacokinetic and pharmaco-dynamic analysis of sedative and amnesic effects of lorazepam in healthy volunteers. *Clin Neuropharmacol*, 24, 71–81.

Brédart, S., & Docquier, M. (1989). The Moses illusion: A follow-up on the focalisation effect. *Cahiers de Psychologie Cognitive/European Bulletin of Cognitive Psychology*, 9, 357–362.

Brédart, S., & Modolo, K. (1988). Moses strikes again: Focalization effect on a semantic illusion. *Acta Psychologica: International Journal of Psychonomics*, 67, 135–144.

Brown, A. S. (1991). A review of the tip-of-the-tongue experience. *Psychological Bulletin*, 109, 204–223.

(2012). *The tip of the tongue state (essays in cognitive psychology)*. New York: Psychology Press.

Brown, J., Lewis, V., Brown, M., Horn, G., & Bowes, J. B. (1982). A comparison between transient amnesias induced by two drugs (diazepam or lorazepam) and amnesia of organic origin. *Neuropsychologia*, 20, 55–70.

Brown, R., & McNeill, D. (1966). The tip of the tongue experience. *Psychological Bulletin*, 1090, 339–347.

Buffett-Jerrott, S. E., & Stewart, S. H. (2002). Cognitive and sedative effects of benzodiazepine use. *Curr Pharm Des*, 8, 45–58.

Burke, D. M., MacKay, D. G., Worthley, J. S., & Wade, E. (1991). On the tip of the tongue: What causes word finding failures in young and older adults? *Journal of Memory and Language*, 30, 542–579.

Choi, H., & Smith, S. M. (2005). Incubation and the resolution of tip-of-the-tongue states. *Journal of General Psychology*, 132, 365–376.

Costermans, J., Lories, G., & Ansay, C. (1992). Confidence level and feeling of knowing in question answering: The weight of inferential processes. *J Exp Psychol [Learn Mem Cognit]*, 18, 142–150.

Curran, H. V. (1991). Benzodiazepines, memory and mood: A review. *Psychopharmacology*, 105, 1–8.

(1999). Effects of anxiolytics on memory. *Hum Psychopharmacol*, 14, 72–79.

(2000). Psychopharmacological approaches to human memory. In M. S. Gazzaniga (Ed.), *The new cognitive neuro-sciences*, 2nd edn. (pp. 797–804). Boston, MA: MIT Press.

Curran, H. V., Bond, A., O'Sullivan, G., Bruce, M., Marks, I., Lelliot, P., Shine, P., & Lader, M. (1994). Memory functions, alprazolam and exposure therapy: A controlled longitudinal study of agoraphobia with panic disorder. *Psychological Medicine*, 24, 969–976.

Curran, H. V., Gardiner, J. M., Java, R. I., & Allen, D. (1993). Effects of lorazepam upon recollective experience in recognition memory. *Psychopharmacology*, 110, 374–378.

Curran, H. V., Schiwy, W., & Lader, M. (1987). Differential amnesic properties of benzodiazepines: A dose-response comparison of two drugs with similar elimination half-lifes. *Psychopharmacology*, 92, 358–364.

Danion, J. M. (1994). Drugs as tools for investigating memory. *Eur Neuropsychopharmacol*, 4, 179–180.

Danion, J. M., Peretti, S., Grange, D., Bilik, M., Imbs, J. L., & Singer, L. (1992). Effects of chlorpromazine and lorazepam on explicit memory, repetition priming and cognitive skill learning in healthy volunteers. *Psychopharmacology*, 108, 345–351.

Danion, J. M., Zimmermann, M. A., Willard-Schroeder, D., Grangé, D., & Singer, L. (1989). Diazepam induces a dissociation between explicit and implicit memory. *Psychopharmacology*, 99, 238–243.

Duka, T., Curran, H. V., Rusted, J. M., & Weingartner, H. J. (1996). Perspectives on cognitive psychopharmacology research. *Behav Pharmacol*, 7, 401–410.

Duka, T., Redemann, B., & Voet, B. (1995). Scopolamine and lorazepam exert different patterns of effects in a test battery assessing stages of information processing. *Psychopharmacology*, 119, 315–324.

Ecke, P. (1997). *Tip of the tongue states in first and foreign languages: Similarities and differences of lexical retrieval failures.* In Proceedings of the EUROSLA 7 Conference (pp. 505–514). Barcelona, Spain.

Erickson, T. A., & Mattson, M. E. (1981). From words to meaning: A semantic illusion. *Journal of Verbal Learning and Verbal Behavior*, 20, 540–552.

Ferrara, S. D., Giorgetti, R., Zancaner, S., Orlando, R., Tagliabracci, A., Cavarzeran, F., & Palatini, P. (1999). Effects of single dose of gamma-hydroxybutyric acid and lorazepam on psychomotor performance and subjective feeling in healthy volunteers. *Eur J Clin Pharmacol*, 54, 821–827.

File, S. E., Sharma, R., & Shaffer, J. (1992). Is lorazepam-induced amnesia specific to the type of memory or to the task used to assess it? *J Psychopharmacol*, 6, 76–80.

Fluck, E., File, S. E., Springett, J., Kopelman, M. D., Rees, J., & Orgill, J. (1998). Does the sedation resulting from sleep deprivation and lorazepam cause similar cognitive deficits? *Pharmacol Biochem Behav*, 59, 909–915.

Gollan, T. H., & Acenas, L. A. (2004). What is a TOT? Cognate and translation effects on tip-of-the-tongue states in Spanish-English and Tagalog-English bilinguals. *Journal of Experimental Psychology: Learning, Memory, and Cognition*, 30, 246–269.

Goodman, L. A., & Kruskal, W. H. (1954). Measures of association for cross classifications. *Journal of the American Statistical Association*, 49, 732–764.

Gorenstein, C., Bernik, M. A., Pompéia, S., & Marcourakis, T. (1995). Impairment of performance associated with long-term use of benzodiazepines. *J Psychopharmacol*, 9, 313–318.

Green, J. F., McElhom, A., & King, D. J. (1996). A comparison of the sedative and amnestic effects of chlorpromazine and lorazepam. *Psycho-pharmacology*, 128, 67–73.

Hamberger, M. J., & Seidel, W. T. (2003). Auditory and visual naming tests: Normative and patient data for accuracy, response time, and tip-of-the-tongue. *Journal of International Neuropsychological Society*, 9, 479–489.

Hannon, B., & Daneman, M. (2001). Susceptibility to semantic illusions: An individual-differences perspective. *Memory and Cognition*, 29(3), 449–461.

Harvey, S. C. (1980). Hypnotics and sedatives. In A. Goodman Gilman, L. S. Goodman, & A. Gilman (Eds.), *The pharmacological basis of therapeutics* (chapter 17, pp. 339–375). New York: Macmillan.

Hinrichs, J. V., Mewaldt, S. T., Ghoneim, M. M., & Berie, J. L. (1982). Diazepam and learning: Assessment of acquisition deficits. *Pharmacol Biochem Behav*, 17, 165–170.

Huron, C., Giersch, A., & Danion, J. M. (2002). Lorazepam, sedation and conscious recollection: A dose-response study with healthy volunteers. *Int Clin Psychopharmacol*, 17, 19–26.

Izaute, M., & Bacon, E. (2006). Effects of the amnesic drug lorazepam on complete and partial information retrieval and monitoring accuracy. *Psychopharmacology*, 188(4), 472–481.

Izaute, M., Paire-Ficout, L., & Bacon, E. (2004). Benzodiazepines and semantic memory: Effects of lorazepam on the Moses illusion. *Psychopharmacology*, 172, 309–315.

Kamas, E. N., Reder, L. M., & Ayers, M. S. (1996). Partial matching in the Moses illusion: Response bias not sensitivity. *Mem Cognit*, 24, 687–699.

Kelley, C. M., & Lindsay, D. S. (1993). Remembering mistaken for knowing: Ease of retrieval as a basis for confidence in answer to general knowledge questions. *J Mem Lang*, 32, 1–24.

Kleven, M. S., & Koek, W. (1999). Effects of benzodiazepine agonists on punished responding in pigeons and their relationship with clinical doses in humans. *Psychopharmacology*, 141, 206–212.

Koriat, A. (1993). How do we know that we know? The accessibility model of the feeling of knowing. *Psychol Rev*, 100, 609–639.

(1994). Memory's knowledge of its own knowledge: The accessibility account of the feeling of knowing. In J. Metcalfe & A. P. Shimamura (Eds.), *Metacognition: Knowing about knowing. A Bradford Book* (pp. 115–135). Cambridge, MA and London: MIT Press.

(1995). Dissociating knowing and the feeling of knowing: Further evidence for the accessibility model. *J Exp Psychol* [Gen Sect], 124, 311–333.

(1997). Monitoring one's knowledge during study: A cue-utilization approach to judgments of learning. *Journal of Experimental Psychology: General*, 126, 349–370.

(1998). Metamemory: The feeling of knowing and its vagaries. In M. Sabourin, F. Craik, & M. Robert (Eds.), *Advances in psychological science*. Hove, UK: Psychology Press.

Koriat, A., & Goldsmith, M. (1994). Memory in naturalistic and laboratory contexts: Distinguishing the accuracy-oriented and quantity-oriented approaches to memory assessment. *J Exp Psychol Gen*, 123, 297–315.

(1996a). Memory metaphors and the real-life/laboratory controversy: Correspondence versus storehouse conceptions of memory. *Behav Brain Sci*, 19, 167–228.

(1996b). Monitoring and control processes in the strategic regulation of memory accuracy. *Psychol Rev*, 103, 490–517.

Koriat, A., & Levy-Sadot, R. (1999). Processes underlying metacognitive judgments: Information-based and experience-based monitoring of one's own knowledge. In S. Chaiken & Y. Trope (Eds.), *Dual process theories in social psychology*. New York: Guilford Publication.

Koriat, A., Levy-Sadot, R., Edry, E., & Marcas, S. (2003). What do we know about what we cannot remember? Accessing the semantic attributes of words that cannot be recalled. *J Exp Psychol*, 29, 1095–1105.

Kumar, R., Mac, D. S., Gabrielli, W. F., & Goodwin, D. W. (1987). Anxiolytics and memory: A comparison of lorazepam and alprazolam. *J Clin Psychiatry*, 48, 158–160.

Legrand, F., Vidailhet, P., Danion, J. M., Grangé, D., Giersch, A., Van der Linden, M., & Singer, L. (1995). Differential effects of diazepam and lorazepam on repetition priming on healthy volunteers. *Psychopharmacology*, 118, 475–479.

Lesk, V. E., & Womble, S. P. (2004). Caffeine, priming and tip of the tongue: Evidence for plasticity in the phonological system. *Behavioral Neuroscience,* 118, 453–461.

Lobo, B. L., & Greene, W. L. (1997). Zolpidem: Distinct from triazolam? *Ann Pharmacother,* 31, 625–632.

Mac, D. S., Kumar, R., & Goodwin, D. W. (1985). Anterograde amnesia with oral lorazepam. *J Clin Psychiatry,* 46, 137–138.

Mallick, J. L., Kirby, K. C., Martin, F., Philp, M., & Hennessy, M. J. (1993). A comparison of the amnesic effects of lorazepam in alcoholics and non-alcoholics. *Psychopharmacology,* 110, 181–186.

Maril, A., Simons, J. S., Mitchell, J. P., Schwartz, B. L., & Schacter, D. L. (2003). Feeling-of-knowing in episodic memory: An event-related fMRI study. *NeuroImage,* 18, 827–836.

Maril, A., Simons, J. S., Weaver, J. J., & Schacter, D. L. (2005). Graded recall success: An event-related fMRI comparison of tip of the tongue and feeling of knowing. *NeuroImage,* 24, 1130–1138.

Massin-Krauss, M., Bacon, E., & Danion, J. M. (2002). Effects of the benzodiazepine lorazepam on monitoring and control processes in semantic memory. *Conscious Cognit,* 11, 123–137.

Matthews, A., Kirkby, K. C., & Martin, F. (2002). The effects of single-dose lorazepam on memory and behavioural learning. *J Psychopharmacol,* 16, 345–354.

Mattila, M. J., Vanakoski, J., Kalska, H., & Seppala, T. (1998). Effects of alcohol, zolpidem, and some other sedatives and hypnotics on human performance and memory. *Pharmacol Biochem Behav,* 59, 917–923.

Mazzoni, G., & Nelson, T. O. (1995). Judgments of learning are affected by the kind of encoding in ways that cannot be attributed to the level of recall. *J Exp Psychol [Learn Mem Cognit],* 21, 1263–1274.

Metcalfe, J., & Shimamura, A. (1994). *Metacognition: Knowing about knowing.* Cambridge, MA: MIT Press.

Melzack, R., Coderre, T. J., Katz, J., & Vaccarino, A. L. (2001). Central neuroplasticity and pathological pain. *Annual reports of New York Academy of Sciences,* 933, 157–174.

Metcalfe, J., Schwartz, B. L., & Joaquim, S. G. (1993). The cue-familiarity heuristic in metacognition. *J Exp Psychol [Learn Mem Cognit],* 19, 851–961.

Mintzer, M. Z., Frey, J. M., Yingling, J. E., & Griffiths, R. R. (1997). Triazolam and zolpidem: A comparison of their psychomotor, cognitive, and subjective effects in healthy volunteers. *Behav Pharmacol,* 8, 561–574.

Mintzer, M. Z., & Griffiths, R. R. (1999). Selective effects of zolpidem on human memory functions. *J Psychopharmacol,* 13, 18–31.

(2003). Lorazepam and scopolamine: A single-dose comparison of effects on human memory and attentional processes. *Exp Clin Psychopharmacol,* 11, 56–72.

(2005). Drugs, memory, and metamemory: A dose-effect study with lorazepam and scopolamine. *Exp Clin Psychopharmacol,* 13, 336–347.

Miozzo, M., & Caramazza, A. (1997). Retrieval of lexical-syntactic features in tip-of-the-tongue states. *Journal of Experimental Psychology: Learning, Memory, and Cognition,* 23, 1410–1423.

Nelson, T. O. (1984). A comparison of current measures of the accuracy of feeling of knowing predictions. *Psychol Bull,* 95, 109–133.

Nelson, T. O., & Narens, L. (1990). Metamemory: A theoretical framework and new findings. In G. H. Bower (Ed.), *The psychology of learning and motivation* (pp. 1–45). New York: Academic.

(1994). Why investigate metacognition. In J. Metcalfe & A. P. Shimamura (Eds.), *Metacognition: Knowing about knowing* (pp 1–25). Cambridge, MA and London: MIT Press.

Patat, A., Paty, I., & Hindmarch, I. (2001). Pharmacodynamic profile of zaleplon, a new non-benzodiazepine hypnotic agent. *Hum Psychopharmacol,* 16, 369–392.

Patat, A., Perault, M. C., Vandel, B., Ulliac, N., Zieleniuk, I., & Rosenzweig, J. (1995). Lack of interaction between a new antihistamine, mizolastine, and lorazepam on psychomotor performance and memory in healthy volunteers. *Br J Clin Pharmacol,* 39, 31–38.

Pompeia, S., Bueno, O. F., Lucchesi, L. M., Manzano, G. M., Galduroz, J. C., & Tufik, S. (2000). A double-dissociation of behavioural and event-related potential effects of two benzodiazepines with similar potencies. *J Psychopharmacol,* 14, 288–298.

Reason, J., & Lucas, D. (1984). Using cognitive diaries to investigate naturally occurring memory blocks. In J. E. Harris & P. E. Morris (Eds.), *Everyday memory, actions, and absentmindedness* (pp. 53–70). London: Academic.

Reder, L.M., Cleeremans, A. (1990). The role of partial matches in comprehension: the Moses illusion revisited. In: Graesser A, Bower GH (Eds.) *The Psychology of Learning and Motivation* (vol. 25 pp. 233–258). Academic Press: New York.

Reder, L. M., & Kusbit, G. W. (1991). Locus of the Moses Illusion: Imperfect encoding, retrieval, or match? *Journal of Memory and Language,* 30, 385–406.

Reder, L. M., & Ritter, F. E. (1992). What determines initial feeling of knowing? Familiarity with question terms, not with the answer. *J Exp Psychol [Learn Mem Cognit],* 18, 435–451.

Rush, C. R., Armstrong, D. L., Ali, J. A., & Pazzaglia, P. J. (1998). Benzodiazepine-receptor ligands in humans: Acute performance-impairing, subject-rated and observer-rated effects. *J Clin Psychopharmacol,* 18, 154–165.

Rush, C. R., & Griffiths, R. R. (1996). Zolpidem, triazolam, and temazepam: Behavioural and subject-rated effects in normal volunteers. *J Clin Psychopharmacol,* 16, 146–157.

Schacter, D. L. (1999). The seven sins of memory: Insight from psychology and cognitive neuroscience. *American Psychologist,* 54, 182–203.

Schwartz, B. L. (1998). Illusory tip-of-the-tongue states. *Memory,* 6, 623–642.

(2002a). The phenomenology of naturally-occurring tip-of-the-tongue states: A diary study. In S. P. Shohov (Ed.), *Advances in psychology research* (Vol. 8, pp. 71–84). New York: Nova Sciences.

(2002b). *Tip-of-the-tongue states: Phenomenology, mechanism, and lexical retrieval.* Mahwah, NJ: Erlbaum.

Schwartz, B. L., & Bacon, E. (2008). Metacognitive neuroscience. In J. Dunlosky & R. A. Bjork (Eds.), *Handbook of Memory and Metamemory: Essays in Honor of Thomas O. Nelson* (pp. 355–371). New York: Psychology Press.

Schwartz, B. L., & Metcalfe, J. (2011). Tip-of-the-tongue (TOT) states: Retrieval, behavior, and experience. *Mem Cognit,* July 39(5), 737–749.

Schwartz, B. L., Travis, D. M., Castro, A. M., & Smith, S. M. (2000). The phenomenology of real and illusory tip-of-the-tongue states. *Memory and Cognition,* 28, 18–27.

Shafto, M., & McKay, D. G. (2000). The Moses, mega-Moses, and Armstrong illusions: Integrating language comprehension and semantic memory. *Psychol Sci,* 11, 372–378.

Smith, S. M. (1994). Frustrated feelings of imminent recall: On the tip-of-the tongue. In J. Metcalfe & A. P. Shimamura (Eds.), *Metacognition: Knowing about knowing* (pp. 27–46). Cambridge, MA: MIT Press.

Stewart, S. A. (2005). The effects of benzodiazepines on cognition. *J Clin Psychiatry,* 66(Suppl 2), 9–13.

Tata, P. R., Philip, R., Rollings, J., Collins, M., Pickering, A., & Jacobson, R. R. (1994). Lack of cognitive recovery following withdrawal from long-term benzodiazepine use. *Psychol Med,* 24, 203–213.

Vanover, K. E., Robledo, S., Huber, M., & Carter, R. B. (1999). Pharmacological evaluation of a modified conflict procedure: Punished drinking in non-water-deprived rats. *Psychopharmacology,* 145, 333–341.

Van Oostendorp, H., & de Mul, S. (1990). Moses beats Adam: A semantic relatedness effect on a semantic illusion. *Acta Psychologica,* 74, 35–46.

Van Oostendorp, H., & Kok, I. (1990). Failing to notice errors in sentences. *Languages and Cognitive Processes,* 5, 105–113.

Vermeeren, A., Jackson, J. L., Muntjewerff, N. D., Quint, P. J., Harrison, E. M., & O'Hanlon, J. F. (1995). Comparison of acute alprazolam (0.25, 0.50 and 1.0 mg) effects versus those of lorazepam 2 mg and placebo on memory in healthy volunteers using laboratory and telephone tests. *Psychopharmacology,* 118, 1–9.

Vidailhet, P., Kazès, M., Danion, J. M., Kauffmann-Muller, F., & Grangé, D. (1996). Effects of lorazepam and diazepam on conscious and automatic memory processes. *Psychopharmacology,* 127, 63–72.

Vigliocco, G., Antonini, T., & Garrett, M. F. (1997). Grammatical gender is on the tip of Italian tongues. *Psychological Science,* 8, 314–317.

Wechsler, D. (1987). *Wechsler memory scale, revised manual.* San Antonio, TX: Psychological Corporation.

Weingartner, H. J., Joyce, E. M., Sirocco, K. Y., Adams, C. M., Eckardt, M. J., George, T., Lister, R. G. (1993). Specific memory and sedative effects of the benzodiazepine triazolam. *J Psychopharmacol,* 7, 305–315.

Widner, R. L., Smith, S. M., & Graziano, W. G. (1996). The effects of demand characteristics on the reporting of tip-of-the-tongue and feeling-of-knowing states. *American Journal of Psychology,* 109, 525–538.

10

Neurofunctional Correlates of the
Tip-of-the-Tongue State

FERNANDO DÍAZ, MÓNICA LINDÍN, SANTIAGO
GALDO-ÁLVAREZ, AND ANA BUJÁN

INTRODUCTION

Naming is the result of complex cognitive processes, as it involves remembering the verbal label associated with an object, action, place, animal, or person. Naming requires retrieval of a label and its spoken or written production. However, although we know the names of many people, animals, or things, in the course of daily life, the naming of known names can fail momentarily. A universal experience is the annoying feeling of wanting to say a word and not being able to, while being completely sure that we know it, that we have recalled it in the past, and that we are on the verge of retrieving it. This experience is, of course, the "tip-of-the-tongue state" (TOT).

One of the main features of the phenomenon lies in the temporary inability to access information that is undoubtedly registered in the memory stores of the person who presents a TOT. Understanding how this phenomenon occurs, therefore, may be helpful to understand how the mechanisms of accessing information stored in memory take place. We also think that TOTs can aid our understanding of memory retrieval disorders.

The vast majority of studies have focused on the behavioral (and therefore directly observable) characteristics of the TOT phenomenon. However, in recent decades, researchers have made important advances in the development of techniques that allow neuroscientists to study brain function in vivo and, therefore, to assess brain activity associated with cognitive

This work was financially supported by funds from the Spanish Ministerio de Economía y Competitividad (PSI2010–22224-C03–03), and from the Galician government: Consellería de Industria e Innovación/Economía e Industria (10 PXIB 211070 PR), and Consellería de Cultura, Educación e Ordenación Universitaria (Axudas para a consolidación e estruturación de unidades de investigación competitivas do sistema universitario de Galicia 2012. CN 2012/033).

processes and behavior in human beings. Consequently, these neuroscientific techniques may provide relevant information to understand *where*, *when*, and *how* the processes involved in successful name retrieval and the TOT phenomenon take place in the brain.

In this chapter, after a brief summary of the main cognitive models that explain the TOT phenomenon and the main contributions and limitations of behavioral studies on the characterization of this phenomenon, we analyze the contributions of neurophysiological techniques to study cognitive processes, beginning with the description of the basic features of such techniques, the information they provide, their limitations, and precautions that should be taken into account in the design of tasks, in recording brain activity, and in the interpretation of results obtained. Then, we present the main results of the study of the TOT phenomenon using such techniques, specifically the techniques of functional magnetic resonance imaging (fMRI), event-related potentials (ERP), and magnetoencephalography (MEG). Finally, an integration of neurocognitive results with cognitive models of the TOT is presented.

Cognitive Models Explaining the TOT

One aspect that has generated research on the TOT phenomenon is the study of the mechanisms through which it is generated, developed, and maintained. Several explanatory hypotheses seek to answer these questions, which may fall into three areas of psychology: psycholinguistics, memory, and metacognition. From these approaches, several models have been proposed that can be arranged, according to Brown (2012) and Schwartz and Metcalfe (2011), in two main types: direct access models and inferential models.

Direct access models propose that the TOT phenomenon reflects partial or incomplete activation of the stored information. Two main interpretations have been proposed from this perspective. The *hypothesis of blocking inhibition* (Woodworth, 1929; see Jones, 1989) suggests that the TOT phenomenon is due to the fact that name retrieval is inhibited or blocked by intrusive words. In contrast, the *transmission deficit hypothesis* (Burke, MacKay, Worthley, & Wade, 1991; MacKay & Burke, 1990), which has received substantial empirical support (Burke et al., 1991; James & Burke, 2000; White & Abrams, 2002; see Harley & MacAndrew, Chapter 6, this volume), argues that the TOTs occur when activation fails to be fully transmitted from the semantic to the phonological system, that is, when phonological activation of an unrecalled item is insufficient or partial. This transmission deficit is modulated by three variables: the frequency (how often a word is used) and recency (how recently a word has been used) of word usage and age of the person. Indeed, the incidence of TOTs seems to increase in less recent words (Bonin, Perret, Méot, Ferrand, & Mermillod, 2008; Burke et al., 1991; Cleary, 2006; Cleary & Reyes, 2009; Cleary & Specker, 2007) and low-frequency words (Brown & McNeill, 1966; Burke et al., 1991; Hanly & Vandenberg, 2010; Vitevitch & Sommers, 2003), as well as in older participants (Burke, Locantore, Austin, & Chase, 2004; Burke et al., 1991; Cohen & Faulkner, 1986; Cross & Burke, 2004; Evrard, 2002; Galdo-Álvarez, Lindín, & Díaz, 2009a, 2009b; Gollan & Brown, 2006; Heine, Ober, & Shenaut, 1999; James, 2006; James & Burke, 2000).

Inferential models maintain that TOT states reflect people's judgments about their knowledge (that is, aspects related to metamemory or meta-cognition), rather than the actual contents of memory (Schwartz, 1994). Within these models, two approaches can also be distinguished: First, the *cue familiarity hypothesis* (Metcalfe, Schwartz, & Joaquim, 1993) claims that TOT are based on the familiarity of the present cue information, predicting that the more knowledge you have of a particular issue, the more probability exists to present a TOT. Second, the *accessibility heuristic hypothesis* (Koriat, 1993) suggests that the TOT experience is the result of an assessment of the retrieval when only partial information (even if this information is not related to the current word) is recalled. In general, this perspective accepts that both hypotheses are complementary (Koriat & Levy-Sadot, 2001).

STUDIES ON THE TOT PHENOMENON

Behavioral Studies: Contributions and Limitations

In 1966, Brown and McNeill conducted the first systematic experimental study concerning the TOT phenomenon, which is defined as a failure to recall a word when you are sure you know it, and feel as if its recall is imminent (Brown & McNeill, 1966). Since this seminal work, scholars have conducted numerous behavioral studies to describe the characteristics of the phenomenon (see Brown, 2012). Two general approaches have been mainly used to characterize the TOT phenomenon: diary studies and experimental-naming tasks.

In *diary studies*, participants must record in a notebook TOTs that occur in everyday life. In addition to the TOT itself, participants are expected to include certain characteristics associated with the phenomenon (information they can retrieve, time and circumstances of the resolution of the phenomenon, etc.). This methodology allows researchers to contrast the incidence of TOTs in daily life, and provides qualitative information for the characterization of this phenomenon. However, it does not allow manipulating experimentally the characteristics of the stimuli that cause the TOT, thus limiting the predictive power of the causes of the phenomenon.

The *experimental-naming task* involves inducing TOTs in participants in the laboratory. The tasks and stimuli used are diverse: word definitions, pictures, photographs of faces, definitions associated with pictures, and paired associates (see Brown, 2012, for a review). The data obtained in these studies include, among others, the incidence (number or percentage of TOTs) and performance measures such as reaction times – both for initial recall and for how long people need to determine that they are in a TOT.

The results of the behavioral studies showed that the TOT appears to be a universal phenomenon; its presence has been found in virtually all cultures (Schwartz, 1999); in all age groups, from infancy (Hanly & Vandenberg, 2010) to old age (Burke et al., 1991). Moreover, in diary studies, TOTs seem to occur in everyday life around once a week (Burke et al., 1991; Cohen & Faulkner, 1986; Gollan, Montoya, & Bonainni, 2005; Heine et al., 1999; Reason & Lucas, 1984); in laboratory experimental tasks the average incidence to the different tasks used is around 15 percent, although the ratio changes using different types of stimuli (Brown, 2012). Research also finds that TOTs are more frequent for proper names, especially the names of people, than for common nouns (Brown, 1991; Burke et al., 1991, Cohen & Faulkner, 1986; Evrard, 2002; Gollan et al., 2005; Hanley, 2011; Rastle & Burke, 1996). Moreover, the experimental work shows that during a TOT, people can retrieve fairly accurate semantic information (Bock & Levelt, 1994; Hay, Young, & Ellis, 1991), syntactic information (Caramazza & Miozzo, 1997; Miozzo & Caramazza, 1997), and even partial phonological information (Brown & McNeill, 1966; Brown & Nix, 1996; Burke et al., 1991; Caramazza & Miozzo, 1997; Gollan et al., 2005; Hanley & Chapman, 2008; Yarmey, 1973).

Although the contributions of behavioral studies have allowed characterization of the TOT phenomenon and have provided evidence about its possible causes, such studies have important limitations. One such limitation is the difficulty of behavioral studies to delve into issues such as the differential mental chronometry of processes involved in successful retrieval and TOTs, or what cognitive control mechanisms are engaged once the problem of inaccessibility of information begins. The main difficulty in behavioral studies stems from the type of measures available, such as the ratio of TOTs to the number of correct names, or the reaction time of recall in different conditions. These measures, although they are readily available, are limited because they constitute the final result of the retrieval process, regardless of whether the retrieval is successful, and therefore they limit the exploration of processes involved, such as the smaller activation of phonological information than of other types of information, or the metacognitive process of deciding whether sufficient information is accessible to output a response. In these cases, differences in behavioral measures may not always be attributable to a particular process, complicating the interpretation of which factors may be a cause or a consequence of the TOT, that is, which factors trigger the TOT and which factors contribute to its maintenance over time.

To overcome these limitations, online measures are needed to distinguish what processes are affected during a TOT. In this sense, the discipline that can provide this type of measures, and thus elucidate the mechanisms underlying TOTs, is cognitive neuroscience.

Neurocognitive Studies

Cognitive neuroscience bridges cognitive science and cognitive psychology, on one hand, and biology and neuroscience, on the other. It has emerged as a distinct enterprise only recently and has been driven by methodological advances that enable the study of the human brain safely in the laboratory (Ward, 2010). Cognitive neuroscience is concerned with the scientific study of neural substrates of mental processes and their behavioral manifestations. To this aim, it has taken advantage of techniques from various scientific fields, such as neuroradiology, experimental psychology, psychobiology, bioengineering, physics, neurophysiology, and computer science, among others.

Research Techniques in Cognitive Neuroscience
In recent decades, researchers have developed a number of tools to study human brain activity during performance of cognitive tasks. These techniques include neuroimaging techniques, such as positron emission tomography (PET) and functional magnetic resonance imaging (fMRI) and techniques to study the electromagnetic changes occurring in neuronal populations of the brain during cognitive processes, such as electroencephalography/event-related potentials (EEG/ERP) and magnetoencephalography (MEG). These techniques have in common that the signal and information that is gathered on brain function covary with the mental process of interest. They have revolutionized the study of the biological substrates of the

behavior in humans, because of their remarkable spatial and/or temporal resolution and because of their noninvasive or minimally invasive nature.

Each of these techniques measures human brain activity in a different manner. Some of them record changes in electrical potentials (EEG/ERP) or magnetic fields (MEG) generated in the membranes of neurons, whereas others record changes in the level of blood oxygenation of the regional cerebral blood flow (fMRI), or metabolic changes (PET), derived from neuronal activity. Each technique uses specific procedures and recording devices, as well as methods of analysis of the obtained signal. These differences determine the differences of the degree of precision or the level of spatial and temporal resolution of each of the techniques.

Spatial resolution refers to the level of precision with which we can determine *where* in the brain functional changes are occurring, associated with a particular event. At present, the functional brain imaging technique with highest spatial resolution is the fMRI, with an accuracy in the order of 0.5 to 3 mm (Menon & Kim, 1999; Meyer-Lindenberger, 2010; Pfeuffer et al., 2002), which is followed by the MEG, multichannel EEG/ERP and PET, with accuracies between 3 and 10 mm (Hämäläinen, Hari, Ilmoniemi, Knuutila, & Lounasmaa, 1993; Meyer-Lindenberger, 2010; Yang, Wilke, Brinkmann, Worrell, & He, 2011).

Temporal resolution refers to how accurately we can determine *when*, or at what time, there is a change in the brain function associated with a particular event. The higher temporal resolution techniques are the ERP and MEG, with an accuracy on the order of milliseconds, followed by the fMRI and PET with less precision, from several hundred milliseconds to seconds (Meyer-Lindenberger, 2010; Pfeuffer et al., 2002). Next, we briefly describe the techniques used to characterize the TOT phenomenon.

The MRI technique allows imaging of brain tissue by applying a magnetic field of high intensity, which orients the protons of some atoms in the same direction. When the protons are in the aligned state, a brief radio frequency pulse is applied that changes the orientation of the aligned protons by 90 degrees to their original orientation. As the protons spin in this state, they produce a change in the magnetic field. When the magnetic field is stopped, the protons return to their original positions, releasing energy. Depending on the nature of the tissue, the time taken to return to the initial situation is different, which forms the basis for measurement of this technique. Building on these physical bases, and using the same type of scanner, the functional MRI (fMRI) technique detects changes in the concentration of oxyhemoglobin/deoxyhemoglobin in blood flow in and out of different brain areas (that is, the blood oxygenation level dependent–BOLD signal).

Because blood flow and oxygen consumption increase in regions that are activated at a given task, this technique provides information on which areas have demanded increased blood supply and consumed more oxygen while a participant is performing a cognitive process. By correlating behavior with the changes in the BOLD signal in particular brain regions, we can infer the nature of the neural processes. Therefore, this technique allows us to map different neural networks in the brain (cortical and subcortical regions) associated with specific cognitive functions.

The potential of this technique is undeniable for the study of the TOT phenomenon. For example, to test the transmission deficit hypothesis (Burke et al., 1991), we might study which regions are involved in phonological processing, and then we could check if these regions are less activated in the TOT than in the successful naming condition (e.g., Shafto, Stamatakis, Tam, & Tyler, 2010).

Despite its high spatial resolution, the fMRI technique has limitations. First, its low temporal resolution is on the order of hundreds of milliseconds, so it is an imprecise technique to study the chronometry of mental processes that often take place in the range of milliseconds. Second, this limitation complicates the interpretation of results in experimental designs comparing conditions in which more than one component of cognitive processing differ. Third, the fMRI technique is very sensitive to technical artifacts. For example, the participant must refrain from making head movements for the fMRI to get a good signal. Fourth, the MRI scanner emits a loud noise that can interfere with auditory stimulation. Finally, for much research, the relatively high cost of fMRI prevents the carrying out of studies. Despite these limitations, fMRI has proven useful in the study of complex cognitive processes.

Other neuroimaging techniques, such as EEG/ERP and MEG, measure task-related changes that occur in the electromagnetic brain activity. The basic principle of both EEG and MEG is the same: the activity of the neurons consists in variations of the distribution of electrical charges within and outside neurons due to ion exchanges across plasmatic membranes. These current flows (or the magnetic fields produced by these flows) in large synchronously active populations of neurons can be detected by sensors attached on the scalp. These sensors are electrodes that record the electrical activity in the case of EEG, or magnetic field sensors (SQUID) in the case of MEG. The time resolution of these techniques is in the order of one millisecond, thus they are especially suitable for the study of the timing of cognitive processes.

ERPs (event-related potentials) are changes in EEG activity associated with certain events (physical stimuli, mental processes, or motor execution).

Because these changes are very small in voltage (relative to the spontaneous brain electrical activity, i.e., EEG), it is necessary to repeatedly present a stimulus so that, after averaging the EEG activity related to these events, the voltage changes associated therewith remain (that is, ERP), whereas the rest of the EEG activity, by its random nature, tends to cancel itself out.

ERPs are measured as positive and negative waves with different latencies with respect to the event of interest. For example, a repetitive visual flash is associated with a positive wave around 100 ms, called P1 or P100, which is related to the visual processing in the extrastriate visual cortex in the occipital lobe. Some of these waves or components (for a distinction between these concepts, and a deepening of the basis of this technique, see Luck, 2005; Luck & Kappenman, 2008) have been related to attention (N1, MMN, P3a), syntactic processing (ELAN, LAN, P600), and semantic processing (N400), or the preparation of the response (Readiness Potential, Lateralized Readiness Potential), among others.

Like each technique, the ERP technique has limitations. The ERP technique is very sensitive to artifacts such as eye or head movements, as well as muscle contractions, which present a greater magnitude than the EEG signal and mask the activity to be analyzed. For obtaining ERP waveforms, it is necessary to average a sufficient number of epochs (EEG segments related with the event of interest) free of artifacts, which means that the tasks are usually lengthy for the participants, especially under conditions that involve complex processes. So, to study the TOT phenomenon with ERP, researchers must evoke at least 20 or 30 TOT states free of such artifacts. Given that TOTs usually represent about 20 percent of presented stimuli in our experiments, it is necessary to provide 200 to 400 (or even more) stimuli (Buján, Galdo-Álvarez, Lindín, & Díaz, 2012; Díaz, Lindín, Galdo-Álvarez, Facal, & Juncos-Rabadán, 2007; Galdo-Álvarez et al., 2009a; Lindín & Díaz, 2010).

Another issue to consider is that many cognitive processes occur in parallel, so that an overlap occurs between the ERP components associated with each of the processes in progress, making it difficult to measure the ERP and disentangle the multiple cognitive processes. To differentiate these components, experimental designs are required for achieving a dissociation of the cognitive process under study, as well as analysis methods to isolate the components of interest. Finally, the spatial resolution of the ERP technique is limited, because EEG activity is recorded at the scalp and is the result of the sum of activity of large populations of neurons mostly in the cortex. In addition, the different tissues between the brain and the electrodes (meninges, skull, skin, etc.) act both as electrical conductors (so that the activity generated in a particular brain region is recorded by the various electrodes placed on the scalp) and as electric resistors that distort and attenuate the original activity.

Scholars have developed algorithms to estimate the neural sources of ERP, such as the low-resolution tomography algorithm: LORETA (Pascual-Marqui, 1999, 2002; Pascual-Marqui, Esslen, Kochi, & Lehmann, 2002; Pascual-Marqui, Michel, & Lehmann, 1994). However, despite the promise of these algorithms, we should be cautious in interpreting these estimates and be aware of the low spatial resolution of the technique.

Magnetoencephalography (MEG) technique provides higher spatial resolution than the ERP, maintaining temporal resolution to the order of milliseconds. The sensors (SQUIDs) capture the magnetic fields generated by the flow of electric current of neurons. Magnetic fields are not distorted or attenuated by the tissues between the cortex and the sensors, which allows the technique to locate the brain sources of MEG components more accurately than with ERP. However, MEG does not achieve the spatial resolution level of fMRI technique.[1] MEG also has the disadvantage that the necessary equipment and its maintenance are expensive.

Therefore, each technique has distinct advantages and important limitations to consider when designing experimental tasks. Nonetheless, each of the techniques will be useful for understanding the TOT phenomenon. As outlined later in this chapter, different paradigms have been developed that have shed light on the neurofunctional characteristics of the TOT phenomenon, helping to clarify its genesis and maintenance.

Where? Spatial Information: What Brain Regions Are
Involved in the TOT State?

The first studies using any imaging technique to describe brain activity in the TOT state used the fMRI technique (Kikyo, Ohki, & Sekihara, 2001; Maril, Simons, Weaver, & Schacter, 2005; Maril, Wagner, & Schacter, 2001).

Kikyo and colleagues (2001) asked participants questions about famous people (e.g., "Who established Sony?"), and the participants were required to recall the names as quickly and accurately as possible. When they retrieved the target name or they did not retrieve the target, they had to press either of two different buttons with the right hand. The authors differentiated the Retrieval phase (which followed the questions and lasted up until one second before the participants gave their responses) and "Hit-on" or "Give-up" phases, which extended for one second just before the participants gave their responses, when the target name was or was not retrieved, respectively. Finally, only TOT states were evaluated, and the only difference between them was that in some cases they were resolved (Hit-on)

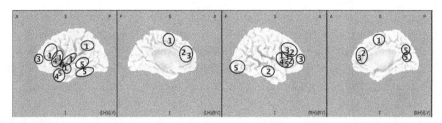

FIGURE 10.1. Schematic representation of the brain areas that showed greater activation in TOT than in K conditions in fMRI and MEG studies. Each number refers to the following study: 1- Kikyo and colleagues (2001), 2- Maril and colleagues (2001), 3- Maril and colleagues (2005), 4- Shafto and colleagues (2010), 5- Lindín and colleagues (2010).

and in other cases they were not (Give-up). Kikyo and colleagues observed bilateral activation of the dorsolateral prefrontal cortex, supramarginal gyrus, superior temporal gyrus, supplementary motor area and anterior cingulate cortex (ACC), as well as inferior frontal gyrus and motor/sensory area, during the Retrieval phase in those tests in which the name was retrieved. In addition, they noted activation of the left dorsolateral prefrontal cortex and of the ACC in the Hit-on phase (Figure 10.1). However, activation of these cortical areas was not observed in the Give-up phase. The study therefore provided interesting information on the neural correlates of the retrieval process when the TOT had already been produced, and of the resolution of the state, but did not provide any information about the spatial-temporal dynamics of the brain activity involved in genesis of the TOT state.

Maril and colleagues (2001) presented participants with general knowledge questions in the form of pairs of semantic cues (e.g., Iraq + capital) that converged on a target (e.g., Baghdad). The participants responded to each question by pressing one of the three response keys available to indicate their retrieval outcome: successful (KNOW), unsuccessful retrieval accompanied by a TOT, or unsuccessful retrieval not accompanied by a TOT (DON'T KNOW). On comparing trials, the authors obtained significantly greater activation for TOT than for the KNOW condition in the ACC, right inferior prefrontal cortex, and right dorsolateral prefrontal cortex (Figure 10.1).

In a later study involving a similar task (Maril et al., 2005), the authors observed significant TOT-related activation in the ACC and the right dorsolateral prefrontal cortex, as well as in the bilateral anterior frontal cortex (Figure 10.1), and interpreted the TOT-related activation in terms of cognitive processes that specifically characterize the TOT, such as retrieval and evaluation of partial information. They reported that some of this activation might also reflect a metacognitive process, such as evaluation by the subject of their level of knowledge on a topic, and evaluation of the probability of them getting the correct answer in time and deciding on a response.

Subsequently, Shafto, Burke, Stamatakis, Tam, and Tyler (2007) using structural magnetic resonance imaging technique (MRI), and Shafto and colleagues (2010) using fMRI, found that the left insula had a role in phonological retrieval, and therefore, it was especially responsible for the phonological deficits correlated with TOTs.

Shafto and colleagues (2007) measured the volume of gray matter in brain structural MRI images in people between 19 and 88 years. In a separate session, participants performed two tests: the Raven's Progressive Matrices test (Raven, 1958) and a celebrity-naming task using stimuli consisting of photographs and descriptions of famous people. The authors found correlations between atrophy of the left insular region, which has been associated with phonological processing (Blank, Scott, Murphy, Warburton, & Wise, 2002) and the number of TOTs, even when the effects of age were controlled. Moreover, the atrophy was not related to performance on the Raven test, which does not involve phonological processing. According to the authors, this result supported the *transmission deficit hypothesis* (Burke et al., 1991) as an explanatory model of the TOT state. But the conclusions drawn from that study were inferences from correlations between behavioral and brain structural measures obtained at different times because no comparisons of insula activity were made during correct naming processes and TOT states. Furthermore, the results did not provide information about the possible role of prefrontal and anterior cingulate gyrus that were related to the TOT phenomenon in previous studies.

To overcome these limitations, in a second study, Shafto and colleagues (2010), using a celebrity-naming task similar to that used by Díaz and colleagues (2007), recorded brain activity with the fMRI technique. They compared the changes in brain activity of younger and older participants in three conditions: successful naming (K), not knowing the name (DK), and TOTs. The authors again found a relation between the insula and phonological processing, and that the greatest degree of atrophy of this region in older people could contribute to the age-related increase of TOT experiences. Furthermore, similar to Maril and colleagues' (2001, 2005) findings, they found higher activation in the anterior cingulate and inferior frontal cortex in the TOT condition than in the K condition, indicating that these regions are recruited when difficulties in access to the required information are observed (Figure 10.1).

In summary, studies with MRI and fMRI have shown that there are differences in brain activation between conditions of successful name retrieval and TOT state. The atrophy of the insula would be related to the unsuccessful access to names of people, whereas TOT states would be associated with the activation of brain areas such as the anterior cingulate cortex, the right prefrontal cortex, and bilateral anterior frontal cortex, which have been related to conflict resolution. Thus, the fMRI studies also support a metacognitive component of the TOT experience (Schwartz & Bacon, 2008; Schwartz & Metcalfe, 2011).

The When of TOTs: Electromagnetic Indexes of the Genesis and Maintenance of TOTs

Díaz and colleagues (2007) studied TOTs for the first time using ERPs in a face-naming task. They compared a condition of successful name retrieval with conditions in which the retrieval failed, either by not knowing the name or with a TOT. The experimental task consisted of the presentation of photographs of famous people to which participants responded by pressing a button if they were sure they knew the name of the famous person, and they pressed another button if they did not know. Immediately after the manual response, participants had to give a verbal response that could be classified into three categories: 1) K: he/she knew the name and said it correctly, 2) DK: he/she does not know the name of the character, and then said "I do not know," and 3) TOT: he/she was sure of knowing the name, was on the verge of retrieving it, but it was not accessible, and said "I can't retrieve it" (in Spanish: "*no me sale*") (see Figure 10.2).

When the response to a photo was "I can't retrieve it" (TOT response), the participant was then presented with a randomly ordered sequence of three words that s/he was required to read aloud. Each word remained on the screen until the participant had read it completely, and after one second, the next word of the series appeared. One of these three words, the cue word, shared with the target name two of the following characteristics: the same first syllable, the same last syllable, the same number of syllables, the same syllables stress pattern, or the same terminal vowel rhyme. The other two words (the foils) did not share any of these characteristics with the target name. Two seconds after the third word had been read, the participants were then presented again with the same photo (second presentation) and were required to respond again, following the same procedure as at the first presentation. The next photo in the series was then presented 2,500 ms after

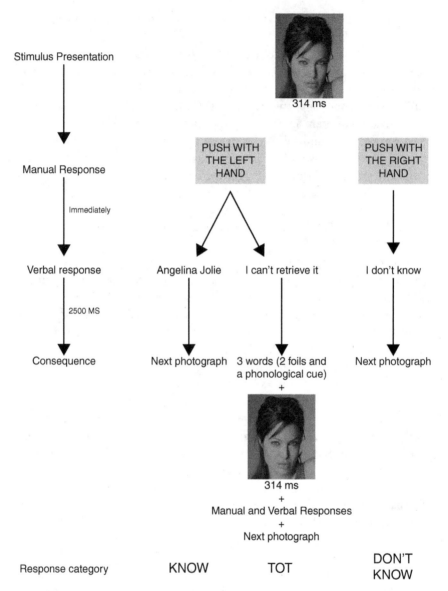

FIGURE 10.2. Face-naming task utilized in Díaz and colleagues' (2007) study.

the key press in response to this second presentation. Therefore, each photo was presented a first time (first presentation), and only faces receiving a TOT response were presented a second time (second presentation).

We used faces of famous people to produce TOT states for the following reasons: a) the faces could be homogenized regarding various physical characteristics such as luminance, color, size, and duration of stimulus presentation, which is more difficult to achieve with definitions or word pairs; b) by using celebrities across different decades, we expected to get a sufficient number of trials with K, DK, and TOT responses in participants of different ages; c) proper names result in a higher percentage of TOT states than common names, which facilitates producing enough TOT episodes to obtain ERP waveforms with a good signal-to-noise ratio; d) the faces are socially relevant stimuli; e) they have been frequently studied in neuroscience, thus various neuroimaging studies and intracranial ERP recordings have identified neural networks involved in face processing (Allison, Puce, Spencer, & McCarthy, 1999; Barbeau et al., 2008; Haxby, Hoffman, & Gobbini, 2000, 2002; Ishai, 2008; McCarthy, Puce, Belger, & Allison, 1999; Puce, Allison, & McCarthy, 1999). In addition, several studies have linked ERP components with phases of face processing (see a comprehensive review in Galdo-Álvarez, Lindín, & Díaz, 2009c). The N170 component, a negative with larger amplitude at lateral posterior electrode sites, has been related to the face structural coding; P2, a positive wave with maximum amplitude at posterior electrodes, has been associated with face recognition; and ERP components in the range between 300 and 600 ms (early P3, N400) have been associated with access to person-specific information, such as semantic, lexical, and phonological information.

In the first presentation of faces, Díaz and colleagues (2007) obtained no differences between K and TOT prior to 450 ms, confirming that processing during the initial stages of perception (P100), structural encoding (N170), face recognition (P2 and N2), and access to person-specific information (early P3) was similar between successful naming and TOT state conditions. Subsequently, another component called late-P3 (l-P3) with a peak around 676 ms and the maximum amplitude at parietal electrodes (which the authors associated with the P600 component or LPC identified in previous studies with faces), was associated with the categorization of the stimulus. The absence of differences in the l-P3 latency between response conditions led the authors to conclude that the time needed to classify the stimulus was similar between the successful name retrieval and the TOT state. The mean amplitude in the 550–750 ms interval, in which l-P3 was identified, was larger in the K condition than in TOT (Figure 10.3, top). It is likely that this difference was related to the different amount of processing resources dedicated to the categorization of the stimulus. We thought it was smaller in TOT than in K, because during TOTs, the participants' attention was divided between the categorization of the stimulus and the intense search for phonological information of the name.

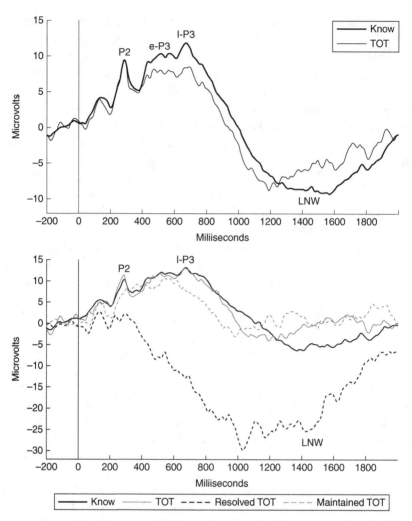

FIGURE 10.3. Grand-averaged ERP waveforms at Pz electrode site, for the first presentation of the face (top; N = 18), and for the first versus second presentation of the face after a TOT state (bottom; N = 9). (Modified from Díaz and colleagues, 2007).

The last component identified in this study was a negative wave (late negative wave -LNW-) in the 1,350–1,550 ms interval. LNW showed a gradation in its amplitude, being larger in DK, followed by K, and the smallest in TOT (Figure 10.3, top), which led the authors to propose that this component could be related to a mechanism of reviewing the categorization of the stimulus and/or the selected response.

After a TOT, the presentation of phonetic cues facilitated resolution of TOTs on 35 percent of the trials. In such cases, the same face was presented again and ERP waveforms were obtained. In the ERP waveform to the second presentation of the face, the N2, e-P3, and l-P3 components were absent (Figure 10.3, bottom). The fact that these components were not identified supported the supposition that the phonetic cue presented after a TOT state facilitated its resolution, enabling access to the name even before the face was presented again. In consequence, it would be sufficient to compare the face with its structural pattern maintained in memory (the correlate of this comparison being the P2 component), to confirm the identity of the person's face and retrieve the corresponding name.

When the presentation of the phonetic cue did not facilitate TOT resolution (56% of the time), the ERP waveforms to the second presentation of the face were similar to those of the first presentation; thus, changes in the morphology and amplitude of ERPs were not detected, which the authors attributed to the stability of the TOT. A reduction in the latencies of N2, early P3, late P3, and LNW with respect to the first presentation of the face (Figure 10.3, bottom) was observed, however, which was interpreted as evidence that the repeated presentation of the face seems to give rise to a repetition priming effect, that is, a facilitation of information transmission.

In a second study, Galdo-Álvarez and colleagues (2009b) investigated the ERP correlates of correct naming and the TOT in young and old participants, using the same task Díaz and colleagues (2007) used. The authors found no age-related differences in the ERP correlates of the TOT, indicating that TOT is a stable phenomenon throughout life. However, they obtained smaller amplitudes in the old than in young participants for the successful naming condition. This result could indicate a lower basal activation of information in memory in the older participants, which would explain why the older participants have a higher incidence of failures in word recall (Burke et al., 1991; Shafto et al., 2010; Wierenga et al., 2008).

Lindín and Díaz (2010) used a variant of the face naming task Díaz and colleagues (2007) employed. They used a larger number of stimuli (800) for improving the signal-to-noise ratio in the ERP waveforms. Lindín and Díaz also changed the response mode; participants pushed three different buttons depending on the response, that is, one for K, one for TOT, and one for DK. The study also established a delay between pressing the button and the verbal response, beyond the two seconds of the EEG epoch evaluated, with the aim of avoiding modulation of the brain activity associated with the verbal response on the LNW. Furthermore, unlike the task Díaz and

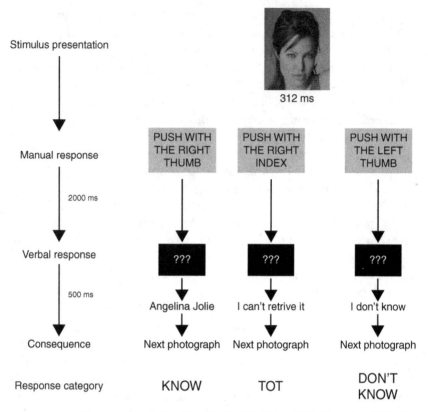

FIGURE 10.4. Face-naming task utilized in the Lindín and Díaz (2010) and Lindín and colleagues (2010) studies. The main differences regarding the task used in Díaz and colleagues' (2007) study were: the use of three response buttons (one for each response category), the time interval between the manual and the verbal responses (2000 ms), being the verbal response indicated by three question marks on the screen; and the short (about 500 ms) interval between the verbal response and the presentation of the next photograph.

colleagues (2007) used, there was not a second presentation of those faces that evoked a TOT state (Figure 10.4).

Lindín and Díaz (2010) partially replicated the results Díaz and colleagues (2007) obtained, although they obtained differences between response conditions for early P3 (300–460 ms interval) and N450 (a component of the N400 family, into the 370–560 ms interval) latencies, both of which were longer in TOT than in the K condition (Figure 10.5). From these results, they concluded that access to semantic and lexical information occurred later in TOT than in K when greater specificity is required

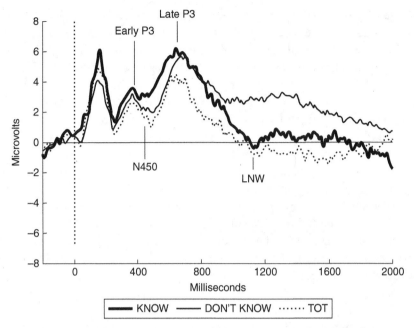

FIGURE 10.5. Grand-averaged ERP waveforms at Pz electrode site, for the K, DK, and TOT response categories. (Modified from Lindín & Díaz, 2010).

when categorizing the stimulus. Unlike the previous study (Díaz et al., 2007), Lindín and Díaz required participants to press a specific button for K and one for TOT (not the same button for both categories), so participants should have accessed the phonological information of the name before making the manual response.

The second major difference regarding Díaz and colleagues' study (2007) was that differences in the LNW amplitude among response categories were not obtained (Figure 10.5), which Lindín and Díaz interpreted as meaning that the differences observed in this component in Díaz and colleagues' (2007) study could be due to a modulation of the ERP waveform by motor components associated with the preparation and/or execution of verbal responses, as Buján, Lindín, and Díaz (2009) had confirmed.

Buján and colleagues (2009) evaluated the manual and speech Movement-Related Cortical Potentials (MRCP) in a subsample of the young participants involved in the previous study (Díaz et al., 2007). The results indicated that the LNW occurred in TOT at the same time as the negative slope of the MRCP, but in the K and DK conditions, LNW coincided with the interval corresponding to the speech-related motor potential

(Figure 10.6). The authors concluded that the differences Díaz and colleagues (2007) obtained in LNW amplitude among response categories (DK > K > TOT) might have been partly caused by the larger amplitude of the speech-related motor potential than the negative slope, and the different modulation of both motor components on the stimulus-related LNW component in K and DK regarding TOT conditions. Thus, this overlap of motor potentials might have masked the ERP correlates of the TOT experience and its consequences in the previous studies.

Furthermore, Buján and colleagues (2009) observed that while in the DK and K categories, a general mobilization of necessary resources was produced to preprogram the motor action (as is reflected in the adequate development of the first component of the readiness potential -1st-RP-). In the TOT, a temporal blockage of this mechanism is produced until completing categorization of the stimulus (whose ERP correlate is the late-P3 component). This blockage was considered the result of the division of processing resources between the fruitless search for semantic and lexical-phonological information about the famous person and the motor programming in the TOT.

Buján, Lindín, and Díaz (2010) showed with older adults a blockage in the development of 1st-RP in the TOT condition, but in a different time than the young participants. Thus, in older adults, more motor resources were allocated at the beginning of motor programming. Furthermore, the division of the processing resources started from the most demanding processing stages (stimulus categorization and review of the categorization and/or of the selected response), when the participant tries unsuccessfully to resolve the conflict between recognizing the famous person and knowing his/her name, but being unable to recall the complete phonology of the name. Buján and colleagues (2010) concluded that the interruption in the progression of the 1st-RP, in both young and older participants, could explain the specific behavioral slowing in TOT category with respect to the other response categories (K and DK).

Although the previous studies shed light about the electrophysiological characterization of face processing and the TOT phenomenon, several relevant aspects about the causes and consequences of the TOT remained unanswered. First, it was necessary to establish clearly if TOTs are due to a transmission deficit in earlier stages of processing (recognition, semantic, and/or lemma access). To achieve this goal, it would be necessary to compare this condition with a category in which no recognition and access to person-specific information take place. Comparison between ERP components associated with processes prior to the response decision was not

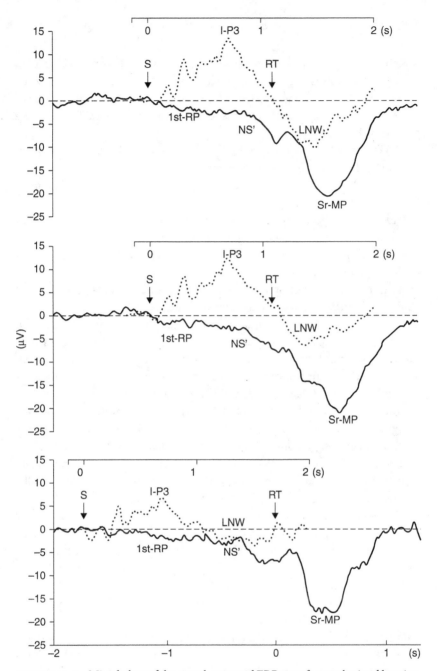

FIGURE 10.6. Mixed plots of the grand-averaged ERP waveforms obtained by stimulus-onset average in Pz electrode site (dotted line) and by response-onset average in Cz electrode site (solid line) for the DK (top), K (middle) and TOT (bottom) response categories (S: stimulus presentation; RT: reaction time; l-P3: late-P3; NS': negative slope; LNW: late negative wave; Sr-MP: speech-related motor potential). (From Buján et al., 2009).

possible in the previous studies because the DK category was poorly defined (as it did not allow differentiation of whether the participant recognized the character of the picture whose name he/she did not know). Second, none of these studies had definitively established the temporal interval in which the genesis of TOT state occurs.

Therefore, and to advance in the electrophysiological characterization of the TOT phenomenon in particular, and of the face processing and naming in general, Buján and colleagues (2012) conducted a new study with a modified face-naming task (Figure 10.7). As in Lindín and Díaz (2010), the task included a delay between the two motor responses (manual and verbal) to avoid the influence of the electrophysiological activity related to the verbal response in order to compare the latter temporal intervals of direct waveforms between the categories.

With the new task design, we tried to determine whether previous ERP studies may have masked differences between the KNOW and TOT conditions, which both may include successful access to semantic and lexical information. To test this hypothesis, the participants had to press a button with one hand if they knew the name of the famous person and press another button with the other hand if they did not know the name, but halfway through the task, in a second block of stimuli, the participants were instructed to change their hands to respond to each condition (knowledge vs. ignorance of the name). This change was necessary to isolate an ERP component named the *lateralized readiness potential* (LRP, a motor component associated to the selection of the response), which informs of the time required to access the necessary information to respond.[2] Specifically, researchers have used the onset latency of the stimulus-locked LRP (s-LRP) as an index of the timing of response selection (Kolev, Falkenstein, & Yordanova, 2006; Praamstra, Plat, Meyer, & Horstink, 1999), and in previous studies researchers have used it as an indirect measure of the access to phonological information required to select a response (Abdel-Rahman, Sommer, & Schweinberger, 2002; Van Turennout, Hagoort, & Brown, 1997). Thus, the s-LRP could represent an appropriate index to measure when the availability of phonological information differed between the successful naming and the TOT state. In addition, in the case of both the DK and the TOT state, several control questions were presented to ensure that TOTs were positive (that is, that participants' missing target was the correct one), and to confirm that in the DK the participant had no knowledge of the person seen in the photo. Finally, the onset latency of the response-locked LRP (r-LRP), which researchers have used as an index of the motor processing (Van der Lubbe & Verleger, 2002), was compared between the response

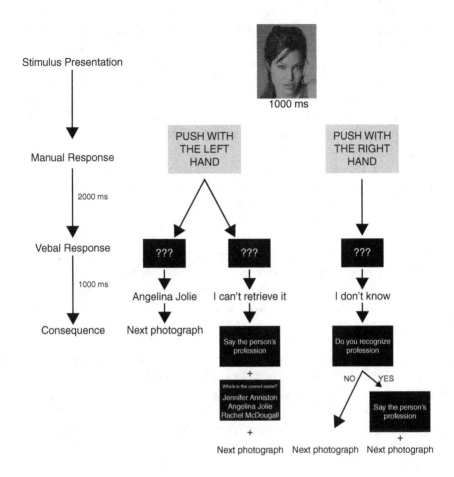

FIGURE 10.7. Face-naming task utilized in Buján and colleagues' (2012) study. The main differences regarding the previous tasks consisted of the improved characterization of the TOT and DK response categories, the time interval between the manual and the verbal responses and between the verbal response and the consequence, as well as a longer stimulus presentation time.

categories, which might clarify how the consequences of the TOT could affect the initiation of the motor processes.

The aims of Buján and colleagues' (2012) study were: 1) to investigate the main causes and consequences of TOTs, 2) to determine whether the access to semantic and lexical information is similar between the TOT state and successful naming, 3) to determine the moment at which the selection of the response takes place in successful naming (and therefore the access to enough information to emit a response), 4) to establish the temporal interval of TOT genesis by means of the stimulus locked lateralized readiness potential (s-LRP) analysis in both response categories (TOT and successful naming), and 5) to obtain the electrophysiological correlates of the TOT consequences (i.e., continuous search for information and conflict monitoring once the TOT is established).

The results again confirmed the similarities between successful naming (K) and TOTs, as they did not show differences in the ERP components related to the processing of faces (P1, N170, P2) and the access to specific information of the person (early P3, N450), although there were differences between both K and TOT and the DK category. However, as reflected by the s-LRP onset, the response was selected around 300 ms in the K category, whereas in the TOT category a delay occurred in the selection of the response (Figure 10.8). This data would indicate that around 300 ms enough information to carry out a successful naming was only retrieved in the K category, supporting the hypothesis of early hypoactivation in TOT for explaining the genesis of the TOT.

In addition, at later stages of processing (from 750 ms onward), researchers observed a smaller amplitude in the TOT category than in the K and DK categories, which they attributed to the devotion of many resources in later stages of processing in the TOT state to conflict management and a continued search of the name in memory. This metacognitive control of the attempt of name retrieval during the TOT state was supported by findings from behavioral studies that related TOTs to retrieval time in recall (Schwartz, 2001) and to the ways people attempt retrieval (Schwartz, 2002), and by findings from fMRI studies (Maril et al., 2001, 2005).

How? An Approximation to the Temporal-Spatial Information: The Sequence of Brain Activation in Successful Naming and TOTs
Lindín, Díaz, Capilla, Ortiz, and Maestú (2010) recorded, simultaneously with brain electrical activity (see Lindín & Díaz, 2010), the magnetoencephalography activity (using the MEG technique) to examine name retrieval and TOTs (see Figure 10.4). Because MEG presents a higher spatial resolution than EEG, the goal was to identify the network of brain areas that respond differently during successful naming (K response category) and failed naming of known faces (TOT response category), in order to delimit the brain regions associated with and the timing of the TOT.

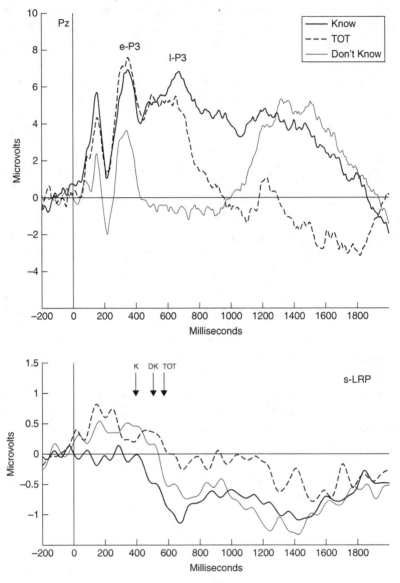

FIGURE 10.8. Grand-averaged ERP waveforms at Pz electrode site (top) and grand-averaged stimulus-locked LRP (s-LRP) waveforms (bottom), for the K, DK, and TOT response categories. The onset of the s-LRP in each category is indicated by arrows. (Modified from Buján et al., 2012).

Consistent with the results of ERP studies, in the first 210 ms in face processing, no differences appeared between both states, consistent with models of face processing and naming (e.g., Bruce & Young, 1986; Valentine, Brennen, & Brédart, 1996). Significantly greater activation in K than in TOT was observed in the 210–310 ms interval in the left anterior medial prefrontal cortex, the left orbitofrontal gyrus, the left superior temporal pole, and the left inferior and anterior middle temporal gyri, a network that could contribute to successful naming. In addition, in the 310–520 ms interval, Lindín and colleagues (2010) identified a smaller activation in TOT than in K in left frontal and temporal areas, bilateral parahippocampal gyrus and right fusiform gyrus, which was associated with the failure to retrieve the complete phonology of the name, that is, the genesis of the TOT state. In a later interval (between 740–820 ms), they observed greater activation in TOT than in K in bilateral occipital, left temporal and right frontal and parietal regions, what they interpreted as reflecting the active but fruitless search of the name in the TOT condition (Figure 10.9; see also Figure 10.1).

Galdo-Álvarez, Lindín, and Díaz (2011) compared, by means of the LORETA program, the temporal sequences of activation of ERP neural sources for the K and TOT conditions using Díaz and colleagues' (2007) face-naming task. The authors found significant differences in activation between the two conditions during the interval 538–698 ms (Figure 10.10), with greater activation for the K than for the TOT condition, in the anterior cingulate cortex and supplementary motor area (SMA), which was interpreted as a reflection of the preparation of the motor response and the successful retrieval of semantic and phonological information in the K condition. However, in late intervals (1000–1500 ms), they only observed activation in the anterior cingulate in the TOT condition, a result they attributed to the TOT experience once it has been established, as the cognitive control to search for the name in this category.

CLOSING THE CIRCLE: INTEGRATION OF NEUROCOGNITIVE
DATA WITH CURRENT MODELS OF TOT PHENOMENON

From 2001 to the present, 14 papers have been published about brain functional correlates of TOTs. Each study, given the type of technique used by the experimental design, has provided various clues to understanding the TOT phenomenon. A comprehensive understanding of how the TOT state occurs and how it progresses requires exploring the spatiotemporal sequence of activation of neural networks involved in accessing information in memory and naming.

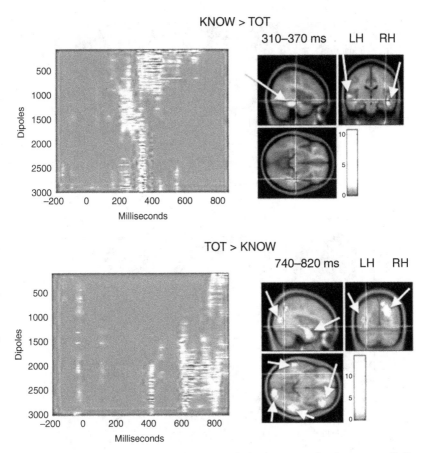

FIGURE 10.9. Temporal windows that showed a higher MEG dipolar activity (left), and some brain areas that showed significantly greater activation (right), in KNOW than in TOT response category (top), and in TOT than in KNOW response category (bottom). The color scale indicates the T values obtained in the t-tests. (Modified from Lindín et al., 2010).

The data obtained up to now with ERP and MEG to face-naming tasks suggest that the origin of the TOT could be due to an early hypoactivation (from approximately 300 ms) of brain regions involved in access to lexical and phonological information in memory, including insula and the left frontal and temporal lobes, along with the bilateral activation of the parahippocampal and fusiform gyri. In addition, greater activation for K than for the TOT condition in the interval between 538–698 ms, in the anterior cingulate cortex and the supplementary motor area, could reflect the actual preparation of the motor response in the successful naming condition (K)

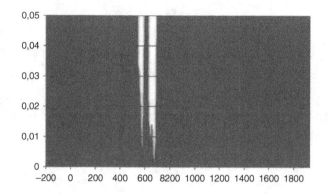

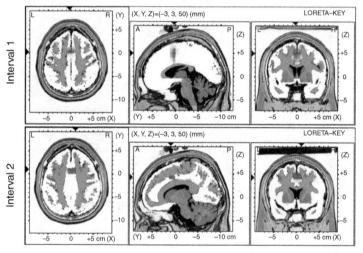

Interval 1: (X= –3, Y=3, Z=50) BA 24/32/6: Left ACC and SMA

Interval 2: (X= 11, Y=10, Z=43; X=–3, Y=10, Z=43) BA 32: Bilateral ACC

FIGURE 10.10. TANOVA results with the LORETA software: Top Panel: p values of the comparison throughout the entire ERP waveforms between the K and the TOT conditions; the graphical representation shows two time intervals presenting significant differences (p<.05). Bottom panel: LORETA t-tests images showing significantly more active brain areas in the KNOW condition than in the TOT condition for two time intervals. Top: Interval 1 (538–598 ms). Bottom: Interval 2 (622–698 ms). (From Galdo-Álvarez et al., 2011).

once successful information retrieval about the person, including the name, has taken place.

The neurocognitive data seems, therefore, to rule out that the TOT may be due to activation of intrusive words, which would result in a similar or higher brain activation in the TOT than in the K condition in the early stages of the processing, in line with behavioral results (see Brown, 2012). The transmission deficit hypothesis (Burke et al., 1991) seems, therefore, a more appropriate explanatory hypothesis to understand how TOTs arise. Successful access to the name allows one to prepare the response faster than when in a TOT, which explains the shorter reaction times commonly found in successful naming when comparing this condition with the TOT state (Buján et al., 2012; Díaz et al., 2007; Galdo-Álvarez et al., 2009a).

The transmission deficit hypothesis (Burke et al., 1991) explains how the TOT state originates, but does not explain the features, the consequences, and the processes that occur once a TOT has been initiated. In this concern, the neurocognitive data indicate greater activation in the TOT state than in the successful naming condition, from approximately 750 ms onward, of the bilateral occipital, left temporal, right frontal, and parietal areas, and the anterior cingulate cortex (see Kikyo et al., 2001; Lindín et al., 2010; Maril et al., 2001, 2005), which could be associated with conflict management and with the unfruitful search in the memory for the name corresponding to the face once the TOT state was established, in line with the inferential theories of TOT.

In summary, neuroimaging techniques are useful tools to delve into explanatory mechanisms and characteristics of the TOT phenomenon. Neuroimaging is also critical in understanding the mechanisms of access to semantic, lexical, and phonological information in memory and naming. We examined, using ERP and MEG, the origin and consequences of TOT. Confirming the data obtained through behavioral studies, we have found similarities between the successful naming and the TOT state, while finding only subtle differences in brain activation (hypoactivation of areas involved in the retrieval of lexical-phonological information) in early processing stages. We assert that this hypoactivation serves as the genesis of the TOT. Moreover, a complete characterization of the TOT phenomenon requires attention to metacognitive conflict management once this has occurred, including the continued search for information that has not been retrieved, and that is reflected in activation of specific brain regions, including the ACC, in late processing stages.

NOTES

1. The MEG records magnetic fields only from cortical, not subcortical neurons, and the magnetic field should be perpendicular to the sensors for being recorded. Given that the brain cortex is folded forming ridges (named gyri) and furrows (named sulci), the activity this technique measures corresponds to

populations of pyramidal neurons in cortical sulci disposed parallel to the scalp, being a technique relatively blind to neuronal activity in the cortical gyri.

2. The LRP is the result of isolating the larger activity of the motor cortex contralateral to the hand that executed the movement. Thus, a larger negativity is observed at contralateral than at ipsilateral central electrodes when the participant is performing a response with a hand. The hand selection is associated with the access to the required information in tasks in which the response depends on the retrieval of specific information.

REFERENCES

Abdel-Rahman, R., Sommer, W., & Schweinberger, S. R. (2002). Brain-potential evidence for the time course of access to biographical facts and names of familiar persons. *Journal of Experimental Psychology: Learning, Memory, and Cognition, 28(2)*, 366–373.

Allison, T., Puce, A., Spencer, D. D., & McCarthy, G. (1999). Electrophysiological studies of human face perception. I: Potentials generated in occipitotemporal cortex by face and non-face stimuli. *Cerebral Cortex, 9(5)*, 415–430.

Barbeau, E. J., Taylor, M. J., Regis, J., Marquis, P., Chauvel, P., & Liégeois-Chauvel, C. (2008). Spatio temporal dynamics of face recognition. *Cerebral Cortex, 18*, 997–1009.

Blank, S., Scott, S., Murphy, K., Warburton, E., & Wise, R., (2002). Speech production: Wernicke, Broca and beyond. *Brain, 125*, 1829–1838.

Bock, K., & Levelt, W. J. M. (1994). Language production: Grammatical encoding. In M. A. Gernsbacher (Ed.), *Handbook of Psycholinguistics* (pp. 945–984). San Diego, CA: Academic Press.

Bonin, P., Perret, C., Méot, A., Ferrand, L., & Mermillod, M. (2008). Psycholinguistic norms and face naming times for photographs of celebrities in French. *Behavior Research Methods, 40(1)*, 137–146.

Brown, A. S. (1991). A review of the tip-of-the-tongue experience. *Psychological Bulletin, 109(2)*, 204–223.

(2012). *The tip of the tongue state*. New York: Psychology Press.

Brown, A. S., & Nix, L. A. (1996). Age-related changes in the tip-of-the-tongue experience. *The American Journal of Psychology, 109(1)*, 79–91.

Brown, R., & McNeill, D. (1966). The "tip of the tongue" phenomenon. *Journal of Verbal Learning and Verbal Behavior, 5(4)*, 325–337.

Bruce, V., & Young, A. W. (1986). Understanding face recognition. *British Journal of Psychology, 77*, 305–327.

Buján, A., Galdo-Álvarez, S., Lindín, M., & Díaz, F. (2012). An event-related potentials study of face naming: Evidence of phonological retrieval deficit in the tip-of-the-tongue state. *Psychophysiology, 49*, 980–990.

Buján, A., Lindín, M., & Díaz, F. (2009). Movement related cortical potentials in a face naming task: Influence of the tip-of-the-tongue state. *International Journal of Psychophysiology, 72*, 235–245.

(2010). The effect of aging on movement related cortical potentials during a face naming task. *International Journal of Psychophysiology, 78*, 169–178.

Burke, D. M., Locantore, J. K., Austin, A. A., & Chae, B. (2004). Cherry pit primes Brad Pitt: Homophone priming effects on young and older adults' production of proper names. *Psychological Science, 15*(3), 164–170.

Burke, D. M., MacKay, D. G., Worthley, J. S., & Wade, E. (1991). On the tip of the tongue: What causes word finding failures in young and older adults? *Journal of Memory and Language, 30*(5), 542–579.

Caramazza, A., & Miozzo, M. (1997). The relation between syntactic and phonological knowledge in lexical access: Evidence from the "tip-of-the-tongue" phenomenon. *Cognition, 64*(3), 309–343.

Cleary, A. M. (2006). Relating familiarity-based recognition and the tip-of-the-tongue phenomenon: Detecting a word's recency in the absence of access to the word. *Memory & Cognition, 34*(4), 804–816.

Cleary, A. M., & Reyes, N. L. (2009). Scene recognition without identification. *Acta Psychologica, 131*(1), 53–62.

Cleary, A. M., & Specker, L. E. (2007). Recognition without face identification. *Memory & Cognition, 35*(7), 1610–1619.

Cohen, G., & Faulkner, D. (1986). Memory for proper names: Age differences in retrieval. *British Journal of Developmental Psychology, 4*(2), 187–197.

Cross, E. S., & Burke, D. M. (2004). Do alternative names block young and older adults' retrieval of proper names? *Brain and Language, 89*(1), 174–181.

Díaz, F., Lindín, M., Galdo-Álvarez, S., Facal, D., & Juncos-Rabadán, O. (2007). An event-related potentials study of face identification and naming: The tip-of-the-tongue state. *Psychophysiology, 44*(1), 50–68.

Evrard, M. (2002). Ageing and lexical access to common and proper names in picture naming. *Brain and Language, 81*(1–3), 174–179.

Galdo-Álvarez, S., Lindín, M., & Díaz, F. (2009a). Age-related prefrontal over-recruitment in semantic memory retrieval: Evidence from successful face naming and the tip-of-the-tongue state. *Biological Psychology, 82*(1), 89–96.

(2009b). The effect of age on event-related potentials (ERP) associated with face naming and with the tip-of-the-tongue (TOT) state. *Biological Psychology, 81,* 14–23.

(2009c). Naming faces: A multidisciplinary and integrated review. *Psicothema, 21*(4), 521–527.

(2011). Brain dynamics associated with face naming and the tip-of-the-tongue state. *Psicothema, 23*(2), 189–195.

Gollan, T. H., & Brown, A. S. (2006). From tip-of-the-tongue (TOT) data to theoretical implications in two steps: When more TOTs means better retrieval. *Journal of Experimental Psychology: General, 135*(3), 462–483.

Gollan, T. H., Montoya, R. I., & Bonanni, M. P. (2005). Proper names get stuck on bilingual and monolingual speakers' tip of the tongue equally often. *Neuropsychology, 19*(3), 278–287.

Hämäläinen, M., Hari, R., Ilmoniemi, R., Knuutila, J., & Lounasmaa, O. (1993). Magnetoencephalography-theory, instrumentation, and applications to non-invasive studies of the working human brain. *Reviews of Modern Physics, 65,* 1–93.

Hanley, J. R. (2011). Why are names of people associated with so many phonological retrieval failures? *Psychonomic Bulletin & Review, 18*(3), 612–617.

Hanley, J. R., & Chapman, E. (2008). Partial knowledge in a tip-of-the-tongue state about two- and three-word proper names. *Psychonomic Bulletin & Review,* 15(1), 156–160.

Hanly, S., & Vandenberg, B. (2010). Tip-of-the-tongue and word retrieval deficits in dyslexia. *Journal of Learning Disabilities,* 43(1), 15–23.

Haxby, J. V., Hoffman, E. A., & Gobbini, M. I. (2000). The distributed human neural system for face perception. *Trends in Cognitive Sciences,* 4(6), 223–233.

(2002). Human neural systems for face recognition and social communication. *Biological Psychiatry,* 51, 59–67.

Hay, D. C., Young, A. W., & Ellis, A. W. (1991). Routes through the face recognition system. *The Quarterly Journal of Experimental Psychology: A Human Experimental Psychology,* 43(4), 761–791.

Heine, M. K., Ober, B. A., & Shenaut, G. K. (1999). Naturally occurring and experimentally induced tip-of-the-tongue experiences in three adult age groups. *Psychology and Aging,* 14(3), 445–457.

Ishai, A. (2008). Let's face it: It's a cortical network. *Neuroimage,* 40, 415–419.

James, L. E. (2006). Specific effects of aging on proper name retrieval: Now you see them, now you don't. *The Journals of Gerontology: Series B, Psychological Sciences and Social Sciences,* 61B(3), 180–183.

James, L. E., & Burke, D. M. (2000). Phonological priming effects on word retrieval and tip-of-the-tongue experiences in young and older adults. *Journal of Experimental Psychology. Learning, Memory, and Cognition,* 26(6), 1378–1391.

Jones, G. V. (1989). Back to Woodworth: Role of interlopers in the tip-of-the-tongue phenomenon. *Memory & Cognition,* 17(1), 69–76.

Kikyo, H., Ohki, K., & Sekihara, K. (2001). Temporal characterization of memory retrieval processes: An fMRI study of the "tip of the tongue" phenomenon. *European Journal of Neuroscience,* 14(5), 887–892.

Kolev, V., Falkenstein, M., & Yordanova, J. (2006). Motor-response generation as a source of aging-related behavioural slowing in choice-reaction tasks. *Neurobiology and Aging,* 27(11), 1719–1730.

Koriat, A. (1993). How do we know that we know? The accessibility model of the feeling of knowing. *Psychological Review,* 100(4), 609–639.

Koriat, A., & Levy-Sadot, R. (2001). The combined contributions of the cue-familiarity and accessibility heuristics to feelings of knowing. *Journal of Experimental Psychology: Learning, Memory, and Cognition,* 27(1), 34–53.

Lindín, M., & Díaz, F. (2010). Event-related potentials in face naming and tip-of-the-tongue state: Further results. *International Journal of Psychophysiology,* 77(1), 53–58.

Lindín, M., Díaz, F., Capilla, A., Ortiz, T., & Maestú, F. (2010). On the characterization of the spatio-temporal profiles of brain activity associated with face naming and the tip-of-the-tongue state: A magnetoencephalographic (MEG) study. *Neuropsychologia,* 48(6), 1757–1766.

Luck, S. J. (2005). *An introduction to the event-related potential technique.* London: MIT Press.

Luck, S. J. & Kappenman, E. (2008). *The Oxford handbook of event-related potential components.* Oxford: Oxford University Press.

MacKay, D. G., & Burke, D. M. (1990). Cognition and aging: A theory of new learning and the use of old connections. In T. M. Hess (Ed.), *Aging and cognition: Knowledge organization and utilization* (pp. 213–263). Oxford: North-Holland.

Maril, A., Simons, J. S., Weaver, J. J., & Schacter, D. L. (2005). Graded recall success: An event-related fMRI comparison of tip of the tongue and feeling of knowing. *NeuroImage,* 24(4), 1130–1138.

Maril, A., Wagner, A. D., & Schacter, D. L. (2001). On the tip of the tongue: An event-related fMRI study of semantic retrieval failure and cognitive conflict. *Neuron,* 31(4), 653–660.

McCarthy, G., Puce, A., Belger, A., & Allison, T. (1999). Electrophysiological studies of human face perception. II: Response properties of face-specific potentials generated in occipitotemporal cortex. *Cerebral Cortex,* 9, 431–444.

Menon R. S., & Kim S. G. (1999). Spatial and temporal limits in cognitive neuroimaging with fMRI. *Trends in Cognitive Sciences,* 3(6), 207–216.

Metcalfe, J., Schwartz, B. L., & Joaquim, S. G. (1993). The cue-familiarity heuristic in metacognition. *Journal of Experimental Psychology: Learning, Memory, and Cognition,* 19(4), 851–864.

Meyer-Lindenberger, A. (2010). From maps to mechanisms through neuroimaging of schizophrenia. *Nature,* 468, 194–202.

Miozzo, M., & Caramazza, A. (1997). Retrieval of lexical-syntactic features in tip-of-the-tongue states. *Journal of Experimental Psychology. Learning, Memory, and Cognition,* 23(6), 1410–1423.

Pascual-Marqui, R. D. (1999). Review of methods for solving the EEG inverse problem. *International Journal of Bioelectromagnetism,* 1, 75–86.

(2002). Standardized low resolution brain electromagnetic tomography (sLORETA): Technical details. *Methods & Findings in Experimental & Clinical Pharmacology,* 24D, 5–12.

Pascual-Marqui, R. D., Esslen, M., Kochi, K., & Lehmann, D. (2002). Functional imaging with low resolution brain electromagnetic tomography (LORETA): A review. *Methods and Findings in Experimental and Clinical Pharmacology,* 24, 91–95.

Pascual-Marqui, R. D., Michel, C. M., & Lehmann, D. (1994). Low resolution electromagnetic tomography: A new method for localizing electrical activity in the brain. *International Journal of Psychophysiology,* 18, 49–65.

Pfeuffer, J., van de Moortele, P. F., Yacoub, E., Shmuel, A., Adriany, G., Andersen, P., Merkle, H., Garwood, M., Ugurbil, K., & Hu, X. (2002). Zoomed functional imaging in the human brain at 7 tesla with simultaneous high spatial and high temporal resolution. *Neuroimage,* 17, 272–286.

Praamstra, P., Plat, E. M., Meyer, A. S., & Horstink, M. W. (1999). Motor cortex activation in Parkinson's disease: Dissociation of electrocortical and peripheral measures of response generation. *Movement Disorders,* 14(5), 790–799.

Puce, A., Allison, T., & McCarthy, G. (1999). Electrophysiological studies of human face perception. III: Effects of top-down processing on face-specific potentials. *Cerebral Cortex,* 9(5), 445–458.

Rastle, K. G., & Burke, D. M. (1996). Priming the tip of the tongue: Effects of prior processing on word retrieval in young and older adults. *Journal of Memory and Language, 35*(4), 586–605.

Raven, J. C. (1958). *The standard progressive matrices.* London: H. K. Lewis.

Reason, J. T., & Lucas, D. (1984). Using cognitive diaries to investigate naturally occurring memory blocks. In J. E. Harris & P. E. Morris (Eds.), *Everyday memory, actions, and absent mindedness* (pp. 53–70). London: Academic Press.

Schwartz, B. L. (1994). Sources of information in metamemory: Judgments of learning and feelings of knowing. *Psychonomic Bulletin & Review,* 1(3), 357–375.

(1999). Sparkling at the end of the tongue: The etiology of tip-of-the-tongue phenomenology. *Psychonomic Bulletin & Review,* 6(3), 379–393.

(2001). The relation of tip-of-the-tongue states and retrieval time. *Memory & Cognition,* 29(1), 117–126.

(2002). The strategic control of retrieval during tip-of-the-tongue states. *Korean Journal of Thinking and Problem-Solving,* 12, 27–38.

Schwartz, B. L., & Bacon, E. (2008). Metacognitive neuroscience. In J. Dunlosky and R. Bjork (Eds.), *Handbook of metamemory and memory* (pp. 355–371). New York: Psychology Press.

Schwartz, B. L., & Metcalfe, J. (2011). Tip-of-the-tongue (TOT) states: Retrieval, behavior, and experience. *Memory & Cognition,* 39(5), 737–749.

Shafto, M. A., Burke, D. M., Stamatakis, E. A., Tam, P. P., & Tyler, L. K. (2007). On the tip-of-the-tongue: Neural correlates of increased word-finding failures in normal aging. *Journal of Cognitive Neuroscience,* 19(12), 2060–2070.

Shafto, M. A., Stamatakis, E., Tam, P., & Tyler, L. (2010). Word retrieval failures in old age: The relationship between structure and function. *Journal of Cognitive Neuroscience,* 22(7), 1530–1540.

Valentine, T., Brennen, T., & Brédart, S. (1996). *The cognitive psychology of proper names.* London: Routledge.

Van der Lubbe, R. H. J., & Verleger, R. (2002). Aging and the Simon task. *Psychophysiology,* 39(1), 100–110.

Van Turennout, M., Hagoort, P., & Brown, C. M. (1997). Electrophysiological evidence on the time course of semantic and phonological processes in speech production. *Journal of Experimental Psychology: Learning, Memory, and Cognition,* 23(4), 787–806.

Vitevitch, M. S., & Sommers, M. S. (2003). The facilitative influence of phonological similarity and neighborhood frequency in speech production in younger and older adults. *Memory & Cognition,* 31(4), 491–504.

Ward, J. (2010). *The student's guide to cognitive neuroscience.* Second Edition. New York: Psychology Press.

White, K. K., & Abrams, L. (2002). Does priming specific syllables during tip-of-the-tongue states facilitate word retrieval in older adults? *Psychology and Aging,* 17(2), 226–235.

Wierenga, C. E., Benjamin, M., Gopinath, K., Perlstein, W. M., Leonard, C. M., Gonzalez Rothi, L. J., Conway, T., Cato, M. A., Briggs, R., & Crosson, B. (2008). Age-related changes in word retrieval: role of bilateral frontal and subcortical networks. *Neurobiology of Aging,* 29, 436–451.

Woodworth, R.S. (1929). *Psychology.* Oxford, UK: Holt.

Yang, L., Wilke, C., Brinkmann, B., Worrell, G. A., & He, B. (2011). Dynamic imaging of ictal oscillations using non-invasive high-resolution EEG. *Neuroimage,* 56(4), 1908–1917.

Yarmey, A. D. (1973). I recognize your face but I can't remember your name: Further evidence on the tip-of-the-tongue phenomenon. *Memory & Cognition,* 1(3), 287–290.

11

The Blank-in-the-Mind Experience: Another Manifestation of the Tip-of-the-Tongue State or Something Else?

ANASTASIA EFKLIDES

INTRODUCTION

Everyday life often creates conditions in which a current (main) task is interrupted to respond to some other secondary task. Multitasking is a requirement in many jobs, and performance can suffer in accuracy or speed as one moves from one task to the other (Monk, Trafton, & Boehm-Davis, 2008). Understanding the processes involved in setting goals and resuming temporarily suspended goals is an issue of interest in current memory research and is closely related to prospective memory (PM) research (Einstein, McDaniel, Williford, Pagan, & Dismukes, 2003; Monk et al., 2008).

Prospective memory failures can take various forms. These include: (1) omission error, namely, not performing the required prospective memory response. This can be due to failure to monitor the cue that should trigger the prospective memory goal. It can also be the outcome of failure to maintain in memory the prospective memory goal; (2) commission error, namely, performing the prospective memory response in the absence of the cue that should have triggered it; and (3) performing the prospective memory response again, because of failure to monitor its execution.

The following examples highlight the various forms of prospective memory failures. Suppose you are at work and you have to take a medicine at 5 o'clock. It is 5 o'clock and you do not take the medicine because, being busy with work, you failed to notice that the time was 5 o'clock. Alternatively, you may look at the watch showing 5 o'clock and wonder what it was that you had to do at 5 o'clock. Thus, you do not take the medicine because you

Address: Anastasia Efklides, School of Psychology, Aristotle University of Thessaloniki, 541 24 Thessaloniki, Greece. Tel.: +30–2310–997374. Fax: +30–2310–997384. E-mail: efklides@psy. auth.gr.

forgot that you had to do it (omission error). Suppose then that later on you realize that you did not take the medicine at 5 o'clock and you should not miss the next dose at 9 o'clock when you go home. You keep reminding yourself that you need to take the medicine, and as soon as you arrive at home, you take the medicine although it is 8 o'clock (commission error). After some time, as 9 o'clock approaches, you start wondering if you have taken your medicine. In the absence of a clear memory of yourself taking the medicine, you take it again or check the medicine looking for clues that can remind you of whether you took the medicine.

Research on prospective memory focuses on the cognitive underpinnings of the relevant responses. However, there are also metacognitive experiences that accompany prospective memory failures. Focusing on the metacognition of prospective memory introduces a number of new questions. Are people aware of their prospective memory failures? What form does this awareness take? Does this awareness affect control decisions? Do people use strategies that can help them have control over their prospective memory? In this chapter, I focus on metacognitive awareness of prospective memory failures. One particular metacognitive experience that is unique to memory of goals is the blank-in-the-mind state (henceforth, BIM, Moraitou & Efklides, 2009). BIM is the awareness that one cannot retrieve the goal that initiated a course of action (why did I do this?) or the goal following a course of action that has been completed (what should I do now?). For example, a person may suddenly become aware that they do not know why they are walking toward a bathroom in their house. Retrieving what they had been doing earlier (perhaps, doing dishes) may help them recall that their actions were intended to get a clean towel from the bathroom. Or a person at work may not recall why they opened their PowerPoint application. Retrieving that they had been working on the payroll may inform them that they have been tasked with making a presentation about salaries. In contrast, tip-of-the-tongue states (henceforth, TOT) also signal memory failure, but they are associated with retrospective and semantic memory. That is, a TOT is a marker that a known word or name is not currently accessible. Thus, a person may be sure that they know the German word for "black" but cannot recall it at the moment. Therefore, the question is whether BIM and TOT are both manifestations of lack of accessibility of memory information or have characteristics that render them distinct phenomena. The aim of this chapter is to present empirical evidence that evaluates the possible mechanism underlying BIM. A second aim is to explore the possible relations of BIM with TOT, two metacognitive experiences related to memory failure. In what follows, I shall refer to metacognitive experiences that are associated with prospective memory failures and then to the phenomenological characteristics of the BIM experience. Theories that could account for BIM are then presented. Three studies that explore BIM will follow, and the implications of their findings will be discussed.

AWARENESS OF PROSPECTIVE MEMORY FAILURES

Koriat, Ben-Zur, and Sheffer (1988) distinguished two types of monitoring processes in prospective memory: input monitoring and output monitoring. *Input monitoring* underlies the recognition of the cue that should trigger goal enactment. Two typical experiences associated with input monitoring are (1) the deliberate and effortful search of the environment for the presence of the prospective memory cue, and (2) the "pop up" experience when the cue is automatically processed and the prospective memory goal comes spontaneously to mind (Einstein et al., 2003; McDaniel & Einstein, 2000; Meier, Zimmerman, & Perrig, 2006). *Output monitoring*, however, is responsible for determining whether the prospective memory response was successfully performed. One typical metacognitive experience in output monitoring is the *uncertainty* that the person experiences as to whether the prospective memory response has been performed (Koriat et al., 1988; Sugimori & Kusumi, 2009). For example, one may be unsure that one locked the front door. In this case, the uncertainty may lead to repetition of the prospective memory response, for example, going back to the door and checking whether it was locked. Omission errors, by contrast, often go unnoticed and denote an output monitoring failure (Marsh, Hicks, Hancock, & Munsayac, 2002). Only later does the person realize that the prospective memory response was not carried out. Thus, the person may not be aware that the door was left unlocked until he or she returns home. A similar post hoc awareness of an error response may occur in commission errors, that is, executing the PM response in the absence of the prospective memory cue. One may lock the front door and then realize (Oops! experience) that they should not have done it because they were only going out, for example, in the garden and need not do it.

Another metacognitive experience in prospective memory is BIM (Moraitou & Efklides, 2009; Efklides & Touroutoglou, 2010), in which the person fails to remember a prospective memory goal while fulfilling a particular task. The BIM experience is presumably the product of monitoring processes, but it involves monitoring of the goal memory rather than the prospective memory response. Goal maintenance in memory is a necessary precondition for the triggering of goal-related actions and successful comparison of the goal with the response outcome. This feedback is essential for concluding the course of action initiated by the goal and triggering the next action necessary to fulfill that goal. For example, if an initial goal was interrupted and triggered action related to a secondary task, then the feedback from output monitoring of the secondary task is necessary for the triggering of the resumption of the main task.

BIM VERSUS TOT EXPERIENCE

To place the BIM experience in everyday life, consider the following example. Suppose you are writing a chapter for a book and need to verify whether the conceptualization of one phenomenon you are writing about is correct. To do this, you interrupt the writing and search for the information in a search engine program. The search engine program produces a number of results and you start reading them. You find an interesting article that you would like to read, and so you open a new window for it. As you read it, you find a new reference you want to check and start searching for it. After a number of such efforts, you suddenly realize that you do not remember why you are reading the particular article you located: "What was I looking for?" "Why am I reading it?" "Why did I start the search in the search engine program?" This is a typical situation in which prospective memory is called on to support the intention to perform a secondary task and resume the main task when a particular cue is present (in our example, when you find the required information). Alternatively, you may carry out successfully the activity related to the secondary goal, but when you need to resume the main task, you experience BIM: "What do I need to do next?" What is failing in this second case is access to the resumption goal.

In such situations, the BIM is associated with a strong sense that the missing goal *cannot* be accessed. Moreover, there is no awareness of some part of the sought-after memory, as is the case in TOT states. On the contrary, there is no clue that could allow guided memory search. This awareness of lack of access to the prospective memory goal is associated with a frustrating feeling, and the only way to regain access to the missing goal is to go back to the main task and the activity that led to the secondary or the resumption goal. Moraitou and Efklides (2009), using a questionnaire addressing BIM, found that the BIM factor correlated positively ($r = .465$) with the Negative Affect factor that comprised items such as "I was distressed," "I was embarrassed," "I got angry with myself."

Phenomenologically, BIM may be different from TOT. TOT is frequently associated with partial or inaccurate information in consciousness (the persistent alternate) and a strong feeling that retrieval is imminent (Bacon, 2010; Metcalfe, 2000; Schwartz, 2002; see Brown, 2012 for a review). Our research suggests that both partial information and the sense of imminence may be lacking in BIM. Moraitou and Efklides (2009) investigated people's ideas about the nature of BIM using a BIM questionnaire. They found that BIM as a total failure to access the goal of an intended activity (e.g., "Suddenly I felt a blank in my thought because I forgot what I wanted to say") is distinct from the experience of "blank" associated with lack of knowledge (e.g., "I did not understand the question at all because it referred to unknown concepts"). In the latter case, one cannot retrieve information from semantic memory, possibly because it was never encoded.

THEORIES OF PROSPECTIVE MEMORY FAILURE

People usually manage suspended goals efficiently. Yet forgetting intentions established after an interruption is present in all ages and particularly in old age (Maylor, Darby, & Della Salla, 2000). Indeed, in demanding situations such as multitasking, forgetting of intentions is rapid (Einstein et al., 2003). This is very important because prospective memory failures (e.g., forgetting to carry out a final task step after the main goal has been accomplished) can lead to accidents (e.g., forget to turn off the electric power switch after you remove a burning pot from the fire) caused by human error (Li, Blandford, Cairns, & Young, 2008).

Preparatory-Attention-and-Memory theory was developed to explain prospective memory failures (Smith, 2003; Smith & Bayen, 2004; see also Hicks, Marsh, & Cook, 2005; Loft, Kearney, & Remington, 2008; Marsh & Hicks, 1998). One of the reasons for prospective memory failure is that prospective memory involves cognitive processes that draw on attention and working memory resources, thus slowing down main task performance when a prospective memory task is added to it. Hence, if the main task is demanding, then insufficient resources are available for the prospective memory task (Einstein, Smith, McDaniel, & Shaw, 1997). Sugimori and Kusumi (2009) showed that limited attention resources influenced not only prospective memory performance, but also prospective memory input and output monitoring, even in cases of correct prospective memory response. That is, people inferred or guessed the presence of the correct prospective memory cue (in old/new judgments) rather than retrieve it and were uncertain whether they had executed the required response. This suggests that increased demands on cognitive resources in the main task could explain prospective memory failures, but could also trigger BIM states when the goal of the prospective memory task is not maintained in memory because of lack of resources.

Study 1: Demands on Cognitive Resources

Efklides and Touroutoglou (2010) tested the hypothesis that increased working memory demands will increase prospective memory failures and BIM as well as other prospective memory failure-related experiences. These include experiences such as TOTs, and awareness of omission and commission errors. They also tested the hypothesis that BIM experiences will not correlate with TOT states, because phenomenologically the two experiences are different, and presumably the outcome of different underlying cognitive processes is different as well (i.e., prospective versus retrospective memory). Moreover, BIM self-reports should not be correlated with reports of omission or commission errors. In the case of omission or commission errors, the person either is not aware they committed an error or realizes that an error was committed after it has been committed (output monitoring). In both cases there is no blank in the mind.

Method

The sample comprised 110 university students of both genders. Participation was voluntary. Participants were tested on a computer that recorded both accuracy of response and reaction time. E-prime (Schneider, Eschman, & Zuccolotto, 2002) was used for the programming of the tasks.

The tasks were as follows: A reading comprehension task was presented. This task formed the context for the prospective memory task. After the participants had read the text, they continued to an arithmetic operations task (ongoing/main task). The researchers instructed participants that when they came across a particular number, they should press the spacebar (prospective memory task) to answer a question on the text they had studied. For example, when a block of arithmetic operations started, the instruction was that when participants came across number 15 – e.g., 27−12 = 15 – they should press SPACE, instead of ENTER, which led to the next item, to answer a text comprehension question. After they had answered the text comprehension question, a new block of arithmetic operations items started and a new number (e.g., 11) was defined as the cue for pressing the SPACE key. There were six blocks of arithmetic operations and six prospective memory responses respectively.

Unlike the typical prospective memory task in which the cue is standard across trials, in this study the cue changed from one block of trials to the next. This was done because repetition of the same cue and prospective memory response strengthens the prospective memory goal and therefore decreases the possibility for the BIM experience. A BIM experience in this type of task would be: "What do I have to press now: Enter or Space?" Moreover, change of the cue from one block to the next increases the probability of cue interference and triggering of a TOT experience. For example, remembering part of the cue number (e.g., "It was 1…, 11 or 15?").

Finally, after the six blocks of items were finished, participants were asked to respond to a Metacognitive Experiences Questionnaire tapping various metacognitive experiences such as BIM, TOT, and others. The instruction was to answer the question "How many times during the previous tasks did you…" Responses were on a five-point Likert-type scale ranging from 1 = never to 5 = all the time. There were 12 items. Example items (and their conceptualization) are given as follows.

How many times did you correctly press the SPACE key? (Awareness of the correct response);

"How many times did you fail to remember what you had to press: The SPACE or the ENTER key?" (Possible[1] BIM);

"How many times could you recall one or more digits of the cue number but failed to recall the whole number?" (Possible TOT);

"How many times did you experience a blank-in-the-mind state?" (Explicit BIM);

"How many times did you experience a tip-of-the-tongue state?" (Explicit TOT);

"How many times did you failed to press the SPACE key?"(Omission error);

"How many times did you recognize the cue but failed to press the SPACE key?" (Omission error);

"How many times did you fail to press ENTER and pressed SPACE instead?" (Commission error); and

"How many times did you feel uncertain as to whether you had pressed the SPACE or the ENTER key?" (Failure of output monitoring).

To test the effects of working memory load, the study used two types of prospective memory tasks: event-based, that is, prospective memory tasks with a specific cue each time (e.g., number 15) and activity-based prospective memory tasks. In the latter case, the participants were instructed to press the SPACE key after they had answered a number of items (e.g., 5). The difference between the two types of task is that in event-based tasks, monitoring of the cue can be based on automatic processes, whereas in the activity-based tasks, monitoring of the number of executed responses is deliberate and effortful. To make the demands on working memory even more pronounced, there were two conditions in each type of task: a high working memory load condition, in which an *n*-back task was embedded in the event- and the activity-based task, and a low working memory load with no *n*-back task embedded. In the *n*-back groups, the participants carried out the event- or activity-based task and at the same time they had to remember the last digit of the first number of the two involved in each arithmetic operation.

Results

Performance. The results showed that only working memory load affected prospective memory performance, $F(1, 101) = 3.99$, $p < .05$, partial $\eta^2 = .03$. (See Table 11.1 for the means of the four groups.) Working memory load decreased correct prospective memory performance ($M = 3.95$ for the *n*-back groups and $M = 4.52$ for the no *n*-back groups, respectively). Type of task did not have any significant effect on correct prospective memory performance. Working memory load also affected the number of omission errors; it increased the number of omission errors, $F(1, 101) = 3.99$, $p < .05$, $\eta^2_p = .03$ ($M = 2.04$ for the *n*-back groups vs. $M = 1.48$ for the no *n*-back groups), as well as the RT, $F(1, 101) = 15.11$, $p < .001$, $\eta^2_p = .13$ ($M = 11233.54$ for the *n*-back groups and $M = 5588.22$ for the no *n*-back groups). Working memory load, however, did not significantly increase the number of commission errors and decreased their RT, $F(1, 101) = 4.78$, $p < .05$, $\eta^2_p = .04$ ($M = 2360.08$ for the *n*-back groups and $M = 6664.08$ for the no *n*-back groups). These findings are in line with the Preparatory-Attention-and-Memory theory because increase of working memory load in the main task left fewer resources available for the prospective memory task and hence increased incorrect prospective memory performance and omission errors, probably because of less effective input monitoring (e.g., not recognizing the cue for the prospective memory response). High working memory load did not increase commission errors, possibly because of lack of resources for keeping the intended response (i.e., SPACE) active in working memory along with the monitoring of the prospective memory cue and the *n*-back task. However, when this rehearsing-of-the-response strategy was used and led to commission errors, the RT was significantly decreased, possibly because the person did not make any effort to monitor the prospective memory cue and execute the *n*-back task.

Metacognitive experiences. The ANOVAs regarding the responses to the Metacognitive Experiences Questionnaire are presented in Table 11.2. (Mean responses to the various items of the Metacognitive Questionnaire

TABLE 11.1. *Means and standard deviations of prospective memory performance and Metacognitive Questionnaire responses in Study 1*

Group	Performance			
	Event-based	Activity-based	Event-based *n*-back	Activity-based *n*-back
Variable	M(SD)	M(SD)	M(SD)	M(SD)
Correct PM response	4.56(1.31)	4.48(1.55)	4.30(1.42)	3.61(1.44)
Omissions	1.44(1.31)	1.52(1.55)	1.70(1.43)	2.39(1.44)
Commissions	0.65(1.31)	0.78(1.18)	0.13(0.55)	0.54(0.74)
RT of correct PM response	14272.92 (8219.45)	20155.66 (11065.48)	24000.39 (13775.02)	15535.11 (8490.36)
RT of omission errors	4575.48 (4216.28)	6600.96 (7075.52)	9804.69 (7640.24)	12662.39 (9644.82)
RT of commission errors	6009.61 (14098.83)	7318.55 (12264.92)	1031.17 (2556.63)	3689.00 (5901.75)
		Metacognitive Questionnaire*		
Explicit BIM	2.34(0.83)	2.48(0.97)	2.83(1.03)	2.53(1.03)
Explicit TOT	2.22(1.18)	2.07(0.87)	2.22(1.17)	2.78(1.10)
Which key to press (possible BIM)	1.66(0.79)	2.04(1.05)	1.61(0.89)	2.71(1.15)
Possible TOT (Remembering only part of the cue)	1.44(0.67)	1.59(0.79)	2.39(1.34)	2.57(1.17)
Awareness of omission errors (not pressing SPACE)	1.88(0.87)	2.19(0.92)	1.91(0.95)	3.03(1.10)
Awareness of omission errors (Awareness of cue and not pressing SPACE)	1.88(1.16)	2.04(1.12)	1.43(0.66)	2.64(1.31)
Awareness of commission errors (press SPACE instead of ENTER)	1.28(0.52)	1.48(0.85)	1.26(0.62)	1.96(1.10)
Uncertainty about response (failure of output monitoring)	1.78(0.66)	2.07(0.83)	2.35(1.11)	3.21(0.99)

Note: The symbols PM, BIM, TOT, and RT denote Prospective memory, Blank in the Mind, Tip of the Tongue, and Response time, respectively.

* The response scale to the Metacognitive Questionnaire items ranged from 1 = never to 5 = all the time.

TABLE 11.2. *Working-memory and type-of-task effects on the items of the Metacognitive Experiences Questionnaire (Study 1)*

Item	Working memory effect	Type of task effect	Working memory X Type of task
Explicit BIM	–	–	–
Explicit TOT	–	–	–
Possible BIM (failing to remember which key to press)	–	$F(1,106) = 15.66$ $p < .001$, $\eta^2_p = .13$	–
Possible TOT (Remembering only part of the cue)	$F(1, 106) = 25.15$ $p < .001$, $\eta^2_p = .19$	–	–
Awareness of omission errors (not pressing SPACE)	$F(1, 106) = 5.77$ $p < .05$, $\eta^2_p = .05$	$F(1, 106) = 15.00$ $p < .001$, $\eta^2_p = .12$	$F(1, 106) = 8.09$ $p < .01$, $\eta^2_p = .07$
Awareness of omission errors (Awareness of cue and not pressing SPACE)	$F(1, 106) = 10.33$ $p < .01$, $\eta^2_p = .09$	–	–
Awareness of commission errors (press SPACE instead of ENTER)		$F(1, 106) = 8.55$ $p < .01$, $\eta^2_p = .07$	
Uncertainty about response (failure of output monitoring)	$F(1, 106) = 24.56$ $p < .001$, $\eta^2_p = .19$	$F(1, 106) = 11.33$ $p < .001$, $\eta^2_p = .09$	–

are shown in Table 11.1.) What is worth noting in Table 11.2 is that neither working memory load nor type of task had any effect on the self-reported incidence of BIM or TOT states, although participants did report having experienced occasionally both BIM and TOT. Moreover, in contrast with the performance and RT data, working memory load was not the only factor that differentiated responses on metacognitive experiences; type of task was also a significant factor. Specifically, activity-based prospective memory groups reported higher (a) incidence of failure to remember which key to press (possible BIM) ($M = 2.37$) and (b) awareness of commission errors ($M = 1.72$) than the event-based prospective memory groups ($M = 1.63$ and $M = 1.27$ for possible BIM and commission errors, respectively). Working memory load influenced the self-reported frequency of (a) remembering only part of the cue (possible TOT) ($M = 2.48$ for the *n*-back groups and $M = 1.51$ for the no *n*-back groups) and (b) being aware of the cue and not pressing SPACE (awareness of omission errors) (M = 2.03 for the n-back groups and M = 1.96 for the no n-back groups). Both working memory load and type of task influenced responses to the items tapping "not pressing the SPACE key" (omission errors) and uncertainty about the execution of the intended action (failure of output monitoring). The n-back groups reported more omission errors (M = 2.47) than the no n-back groups (M = 2.03), and the activity-based groups (M = 2.61) more omission errors than the event-based groups (M = 1.89). Uncertainty was higher in the n-back groups (M = 2.78) compared to the no n-back groups (M = 1.92) and so was in the activity-based groups (M = 2.64) compared to the event-based groups (M = 2.06).

Finally, the correlations between the items directly addressing BIM and TOT with any of the performance measures (correct performance, number of omission errors, and number of commission errors) were not significant. The BIM and TOT items did not correlate between them either, nor with any of the other metacognitive experiences responses. The only correlations of the item tapping possible BIM (i.e., failure to retrieve which key to press) were with actual commission errors (r = .78, p < .01) and the RT of commission errors (r = .71, p < .01) in the event-based/n-back group.

Summary and Discussion
To summarize, the Efklides and Touroutoglou (2010) study provided evidence that working memory load negatively affected prospective memory performance, as Hypothesis 1 had predicted. This prospective memory failure was associated with increased number of omission errors as well as higher awareness of omission errors, (possible) TOTs (remembering only part of the cue), and uncertainty about the execution of the prospective memory response. These findings are in line with Hypothesis 1 as well. However, working memory load did not affect self-reports of TOT, BIM, and commission errors, contrary to Hypothesis 1. These findings suggest that the Preparatory-Attention-and-Memory theory cannot explain all of the metacognitive experiences in a prospective memory task. Working memory load, however, has been found by Schwartz (2008) to decrease the number of TOTs in a general knowledge task, contrary to the findings of this study. An explanation could be that in Schwartz's study, TOT was defined as imminence of recall rather than as lack of accessibility or partial accessibility of the targeted information as in the case of (possible) TOT in this study. Therefore, it is not clear if the apparently contradictory findings as regards the effect of working memory load on TOTs are due to the

prospective character of the present task or to different conceptualization of the phenomena related to TOT states.

The results also showed that although type of task, that is, event-/activity-based prospective memory task, did not have any effect at the cognitive level (performance or RT), it did have on some of the metacognitive experiences. Specifically, in the activity-based groups there was increased awareness of (possible) BIMs and commission errors as well as of omission errors and uncertainty about the execution of the prospective memory response. In the case of the latter two responses, one could argue that explicit monitoring of the number of responses performed added to the working memory load already imposed by the n-back task, and hence the Preparatory-Attention-and-Memory theory can explain the effect of type of task. But this explanation cannot account for the finding that type of task did not have any effect at the cognitive level. It cannot explain either why the activity-based task had an effect on the reporting of possible BIM and commission errors. An alternative explanation could be that the engagement with explicit monitoring of the number of responses performed in the activity-based groups created the sense that participants could not remember which key they should press (possible BIM), and hence they should focus on the rehearsing of the prospective memory response (SPACE). The latter led to the perception that they had pressed SPACE even in the absence of the prospective memory cue (i.e., commission errors). Similarly, explicit monitoring of the number of responses performed in the activity-based groups increased the uncertainty about the prospective memory response carried out, and hence created the sense that they had omitted it.

However, when participants were directly asked if they had experienced BIM or TOT, their response was not affected by either working memory load or type of task. These findings are in contrast with the findings that awareness of possible BIM and TOT were influenced by the type of task and working memory load, respectively. One explanation could be that the items on possible BIM or TOT captured only a limited aspect of the broader phenomena of BIM and TOT, as conceptualized by the participants. One limitation of the study was that participants were not given instructions on the conceptualization of BIM and TOT.

The lack of any correlation between the direct BIM and direct TOT items, and between them and the other items of the Metacognitive Experiences Questionnaire may reflect the fact that responses on BIM, TOT, and the other metacognitive experiences are influenced by different factors, as Hypothesis 2 and Hypothesis 3 predicted. However, it may also be the case that the conceptualization of BIM and TOT was not clear. A further word of caution is needed here, because self-reports of metacognitive experiences were retrospective; that is, they were made after the completion of the whole set of arithmetic items and not immediately after the prospective memory responses. This may have compromised the accuracy of self-reports.

Study 2: Interruption and Prospective Memory

The fact that working memory load did not affect the self-reported states of BIM or possible BIM suggests that the Preparatory-Attention-and-Memory theory cannot account for the awareness that the prospective memory goal was not maintained in memory. The assumption underlying our research on BIM is that the prospective memory goal is initially encoded, but then, if not rehearsed to remain active in memory, is losing part of its activation. This creates the experience of blank, namely, not having access to the prospective memory goal although the person knows that the goal was initially present in memory. This assumption implies that what is important for BIM is the memory of goals. Altman and Trafton (2002) have developed a model for the activation of memory for goals. In Study 2, the memory-for-goals framework was adopted and a new experimental paradigm was used. In what follows, the rationale of Study 2 is presented along with the experimental paradigm used and the evidence generated.

When an ongoing task is interrupted, the person forms an intention: to respond to the requirements of the interruption task and then resume the suspended goal (Dodhia & Dismukes, 2009). This is a prospective memory task. Researchers have found, however, that after an interruption, people take longer to resume the interrupted task and may even forget to go back to it. Nevertheless, not all interruptions of an ongoing task have a negative effect on post-interruption performance (Monk et al., 2008). According to Altman and Trafton's (2002) memory-for-goals model, the level of goal activation is critical for post-interruption performance. Goal activation is measured by the time needed to resume the suspended goal. The higher the goal activation, the shorter the time lag is for the resumption of the suspended goal. Activation decay means longer resumption times and even failure to carry out the suspended goal. Frequently sampled or recently encoded or retrieved goals have higher levels of activation and therefore do not suffer activation decay after an interruption. Altman and Trafton (2002) demonstrated that goal activation reaches its highest level about two seconds after the goal is installed. From two to six seconds, there is a sharp activation decrease that reaches an asymptotic level at about 30 seconds. When a goal is interrupted by another goal, the initial goal immediately begins to suffer activation decay. However, because activation decay reaches an asymptotic level after 30 seconds, interruptions that last longer than 30 seconds do not have further implications for goal resumption compared to interruptions that last up to 30 seconds. Einstein and colleagues (2003) showed that forgetting of intentions was rapid when the delay between goal setting and the cue for enactment of the intention lasted 5, 15, or 40 seconds. These findings imply that if BIM is associated with decay of activation of goal memory, the highest incidence of BIM experience should be observed if the interruption occurs between six and 30 to 40 seconds after the initiation of the ongoing task and should be seen less frequently after two-second delays.

Pontikakis[2] (Ποντικάκης, 2011) tested the assumption that if BIM is due to inability to retain the prospective memory goal in memory, then the BIM experience will be more frequent in tasks in which the interruption occurs six seconds after the beginning of an item of the ongoing task rather than after two seconds. Moreover, decrease of goal activation would lead to (a) prospective memory failures due to increase of omission errors; (b) it should not lead to commission errors because in this case, goal activation should be strong in order to control the prospective memory response.

A second aim of the study was to test the accuracy of post hoc self-reports on metacognitive experiences and to compare such reports to BIM and TOT experiences that are measured during the execution of the response to the prospective memory task.

Method
Design and Participants
Sixty participants, including 22 males and 38 females, took part in this study. All of the participants were university students (mean age 23.5 years) and participated voluntarily.

To test the aforementioned predictions, a modified version of the Dodhia and Dismukes (2009) experimental paradigm was used. In this paradigm, there is an ongoing task (e.g., answer general knowledge questions) and an interruption that occurs unexpectedly because some other type of task is presented. When the interrupting task (e.g., carry out arithmetic operations) is completed and the prospective memory cue appears on the screen, the person has to remember to go back to the interrupted task and finish it. (More details are given in the description of the Pontikakis study.)

In the Pontikakis study, participants responded to multiple choice items organized in groups of six items of the same category. There were four categories of items: general information, vocabulary, analogies, and arithmetic operations. In total there were 10 blocks of four groups of six items each

Condition	Ongoing task			Loading screen	PM response	Ongoing task
No Interruption	Block 1: Group 1, 2, 3, 4			Yes	ENTER	Block 2: Group 1, 2, 3, 4
Interruption	Block 1: Group1(Item 1,..)	Int err upt ion	Block 2: Group 1,2,3,4	Yes	SPACE	Block 1: Group 1(cont.), 2, 3, 4

FIGURE 11.1. A diagram of the experimental procedure in Study 1.

(N = 240 items). All four types of groups of items were represented in each block. When the four groups of items of a block had been completed, a screen appeared for two and a half seconds that informed the participant that the next block of items was loading (loading screen). This was the cue that the person had to decide whether to press ENTER to go on with the next block of items or press SPACE in the case of interruptions and go back to the interrupted task and finish it. The decision to press either "SPACE" or "ENTER" was the prospective memory task. There were two groups of participants: One had the interruptions two seconds after the presentation of an item. The other group had the interruptions six seconds after the presentation of an item. In each condition (two or six seconds), there were items that were interrupted and others that were not interrupted at all (this served as the control). Before the item was answered, the screen abruptly changed and a new block of items started. This was the interruption task. The first group of items of the interruption task was always different from the interrupted group. That is, if the interrupted group was arithmetic operations, the new group was one of the following: analogies, vocabulary, or general information. When the interrupting block of items was completed and the loading screen appeared, the person had to remember to press SPACE to go back to the interrupted group and continue with the items of that block. If the person failed to press SPACE and pressed ENTER (omission error), then the next block of items appeared. (A diagrammatic presentation of the procedure is given in Figure 11.1.)

Interruptions. There were seven interruptions in each condition, distributed in different blocks. However, in three of the interruptions, there were participants who had already responded to the item – in the condition of six seconds – before the interruption occurred (i.e., it took them less than six seconds to give the answer to that item). For this reason, only four interruptions were included in the analyses. The first interruption occurred in the first block (first group of items, third item); the second interruption in the fourth block (third group, fifth item); the third interruption occurred in the fifth block (first group, second item); and the fourth interruption occurred in the ninth block (third group, fourth item).

Interruption delay and implications for prospective memory performance and BIM. The time allowed for responding to each item was 15 seconds. If the person did not answer in 15 seconds, the next item of the group appeared on the screen. This implies that the lag between the beginning of a group of items (when the ongoing task goal for that set of items is instated along with the conditional prospective memory goal) and the occurrence of the interruption (re-instatement of the prospective memory goal) ranged from 30 to 45 seconds maximum (first and third interruption, respectively) to 60 and 75 seconds maximum (fourth and second interruption, respectively). However, in terms of true time spent on each item (average RT per item = 7 seconds), the time elapsed between the initial goal instatement and the reinstatement of the prospective memory goal was 14 and 21 seconds for the first and third interruptions and 28 and 35 seconds for the fourth and seconds interruptions, respectively. This implies that the maximum decrease of the prospective memory goal activation should be observed in the fourth and second interruptions.

From the point of view of BIM, the prediction was that the probability for BIM would be higher in the second and fourth interruptions compared to the other two interruptions (first and third) because BIM presupposes a dissociation between the prospective memory goal and the cue (loading screen) for the enactment of the intention. That is, there would be more BIM states if the prospective memory goal were not highly active. In such a case, the person would be wondering which key to press when the loading screen was presented because part of the prospective memory goal – cue pair – would not be available.

Metacognitive experiences. Participants were explicitly instructed at the beginning of the experiment on the meaning of TOT and BIM experience. The instructions were as follows: People often feel that they know an answer, but at that moment they cannot retrieve it or remember only part of the answer. This is experienced as having the answer at the tip of their tongue.

For example, "The Greek revolution took place in 18…" People may also feel that they had something in their mind and knew what they would have to do, but suddenly they do not recall it anymore and it is as if they have a blank in their mind. For example, "What did I have to do now?"

Following all prospective memory responses (i.e., the pressing of ENTER or SPACE after the seven interruptions) and another seven random trials (after a response to an item), a screen appeared in which two questions appeared: "Did you experience BIM? Yes/No" and "Did you experience TOT? Yes/No." These items represented concurrent reports of metacognitive experiences.

After the whole set of blocks of items was answered, the Metacognitive Experiences Questionnaire of Efklides and Touroutoglou (2010) was administered, adapted to the characteristics of the present task. These questions represented retrospective self-reports of metacognitive experiences. Fifteen questions tapped monitoring of correct prospective memory responses, omission and commission errors, BIM, and TOT, as well as experiences denoting possible BIM and TOT, and failure of input and output monitoring (see Appendix A).

Results
As hypothesized, the comparison of the two conditions of interruption showed that the two-second group had more correct prospective memory performance ($M = .80$) than the six-second group in the second interruption ($M = .60$), $t(58) = 11.05$, $p = .002$, Cohen's $d = .87$, and in the fourth interruption, $t = 11.05$, $p = .002$, Cohen's $d = .87$. ($M = .80$ and $M = .60$, for the two-second and six-second group, respectively). In these interruptions, the time lag between the beginning of the group of items and the occurrence of the interruption was about 28 to 35 seconds. The six-second condition had more prospective memory failures than the two-second condition, specifically omission errors, in all interruptions (see Table 11.3). In contrast, there was no difference between conditions in commission error rates. Despite the differences in performance, no RT differences appeared in prospective memory responses (both correct and incorrect) in the two conditions. These results suggest that the difference of two versus six seconds impacted the memory for goals and prospective memory performance, but not RT in the execution of the prospective memory response, probably because the six-second condition had many omission errors, and therefore spent no extra time pondering whether to press ENTER or SPACE.

TABLE 11.3. *Means (and standard deviations) and t-tests of omission errors as a function of interruption condition (Study 2)*

Interruption/ condition	2 s M(SD)	6 s M(SD)	t-test	Cohen's d
Interruption 1	.23 (.43)	.50(.51)	$t(58) = 11.53$, $p = .001$	.89
Interruption 2	.17 (.38)	.37 (.49)	$t(58) = 12.91$, $p = .001$	.94
Interruption 3	.20 (.41)	.63 (.49)	$t(58) = 8.16$, $p = .006$	.75
Interruption 4	.17 (.38)	.37 (.49)	$t(58) = 12.91$, $p = .001$	.94

Concurrent BIM reports on the prospective memory responses (i.e., after interruption) did not differ between the two conditions except for the fourth interruption, in which the six-second group reported more BIM cases ($M = .47$) than the two-second ($M = .27$) group, $t(58) = 7.55$, $p = .008$, Cohen's $d = .72$. No significant difference appeared in TOT responses between the two- and six-second groups. There were also more BIM incidences in two (out of the seven) non-interruption trials in which the BIM and TOT questions were asked, $t(58) = 15.62$, $p < .001$ ($M = .53$ and $M = .20$, for the six-second and two-second condition, respectively). The difference between conditions in TOT responses was not significant in the non-interruption trials. The findings on BIM suggest that BIM is not necessarily associated with prospective memory failure or interruption of processing. The only case in which interruption was associated with BIM was the interruption that had occurred about 30 seconds after the beginning of the group of items (fourth interruption).

Post hoc reports of metacognitive experiences. No significant difference appeared between the two conditions as regards the post hoc reports of metacognitive experiences. However, differences occurred in the pattern of correlations between the responses to the various items in the two conditions (see Table 11.4).

(1) In both groups, the item on the *monitoring of correct prospective memory response* (Item 1) was positively related to the number of correct prospective memory responses ($r = .58$[3] and $r = .69$ for the two-second and six-second condition, respectively). This finding attests

TABLE 11.4. Correlations between items of the Metacognitive Questionnaire (Study 2) related to BIM and TOT as a function of condition (two seconds and six seconds)

Item	1	2	3	4	5	6	7	8	9	10	11	12	13	14	15
3											.58	.58/ .47	-.62	.54	
7															
9											.54			.59	
10														.52	
12		-.55		.58						.50	.60		.52	.71/ .53	
14		-.62		.76				.63/ .56			.57		.62	.53	

Note: Correlations of condition six seconds are given after the "/". All ps <.003

The content of the items is as follows:

1. How many times did you remember to press SPACE when you should?
2. How many times did you press SPACE instead of ENTER?
3. How many times did it happen that you saw the screen "loading the next block" and you were not able to remember what you had to do?
4. How many times do you think you missed to press SPACE when you should?
5. How many times did it happen that you pressed SPACE without there being an interruption?
6. How many times did it happen that you pressed ENTER while you knew it was wrong?
7. How many times did you experience a blank in your mind?
8. How many times did you feel uncertain whether an interruption had taken place as you proceeded with the questions?
9. How many times did it happen that you remembered part of the answer and not the whole of it?
10. How many times did you experience a tip-of-the-tongue state?
11. How many times did you feel uncertain whether you had pressed ENTER or SPACE?
12. How many times did it happen that you were not able to remember what you had to press: ENTER or SPACE?
13. How many times do you think you missed to press ENTER while you should?
14. How many times did you feel that what you wanted to press (ENTER or SPACE) was not the correct response?
15. How many times did it happen that you had the response for a moment in your mind and then felt a blank, and were not able to remember it?

250

to the validity of retrospective self-reports. Moreover, monitoring of correct prospective memory response was negatively related to the number of actual omission errors ($r = -.70$), but only in the six-second condition. This suggests that the monitoring of correct prospective memory responses is taking into consideration failures in the prospective memory response, but such failures need to be quite prominent as in the condition of six seconds. In this condition, there were more omission errors compared to the two-second condition.

(2) The *item directly tapping BIM* (Item 7; "How many times did you experience BIM?") was positively correlated with the concurrent reports of BIM in both conditions ($r = .51$ and $r = .53$ for the two-second and six-second conditions, respectively) and with concurrent BIM ($r = .53$ in non-interruption items) in the two-second condition. There was no correlation of Item 7 with Item 10 that directly tapped TOT or with other items of the Metacognitive Questionnaire.

(3) The item tapping *possible BIM* (Item 3; "How many times did it happen that you saw the loading screen and you were not able to remember what you had to do?") correlated, $r = .58$ and $r = .47$ in the two-second and six-second condition respectively, with Item 12 (possible BIM; "How many times did it happen that you were not able to remember what you had to press: ENTER or SPACE?"). Item 3 also correlated, $r = .53$, with correct prospective memory response and $r = -.55$ with actual number of omission errors, but only in the six-second condition. This means that the possible BIM experience in the six-second condition was successfully resolved, and the momentary blank was replaced by retrieval of the prospective memory goal.

In the two-second group, Item 3 was negatively related to Item 13 (omission of the ENTER response), $r = -.62$, and to Item 14 ("How many times did you feel that what you wanted to press (ENTER or SPACE) was not correct"), $r = .54$. This suggests that the possible BIM in the two-second condition was not successfully resolved and the participants associated it with omission errors or a sense that the response they were to execute was incorrect.

(4) Item 12 (possible BIM; "How many times did it happen that you were not able to remember what you had to press: ENTER or SPACE?") was positively related to Item 14 ("How many times did you feel that the key you wanted to press (ENTER or SPACE) was not the correct response?") in both groups, $r = .71$ and $r = .53$ for the two-second and six-second condition, respectively. Item 12 was also related, $r = .50$,

to Item 10 (explicit TOT), but only in the two-second condition. It seems that in the two-second condition there was some confusion as regards BIM and TOT. That is, failure to remember which key to press was not understood as "blank," but as difficulty with retrieving the required response due to some interference of the ENTER to the SPACE response. In the two-second condition, Item 12 was also negatively related to Item 1 (monitoring of correct response), $r = -.55$, and positively related to Item 4 (omission of SPACE), $r = .58$. Also, Item 12 correlated with Item 11 (failure of output monitoring), $r = .60$, and Item 13 (omission of ENTER), $r = .52$ only in the two-second condition. All these correlations in the two-second condition suggest a strong difficulty with deciding which key to press in the prospective memory response, which gave the sense that one did not respond correctly or omitted the correct response, despite the fact that the actual number of omission errors in this condition was lower than in the six-second condition.

(5) Item 10 *tapping TOT* ("How many times did you experience TOT?") was positively associated with concurrent TOT reports in interruption items in both conditions, $r = .69$ and $.58$, and non-interruption items, $r = .71$ and $.50$ for the two-second and six-second condition, respectively. However, there was no correlation with the other items of the Metacognitive Experiences Questionnaire as with the direct BIM item (Item 7). Only in the two-second condition was Item 10 related, $r = .52$, with Item 14 (feeling that the response ENTER or SPACE was not correct).

(6) Item 9 tapping *possible TOT* ("How many times did it happen that you remembered part of the answer and not the whole of it?") correlated, $r = .54$, with Item 11 ("How many times did you feel uncertain whether you had pressed ENTER or SPACE") and $r = .59$ with Item 14 (feeling that the response ENTER or SPACE was not correct). These findings, along with those of Item 10, suggest that TOT states can be associated with failure of output monitoring or a sense that the prospective memory response was not correct. However, this was specific to the two-second and not the six-second condition.

(7) Item 14 tapping possible TOT ("How many times did you feel that what you wanted to press (ENTER or SPACE) was not the correct response?") was related to item 8 ("How many times did you feel uncertain whether an interruption had taken place as you proceeded with the questions?"), $r = .63$ and $r = .56$, for the two-second and six-second condition, respectively. This finding suggests that the feeling

that the response that comes to mind is not correct was associated with failure of input monitoring, that is, that an interruption had occurred. Moreover, in the two-second condition, Item 14 was negatively related to Item 1 (monitoring of correct prospective memory response), $r = -.62$, and positively, $r = .76$, to Item 4 (omission of SPACE), $r = .57$ to Item 11 (failure of output monitoring) and $r = .62$ to Item 13 (omission of ENTER). These findings are in line with those of Item 9 and suggest that possible TOT was associated in the two-second condition with output monitoring.

Discussion

The study of Pontikakis (Ποντικάκης, 2011) described here provided evidence that goal memory is involved in prospective memory responses. That is, for omission errors, the six-second time lag from the instatement of the item-specific goal was sufficient to decrease the activation of the prospective memory goal and increase omission errors, namely, pressing ENTER instead of SPACE. For correct prospective memory response, the six-second time lag interacted with the time lag between the beginning of a group of items, when the prospective memory goal was instated, and the occurrence of interruption. That is, prospective memory correct response in the six-second condition was significantly lower than in the two-second condition only in cases in which interruption occurred at about 30 or 35 seconds (considering that mean response time per item was about seven seconds) after the initiation of the ongoing task. These findings suggest that omission errors were controlled by the processing of the interrupted item and not by the prospective memory goal. The prospective memory goal suffered from decrease of the memory-for-goal activation. Such a decrease of activation was most pronounced 30–35 seconds after the instatement of the prospective memory goal.

Concurrent reports of BIM were also more frequent in the 30–35-second time lag in the six-second group compared to the two-second condition. It is plausible that failure to reinstate the prospective memory goal when the interruption occurred created a dissociation of the initial prospective memory goal (press SPACE) and the cue (loading screen), and this led to the experience of momentary blank in the mind. However, the six-second group also reported more BIM experiences in non-interruption trials compared to the two-second group, although this was only for two out of seven items. This finding is hard to explain unless it means that BIM was associated with a blank during the execution of response to particular items as well. In this case, BIM might reflect lack of knowledge (see Moraitou &

Efklides, 2009). Finally, TOT concurrent reports did not differ between the two-second and six-second conditions. Therefore, there is some evidence in favor of the memory-for-goals model at the cognitive level, but this evidence is not so strong for BIM.

Post hoc reports of metacognitive experiences, such as awareness of prospective memory correct response, correlated with the number of prospective memory correct responses in both conditions. In the six-second condition, awareness of omission errors correlated with the number of omission errors. Moreover, the post hoc self-reports of BIM (Item 7) and TOT (Item 10) were associated with the respective concurrent reports of BIM and TOT in both conditions. This further attests to the validity of the post hoc reports of BIM and TOT.

As in the Efklides and Touroutoglou (2010) study, no correlation was found between the items directly tapping BIM and TOT in both conditions. Note that in this study participants received explicit instructions on the conceptualization of BIM and TOT. Therefore, this lack of association cannot be attributed to insufficient conceptualization of the two metacognitive states. Nevertheless, in both conditions, Items 3 and 12, denoting possible BIM, correlated between them, but not with Item 7 that directly asked about BIM. This finding suggests that BIM is not identical to what Items 3 and 12 describe, although each of them captures some aspect of the BIM state.

Similar lack of association was found between the item directly tapping TOT (Item 10) and Item 9 tapping possible TOT in both conditions. There was, however, a correlation with Item 14 in the two-second condition. In the two-second condition, TOT was associated with the feeling that the retrieved response was not correct. Item 14 is indicative of the persistent alternate in TOT states. The correlation with the TOT item suggests that, contrary to BIM states, in which there is blank in the mind, in TOT states, there is information in awareness, albeit tagged with the feeling that it is not correct. This feeling that the retrieved response was not correct (Item 14) seems to be also present in states of possible BIM (Item 3 and 12). This might explain why these items did not correlate with the BIM item (Item 7) but correlated with Item 14: they capture a failure in output monitoring (see correlations with Item 11) or conflict as regards the key to press rather than a blank. This explanation, however, requires further investigation because these correlations were only found in the two-second condition. There might be something specific about this condition – that is, there was correct responding at the cognitive level but strong sense of conflict of response at a metacognitive level. This was not the case in the condition

TABLE 11.5. *Position of interruption in the various blocks as a function of group of items and type of content (Study 3)*

Block	Group	Type of task	Position of interruption
1	1	Analogies	2nd item
2	3	Synonyms	6th item
3	2	Analogies	1st item
4	3	Arithmetic operations	5th item
5	1	General information	9th item
6	1	Arithmetic operations	3rd item
7	3	Synonyms	7th item
8	2	General information	1st item
9	3	Arithmetic operations	4th item
10	1	Synonyms	8th item

of six seconds, in which there were omission errors and less conflict over which key to press.

Study 3: More on Interruption and BIM

To replicate and extend the findings of Pontikakis (Ποντικάκης, 2011), Efklides, Dina, and Pontikakis (unpublished data) conducted an experiment following the same experimental paradigm. However, easy items in the Pontikakis study were removed and replaced with more difficult questions. Moreover, items were added in each group ($n = 10$), summing to a total of 400 items per participant. This allowed for more positions for interruption. There was one interruption in each block ($n = 10$). The interruptions occurred in the following positions (see Table 11.5).

The hypothesis was that if the memory-for-goal activation is critical for prospective memory and BIM, and there is sharp decrease after two seconds of goal instatement, then the six-second condition would have lower performance in the prospective memory task and more BIM experiences relative to the two-second condition, regardless of the position of the item that was interrupted. If, however, goal-memory activation continues to decrease in the period up to 30 seconds (Monk et al., 2008) or 40 seconds (Einstein et al., 2003), then there would be no difference in the prospective memory task and the number of BIM experiences between the two conditions (two seconds versus six seconds) in cases when the interruption occurred earlier than 30 seconds because there would still be sufficient activation of memory for the prospective memory goal. Instead, the difference would be located only in interruptions that occur in the period from 30 to 40 seconds, when the decrease of activation is highest, and there would be no difference between conditions in interruptions that occur after 40 seconds because goal decay levels off after this time. This implies that for the interruptions that occur in the first to the third item, there will be no difference between the two conditions (two seconds versus six seconds). Differences would be found in interruptions in the fourth to the sixth item (about 30 to 45 seconds since the beginning of a group of items), and there would be no difference in interruptions that occur in items 7 to 9 (time lag > 40 seconds).

Method

Participants and Design

There were 20 participants, all university students of psychology. Their average age was 20 years. They volunteered after an open invitation to participate in the study.

The task of the Pontikakis study with the modifications mentioned earlier was used. Accuracy of prospective memory response and reaction time of the prospective memory response were also recorded. As in the previous study, after each interruption and the prospective memory response, participants were asked if they had experienced BIM or TOT during their response after the loading screen. Similar questions were asked after response to items without interruption (control items). Finally, the Metacognitive Experiences Questionnaire with 15 items on metacognitive experiences that was administered in the Pontikakis study was used in this study as well.

Results

Prospective Memory Response Accuracy

A series of ANOVAs showed that there was no main effect of condition (two seconds versus six seconds). Furthermore, for interruptions that occurred in the first to the third item there was no difference between conditions (two seconds versus six seconds). For interruptions occurring in Items 4 to 6, there was an interaction of item by condition, $F (1, 18) = 6.785$ $p = 018$, $\eta^2_p = .27$. Prospective memory response in the interruption in Item 6 was more accurate in the two-second condition ($M = .90$) compared to the six-second condition (M = .40), although it was comparable in items 4 and 5. In the interruptions that occurred in the seventh to the ninth item, there was no main effect of condition, nor any interaction of condition with item.

Reaction Time

Unlike response accuracy, RT of prospective memory response did vary across items in interruptions that occurred in the first to the third item, $F(1, 17) = 6.59$, $p = .02$, $\eta^2_p = .28$. RT was longer in the six-second condition ($M = 7.05$) than in the two-second condition ($M = 6.88$). This is probably due to the higher activation of goal memory in the two-second condition. That is, in the six-second condition more time was needed to enact the goal to press SPACE. Despite this difference in RT, prospective memory performance did not differ between conditions in these items. This suggests that in the six-second condition sufficient activation remained to control the prospective memory response, but the activation decay led to higher resumption lag.

Concurrent BIM, TOT, and Retrospective Metacognitive Experiences

There were no significant differences between conditions in the concurrent BIM and TOT responses after the interruptions, although the BIM reports tended to be more in the six-second condition (M = 3.22) than in the two-second condition (M = 2.37). There was also no difference between conditions in the questions tapping BIM or TOT in the Metacognitive Experiences Questionnaire. There was only one difference in the item tapping commission errors with the two-second condition reporting more commission errors (M = 1.90) than the six-second condition (M = 1.20).

Finally, there were significant correlations between concurrent BIM responses and the BIM item and possible BIM items of the Metacognitive Experiences Questionnaire as well as between concurrent TOT responses and the respective post hoc self-reports of TOT and possible TOT. However, in the two-second condition there were also correlations between concurrent BIM responses and the TOT item of the Metacognitive Experiences Questionnaire.

Discussion

The study by Pontikakis had suggested that memory-for-goal activation might be involved in prospective memory responses and the BIM state. However, the current study did not show a consistent advantage of the two-second condition compared to six seconds as regards correct prospective memory response. The difference between the two conditions was limited to one item (the sixth item, about 42 seconds from the instatement of the prospective memory goal). In the Pontikakis study, the difference between conditions was in the fourth and fifth items (about 28 seconds and 35 seconds). This suggests that the critical period for memory-for-goals decay is about 30 to 40 seconds after the instatement of a goal. However, as the RT findings of this study showed, the decrease of goal memory likely starts six seconds after goal instatement, but the decrease has observable effects on behavior at about 30 to 40 seconds. However, unlike the Pontikakis study, there was no difference as regards omission errors between the two-second and six-second condition. Therefore, the goal-for-memory hypothesis was not conclusively confirmed. More research is needed to establish its relevance to prospective memory performance and BIM.

At the metacognitive level, there was no difference between conditions or interruption position as regards the number of concurrent BIM or TOT reported, although there was a tendency for more concurrent BIM in the six-second condition compared to the two-second condition. In the Pontikakis study, there were more concurrent BIM reports in the six-second condition than in the two-second condition, but the difference was significant in one item only. Therefore the puzzle of the mechanism that underlies BIM was not resolved. It should be noted, however, that the lack of significant differences between conditions might be due to the fact that there were more interruptions in this study compared to the Pontikakis study – one per package. This might have strengthened the activation of the prospective memory goal, thus leading to better performance and less BIM experiences.

GENERAL DISCUSSION

The BIM experience is a phenomenon associated with prospective memory failures, although not all prospective memory failures are accompanied by a BIM experience. Moreover, BIM may occur even with correct prospective memory performance, possibly because BIM triggers regulatory processes that end up with correct performance. This regulatory role of metacognitive experiences is also found in judgments of learning (Schwartz & Efklides, 2012) but does not entail that the regulatory strategy selected is always successful. For example, rehearsing of the prospective memory goal at the expense of the prospective memory cue can lead to commission errors, as the Efklides and Touroutoglou (2010) study suggested. In the Pontikakis study and Study 3, possible BIM and TOT states in the two-second condition were related to failure of input and output monitoring and awareness of omission errors. This suggests that possible BIM and TOT were not always able to trigger the prospective memory goal and control the prospective memory response. It might also be the case that prospective memory response was cognitively controlled (e.g., in the two-second condition, prospective memory performance was better or equal to that of six seconds in Pontikakis's study) but associated with an awareness of difficulty to access the cue or prospective memory goal at a metacognitive level. Thus, monitoring of one's metacognitive experiences followed the triggering of the prospective memory response rather than preceding and controlling it. In the six-second condition, the decay of the prospective memory goal created no conflict between the ENTER or SPACE response. Thus, there were fewer correlations of possible BIM or TOT with failures of input and output monitoring compared to the two-second condition. If BIM occurred, it informed on the lack of access to the required cue or goal. This awareness could then trigger a search strategy to resolve the impasse.

Up to now, our understanding of the processes that give rise to BIM has been limited. The studies reported in this chapter represent a first approximation to an understanding of the etiology of the BIM phenomenon. Efklides and Touroutoglou (2010) showed that working memory load increases prospective memory failures but not BIM, whereas the monitoring of memory contents increases BIM but not prospective memory failures. This suggests that BIM is based on monitoring processes, and there was interference between explicit monitoring of memory contents and implicit monitoring of the cue or goal that should trigger the prospective memory response.

The study by Pontikakis tested the hypothesis that BIM monitors memory-for-goal activation and therefore it manifests in cases in which goal activation is decreasing, that is, six seconds after the establishment of the goal. This hypothesis was only partly confirmed because not all interruptions in the six-second condition were associated with BIM. This led to the hypothesis that decreases in the activation of goal for memory in the period between two and six seconds is not so detrimental to produce BIM. Study 3 confirmed this. One could argue that there were many interruptions in Study 3 and therefore participants were keeping the prospective memory goal active in memory and were anticipating the occurrence of interruption in each package of items. This could indirectly argue in favor of the goal-for-memory hypothesis. Nevertheless, it is important to further evaluate the goal-for-memory hypothesis. One could decrease, for example, the number of interruptions to eliminate its impact on goal activation or create distractions that could decrease the anticipation of interruption.

To go back to the question posited in the title of this chapter: "Are BIM and TOT manifestations of the same underlying processes?" The evidence from the three studies reported here is not conclusive. Study 1 suggested that BIM is associated with explicit monitoring of contents of consciousness that limits the available resources for memory for goals. Indeed, decrease of memory-for-goal activation is, at least partly, involved in prospective memory failure and BIM. Memory-for-goal activation is not involved in TOT, and this suggests a different mechanism underlying BIM relative to TOTs. Furthermore, the items on BIM and TOT were not correlated between them in all of the three studies. But in the two-second condition in Study 2 and Study 3, possible BIM and TOT shared relations with awareness of omission errors and failure of input and output monitoring. Moreover, items of possible BIM and TOT correlated with the item tapping the feeling that the retrieved response was not correct. This feeling is characteristic of TOT states, but it seems it was also present in cases in which the person did not remember which key to press – a state representative of BIM. Therefore, in some cases, response interference may be attributed to some "blank" in the mind although TOT is present. This suggests that more complex processes might be at the basis of reports of BIM and TOT. That is, the cognitive component of BIM and TOT (lack of accessibility of memory content) cannot fully account for the role and the characteristics of the metacognitive experiences of BIM and TOT. It is important that future research disentangles the complexities of the two phenomena and the implications for memory monitoring and control.

APPENDIX A

Metacognitive Questionnaire

1. How many times did you remember to press SPACE when you should? (Monitoring of correct response)
2. How many times did you press SPACE instead of ENTER? (Awareness of commission errors)
3. How many times did it happen that you saw the screen "loading the next block" and you were not able to remember what you had to do? (Possible BIM)
4. How many times do you think you missed to press SPACE when you should?(Awareness of omission errors)

5. How many times did it happen that you pressed SPACE without there being an interruption? (Awareness of commission errors)

6. How many times did it happen that you pressed ENTER while you knew it was wrong? (Possible TOT)

7. How many times did you experience a blank in your mind? (BIM)

8. How many times did you feel uncertain whether an interruption had taken place as you proceeded with the questions? (Failure of input monitoring)

9. How many times did it happen to you to remember part of the answer and not the whole of it? (Possible TOT)

10. How many times did you experience a tip-of-the-tongue state? (TOT)

11. How many times did you feel uncertain whether you had pressed ENTER or SPACE? (Failure of output monitoring)

12. How many times did it happen that you were not able to remember what you had to press: ENTER or SPACE? (Possible BIM)

13. How many times do you think you missed to press ENTER while you should? (Awareness of omission errors)

14. How many times did you feel that what you wanted to press (ENTER or SPACE) was not the correct response? (Possible TOT)

15. How many times did it happen that you had the response for a moment in your mind and then felt a blank, and were not able to remember it? (Possible BIM)

NOTES

1. The term *possible* denotes that BIM or TOT are not mentioned explicitly in the item, but the authors' description of the experience was meant to represent BIM or TOT.
2. The study was the MA thesis of Pontikakis under the supervision of the author.
3. All *r*s are significant at $p < .003$.

REFERENCES

Altman, E. F., & Trafton, J. G. (2002). Memory for goals: An activation-based model. *Cognitive Science, 26*, 39–83.

Bacon, E. (2010). Further insight into cognitive and metacognitive processes of the tip-of-the-tongue state with an amnesic drug as cognitive tool. In A. Efklides & P. Misailidi (Eds.), *Trends and prospects in metacognition research* (pp. 81–104). New York: Springer.

Brown, A. S. (2012). *Tip of the tongue state*. New York: Psychology Press.

Dodhia, R. M., & Dismukes, R. K. (2009). Interruptions create prospective memory tasks. *Applied Cognitive Psychology*, 23, 73–89.

Efklides, A., Dina, F., & Pontikakis, N. (unpublished data). Goal memory and blank in the mind. School of Psychology, Aristotle University of Thessaloniki, Greece.

Efklides, A., & Touroutoglou, A. (2010). Prospective memory failure and the metacognitive experience of "blank in the mind." In A. Efklides & P. Misailidi (Eds.), *Trends and prospects in metacognition research* (pp. 105–126). New York: Springer.

Einstein, G. O., McDaniel, M. A., Williford, C. L., Pagan, J. L., & Dismukes, R. K. (2003). Forgetting of intentions in demanding situations is rapid. *Journal of Experimental Psychology: Applied*, 9, 147–162.

Einstein, G. O., Smith, R. E., McDaniel, M. A., & Shaw, P. (1997). Aging and prospective memory: The influence of increased task demands at encoding and retrieval. *Psychology and Aging*, 12(3), 479–488.

Hicks, J. L., Marsh, R. L., & Cook, G. I. (2005). Task interference in time-based, event-based, and dual intention prospective memory conditions. *Journal of Memory and Language*, 53(3), 430–444.

Koriat, A., Ben-Zur, H., & Sheffer, D. (1988). Telling the same story twice: Output monitoring and age. *Journal of Memory and Language*, 27, 23–39.

Li, S. Y. W., Blandford, A., Cairns, P., & Young, R. (2008). The effect of interruptions on postcompletion and other procedural errors: An account based on the activation-based goal memory model. *Journal of Experimental Psychology: Applied*, 14, 314–328.

Loft, S., Kearney, R., & Remington, R. (2008). Is task interference in event-based prospective memory dependent on cue presentation? *Memory and Cognition*, 36, 139–148.

Marsh, R. L., & Hicks, J. L. (1998). Event-based prospective memory and executive control of working memory. *Journal of Experimental Psychology: Learning, Memory, and Cognition*, 24(2), 336–349.

Marsh, R. L., Hicks, J. L., Hancock, T. W., & Munsayac, K. (2002). Investigating the output monitoring component of event-based prospective memory performance. *Memory and Cognition*, 30(2), 302–311.

Maylor, E. A., Darby, R. J., & Della Sala, S. (2000). Retrieval of performed versus to-be-performed tasks: A naturalistic study of the intention-superiority effect in normal aging and dementia. *Applied Cognitive Psychology*, 14, S83–S98.

McDaniel, M. A., & Einstein, G. O. (2000). Strategic and automatic processes in prospective memory retrieval: A multi-process framework. *Applied Cognitive Psychology*, 14, S127–S144.

Meier, B., Zimmerman, T. D., & Perrig, W. J. (2006). Retrieval experience in prospective memory: Strategic monitoring and spontaneous retrieval. *Memory*, 14, 872–889.

Metcalfe, J. (2000). Feelings and judgments of knowing: Is there a special noetic state? *Consciousness and Cognition*, 9, 178–186.

Monk, C. A., Trafton, J. G., & Boehm-Davis, D. A. (2008). The effect of interruption duration and demand on resuming suspended goals. *Journal of Experimental Psychology: Applied*, 14, 299–313.

Moraitou, D., & Efklides, A. (2009). The Blank in the Mind Questionnaire (BIMQ). *European Journal of Psychological Assessment*, 25, 115–122.

Ποντικάκης, Ν. (2011). Κενό στο νου σε συνθήκες προοπτικής μνήμης: Ο ρόλος της κωδικοποίησης. Blank in the mind under conditions of prospective memory: The role of encoding. Unpublished master's thesis, School of Psychology, Aristotle University of Thessaloniki, Greece.

Schneider, W., Eschman, A., & Zuccolotto, A. (2002). *E-prime user's guide*. Pittsburgh, PA: Psychology Software Tools Inc.

Schwartz, B. L. (2002). *Tip-of-the-tongue states: Phenomenology, mechanism, and lexical retrieval*. Mahwah, NJ: Erlbaum.

(2008). Working memory load differentially affects tip-of-the-tongue states and feeling of knowing judgments. *Memory & Cognition*, 36, 9–19.

Schwartz, B. L., & Efklides, A. (2012). Metamemory and memory efficiency: Implications for student learning. *Journal of Applied Research in Memory and Cognition*, 1, 145–151.

Smith, R. E. (2003). The cost of remembering to remember in event-based prospective memory: Investigating the capacity demands of delayed intention performance. *Journal of Experimental Psychology: Learning, Memory, and Cognition*, 29(3), 347–361.

Smith, R. E., & Bayen, U. J. (2004). A multinomial model of event-based prospective memory. *Journal of Experimental Psychology: Learning, Memory, and Cognition*, 30, 756–777.

Sugimori, E., & Kusumi, T. (2009). Limiting attentional resources influences performance and output monitoring of an event-based prospective memory task. *European Journal of Cognitive Psychology*, 21, 112–128.

12

On the Empirical Study of Déjà Vu: Borrowing Methodology from the Study of the Tip-of-the-Tongue Phenomenon

ANNE M. CLEARY

THE DÉJÀ VU EXPERIENCE

Like the tip-of-the-tongue (TOT) experience, déjà vu is a type of subjective cognitive state that most people can relate to or report having experienced at some point in their lives (e.g., Brown, 2003, 2004). Déjà vu is the sometimes eerie experience of feeling as if a new situation has been experienced before, despite knowing that it has actually never been experienced before. When on the platform at the train station in Beijing last summer, preparing to board the bullet train from Beijing to Shanghai, I had this strange feeling of having been there before and of having done that before, despite never having been to Beijing, or ridden on a bullet train, or taken a trip to Shanghai. From where did that feeling arise? What caused it?

Though déjà vu has piqued human interest enough to appear in literature and personal musings for more than 100 years (e.g., Brown, 2004; Brown & Marsh, 2010), experimental scientific research on the phenomenon has been lacking, or at least slow to come about, compared to research on other cognitive phenomena, such as TOT experiences. Both the TOT state and the déjà vu phenomenon have long histories of anecdotal study prior to their becoming topics of laboratory investigation. In fact, though there was half a century of speculation regarding TOTs starting with William James (James, 1893), modern laboratory research on TOTs did not emerge until Brown and McNeill's (1966) groundbreaking piece on the subject. This illustrates some of the difficulty involved in bringing relatively infrequent subjective states of experience into the laboratory for empirical study. As for why déjà vu has taken longer to become an accepted laboratory topic than TOT experiences, Brown and Marsh (2010) suggest some reasons why this may be, including déjà vu's tendency to be associated with paranormal explanations, as well as the rarity with which déjà vu tends to occur according to survey research (Brown, 2003).

STUDYING DÉJÀ VU INDIRECTLY BY STUDYING
MEMORY PROCESSES

Despite the lack of direct experimental work on the phenomenon of déjà vu itself, given that many memory theories of déjà vu exist, memory researchers have attempted to study déjà vu indirectly by examining the memory processes that are hypothesized to give rise to it. According to memory theories of déjà vu, the feeling of déjà vu results from the fact that the person *has* actually experienced the situation (or something like it) before; he or she is simply not consciously recollecting that prior experience (Brown, 2004; Cleary, 2008). In the absence of consciously recollecting the prior experience related to the present situation, the current situation may just seem familiar without explanation. If the person also feels certain that the current situation has never actually been experienced before, then this feeling of familiarity may be interpreted as déjà vu. In short, déjà vu may be a specific case of familiarity-based recognition when normal familiarity processes occur in a situation that also happens to be recognized as new. So, when I felt as if I had been on the train platform in Beijing before, it was likely because I had actually been in a similar situation before. When I mentioned my strange familiarity experience, my spouse reminded me that years ago, he and I had traveled on the Eurostar from Paris to London, that the train platform was similar, and that I was probably reminded of that experience. Once he mentioned it, I agreed that that was probably the source of my familiarity. When I was consciously able to compare the two experiences, they were indeed highly similar.

If déjà vu is indeed driven by normal human memory processes, then it should be possible to indirectly investigate it by studying the memory processes themselves. Jacoby and Whitehouse (1989) took this approach in their study of familiarity as it might relate to déjà vu. They discuss their memory experiments and findings in terms of a description of déjà vu Titchener gave in 1928: a man glances one way to look for traffic before crossing the street, then gets distracted and forgets having just glanced that way. As he glances that way again upon crossing the street, he is perplexed at the feeling of déjà vu. (He believes this to be his first glance, though it is actually his second). Jacoby and Whitehouse relate this example to their finding that a very brief exposure to a stimulus (i.e., a rapidly flashed, masked word) immediately prior to receiving that same stimulus as a recognition test item leads to an increased probability of judging the test item to be old.

Specifically, in their study, Jacoby and Whitehouse gave participants a study list of words followed by a test list containing a mixture of studied and unstudied words. On the test, some of the test words were preceded by a brief flash of a word. For example, after a 500 ms flash of ampersands (&&&&&&), the word "banquet" might flash for 50 ms, followed by another 500 ms flash of ampersands (&&&&&&) to serve as a mask, then the test word would follow and remain on the screen until the participant indicated whether that test word was studied or unstudied. Sometimes, the rapidly flashed word matched the test word (e.g., the flashed word would be "banquet" and the test word would be "banquet"). Sometimes, the rapidly flashed word did not match the test word (e.g., the flashed word would be "airplane" and the test word would be "banquet"). When the flashed word matched the subsequent test word, participants thought it more likely that the test word had been studied than when the flashed word did not match the test word. Presumably, test items for which an identical match was flashed immediately beforehand seemed more familiar because of that prior flash. This does fit with Titchener's suggestion that déjà vu may result from mistaking a familiar second glance for a first.

However, though many researchers have replicated and extended their findings (e.g., Brown & Marsh, 2009; Huber Clark, Curran, & Winkielman, 2008; Westerman, 2008) and have shed light on the possible nature of familiarity, Jacoby and Whitehouse never directly asked participants about whether they were experiencing déjà vu during the experiment. Thus, this is an example of studying déjà vu indirectly through studying the memory processes hypothesized to give rise to it.

Other researchers have also likened familiarity findings, like the Jacoby-Whitehouse (1989) effect, to déjà vu without directly asking participants about whether they were experiencing déjà vu. Westerman (2008) found that the tendency for participants to call identically primed test items old in the Jacoby-Whitehouse paradigm would increase with a decreasing probability of identically primed items in the test list. When the probability of a test item being primed with an immediately preceding brief flash of the identical item was quite low (e.g., only 10%), the familiarity effect was at its highest. This familiarity effect (i.e., the Jacoby-Whitehouse effect) decreased as that probability increased (e.g., 67% or 90% of test items identically primed).

Westerman (2008) argued that this finding may relate to déjà vu in that the feeling of familiarity with an item may be greatest when contrasted with a lack thereof from the surrounding context (the surrounding context in this case being the other test items in the temporal sequence). Perhaps something familiar in an unfamiliar context helps to give rise to that contrast between the feeling of familiarity and recognition of novelty that is characteristic of déjà vu. However, like Jacoby and Whitehouse (1989), Westerman did not directly ask participants about whether they were experiencing déjà vu. The link to déjà vu was inferred based on the assumption that familiarity-types of memory processes are the underlying basis of déjà vu experiences, and that by studying these memory processes themselves, déjà vu can be better understood.

Brown and Marsh (2009) extended the Jacoby-Whitehouse (1989) effect to judgments of pre-experimental experience with novel symbols. In their variant of the Jacoby-Whitehouse paradigm, Brown and Marsh briefly flashed a symbol immediately prior to presenting either the same or a different symbol for a judgment about whether it had been seen pre-experimentally. Some of the symbols were highly familiar symbols that had indeed likely been seen pre-experimentally, while some were lower in familiarity and some were completely novel (i.e., never before experienced outside of the experiment). Interestingly, for the completely novel symbols, participants showed an increased likelihood of judging the symbols to have been seen outside of the context of the experiment when they had been briefly flashed immediately prior to their test presentation. Thus, the initial findings of Jacoby and Whitehouse were extended to a situation in which the judgment was about pre-experimental (i.e., real-world) experience with the test items. In discussing these findings, Brown and Marsh related them to déjà vu. Participants were given a post-experiment questionnaire asking if they had experienced déjà vu at all during the experiment, and 50 percent indicated that they had.

ON THE DIRECT EXPERIMENTAL APPROACH TO STUDYING DÉJÀ VU

In all of the aforementioned studies (e.g., Brown & Marsh, 2009; Jacoby & Whitehouse, 1989; Westerman, 2008), indirect inferences were made about déjà vu on the basis of findings about memory processes. Participants were never directly asked about whether they were experiencing déjà vu on a given experimental trial. Even in the study by Brown and Marsh (2009), participants were only asked at the end of the experiment, and not on a trial-by-trial basis. This general approach to studying déjà vu differs from the approach used to study TOT experiences. In standard TOT research (e.g., see Brown, 2012, or Schwartz, 2002, for a review), researchers generally ask participants to indicate, with a dichotomous judgment, whether they are experiencing a TOT state on each experimental trial. The assumption is that participants understand what a TOT state is and can subjectively report on when it occurs. So why not approach the study of déjà vu in a manner similar to the study of TOT experiences? Doing so would allow for a determination of whether the likelihood of a reported déjà vu experience varies with an experimental manipulation that is predicted to have an effect. Before turning to some of the ways my collaborators and I have attempted to study déjà vu directly in the laboratory, I first discuss some of the potential criticisms of attempting to study déjà vu directly in the lab on a trial-by-trial basis, and some of the possible reasons the direct approach to studying déjà vu has been slow to catch on.

Are Déjà vu Experiences Too Rare to Study in the Lab? As Brown and Marsh (2010) mention in their review chapter on déjà vu, one reason for the scarcity of empirical research on déjà vu may be the relative rarity of the experience itself. According to survey research (Brown, 2003), déjà vu occurs fairly infrequently – about twice per year among young adults. Brown and Marsh suggest that the slow start to empirical investigations of déjà vu may be a result of researchers assuming that eliciting such a rare experience in the laboratory will be difficult or impossible.

However, although déjà vu may be less frequent in daily life than the TOT experience, like the TOT, it should theoretically be possible to increase the probability of the experience by creating circumstances known to drive it. With TOT experiences, the pools of questions are specifically chosen because they have been shown to have a higher likelihood of inducing TOT experiences. With many subjective experiences that researchers study in the lab (e.g., tip-of-the-tongue experiences, familiarity, feelings of knowing), the intent in the laboratory investigations is to drive up the likelihood of those experiences relative to daily life by creating circumstances that favor their occurrence. Understanding the circumstances that tend to lead to these subjective experiences allows laboratory researchers to obtain these same experiences with greater frequency than they occur in real life.

As an example, in a TOT experiment, a person may experience the TOT feeling for 20 different questions out of 80 within the one-hour experiment. One would not ordinarily experience 20 TOT states in one hour, but because the question pool has been selectively constructed to favor or induce tip-of-the-tongue states, one experiences it more often in the one-hour experiment than in a typical hour of one's day.

The same could be said of studying déjà vu in the laboratory through trial-by-trial prompting across different experimental conditions. Because my collaborators and I specifically create circumstances intended to elicit déjà vu based on our hypotheses about how déjà vu operates, it should be theoretically possible to increase the frequency of déjà vu in the lab relative to in day-to-day life. For example, in day-to-day life, it may actually be somewhat rare to encounter a scene that configurally resembles one in memory, or to encounter a scene but fail to recall the previous experience with it. However, if similarity in spatial layout to a prior experience is a driving factor behind déjà vu experiences with places, as is discussed later in this chapter, it should be possible to increase the probability of experiencing déjà vu by creating such a circumstance in the lab.

On Demand Characteristics from Direct Probing. Some may be concerned about demand characteristics in probing participants for a déjà vu decision on a trial-by-trial basis. That is, maybe participants would form impressions of what the experimenters are searching for regarding the hypotheses about déjà vu, and would try to be accommodating in their responses. The same argument could be made about trial-by-trial investigations of the TOT experience. However, what makes this a difficult explanation for experimental results in the case of TOT experiences is that participants only indicate TOT experiences when retrieval of a target word fails. Thus, to assume that TOT results are explainable by demand characteristics, one would have to assume either that a) participants withhold responses to the TOT questions to meet some perceived experimenter expectation (to make it seem like a retrieval failure had occurred when it had not), or b) despite the retrieval failure and lack of access to the target word, participants in TOT studies are aware of on which trials the experimenter should expect them to have a TOT experience and on which trials the experimenter should expect them not to have a TOT experience.

The direct trial-by-trial investigations of déjà vu by my colleagues and I are similar to TOT studies in that we specifically examine those trials in which participants fail to recall the prior study episode for which the current test scene is intended to be a cue. With both these and TOT studies in my lab, we have found that participants are highly motivated to get as many correct as possible in these experiments. In fact, they often ask if they can find out their recall performance at the end of the experiment – they want to know how many they got right. Thus, it is unlikely that participants fake failing to recall a studied scene in response to a test scene to meet some perceived experimenter expectation. Additionally, it would be difficult for participants to identify researcher expectations on a trial-by-trial basis in cases of retrieval failure, where participants do not have access to the critical information that would be needed to make that identification.

Is This the "Real" Déjà Vu? Some may wonder if the reports of déjà vu that are given in response to direct trial-by-trial prompting in the lab reflect the same déjà vu experience that so rarely occurs in day-to-day life. This is a question that one could ask about most phenomena that are studied in cognitive psychology. For example, one could ask whether laboratory visual attention tasks tap the real-life visual selective attention, whether the flicker paradigm relates to the real mechanisms of change blindness that occur in daily existence, whether priming paradigms mimic priming that occurs in our everyday experiences, whether dual-process methods of probing recognition memory really succeed in tapping the type of familiarity-based recognition that occurs in daily life, and finally, whether using general knowledge questions and prompting participants to indicate when TOT experiences occur actually taps the real TOT experiences that occur in daily life. In short, this is not a question unique to déjà vu, and there is nothing "special" about déjà vu that should make it unable to be studied in the laboratory the way that other cognitive phenomena are studied. The general approach of studying déjà vu is similar to that taken in other domains of cognitive psychology: Develop laboratory paradigms meant to elicit the phenomenon in question, use them to test hypotheses about the phenomenon and develop theories, and eventually attempt to examine the ecological validity by developing real-world extensions of the paradigms.

On Relying on Subjective Reports. Given the controversy surrounding the reliance on participants' subjective judgments of their own memory processes in studies of recognition memory, some may have concerns about relying on participants' subjective reports of déjà vu. For example, with the remember-know paradigm, participants provide a subjective judgment of the basis of their recognition decision on each recognition test trial (e.g., Gardiner, 1988; Gardiner & Java, 1993; Gardiner & Parkin, 1990; Rajaram, 1993; Rajaram & Geraci, 2000; Tulving, 1985). Whenever they judge a test item to have been studied, they indicate the basis of that judgment: participants give a "remember" judgment whenever the decision is based on conscious recollection of the item from the study list, and a "know" judgment whenever the decision is based on a mere sense of familiarity with the test item. This approach is controversial because some mathematical models can account for the patterns of results without assuming two different processes (e.g., Dunn, 2004). Thus, at issue in the controversy is whether subjects really have access to different processes underlying their decisions in a way that allows differentiation.

Like TOT states, déjà vu experiences are subjective experiences. With TOT experiences, it would not suffice to infer their occurrence solely on the basis of some experimenter-established criteria for determining whether such a state occurred. Because it is a subjective experience, the subject's report is essential as merely inferring a TOT on the basis of some other independent criteria might lead to inferred TOT states that do not correspond to participants' subjective sense of whether a TOT occurred. A researcher cannot be certain that a TOT actually occurred without asking people if they are experiencing it. The déjà vu state can be viewed as similar to the TOT state; because it is a specific type of subjective state, a researcher cannot be certain that it actually occurred without asking people if they are experiencing it.

Along these same lines, another consideration is that survey research (e.g., Brown, 2003) and case studies (e.g., O'Connor & Moulin, 2008) of déjà vu also rely on subjective reports. In survey studies, participants are asked to reflect on their past experiences with déjà vu, relying not just on subjective reporting, but on memory of the past subjective experiences. In case studies of people who experience chronic déjà vu, the fact that they experience chronic déjà vu is known only from their subjective reporting on the experience. Thus, all methods of studying déjà vu rely on subjective reporting on the experience.

Does Repeated Prompting Influence Déjà Vu Reports? It is an interesting question whether repeatedly prompting about déjà vu itself influences the likelihood of experiencing or reporting déjà vu. Schwartz (2011) investigated this issue with TOTs. He examined how being in a TOT state influences the likelihood of reporting a TOT state on a subsequent trial and found that despite having no influence on actual recall ability, being in a TOT state on one trial reduced the likelihood of reporting a TOT state on the subsequent trial. It is possible that a similar finding might be obtained when prompting participants about déjà vu states. More specifically, reporting a déjà vu experience may make a person less, rather than more, likely to report a subsequent déjà vu state.

STUDYING DÉJÀ VU DIRECTLY: BORROWING METHODOLOGY
FROM TIP-OF-THE-TONGUE RESEARCH

In recent years, my collaborators and I have used the same approach used in the study of TOT experiences to more directly investigate hypotheses generated by memory explanations of déjà vu. As mentioned earlier, such explanations of déjà vu assume that the experience results from a memory of a prior experience either with, or related to, the current situation. The exact memory is simply not coming to mind at the moment, even though it is driving the feeling of familiarity with the otherwise novel situation. Memory explanations of déjà vu generally assume that it is itself a manifestation of familiarity processes. Therefore, to the extent that one can generate hypotheses about how manipulations should affect familiarity processes, one can also examine whether such manipulations affect the probability of reporting a déjà vu experience.

In one study in which my collaborators and I used the TOT approach to study déjà vu, we examined the hypothesis that the probability of reporting a déjà vu experience would be increased among test items that were highly similar to earlier-presented studied items that failed to be recalled (Cleary, Ryals, & Nomi, 2009). We used a variant of the recognition without cued recall paradigm (Cleary, 2004; Ryals & Cleary, 2012), in which participants first view a study list of items and are then tested with cues that potentially resemble studied items on some feature dimension. For example, some of the test cues may resemble studied items in their visual appearance while some do not. This was thought to be a useful paradigm for examining déjà vu because all of the test cues are actually novel, in that none of them were actually studied. In this paradigm, participants are to use each cue to attempt to recollect a studied item from the earlier list. Even when they fail to do so, participants are still asked to judge the familiarity of the test cue. The usual finding is that, among cues for which recall failed, participants will still rate cues that resemble studied items as seeming more familiar than cues that do not resemble studied items.

To apply this paradigm to the study of déjà vu, we had participants study black and white line drawings of various scenes, like that shown in the left-hand panel of Figure 12.1 (Cleary et al., 2009). At test, participants were presented with a list of novel scenes, each of which potentially resembled a studied scene, especially in the layout of its elements, like that shown in the right-hand panel of Figure 12.1. For each scene presented on the test, participants were asked if they could recall a similar scene from the study list. If they thought they could, they were asked to type in its name. The scenes had been tested previously for ease of naming to determine that if participants could recollect the scene itself, they could nearly always name it (99% of the time). The primary interest was in those situations in which participants failed to recall the corresponding studied scene. They were still asked to give familiarity ratings to the test scenes using a scale of 0 (very unfamiliar) to 10 (very familiar), and to indicate whether or a déjà vu state was present.

Indeed, the probability of a reported déjà vu experience was correlated with the recognition without cued recall effect. Just as participants gave higher familiarity ratings to novel test scenes that resembled studied scenes (but for which recall failed) than for novel test scenes that did not resemble studied scenes (the recognition without cued recall effect), they indicated

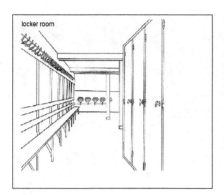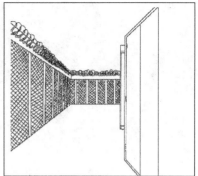

FIGURE 12.1. On the left is an example of a study scene (a locker room) and on the right is an example of its corresponding similar but novel test scene (a prison) used by Cleary and colleagues (2009).

déjà vu more often among novel test scenes that resembled studied scenes (but for which recall failed) than among novel test scenes that did not resemble studied scenes. The mean probability of a reported déjà vu state in the former situation was .17, whereas in the latter it was .13.

In another experiment, this effect was extended to a situation in which, instead of indicating "yes" or "no" regarding whether a déjà vu state was present, participants rated their feeling of déjà vu on a scale of 0 (no déjà vu at all) to 10 (very strong déjà vu). Participants were not given a definition of déjà vu, nor were they told to judge the familiarity of the test items. Despite the lack of juxtaposing familiarity and déjà vu judgments, and not being provided a definition of déjà vu, when recall failed déjà vu ratings were higher for scenes that resembled studied scenes than for scenes that did not. In a between-subjects comparison, the magnitude of this ratings effect was comparable to the recognition without cued recall effect found in the standard condition in which familiarity ratings were used.

In another study, my colleagues and I took this paradigm a step further using virtual reality technology (Cleary et al., 2012). We investigated the Gestalt familiarity hypothesis (e.g., Brown, 2004; Brown & Marsh, 2010; Dashiell, 1937), according to which déjà vu can result from similarity in the spatial layout of the current situation to one stored in memory. For example, maybe I experience a feeling of déjà vu upon viewing a museum display while roaming around inside of a museum. The source of that déjà vu experience may actually be an unretrieved memory of a previous experience in which the spatial layout was highly similar. Maybe the arrangement of the museum pieces relative to one another is similar to the arrangement of

FIGURE 12.2. Example screenshot of a study scene (bowling alley) on the left, and the configurally similar test scene on the right.

statues, plants, and benches at a park that I had visited at some point in my past, but which I was failing to currently recall. Without recalling that past experience, I am left only with a feeling of having experienced this current situation before, even though I know that I have never been to this museum or seen this display before.

To test the Gestalt familiarity hypothesis using virtual reality, we again used the approach taken by researchers of TOT experiences. We manipulated the similarity of the virtual reality scenes from study to test, and asked people to report on when they experienced déjà vu throughout the test portions of the experiment. Specifically, participants viewed a study list of 3-D scenes in which they were immersed such that they could look around inside each scene by turning their heads, as if they were physically present within the scene but in a stationary spot. An example of a study scene is shown in the 2-D screenshot on the left-hand side of Figure 12.2 (the bowling alley). The test cues were also 3-D scenes in which participants were immersed and could look around. A grid had been used to place elements in the same locations from study scenes to test scenes to create the same spatial configuration from study to test, as can be seen on the right-hand side test scene in Figure 12.2.

In Experiment 1, all of the test scenes were novel (i.e., not studied), but half had the same spatial configuration as a studied scene and half did not. While viewing a test scene, participants were asked to attempt to recall a study scene that resembled that test scene. They were also asked to rate the familiarity of the test scene itself using a scale of 0 (very unfamiliar) to 10 (very familiar), and to indicate whether they were experiencing a déjà vu state while looking at the test scene. As was found by Cleary and colleagues (2009), among test scenes for which recall of corresponding studied scenes failed, the probability of a déjà vu report was significantly higher among those novel test scenes that had the same spatial layout as a studied scene (.35) than among those novel test scenes that did not have the same spatial layout as a studied scene (.20).

In Experiment 2, one third of the virtual reality test scenes were exactly the same as at study (i.e., if the bowling alley had been studied, it would be presented again at test), one third were novel but had the same spatial layout as a studied scene (as on the right-hand side of Figure 12.2), and one third were novel and did not share a spatial layout with any studied scene. Participants were asked to indicate if a test scene was old or new, to rate the familiarity of the test scene, and to indicate if they were experiencing déjà vu. Because déjà vu is defined as a simultaneous feeling of familiarity alongside a recognition of newness or novelty, the interest in this experiment was in test scenes that participants determined to be new (i.e., not studied). Among these, the probability of reporting a déjà vu experience was highest for scenes that were actually studied (i.e., old) but that participants failed to recognize as such (.58). Déjà vu probabilities were next highest among new scenes that had the same spatial layout as a studied scene (.35), and lowest among new scenes that did not share the same spatial layout as a studied scene (.19). The déjà vu probabilities followed the same pattern as familiarity. This finding supports the idea that déjà vu represents a specific case of familiarity-based recognition, and that the greater the degree of match between the current situation and the unrecalled one in memory, the greater the sense of familiarity and the higher the likelihood of déjà vu.

A potential criticism of the results reported by Cleary and colleagues (2009) and Cleary and colleagues (2012) is that the base rates of déjà vu reports seem high, defined as the frequency of déjà vu reports in control conditions. As discussed by Cleary and colleagues (2009), one reason for base rates that seem much higher than zero may be the interstimulus similarity (e.g., Cleary, Morris, & Langley, 2007) from study to test. For the same reason that similarity to a studied item increases familiarity in the absence of recall, as the pool of study and test items become more similar to each other, so does the sense of familiarity with each item. More specifically, the stimuli used by Cleary and colleagues (2009) were all black and white line drawings of places, and the virtual reality scenes used by Cleary and colleagues (2012) were all created using the same gaming software (The Sims). Thus, the degree of interstimulus similarity was greater than one would normally experience in daily life, which could contribute to an elevated base rate of reported déjà vu experiences relative to the expected base rate of near zero. Thus, the elevated base rates may be for the very same reasons our similarity manipulation had an effect on déjà vu.

In relation to the concern that demand characteristics might drive trial-by-trial déjà vu reports (in the section "On Demand Characteristics"), when participants fail to recall a prior scene that resembles the test scene, they presumably have no way of knowing that the test scene does in fact resemble a studied scene (as half of the test scenes do not resemble studied scenes and they are told this beforehand). This uncertainty regarding which test scenes do, and do not, resemble studied scenes would make it difficult to deliberately attempt to alter one's déjà vu reports to accommodate experimenter expectations. Presumably, in the absence of recall, the test scene will elicit some varying degree of familiarity (strongly familiar, somewhat familiar, mildly familiar, or completely unfamiliar). The variable familiarity levels of the test scenes may be the main basis on which participants can make judgments in cases of recall failure. This variability in familiarity is thought to underlie the recognition without cued recall effect, and likely forms the basis of people's déjà vu judgments as well.

However, if participants are indeed basing their déjà vu judgments on the level of familiarity for a test scene, then that leaves open the possibility that participants only equate déjà vu with familiarity because they expect that the experimenters are equating the two in that same way. Such a demand characteristic is plausible in Experiment 1 of Cleary and colleagues (2009), where we juxtaposed a question about familiarity with a question about déjà vu. That is, we asked participants both to rate how familiar the scene seemed and to indicate whether they were experiencing a déjà vu state.

To address this possibility of response bias, in Experiment 2a of Cleary and colleagues (2009), participants indicated whether they were experiencing déjà vu on each trial, without a familiarity rating or even a definition of déjà vu. In this situation, the probability of reporting a déjà vu experience was still greater among test scenes that resembled unrecalled studied scenes than among those that did not. In Experiment 2b of the same study, participants were instead asked to rate the intensity of their déjà vu experience, again without any reference to familiarity or a definition of déjà vu. Participants still gave higher déjà vu ratings to scenes that resembled unrecalled studied scenes than to those that did not, and the magnitude of this effect was comparable to that found in a standard familiarity rating version of the experiment.

These results suggest that participants tend to base their déjà vu judgments on the familiarity of the test scenes, with higher familiarity leading to a higher likelihood of déjà vu and lower familiarity leading to a lower likelihood of déjà vu. Note that this is consistent with memory interpretations of déjà vu. As discussed earlier ("Studying Déjà vu Indirectly by Studying Memory Processes"), déjà vu has previously been indirectly investigated by examining memory processes thought to be familiarity based. Thus, if participants do indeed base their déjà vu judgments on familiarity, this would lend support for the idea that déjà vu can be understood through investigating familiarity processes.

However, might participants only be basing déjà vu judgments on familiarity because of demand characteristics, whereby they assume that this is how the experimenter is defining déjà vu? In a questionnaire study, 92 participants were asked to define déjà vu (without having participated in a study of déjà vu), and 79 percent independently defined it as a sense of having experienced something before. This is indeed how one would generally define familiarity as well. Thus, it supports the notion that participants from our population of young adult college students do tend to treat déjà vu as a form of familiarity, independently of any inferred experimenter definition.

In summary, it is unlikely that demand characteristics are responsible for the déjà vu results found in studies directly asking participants to report on when they experience déjà vu. The experimental manipulations had their predicted effect on the likelihood of these reports (e.g., Cleary et al., 2012; Cleary et al., 2009), suggesting that déjà vu behaves like familiarity. Furthermore, the fact that subjects equate déjà vu and familiarity in their independent definitions of déjà vu suggests that the a priori assumption researchers made in those investigations of déjà vu using indirect measures (discussed earlier) may have validity. Finally, a recent research study by Sugimori and Kusumi (2014) provides some external validity for Cleary and colleagues' (2009) déjà vu study. Their findings suggest that the frequency of déjà vu in real-life, as indicated in survey reports, is positively correlated with the ability to detect the similarity between two configurally similar scenes among the scenes used by Cleary et al. (2009). Future research should further examine the validity of the assumption that déjà vu can be understood through laboratory paradigms aimed at probing familiarity. For example, perhaps survey studies could compare the frequency of reported familiarity experiences with the frequency of reported déjà vu experiences to see how they compare in day-to-day life.

FUTURE DIRECTIONS

Future research on déjà vu should examine whether previously reported findings that were aimed at indirectly studying the mechanisms of déjà vu (such as by investigating familiarity processes with the assumption that those processes are responsible for the experience of déjà vu) apply to reports of déjà vu when directly prompted. For example, in the Jacoby-Whitehouse (1989) paradigm, would participants be more likely to report experiencing déjà vu in the condition in which a rapidly flashed, difficult-to-see match to the test item immediately precedes the test item? In the real-world variation of this task used by Brown and Marsh (2009), would participants be more likely to report déjà vu when novel symbols are primed with rapidly flashed matches than when they are primed with mismatches or than when familiar symbols are primed with matches or mismatches? Finally, are participants more likely to report déjà vu when a familiar item is presented against a background of novel items (e.g., Westerman, 2008)?

Future research should also continue using virtual reality to probe déjà vu experiences. In the virtual reality study by Cleary and colleagues (2012), the effects of the similarity manipulations on déjà vu likelihood were greater than in prior work with 2-D black and white line drawings (Cleary et al., 2009), suggesting that the more realistic scenes afforded by virtual reality may be more conducive to studying déjà vu than more typical laboratory stimuli. Virtual reality can be used to examine many other hypotheses about déjà vu, such as the single-element theory (Brown, 2004), the multiple-element theory (Brown, 2004), and even how variables such as full versus divided attention at encoding affect the subsequent likelihood of déjà vu for similar scenes for which recall of the source of the similarity fails.

REFERENCES

Brown, A. S. (2003). A review of the déjà vu experience. *Psychological Bulletin, 129*, 394–413.
(2004). *The déjà vu experience.* New York: Psychology Press.
(2012). *Tip of the tongue states.* New York: Psychology Press.
Brown, A. S., & Marsh, E. J. (2008). Evoking false beliefs about autobiographical experience. *Psychonomic Bulletin & Review, 15*, 186–190.
(2009). Creating illusions of past encounter through brief exposure. *Psychological Science, 20*, 534–538.
(2010). Digging into déjà vu: Recent research findings on possible mechanisms. In B. H. Ross (Ed.), *The Psychology of Learning and Motivation, Vol. 53* pp. 33–62). Burlington, VT: Academic Press.
Brown, R., & McNeill, D. (1966). The "tip of the tongue" phenomenon. *Journal of Verbal Learning and Verbal Behavior, 5*, 325–337.
Cleary, A. M. (2004). Orthography, phonology, and meaning: Word features that give rise to feelings of familiarity in recognition. *Psychonomic Bulletin & Review, 11*, 446–451.

(2008). Recognition memory, familiarity, and déjà vu experiences. *Current Directions in Psychological Science*, 17, 353–357.

Cleary, A. M., Brown, A. S., Sawyer, B. D., Nomi, J. S., Ajoku, A. C., & Ryals, A. J. (2012). Familiarity from the configuration of objects in 3-dimensional space and its relation to déjà vu: A virtual reality investigation. *Consciousness and Cognition*, 21, 969–975.

Cleary, A. M., Morris, A. L., & Langley, M. M. (2007). Recognition memory for novel stimuli: The structural regularity hypothesis. *Journal of Experimental Psychology: Learning, Memory, and Cognition*, 33, 379–393.

Cleary, A. M., Ryals, A. J., & Nomi, J. S. (2009). Can déjà vu result from similarity to a prior experience? Support for the similarity hypothesis of déjà vu. *Psychonomic Bulletin & Review*, 16, 1082–1088.

Dashiell, J. (1937). *Fundamentals of general psychology*. Boston, MA: Houghton Mifflin Company.

Dunn, J. C. (2004). Remember-know: A matter of confidence. *Psychological Review*, 111, 524–542.

Gardiner, J. M. (1988). Functional aspects of recollective experience. *Memory & Cognition*, 16, 309–313.

Gardiner, J. M., & Java, R. I. (1993). Recognizing and remembering. In S. E. Gathercole, M. A. Conway, P. E. Morris, & A. F. Collins (Eds.), *Theories of memory* (pp. 163–188). Hove, England: Erlbaum.

Gardiner, J. M., & Parkin, A. J. (1990). Attention and recollective experience in recognition memory. *Memory & Cognition*, 18, 579–583.

Huber, D. E., Clark, T. F., Curran, T., & Winkielman, P. (2008). Effects of repetition priming on recognition memory: Testing a perceptual fluency-disfluency model. *Journal of Experimental Psychology: Learning Memory and Cognition*, 34, 1305–1324.

Jacoby, L. L., & Whitehouse, K. (1989). An illusion of memory: False recognition influenced by unconscious perception. *Journal of Experimental Psychology: General*, 118, 126–135.

James, W. (1893). *The Principles of Psychology (Volume 2)*. New York: Henry Holt and Company.

O'Connor, A. R., & Moulin, C. J. A. (2008). The persistence of erroneous familiarity in an epileptic male: Challenging perceptual theories of déjà vu activation. *Brain and Cognition*, 68, 144–147.

Rajaram, S. (1993). Remembering and knowing: Two means of access to the personal past. *Memory & Cognition*, 21, 89–102.

Rajaram, S., & Geraci, L. (2000). Conceptual fluency selectively influences knowing. *Journal of Experimental Psychology: Learning, Memory, and Cognition*, 26, 1070–1074.

Ryals, A. J., & Cleary, A. M. (2012). The recognition without cued recall phenomenon: Support for a feature-matching theory over a partial recollection account. *Journal of Memory and Language*, 66, 747–762.

Schwartz, B. L. (2002). *Tip-of-the-tongue states: Phenomenology, mechanism, and lexical retrieval*. Mahwah, NJ: Lawrence Erlbaum Associates.

(2011). The effect of being in a tip-of-the-tongue state on subsequent items. *Memory & Cognition*, 39, 245–250.

Sugimori, E., & Kusumi, T. (2014). The similarity hypothesis of déjà vu: On the relationship between frequency of real-life déjà vu experiences and sensitivity to configural resemblance. *Journal of Cognitive Psychology*, 26, 48–57.

Titchener, E. B. (1928). *A text-book of psychology*. New York: Macmillan.

Tulving, E. (1985). Memory and consciousness. *Canadian Psychologist*, 25, 1–12.

Westerman, D. L. (2008). Relative fluency and illusions of recognition memory. *Psychonomic Bulletin & Review*, 15, 1196–1200.

13

Déjà Vu in Older Adults

CHRIS J. A. MOULIN, CELINE SOUCHAY, SARAH
BUCHANAN, ROSEMARY BRADLEY, DILAY ZEYNEP
KARADOLLER, AND MELISA AKAN

On the bus with my Uni friends and [I] felt like I had been there before, had the same conversation and people had the same positions, although I don't remember seeing the faces before but when I was on the bus in that position the faces I saw fitted the vision perfectly.
Research participant

It does not come round in hundreds of thousands of years,
It comes round in the split of a wink, you will be sitting exactly
Where you are now and scratching your elbow, the train
Will be passing exactly as now and saying It does not come round,
It does not come round, It does not come round
Louis MacNeice, "Déjà vu" (1963)

OVERVIEW

Déjà vu is the "phenomenological experience of recognising a current situation and the awareness that this feeling of recognition is false" captured in the two quotes cited at the beginning of this chapter (O'Connor & Moulin, 2010). Brown (2004) reports an average lifetime prevalence of 67 percent across 41 studies; approximately two-thirds of the population have had at least one déjà vu experience in their lifetime. The focus of the current chapter is whether the incidence of déjà vu increases or decreases with age, and what that might tell us about the nature of the experience and, possibly, the aging process. We report two studies on déjà vu incidence in younger and older adults, assess the relationship of déjà vu with other relatively infrequent and notable experiences – intrusive memories and the tip-of-

Address for Correspondence: Chris Moulin, LEAD CNRS UMR 5022, University of Bourgogne, Pole AAFE, 21065 Dijon, France.

the-tongue state – and finish with an overview of theories of déjà vu formation, and how the reduction in déjà vu experiences in older adults might be
interpreted.

A review of the literature suggests that older people report fewer
instances of déjà vu (Brown, 2004). Chapman and Mensh (1951) found a
negative correlation between déjà vu experience and age of -.23; Adachi and
colleagues found negative correlations of -.38 (Adachi, Adachi, Akanuma,
Matsubara, & Ito, 2007; Adachi et al., 2003), -.34 (Adachi et al., 2008), and
-.37 (Adachi et al., 2010); Sno, Schalken, de Jonghe, and Koeter (1994) found
a negative correlation of -.22, and Kohr (1980) of -.31. In a review of studies
that report mean age, Brown (2004) found that those studies with an older
sample had a lower lifetime incidence of the phenomenon, r(13) = -.44. As
such, correlational studies are clear: the older you are, the less frequently
you have experienced déjà vu.

This is a critical issue because contemporary theories of déjà vu formation connect it with episodic memory function, and so we might expect it to
increase with age, not decrease, because episodic memory declines as part of
the healthy aging process. This was the angle Nobel laureate Tonegawa[1] and
his colleagues adopted when interpreting their data from a mouse model of
Alzheimer's disease.

> Déjà vu is a memory problem, Tonegawa explained, occurring when our
> brains struggle to tell the difference between two extremely similar situ-
> ations. As people age, Tonegawa said, déjà-vu-like confusion happens
> more often – and it also happens in people suffering from brain diseases
> like Alzheimer's. "It's not surprising," he said, "when you consider the
> fact that there's a loss of or damage to cells in the dentate gyrus."
>
> (Mosher, 2007)

This idea is a logical continuation of the temporal lobe pattern-matching theory of déjà vu formation (Spatt, 2002), and is theoretically feasible. According
to this view, older adults have subtle memory deficits that manifest as an
increased likelihood to have déjà vu experiences; they *mismatch* current perception with stored representations. Thus, while there is some empirical evidence that aging leads to a *decrease* in déjà vu experiences, at least one theory
of déjà vu formation (pattern mismatch) suggests it might *increase* with age.

COHORT EFFECTS AND DÉJÀ VU

There seems, then, to be overwhelming evidence that the frequency of déjà
vu experiences does indeed decrease with age. However, all the studies that

examine this issue have been cross-sectional, that is, comparing groups of people of different ages, rather than longitudinal, following the same individuals over time. In aging research, such designs can fall foul of cohort effects, whereby the differences that we intend to measure between different age groups actually reflect differences in the cultural and environmental differences between those groups rather than the internal psychological processes at work in the aging individual, or age per se (Back & Bourque, 1970). A classic example is the influence of the Second World War, an event that caused a massive shift in societal values, traumatic events, and even nutrition (at least in the United Kingdom, where there was rationing) amongst a whole cohort of people. Such a major event will undoubtedly shape the psychology and biology of people born in 1940, in a way that it would not for a group of people born in 1980. Of course, the best way to control for cohort effects is to use a longitudinal design, which also has its disadvantages, and the differences between cross-sectional and longitudinal designs mirror those of between and within subject designs, respectively. There are no known longitudinal studies of déjà vu incidence, and for reasons of cost, time, and patience, we are not suggesting one here. The critical point is that cohort effects may well influence both the rates of experiencing and reporting déjà vu in older adults (i.e., perhaps old people had fewer déjà vu experiences even when they were young).

The more likely explanation would be a change in the reporting over time (here we are assuming that brains and memory systems remain relatively stable through the ages, whereas cultural trends and linguistic usage is relatively changeable). That is, there could be differences in the déjà vu experience across the lifespan due to a shift in cultural or environmental factors influencing the individual, rather than due to cognitive changes. It is possible that fewer older adults report experiencing déjà vu simply because it is a concept with which they are less comfortable. Déjà vu is a nebulous and complex experience with a loose definition, which may therefore see some change over time. Indeed, one major problem for aging studies is that the belief in or acceptance of the existence of déjà vu has increased in recent years. Gallup and Newport (1991) reported that from 1978 to 1990, déjà vu experients increased from 30 percent of the population to 55 percent. Figure 13.1 presents an overview of Brown's (2004) review, plotting the lifetime incidence of déjà vu against population year for 41 studies. This shows a relationship between when the survey was conducted and how many people say that they have had the experience, $r(41) = .50$, $p<.01$.

Thus, changes in collective societal beliefs may account for age differences mentioned in previous studies; these findings might not reflect

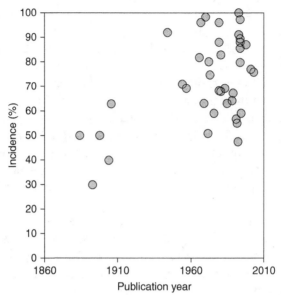

FIGURE 13.1. Relationship between lifetime incidence of déjà vu and date of publication, taken from Brown (2004).

genuine age differences but rather cohort effects: "older cohorts matured during an era in which belief in déjà vu was not as accepted as it is today" (Brown, 2003, p. 400). That is, perhaps older adults do not understand the term or have not experienced the use of the phrase in relation to cognitive difficulties, and this creates a false impression of reduced déjà vu in old age. In fact, there seems to be a slippage of the term toward a meaning applied to any repeated action, for example, "déjà vu in every gulp" (Pepsi Advertising, 2005).

In summary, there seems to be empirical evidence that déjà vu experiences decrease with age, while a few researchers have suggested they should increase with age. Whether déjà vu does increase or decrease with age is an important issue, because it may shed some light on the mechanisms of déjà vu formation, and more generally the nature of beliefs about memory function in older adults. The present studies aim to shed light on the incidence of déjà vu in older adults. In particular, we will address possible cohort effects in the understanding of the term *déjà vu*, by presenting participants with a definition (Study 1) and by assessing whether the groups can correctly define the term (Study 2). In turn, to put the rates of experience in some sort of context, and to make links with other memory-related phenomena, we also measure in the same individuals the rates of involuntary memories (Study 1) and the tip-of-the-tongue experience (Study 2). We finish by presenting two current hypotheses of déjà vu formation, and how the aging process may relate to those.

Study 1

The motivation behind this study was to examine the incidence of déjà vu in a group of older adults who had been provided with a definition of the sensation. We examined participants' estimates of déjà vu occurrence in the past year and more generally in their life. If aging leads to experiencing déjà vu less frequently, we would expect that, whereas recent experiences might be reduced, the lifetime incidence should be similar to that reported by younger people. We also asked about the frequency of intrusive memories.

Method
Participants
There were 131 participants, with 74 younger adults ($\underline{M}$ = 18.59 years, $\underline{SD}$ = .94, range = 18–24 years, 92% women) and 56 older adults ($\underline{M}$ = 71.00, $\underline{SD}$ = 6.50, range = 60–84 years, 72% women). The two groups had equivalent levels of education, having completed education until a mean age of 18.08 years (older group) and 18.23 years (younger group), t<1. Participants in the older adult group were recruited from an open day at the Leeds Memory Group, and as such all had experience of taking part in memory experiments and the notion of psychological research. Participants in the younger adult group were all undergraduate students taking a degree in psychology.

Materials and Procedure
Participants received a simple one-page questionnaire. They reported gender and age and the age at which they left school. They were asked about their memory efficacy: "How would you say your memory is compared to other people your age?" They answered on a three-point scale: better, about the same, or worse. We then asked them about déjà vu and involuntary memory incidence:

> How often would you say you experienced "involuntary memories," where scenes from your past life pop into your head? ("Involuntary memories are conscious and unintentional recollections of personal experiences and have been described as being peculiarly vivid and emotional and having a strong feeling of immediacy." daily / once a week / once a month / once every six months / never

How often would you say you experience "déjà vu," where you have the feeling that you've experienced something before, but know that you haven't? ("Déjà vu is a feeling of familiarity when you know that in fact you can't have experienced the present moment before.") How many times have you had déjà vu in the last year? How many times have you had déjà vu in your life?

Participants responded with integers for the déjà vu questions. Where they responded with a range, such as 10–15, the higher value was entered. The textual answers, such as "several" were not analyzed, except where they could be interpreted as numbers, that is, "never" = 0, "couple" = 2.

Results and Discussion
Incidence of déjà vu experiences. Table 13.1 shows the incidence of déjà vu. First we present the frequency of experience for the whole sample that generated meaningful, numeric responses (the differences in the sample sizes reflect data missing because of non-numeric responses). Twenty-two older adult participants said that they had not had déjà vu in the past year (39% of the sample). Only eight people in the younger group (11%) said that they had not had déjà vu in the past year. The difference between the mean number of déjà vu experiences between the groups was significant, $t(128) = 3.08$, $p=.003$, with the older adults having had fewer déjà vu experiences in the past year. There was a marginally significant difference in lifetime incidence, with the older adults reporting fewer instances of déjà vu in their lifespan – despite having lived considerably longer, $t(102)=1.85$, $p=.068$. By way of reference, Brown (2004) found that on average, people between the ages of 15 and 24 experience déjà vu between two and three times a year, somewhat less than our undergraduate sample, who on average reported having had it nine times in the past year.

The rates of déjà vu varied considerably across individuals, and responses such as "too many times to count," "countless," and "lots" may reflect that this is a particularly difficult estimation task. One issue is that perhaps people forget when they last had déjà vu. That might explain age differences in reporting the experience, as the older adults are likely to be more forgetful. We also note that there is a very large standard deviation in the responses for the whole sample, with the range of responses between 0–100 in the incidence in the last year, and 0–1,000 in the lifetime experience. Moreover, the frequency in the past year statistic may reflect differences according to those people who report never having had déjà vu in their lifetime (six in the old sample, and five in the young sample).

TABLE 13.1. *Mean (and standard deviation) of frequency of déjà vu experiences in the past year and across the lifetime, Study 1*

	In the past year	Lifetime
Whole sample		
Young	8.94 (15.86) n=70	68.57 (159.08) n= 65
Old	1.60 (2.29) n=45	20.15 (48.82) n= 39
Clean sample		
Young	6.62 (6.95) n= 60	45.71 (53.10) n=59
Old	1.41 (1.68) n=29	23.31 (53.11) n=32

To address this, a clean sample removed individuals who did not report déjà vu at all in their lifetime, and removed any responses that were three standard deviations above the aggregate mean for the two groups on either the incidence in the past year or in their lifetime. On this basis, three people were removed from the young sample with incidences of more than 40 in the past year, and 800–1,000 lifetime experiences. With this clean sample (see Table 13.1), there was still a highly significant difference in levels of the experience in the past year, $t(87)=3.96$, $p<.001$, although the difference in lifetime experiences was still only marginally significant, $t(89)=1.92$, $p=.058$. Bear in mind that we asked participants about the lifetime incidence in total, however, and if we adjust the scores according to the ages of the participants, these marginally significant raw scores come out as very significantly different, with older adults having less than one déjà vu experience per year, and the younger adults having about three a year – which is in concert with Brown's (2004) estimate.

We did not find an age difference in the rates at which our young and old groups experienced involuntary memories (an ANOVA on the ratings scores and a chi-squared both revealed no group differences, nor did the rating of frequency of involuntary memory correlate with age). Both young and old participants indicated that on average they experienced an involuntary memory between once a week and once a month, although 11 percent of each sample reported having an involuntary memory once a day.

Correlational Analyses. We ran nonparametric correlations separately within each group. Within the older group, there was a negative correlation between age and the incidence of déjà vu in the past year $r(44)=-.356$, $p=.018$, but not lifetime incidence of déjà vu $r(38) = .-072$, $p=.668$. Education level did not correlate with any other variable, nor did self-rated memory performance. The number of involuntary memories correlated with déjà vu – such that more involuntary memories were reported with higher levels of déjà vu, r(44)=.723, p<.001. The lifetime and past year incidences of déjà vu correlated with each other, r(35)=.521, p<.001. The young people's correlations with age were null, as you might expect with age being such a restricted range. But the relationship between involuntary memories and déjà vu was not borne out in the young group, although the two ratings of déjà vu correlated with each other very highly, r(66)=.90, p<.001.

In summary, this study replicates the previously demonstrated reductions in incidence and frequency of déjà vu in older adults. Critically, the novelty of this finding is that this lower level of déjà vu in older adults is found even when we provide older adults with a description of the experience. However, we do find some evidence of a cohort effect: the older group report lower incidence of déjà vu in total across their lifespan compared to young people. That is, although we have controlled for whether or not each group is using a different definition of the experience, the older adult group reported fewer instances of déjà vu for the past year, and also for their life in general. Naturally, one does not keep a tally of one's infrequent mental experiences, and of course, it is possible that to gauge lifetime incidence one looks back over the past year – this of course would explain why the two measures of déjà vu incidence were correlated. Critically, there was not a difference in how the two groups rated their involuntary memories, although both groups had involuntary memories more frequently than they had déjà vu. The incidence of déjà vu and involuntary memory was related in our older sample, though, and we return to this issue later in this chapter.

Study 2

The second study focused on three issues. First, we were interested in how older adults assess déjà vu in comparison to a similar mental event, the TOT experience (e.g., Brown, 2012). Second, we were interested in how well older adults can define déjà vu (and whether younger and older groups differ in how they define it). Finally, we investigated if participants can report a previous example of a déjà vu experience. One interpretation of the difference in déjà vu experiences between the young and old is that they experience it equally frequently, but that the older adults forget that they have had it.

Method
Participants
The sample consisted of 347 participants. The sample had a mean (and standard deviation) age of 31.9 years (17.76) and an age range of 18–90, and was 59 percent female. To offer a comparison with Study 1, 64 percent of the

sample was aged in the range of the young sample, and 14 percent were aged 60 and older, although we did not recruit separate groups in this study, nor did we analyze the data split by age.

Procedure and Materials

The study was conducted by means of an online questionnaire, made available to the general public. Participants were not explicitly informed that the study was related to age and memory, only that it was exploring certain "phenomena of memory." Ethical approval was obtained from the ethics committee of the Institute of Psychological Sciences at the University of Leeds.

The questionnaire consisted of a number of items concerning déjà vu. The first item involved participants selecting which they believed to be the correct definition from a set of three. The correct answer (a) includes the dissociation necessary for a déjà vu experience, whereas (c) gives the incorrect but popular conception of a repeated experience:

> Which of the following definitions most closely resembles your idea of what déjà vu is?
> a) The unsettling feeling of having been in a particular situation before, although you know it is highly unlikely that you ever were.
> b) Suddenly feeling outside of a situation, as if you're on the outside looking in.
> c) When a conversation you've had before comes up, and you go through the same topics all over again.

The following items assessed how recently the person had experienced déjà vu and asked three questions on specific forms of déjà vu and their general frequency of experience.

The questionnaire's website address was posted on several social networking sites (including MSN Groups and AOL Community) in English. It was arranged as a series of pages; when one page was completed, the participant was required to press "submit" before moving on to the next page. The questionnaire began with a number of demographic questions, including gender, age, and level of education achieved, as well as the number of medications taken. Participants were then asked to select what they thought was the best definition of déjà vu, from a selection of three possible definitions (see appendix). Following this, participants responded to items relating to the participants' own déjà vu and tip-of-the-tongue experiences, mainly in a closed, tick-box format, and text boxes were provided that allowed participants to put in any additional information they thought might be relevant.

Results and Discussion

Correct understanding of definitions. Overall, 54 (15.6%) participants incorrectly defined the déjà vu phenomenon. Relatively more of the older adults failed to correctly define déjà vu; of the 50 older adults (i.e., people 60 and older), 32 percent gave the incorrect definition. An independent samples t-test showed that the people who incorrectly defined déjà vu were significantly older than those who correctly defined it (M=41.37 vs. M=30.23, t(344)=-4.336, p<.001). For the following analyses, we exclude people who incorrectly defined the déjà vu phenomenon, in order to focus on the incidence and quality of déjà vu in older adults.

Analysis of lifetime déjà vu incidence. We explicitly asked whether participants had ever had the experience, as part of a question assessing whether the experience had decreased or increased with age. Eight people (3.1%) responded that they had never had the experience. These eight people had a mean age of 22.75 years (range 19–37), that is, none of them were older adults. Thus, to address the issue of whether déjà vu increased or decreased with age, we had a select sample of people who had reported having déjà vu on at least one occasion and who could correctly define the term. However, this clean sample included only 29 older adults.

Memory of last déjà vu experience. Participants used a rating scale to report when they had had their last déjà vu or TOT experience. This rating scale included five points that assessed recency: in the past day, past week, past month, past six months, and past year, and the final point on the scale was used if participants could not remember their last déjà vu experience. Forty-six percent of older adults could not remember their last déjà vu experience. If we exclude those people who could not remember their last experience and run a correlation between age and recency of last déjà vu experience, we find exactly what Study 1 would predict: the younger people have experienced déjà vu more recently, r(196) = .240, p=.001. However, this clean sample of 196 people contains only 14 older adults, an unreasonable subsample size that clearly stretches the generalizability of our results.

If we exclude older adults who have never had the experience, who fail to define the experience correctly, and who cannot remember the last instance of the experience, we are left with only a very limited sample, but we still have evidence that déjà vu decreases as one gets older. Certainly, this approach is a little conservative, and for instance, if older adults genuinely do have reductions in their déjà vu experience, it is not unreasonable that they last occurred so long ago that they are difficult to remember. If we group together the ends of our scales for recency of experience, so that we interpret the inability to remember the last déjà vu experience as a statement about how long ago it occurred, and group together "in the past day" and "in the past week," we are left with a four-point scale of recency. If, using this scale, we switch back to using our full sample regardless of the understanding of the déjà vu term, we continue to find a significant nonparametric correlation between age and recency, $r(306) = .226$, $p<.001$; people who are older rate their last déjà vu experience as having occurred less recently. At this stage, we support the idea that older adults have fewer experiences of déjà vu. It is also clear that older adults struggle to remember their last déjà vu experience, which may point to them making inaccurate assessments of how frequently it occurs (i.e., they experience it, but forget that they do so); or it may be a genuine finding that because they have it less frequently, older adults have to look a lot further back to retrieve the last instance of déjà vu. This is a finding to take into the laboratory: we could investigate the characteristics of memories of mental experiences such as déjà vu, TOT, and involuntary memory in different age groups.

Déjà vu and tip-of-the-tongue experiences. Another aim was to set the questionnaire in the context of the tip-of-the-tongue experience. Using the same scale for recency and the large, untrimmed sample showed no correlation between age and TOT experience, $r(306)=.025$. However, there was a significant correlation between TOT and déjà vu experiences – people who had had a déjà vu experience more recently also reported having had a TOT more recently, $r(306)=.19$, $p=.001$. A comparison of the scales used to rate recency of experience using a paired samples t-test showed that people had experienced a TOT significantly more recently than déjà vu, $t(213)=11.46$, $p<.001$.

The questionnaire also included a number of specific questions about the frequencies of various types of déjà vu and TOT experiences (see Table 13.2). This showed that of our nine comparisons between déjà vu and TOT experiences, six were significant, and the other three were marginally significant (all $p<.13$).[2] That is, in general, people who report déjà vu more frequently report having TOT more frequently.

However, also note that correlations with age were a little unusual with these questions in Table 13.2, possibly reflecting the fact that a large number of the older adults in the sample did not endorse the correct definition of déjà vu. For instance, there was a positive correlation with age for the frequency of feeling that a conversation was repeating, $r(323)=.241$, $p<.001$, suggesting that older people have this feeling more often, contrary to Study 1 and the foregoing analyses. (The other two questions about déjà vu had nonsignificant correlations with age.) The TOT questions yielded results closer to what would be expected with regards to age, significant

TABLE 13.2. *Correlations between déjà vu and TOT experiences, across all participants, Study 2*

	2	3	4	5	6
1	.50**	.23**	.18**	.09	.24**
2		.24**	.10	.10	.19**
3			.12*	.16**	.21**
4				.33**	.29**
5					.28**

Notes: Déjà vu: 1. Same conversation before, 2. Same room before, 3. Same information before. TOT: 4. Can't access actor's name, 5. Can't access place name, 6. Can't find the right word

correlations with age for the frequency of TOTs for actors' names and word finding, $r(322) = .135$, $p=.016$ and $r(322)=.152$, $p=.006$, respectively, although the correlation between TOTs for place names and age was nonsignificant.

In summary, our second study confirms the age differences in déjà vu experiences. There is also evidence on this study that older adults do not endorse the correct definition of déjà vu, in line with our hypothesis that cohort effects in the understanding of the definition may lie behind the differences in young and old rates of déjà vu. Study 2 also shows a relationship between déjà vu experiences and the tip-of-the-tongue experience, in that people who have more TOT experiences have more déjà vu experiences. We also showed that TOTs were reported more recently than déjà vu experiences, in line with them being experienced more frequently.

DISCUSSION: DÉJÀ VU AS METACOGNITION

We started this chapter with the idea that déjà vu results from a pattern mismatch. Pattern mismatch in itself should not lead to déjà vu – it is only half the story. Déjà vu requires two simultaneous evaluations. One – which could be a mismatch – is the sensation that a particular event or instance matches a previous one. The second critical one is the knowledge that this feeling is false. If an older adult visits a place that they erroneously match with a previous place, they won't necessarily recognize that this feeling is false. However, if they mismatch the memory AND are aware of this erroneous match – or know the place to be novel, they will be left with a "clash in mental evaluations," which is at the heart of the déjà vu experience.

We have recently put forward the idea that like other brief and nebulous experiences such as the tip-of-the-tongue state, déjà vu is, in some regards, metacognitive (e.g. Moulin & Souchay, 2013) for a description of TOTs as metacognitive, see Bacon, Schwartz, Paire-Ficout, & Izaute, 2007). It is only because we are able to metacognitively reflect on the error at the heart of the illusion of familiarity that we are aware of it at all. If we are not aware that the feeling of familiarity is false, we do not have déjà vu – we presumably just accept our feeling that the current location or conversation, is, in fact a repetition of one we have encountered previously. That is, déjà vu must derive from some feeling, belief, or knowledge that the familiarity is false. In this way, the déjà vu state suggests that there are two levels of evidence at play in recognition memory, and two different forms of epistemic information in consciousness, a fast and obligatorily sensed feeling that something is familiar, and an evaluation that this feeling is in fact false (see Arango, 2010; de Sousa, 2009; Moulin & Souchay, 2013, for accounts of two levels of metacognition and this notion of epistemic feelings).

TWO THEORIES OF DÉJÀ VU FORMATION

We have previously complained that there is probably a little too much theorizing about déjà vu in the absence of a strong empirical basis for said theories (Moulin & Chauvel, 2010). At least one popular theory, the idea that déjà vu is caused by information from one eye being processed in advance of the other, for instance, was dispatched with the most minimal of empirical work – the demonstration of déjà vu in a blind subject (O'Connor & Moulin, 2006). But other theories of déjà vu based on dreams, for instance, are pervasive among the population more widely, and are difficult to shift, but should receive a little more attention from empirical work. For dreaming, our view is that when faced with a strange and inexplicable feeling of familiarity, people are drawn to dreams as a way of explaining the sensation – the feeling can be made sense of with the post hoc justification that it was encountered in dream. If one has a robust paradigm for generating déjà vu, this would be an easy idea to test.

There are two broad theories of déjà vu formation, which draw on different literatures, but are sustainable according to current views of memory function. Here we outline these two: the Gestalt similarity hypothesis (e.g., Cleary et al., 2012; Dashiel, 1937) and the decoupled familiarity hypothesis (e.g., Illman et al., 2012; Penfield, 1955). We then offer an explanation of how they may be seen in the healthy aging process.

The Gestalt Similarity Hypothesis

The key feature of the similarity hypothesis is that there is some overlap between a perceptual experience (which is responsible for triggering the déjà vu) and a previously stored representation, not unlike the pattern mismatch idea. The "Gestalt" in the title refers to an overarching "form" or "structure" into which perceptual elements can fall:

> [D]éjà vu is elicited by familiarity with the arrangement of the elements within a scene. For example, when visiting a friend's home for the first time, one may have a strange sense of having been in that living room before. Perhaps the arrangement of the furniture in the new friend's living room (e.g., the way that the couches, tables and lamps are arranged) maps onto an arrangement that was seen before, perhaps in the person's doctor's office waiting area. The inability to recall the doctor's office waiting area as the source of this familiarity leads to the experience of déjà vu. Cleary and colleagues (2012, p. 969)

The critical issue is developed in the last sentence: the experient should be unaware of the source of the familiarity, and this would lead to the inherent conflict in feelings in a déjà vu experience. The beauty of this account of déjà vu is that it lends itself to an existing laboratory task, the recognition without identification paradigm, which is where it is possible to make a stimulus familiar in such a way that the participant is not aware of the source of the familiarity (e.g., Cleary et al., 2012; Cleary et al., 2009; Cleary & Reyes, 2009; Cleary, 2008). For instance, in perhaps its most elegant manifestation (Cleary et al., 2012), participants studied rooms in a virtual reality environment (where the experimenter provided a label, such as "bedroom"). Participants then encountered similar and dissimilar rooms in a test (Exp. 1; or similar, dissimilar, and identical rooms, Exp. 2). Participants reported whether they could recall the label, followed by a rating of familiarity for the room and a report (yes/no) as to whether they were experiencing déjà vu. Cleary and colleagues arranged the rooms such that half matched the studied rooms configurally, and half did not. In Experiment 1, they report that participants could recall the label of nearly half the configurally similar rooms, leaving a set of rooms that are similar in some way, but in which the similarity is undetected. These similar rooms can be compared to the rooms that do not resemble previously encountered rooms. Déjà vu was measured for these rooms with a yes/no question, with 27 percent of similar rooms giving rise to déjà vu, significantly higher than for the dissimilar rooms (17%). Furthermore, the familiarity ratings were higher for the configurally similar scenes, and an item-by-item correlation showed that the more familiar a room feels, the more likely it is to give rise to a feeling of déjà vu. Experiment 2 produced similar results, with participants again reporting déjà vu experiences on about a third of items.

Experiment 2 is also of interest, because it re-presented participants with rooms at test that were identical to studied rooms, as would be usual in tests of recognition memory ("old" items). Naturally, because these test items actually are a repetition of a previous stimulus, we should not expect them to generate a feeling of déjà vu: standard recognition memory tests do not routinely give rise to déjà vu. Indeed, Cleary and colleagues (p. 973) state that "we defined déjà vu as a simultaneous recognition of newness alongside a feeling of familiarity" and report that two participants gave déjà vu responses for 100 percent of old items, consistent with a misunderstanding of the definition of déjà vu. In line with our reasoning, and our approach, these subjects highlight the difficulties in working with such an ephemeral and subjective experience, and their data was removed from the study, as we did in our analysis. In sum, Cleary and colleagues present experimental support for the idea that déjà vu arises when scenes (for instance) have some overlap with a prior scene, giving rise to a feeling of familiarity, but for which the cause for this familiarity is undetected.

The Decoupled Familiarity Hypothesis

An alternate (but not necessarily incompatible) view is that déjà vu arises when the sensation of familiarity becomes decoupled from the current outputs of memory processing, such that there is a false feeling of familiarity independent from what is actually perceived in the environment. The chief support for this idea has been neuropsychological, arising from data from neuropsychological populations, most particularly temporal lobe epilepsy (TLE; see Illman et al., 2012). An early presentation of this idea (O'Connor and Moulin, 2008) emphasized that déjà vu is not connected to what was received from the perceptual system – it is a higher-order error caused by processing problems in the brain. The genesis of this idea was the observation that in cases of TLE, the feeling of déjà vu is essentially unpredictable, and when it does occur, it is felt for all domains and modalities, and does not reduce according to what the experient pays attention to (the same occurs in other pathologies, e.g., Kalra et al., 2007).

The decoupled familiarity hypothesis does not lend itself so readily to experimentation in healthy subjects, and thus the chief evidence for this idea rests with clinical reports and our knowledge of the memory system. In brief, in TLE there is a disturbance in the synchronization of brain waves in

the region responsible for memory, with the result that the feeling of familiarity can be activated independently of retrieval from memory. Indeed,
this can also be achieved artificially. Direct application of electrical current
to the cortex of the temporal lobes produces sensations of déjà vu in epileptic patients (who have this procedure to "map" brain areas responsible
for symptomology and function prior to surgery; Bartolomei et al., 2004;
Penfield & Perot, 1963).

Like many areas of cognitive neuropsychology, the deficit and dysfunction in TLE hints at how the healthy brain is organized and how it operates.
In the healthy experient, the idea is that a physiological event akin to a brief
and otherwise inconsequential epileptic glitch activates a feeling of familiarity. The fact that tiredness and intoxication are related to déjà vu experiences (Brown, 2003) supports the idea that there is a physiological basis for
déjà vu. Moreover, observations such as déjà vu being experienced more
by people who travel more (Brown, 2003) can be explained by the fact that
only when in a novel situation would one notice that there has been an erroneous activation of familiarity. Of course, there are many interpretations of
such a correlation; not least, it is educated people who travel more and it is
educated people who are more tuned in to their mental experiences.

The difficulty in using neuropsychological cases and phenomena like
this is making a link between healthy and pathological déjà vu. Several
researchers have examined the quality of déjà vu in TLE, with some finding
that déjà vu is phenomenologically the same in healthy and epileptic forms
(e.g., Warren-Gash & Zeman, in press) and others finding that epileptics
can differentiate between seizure related and non-seizure related déjà vu –
although this is largely due to the fact that seizure-related déjà vu is related
to other experiential phenomena, what Warren-Gash and Zeman (in press)
refer to as the "company that déjà vu keeps." The investigation of the phenomenology and quality of déjà vu when it occurs naturally is somewhat
limited by the inventory commonly used to assess it, which predates the
recent resurgence of interest shown in déjà vu by cognitive psychologists
since Brown's review and the two principal theories of formation outlined
here. A priority for future research would be to develop a measure that takes
on board the theoretical insights of the familiarity approaches.

AGING AND THEORIES OF DÉJÀ VU FORMATION

How might our aging data fit into these two theories of déjà vu formation?
In one of her early papers, Cleary offers an interpretation of the Gestalt similarity hypothesis, which hinges on the fact that as we get older, we become

more reliant on familiarity and less able to recollect specifics of a previous scene:

> Because reliance on familiarity likely increases with age, people may become accustomed to experiencing familiarity-based recognition as they age. Thus older people may frequently attribute feelings of familiarity to failures of recalling specific prior experiences or to forgetting rather than labeling them as déjà vu instances. Cleary (2008, p. 356)

By this view, older adults are not metacognitively aware of the inconsistent feelings of familiarity, because they often make assessments based on familiarity, and without being able to recognize the error in their memory attribution. We have developed this idea to include recollective processes (Moulin & Souchay, 2013). Memory researchers commonly contrast two evaluations: recollection and familiarity. One of the main functions of recollection is to minimize memory errors and avoid "illusions of familiarity" (Jacoby et al., 1989). For instance, an eyewitness who has seen two people, a bystander and a perpetrator, needs to be able to recall the information about who was who in order to not be seduced by the overwhelming sensation of familiarity of the bystander. This ability has been termed "recollection rejection" (Brainerd et al., 2003), and consists in correctly rejecting errors on the basis of recollection, for example, remembering that the man with glasses was the man who sat opposite on the bus, not the one who ran off with the iPad. Recollection is also involved in reducing susceptibility to memory distortions such as misattribution (i.e., the act of attributing a recollection or idea to an incorrect source).

We suggest that to experience déjà vu one needs intact recollection to produce the clash in evaluations (see Spatt, 2002, for neurological account of this view). In short, many research themes converge on the idea that recollection is impaired in older adults (e.g., Souchay et al., 2007). For example, older adults are less likely to experience memory in the form of "remembering" (e.g., Perfect & Dasgupta, 1997; Souchay et al., 2007). This is a rather specific memory failure: older adults are as capable of recognizing items in a memory test as younger adults, but their subjective experience is different from younger people's: they do not "remember" specifics of the study phase. This view neatly explains the lower rates of déjà vu in older adults – it's because of less recollection.

This view of déjà vu receives support from the temporal lobe epilepsy literature. Martin and colleagues (2012) took two groups of TLE, some of whom did and some of whom did not have déjà vu as part of their seizure manifestation. They show that the patients with TLE who experience déjà vu have a familiarity disorder, as we would predict here. However, a disorder in familiarity did not differentiate those who did and did not experience déjà vu – both groups of TLE patients had a familiarity disorder, whereby they were less able to use familiarity signals to judge whether a stimulus had been previously seen or not. It was recollection that differentiated the groups – those who had déjà vu had significantly *better* recognition scores than the TLE patients without déjà vu. The interpretation of this finding is that recollection is required to be aware of the erroneous familiarity at play in the déjà vu phenomenon. Patients with TLE who have both familiarity and recollection deficits do not possess sufficient memory capacity to detect the error of familiarity.

In sum, younger adults have the requisite processes to detect a clash between two evaluations, whereas the older adults have a diminished ability to detect a clash between familiarity and more objective sources. Older adults either cannot use recollection to reject feelings of familiarity or become habitually used to familiarity-alone assessments of the environment in the absence of recollection. This interpretation follows for both theoretical accounts of the déjà vu phenomena, and cannot differentiate between the two theories outlined earlier. The Gestalt similarity and decoupled familiarity accounts both explain how the familiarity mismatch arises – and either or both may be correct, but the decline in déjà vu experiences in aging, by our view, is most likely linked to a deficit in recollection, or at least a change in the relationship between familiarity and recollection in older adults. The most obvious means for assessing the recollection and familiarity hypothesis is to use Cleary and colleagues' paradigms in older adults. First, we might expect that if these experiments do produce something akin to the real déjà vu experience, that it should be less successful in older adults. Second, we might expect the differences in susceptibility to déjà vu to change with relation to recollection, in line with Martin and colleagues' (2012) results.

DÉJÀ VU: TAKING A LEAD FROM THE TOT AND INVOLUNTARY MEMORY LITERATURES

Finally, because we have looked at other phenomena in the empirical literature in this chapter, we wanted to outline some thoughts for future work based on research into these other phenomena. We have previously outlined the differences and similarities between déjà vu and the tip-of-the-tongue experiences. Both can be thought of as metacognitive and as infrequent memory errors that expose the epistemic feelings at play in cognition (Arango -Muñoz, 2010). In this study, we found a relationship between the two: people who experienced a TOT more recently (our proxy for frequency of experience) had also experienced déjà vu more frequently. And yet, déjà vu was a less frequent memory error. This correlation may point to the fact that some people are more aware of their cognitive failings and epistemic feelings than others.

The main issue we want to draw out here is the relationship between laboratory and questionnaire evaluations of TOT and déjà vu. Despite Cleary and colleagues' clear successes in laboratory analogs of déjà vu, it is remains rather difficult to produce in the laboratory and is something of a ephemeral entity. One criticism of the laboratory variety of déjà vu is that it is produced somewhat too successfully, that is, the déjà vu rates are higher than anything one might observe naturally (see O'Connor & Moulin, 2010, for a critique). The TOT is easier to produce in the laboratory than déjà vu, being that it can be elicited reliably by a set of purposefully designed general knowledge questions, but even here, it too has been criticized for being too easy to produce in the laboratory, with a common criticism being that the real-world and laboratory experiences may not share phenomenology or even the same cause. Typically, the TOT might be experienced multiple times on one test in the laboratory, whereas diary studies indicate that it is experienced only about once a week in young adults, and once a day in the oldest old (Brown, 2012). Heine and colleagues (1999) examined diary TOT and laboratory TOT rates in the same groups of participants. In the laboratory, their group of young adults (mean age 21 years) generated 23 TOTs on a 112-item test. In the real world, over a four-week period, the same group repeated a mean of 5.21 TOTs. Similar figures are found in déjà vu, too. Cleary and Reyes (2009) found 87 percent of participants (33 of 38) report at least one incidence of déjà vu in their experiment. This is striking in that the generation of déjà vu is almost as frequent as the generation of the TOT state, which was achieved in 97 percent of participants in the same experiment. Unlike in the TOT literature, there are no studies that attempt to reconcile rates of déjà vu in the laboratory and in the real world, and this is a priority for future research.

The déjà vu literature needs to develop in the manner of the TOT literature, where researchers share a generally accepted definition, and a central paradigm behind which researchers can align themselves. The TOT has the advantage that there are behavioral consequences of the feeling (such as search time, and the production of associated information, and the effects of a concurrent task; Schwartz, 2001, 2002, 2008). In comparison, it is difficult to see what the behavioral consequences of a déjà vu experience are.

One promising idea is to examine the after effects of the déjà vu-eliciting trial. If the experimenter really has produced an attention-grabbing experience, one might expect a cost to processing on the next trial (or possibly on a dual task). In an elegant demonstration of this idea, Schwartz (2011) has shown that TOTs are less likely to occur in the trial after a TOT has been reported, with the interpretation being that the high level of resources required to generate a metacognitive evaluation have been depleted, and take a while to recover. This occurs even though recall is not affected for the subsequent trial.

We examined involuntary memories in Study 1 and would like to briefly point to areas ripe for future research. In a similar way to the TOT literature, there is mixed evidence about involuntary memories in older adults according to differing methodology. Questionnaires by Berntsen and Rubin (2002) and diary studies by Schlagman and colleagues (2009) found that older adults report fewer involuntary memories than younger people during their day-to-day lives, but a later study by Rubin and Berntsen (2009) with participants aged 15 to older than 90 concluded that involuntary memories had similar frequencies. Again, the involuntary memory literature is at pains to discuss and comprehend the differences between the real-world phenomenon and its laboratory analog, and how aging might help us understand that picture. But the point here is that when there is a divergent pattern between age changes in laboratory and field studies, it should tell us something about the processes involved in the phenomena and the validity of the theory. In the current chapter, we showed that déjà vu was related to involuntary memory – at least in the older adult group. Involuntary memories are more frequently experienced than déjà vu. We have previously suggested that according to the decoupled familiarity hypothesis, these two experiences should be related. Indeed, in TLE, when the erroneous neural firing is sufficient, whole veridical memories are intruded into consciousness rather than just a feeling of familiarity (Vignal et al., 2007). We have presented the idea that in TLE there is a continuum between déjà vu feelings and the retrieval of prior events (Illman et al., 2012), but this idea needs development in healthy groups.

CONCLUSIONS

The idea that déjà vu decreases with age is not new – déjà vu all over again – and before this empirical chapter there were datasets larger and more detailed than ours that clearly showed that it decreased with age. The data reported here add to this picture, however, and neatly illustrate that as well as a genuine decline according to age (which might be confirmed with laboratory investigations of déjà vu in older adults) there are also cohort differences in the understanding of the term and in estimates of lifetime incidence. Once these factors are taken into consideration, however, there is still a clear finding that déjà vu is experienced less frequency by older adults.

We have presented a summary of theories of déjà vu formation and offered a couple of suggestions for future research. In sum, we argue that déjà vu rests not only on falsely finding an event or location familiar, but also on detecting that familiarity as inappropriate, and it is in this second factor, in line with neuropsychological evidence from TLE, in which we hypothesize that older adults are particularly impaired. The ability to know that a familiar event is not in fact a repetition of a similar occurrence presumably relies on some recall or recollection process requiring the retrieval of specifics and a sense of certainty, and current theories of memory in older adults suggest that this type of memory is impaired.

NOTES

1. Of interest, Tonegawa's willingness to forward his own personal theory on déjà vu (based on his experience) is at odds with Brown's (2004) observation that there might be less research into déjà vu than other memory phenomena because it occurs less with age, and as such more "mature" researchers might just not find it personally relevant or interesting.
2. Note that if we correct for multiple comparisons using Bonferroni corrections, five of these correlations remain significant.

REFERENCES

Adachi, N., Adachi, T., Akanuma, N., Matsubara, R., & Ito, M. (2007). Déjà vu experiences in schizophrenia: Relations with psychopathology and antipsychotic medication. *Comprehensive Psychiatry*, 48, 592–596.

Adachi, N., Adachi, T., Kimura, M., Akanuma, N., Takekawa, Y., & Kato, M. (2003). Demographic and psychological features of déjà vu experiences in a nonclinical Japanese population. *Journal of Nervous and Mental Disease*, 191, 242–247.

Adachi, N., Akanuma, N., Akanu, N., Adachi, T., Takekawa, Y., Adachi, Y., Ito, M., et al. (2008). Déjà vu experiences are rarely associated with pathological dissociation. *The Journal of Nervous and Mental Disease*, 196(5), 417–419.

Adachi, N., Akanuma, N., Ito, M., Adachi, T., Takekawa, Y., Adachi, Y., Matsuura, M., et al. (2010). Two forms of déjà vu experiences in patients with epilepsy. *Epilepsy & Behavior: E&B*, 18(3), 218–222.

Arango-Muñoz, S. (2010). Two levels of metacognition. *Philosophia*, 39(1), 71–82.

Back, K. W., & Bourque, L. B. (1970). Life graphs: Aging and cohort effect. *Journal of Gerontology*, 25: 249–255.

Bacon, E., Schwartz, B. L., Paire-Ficout, L., & Izaute, M. (2007). Dissociation between the cognitive process and the phenomenological experience of TOT: Effect of the anxiolytic drug lorazepam on TOT states. *Consciousness & Cognition*, 16, 360–373.

Bartolomei, F., Barbeau, E., Gavaret, M., Guye, M., & Mcgonigal, A. (2004). Cortical stimulation study of the role of rhinal cortex in déjà vu and reminiscence of memories. *Neurology*, 63, 858–864.

Berntsen, D., & Rubin, D. C. (2002). Emotionally charged autobiographical memories across the life span: The recall of happy, sad, traumatic, and involuntary memories. *Psychology and Aging*, 17(4), 636–652.

Brainerd, C. J., Reyna, V. F., Wright, R., & Mojarding, A. H. (2003). Recollection rejection: False-memory editing in children and adults. *Psychological Review*, 110, 762–784.

Brown, A. S. (2003). A review of the déjà vu experience. *Psychological Bulletin*, 129, 394–413.

(2004). *The déjà vu experience*. London: Psychology Press.

(2012). *The tip of the tongue state*. New York: Psychology Press.

Chapman, A. H., & Mensh, I. N. (1951). Déjà vu experience and conscious fantasy in adults. *Psychiatric Quarterly Supplement*, 25, 163–175.

Cleary, A. M. (2008). Recognition memory, familiarity, and déjà vu experiences. *Current Directions in Psychological Science*, 17: 353–357.

Cleary, A. M., Brown, A. S., Sawyer, B. D., Nomi, J. S., Ajoku, A. C., & Ryals, A. J. (2012). Familiarity from the configuration of objects in 3-dimensional space and its relation to déjà vu: A virtual reality investigation. *Consciousness and Cognition*, 21(2), 969–975.

Cleary, A. M., & Reyes, N. L. (2009). Scene recognition without identification. *Acta Psychologica*, 131(1), 53–62.

Cleary, A. M., Ryals, A. J., & Nomi, J. S. (2009). Can déjà vu result from similarity to a prior experience? Support for the similarity hypothesis of déjà vu. *Psychonomic Bulletin & Review*, 16(6), 1082–1088.

Dashiell, J. (1937). *Fundamentals of general psychology*. Boston, MA: Houghton Mifflin Company.

de Sousa, R. (2009). Epistemic feelings. *Mind and Matter*, 7(2), 139–161.

Gallup, G. H., & Newport, F. (1991). Belief in paranormal phenomena among adult Americans. *Skeptical Inquirer*, 15.

Heine, M. K., Ober, B. A., & Shenaut, G. K. (1999). Naturally occurring and experimentally induced tip-of-the-tongue experiences in three adult age groups. *Psychology and Aging*, 14, 445–457.

Illman, N. A., Butler, C. R., Souchay, C., & Moulin, C. J. A. (2012). Deja experiences in temporal lobe epilepsy. *Epilepsy Research and Treatment*, 1–40.

Jacoby, L., Kelley, C., & Dywan, J. (1989). Memory attributions. In H. L. Roediger & F. Craik (Eds.), *Varieties of memory and consciousness* (pp. 391–422). New York: Lawrence Erlbaum Associates.

Kalra, S., Chancellor, A., & Zeman, A. (2007). Recurring déjà vu associated with 5-hydroxytryptophan. *Acta Neuropsychiatrica*, 19, 311–313.

Kohr, R. L. (1980). A survey of psi experiences among members of a special population. *Journal of the American Society for Psychical Research*, 74, 395–412.

Martin, C. B., Mirsattari, S. M., Pruessner, J. C., Pietrantonio, S., Burneo, J. G., Hayman-Abello, B., & Köhler, S. (2012). Déjà vu in unilateral temporal-lobe epilepsy is associated with selective familiarity impairments on experimental tasks of recognition memory. *Neuropsychologia*, 50, 2981–2991.

Mosher, D. (2007). Origin of déjà vu pinpointed. http://www.livescience.com/1589-origin-deja-vu-pinpointed.html. Accessed on January 14, 2014.

Moulin, C. J. A., & Chauvel, P. (2010). Déjà vu: Insights from the dreamy state and memory research. In D. B. Wright & G. Davies (Eds.), *New frontiers in applied memory* (pp 206–235): Hove, UK: Psychology Press.

Moulin, C. J. A., & Souchay, C. (2013). Epistemic feelings and memory. In T. Perfect & S. Lindsay (Eds.), *The Sage handbook of applied memory* (pp. 520–537). SAGE.

O'Connor, A. R., Lever, C., & Moulin, C. J. A. (2010). Novel insights into false recollection: A model of déjà vu. *Cognitive Neuropsychiatry*, 15(1), 118–144.

O'Connor, A. R., & Moulin, C. J. A. (2008). The persistence of erroneous familiarity in an epileptic male: Challenging perceptual theories of déjà vu activation. *Brain and Cognition*, 68, 144–147.

(2006). Normal patterns of déjà experience in a healthy, blind male: Challenging optical pathway delay theory. *Brain and Cognition*, 62(3), 246–249.

(2010). Recognition without identification, erroneous familiarity, and déjà vu. *Current Psychiatry Reports*, 12(3), 165–173.

Penfield, W. (1955). The twenty-ninth Maudsley lecture: The role of the temporal cortex in certain psychical phenomena. *Journal of Mental Science*, 101, 451–465.

Penfield, W., & Perot, P. (1963). The brain's record of auditory and visual experience: A final summary and discussion. *Brain*, 86, 595–696.

Perfect, T. J. and Dasgupta, Z. R. R. (1997). What underlies the deficit in reported recollective experience in old age? *Memory & Cognition*, 25, 849–858.

Rubin, D. C., & Berntsen, D. (2009). The frequency of voluntary and involuntary autobiographical memories across the life span. *Memory & Cognition*, 37(5), 679–688.

Schlagman, S., Kliegel, M., Schulz, J., & Kvavilashvili, L. (2009). Differential effects of age on involuntary and voluntary autobiographical memory. *Psychology and Aging*, 24(2), 397–411.

Schwartz, B. L. (2001). The relationship of tip-of-the tongue states and retrieval time. *Memory & Cognition*, 29, 117–126.

(2002). The strategic control of retrieval during tip-of-the tongue states. *The Korean Journal of Thinking & Problem Solving*, 12, 27–37.

(2008). Working memory load differentially affect tip-of-the tongue states and feeling-of-knowing judgments. *Memory & Cognition*, 36, 9–19.

(2011). The effect of being in a tip-of-the-tongue state on subsequent items. *Memory & Cognition*, 39, 245–250.

Sno, H. N., Schalken, H. F. A., de Jonghe, F., & Koeter, M. W. J. (1994). The inventory for déjà vu experiences assessment. *The Journal of Nervous and Mental Disease*, 182, 27–33.

Souchay, C., Moulin, C. J. A., Clarys, D., Taconnat, L., & Isingrini, M. (2007). Diminished episodic memory awareness in older adults: Evidence from feeling of knowing and recollection. *Consciousness and Cognition*, 16, 769–784.

Spatt, J. (2002). Déjà vu: Possible parahippocampal mechanisms. *Journal of Neuropsychiatry and Clinical Neurosciences*, 14(6–10).

Vignal, J.-P., Maillard, L., McGonigal, A., & Chauvel, P. (2007). The dreamy state: Hallucinations of autobiographic memory evoked by temporal lobe stimulations and seizures. *Brain*, 130, 88–99.

Warren-Gash, C., & Zeman, A. (in press). Is there anything distinctive about epileptic déjà vu? *Journal of Neurology, Neurosurgery and Psychiatry*.

14

Odor Knowledge, Odor Naming, and the "Tip-of-the-Nose" Experience

FREDRIK U. JÖNSSON AND RICHARD J. STEVENSON

The present chapter concerns odor naming. In particular, it focuses on our naming ability and what we know about odors, in terms of both objective and subjective (metacognitive) knowledge, when we cannot name them. Our ability, or perhaps more aptly, our inability, to correctly name odors without the help of visual or other contextual cues has vexed researchers of olfaction for decades. It has even been described as the "most contentious issue in human olfactory processing" (Herz & Engen, 1996, p. 301). Imagine that you look at a lemon, that you have no other input apart from the visual, and are asked to tell its name. You will likely not find it difficult to tell that it is a lemon, as would all healthy observers. If you instead smell the odor of lemon (again without any other sensory input), naming performance drops considerably, even though the odor will feel very familiar. The environment is full of items that anyone within a given culture would name correctly if they see the object, but if they only smell it, the task becomes considerably more difficult. We still do not fully understand why this is so. In the present chapter, we will present some of the main ideas about why it is so difficult to name odors. We will also examine the relatively few studies that have investigated "feelings of knowing" for odors that you cannot name.

Corresponding author: Fredrik U. Jönsson, Department of Psychology, Stockholm University, S-106 91 Stockholm, Sweden. E-mail: fredrik.jonsson@psychology.su.se. Phone: +46 8 163876.
Author note: Richard Stevenson thanks the Australian Research Council for its continued support, and Fredrik Jönsson likewise thanks the Swedish Research Council.

OUR ABILITY TO NAME AND IDENTIFY ODORS

If you let a group of participants try to name a set of familiar everyday odors without the help of other cues, naming performance rarely exceeds 50 percent (e.g., Cain, 1979, 1982; Cain, de Wijk, Lulejian, Schiet, & See, 1998; Desor & Beauchamp, 1974; de Wijk & Cain, 1994a, 1994b; de Wijk, Schab, & Cain, 1995; Distel & Hudson, 2001; Lawless & Engen, 1977; Olsson & Fridén, 2001). For unfamiliar and uncommon odors, naming performance is considerably lower, and successful naming of *any* single item, however common, rarely reaches 100 percent across a group of participants. Note that these performance levels pertain to our ability to correctly name odors presented in a laboratory environment and in the absence of other contextual cues. In everyday life, we often have other cues that help us tell what odor we smell. For example, the sight of the object, or the situational context, might help in identifying the odor. Such cued identification can be simulated in the laboratory. Davis (1981) showed that when odors were presented along with matching or mismatching color cues, matching cues improved identification performance compared to when no cues were present (although mismatching cues decreased performance). Mostly, though, cued identification refers to a task where an odor is presented along with several odor names, where one is correct in a multiple alternatives forced choice format. Cued identification is considerably easier. For example, de Wijk and Cain (1994a) demonstrated that, whereas young adults' free odor naming was around 40 percent correct, performance increased to above 80 percent correct when cued. For a group of middle-aged participants, performance improved from approximately 30 percent to above 80 percent correct responses in the same study. As the chance level was 17 percent for the cued identification test, this increase is statistically substantial. Because normal healthy participants perform well in cued identification tests, they are the method of choice for clinical tests of olfactory ability such as the University of Pennsylvania Smell Identification Test (Doty, Shaman, Kimmelman, & Dann, 1984), the Scandinavian Odor Identification Test (Nordin, Brämerson, Lidén, & Bende, 1998; Nordin, Nyroos, Maunuksela, Niskanen, & Tuorila, 2002), the Connecticut Chemosensory Clinical Research Center Test (Cain, Goodspeed, Gent, & Leonard, 1988), and the Sniffin' Sticks Test (Kobal et al., 1996). In fact, cued identification may be about as good as our ability to discriminate between different odors. *Odor discrimination* refers to our ability to tell whether a set of odors presented are the same or different. For example, two identical or different odors can be sampled immediately one after the other in a trial, varying both the odors and whether they differ. Yet another example is the Sniffin' Sticks Test (Kobal et al., 1996), where three odors are presented in each of 16 trials with the task to tell which of the three is different. In one study, which used six different odor types, de Wijk and Cain (1994b) compared odor quality discrimination to cued identification. When performance measures were corrected for chance, cued identification (chance level = .17) fell just 10 percent below discrimination (chance level = .50) among young adults and only 1 percent below discrimination in a middle-aged group.

Researchers have taken the marked difficulty of odor naming to imply a fundamental asymmetry in the odor-name association. For example, de Wijk Schab and Cain stated that "the compromised relationship between odors and their names appears to be unidirectional: Where presentation of an odor frequently will fail to activate the odor's name in semantic memory, activation of the odor's name by the experimenter, or the context, often leads to unambiguous perception of the odor in terms of the presented name, even when the actual odor presented is a degraded exemplar" (1995, p. 25). Olsson and Jönsson (2008) tested this odor-name association asymmetry hypothesis. They compared the task of smelling an odor and then choosing the name from among three alternatives with that of reading an odor name and then choosing the matching odorant from among three alternatives. Although asymmetries were found in both directions, depending on which odors or odor names were involved, the overall conclusion was that no general asymmetry is evident. It was as difficult to match a name to an odor as an odor to a name, and this was true for odorants of both high and low familiarity and identifiability.

THE DISTINCTION BETWEEN ODOR IDENTIFICATION AND ODOR NAMING

Most research about odor identification has consisted of odor naming tasks (e.g., de Wijk et al., 1995). The typical procedure is to let a group of participants sample different odors, one at a time, without visual or other contextual cues and to then try to name the object from which the odor emanates. This is often referred to as *free identification* in the literature. The underlying assumption is that if a person is able to name something, then he/she normally also knows what it is (see, e.g., Johnson, Paivio, & Clark, 1996, for similar thoughts on picture naming). However, an object can be identified even though its name is not retrieved or even learned. For example, it is possible to recognize someone's face and know much about them, but fail to retrieve their name (e.g., Burton & Bruce, 1992). For this reason, it is important to distinguish between *naming* and *identification*. Contemporary theories of picture naming (McCauley, Parmelee, Sperber, & Carr, 1980; Johnson et al., 1996) and person naming (Burton & Bruce, 1992) use this distinction, separating object identification (which occurs first) from name activation and response generation.

According to this general scheme, an object is first identified, which involves the activation of a perceptually discrete representation that has a unique set of associations with semantic memory. Notice that the further fractionation implied here is between the creation of a perceptually discrete representation and the capacity of this representation to activate links with semantic memory. Following identification, one or more candidate names are activated within semantic memory. Finally, in the third stage, the best candidate name is articulated as an overt response (aloud or in writing). According to Johnson and colleagues (1996), these stages are usually assumed to occur more or less sequentially, with each process dissociable from the other. Hence, an object can be discriminable from other objects with little being known about it, it can be identified without its name being activated (i.e., in the absence of lexical access), and a name can be activated without it being overtly expressed. An olfactory example of identification without naming would be if you smelled juniper and could discriminate it from other odors (i.e., perceptually discrete), but know nothing further about it. Another example would be that you could discriminate juniper odor and imagine the tree on which it grows, how the juniper berries look, and that it is an ingredient in gin (i.e., associations with semantic memory), but you could not retrieve its name. Obviously, if you can name something correctly, the object will normally also be identified, but the opposite may not be true.

Holley argued that odors are nothing but "attributes of objects and substances whose natural function is to reveal the presence of those objects and substances in the environment. Consequently, odor naming turns out to be odor-source naming" (2002, p. 19). In line with this view, we utilize the term *odor naming* in this chapter as the ability to correctly name an odor's source. It is important to bear in mind that this type of name is quite unlike the arbitrary names that we associate with people's faces or with geographical places. Burton and Bruce (1992) suggest that we commonly have problems recalling arbitrary names because they are more sparsely linked to a facial identity node compared to other knowledge about that person. For this reason, they argue, it is easier to recall things you know about a person you see than it is to recall their name. However, the same may not be true for olfaction. Odor names are not arbitrary, and are arguably far more connected with other pieces of knowledge concerning that odor (e.g., "lighter fluid" is a more basic level of categorization than "Zippo" brand) than, say, a person's name (e.g., Jim) is with a particular face. While failure to recall a person's name has few implications for what you may know about that person, failing to recall an odor's name may mean you can know very little about the odor in question.

The second definition we make – and one distinct from odor naming – is *odor identification*, used here to denote identification ability (i.e., perceptually discrete, associations with semantic memory) that is independent of naming ability. As will be shown, an inability to name odors rarely depends on the observer's failure to come up with a proper name for an already identified odor (as would be the case if you could picture the juniper berry or gin bottle, but not be able to come up with the name "juniper"). The inability to name the odor appears to be a consequence of an identification failure (Jönsson, Tchekhova, Lönner, & Olsson, 2005), although it is currently unclear whether this stems from a perceptual failure, a failure to access semantic memory, or some combination of the two. Because we will likely be able to name the odor source when we have identified the odor name, odor naming performance turns out to be a reasonable approximation of odor identification performance.

WHY IS IT SO DIFFICULT TO NAME ODORS?

What characterizes the TOT experience, the primary focus of this book, is the (temporary) inability to retrieve a sought-after name that is very well known. Quite independently of TOT research, olfactory researchers have long wondered about our apparent inability to name even very familiar odors. However, as we will review later on in this chapter, relatively few studies have investigated TOT experiences triggered by olfactory stimuli (Cleary, Konkel, Nomi, & McCabe, 2010; Lawless & Engen, 1977; Jönsson & Olsson, 2003; Jönsson et al., 2005). The different explanations that have been forwarded to account for the apparent difficulty we have in naming even very familiar odors can broadly be divided into *associative* and *perceptual* failures.

ASSOCIATIVE ACCOUNTS OF ODOR
IDENTIFICATION FAILURES

Köster argued that odor identification is not the primary function of our sense of smell, and that odor names lack ecological importance. Therefore, it is not that surprising that we find it difficult to name odors. He stated that "detection, discrimination, and recognition of odors as familiar or unfamiliar are more important than assessments of intensity gradients or verbal identification of the odor" (2002, p. 28). Rather, Köster (2002) and Degel and Köster (1999) have focused on the implicit effects of odors, and argue that although we sense odors most of the time, we typically do not attend to them. Hence, if odor perception is often implicit, meaning that we do not talk that much about or describe them, and if odor identification is not the primary function of the olfactory sense modality, odor naming may not be that ecologically important. This view posits that odor naming fails because we have not properly learned the association between the odor and its name. However, there are occasions when accurate identification of odors is advantageous, if not essential. For example, the failure to identify a kitchen gas leak, spoiled food, or fire all could have detrimental consequences (White & Kurtz, 2003). Note also that positive identification of odors seems to enhance processing at the perceptual level. When odors are identified, we are better at discriminating between them than when they are not (Jönsson, Møller, & Olsson, 2011).

Another possible reason why we have poorly learned the association between an odor and its name is that odor names are nonconsensual. More specifically, Sulmont-Rossé, Issanchou, and Köster (2005) argue that poor performance in odor naming tasks may be due to the lack of social consensus about odor names. People encounter certain odors in different contexts or in different products, which means that which odor is associated with which objects differs between persons and cultures. For example, in their experiment, several participants consistently labeled artificial flower odors as "cleaning supply" or "bathroom freshener." These were not the names expected by the experimenters, but are correct descriptions of the odor sources, because those products are often fragranced with such odors. However, this account cannot explain why it is so difficult to name even common household objects by their smell alone because these have names that are generally agreed upon within a culture.

These explanations all attribute poor odor-name association to deficient learning. This should then be easily repaired with adequate exposure to these associations, and indeed, there is evidence that learning odor names can occur quite rapidly and effectively with training (Cain, 1979). On this basis, then, a failure to explicitly learn odor names in day-to-day life may explain why participants find it hard to name them when they are presented out of context in the laboratory.

Aside from the deficient learning interpretation, another poor-link hypothesis suggests that the link is *inherently* weak in that the verbal areas of the brain are poorly associated with the olfactory processing areas, and that this is more so than for other modalities (Engen, 1987, 1991; Herz & Engen, 1996). Although well cited, the latter hypothesis is not that well supported by empirical evidence. In a similar vein, Lorig (1999) argued that odor information processing and language processing share some of the same cortical resources. Because of this, simultaneous processing of olfactory and language information leads to interference, which in turn would explain why it is so difficult to name odors. De Wijk and colleagues (1995), however, proposed that our inability to name odors is due to a combination of a poor odor-name association (either inherent or due to less learning) and poor odor discrimination ability. The implications of odor quality discrimination failures on identification performance will be further developed in the next section of this chapter.

To conclude, there is some confusion in the literature about associative accounts of odor identification and naming with respect to why there should be a poor link, as well as the exact nature of this link. Such confusion may relate to the fact that there is one association from the perceptual representation to the identity node and another from the identity node to the proper name, and only a few researchers have taken this into account (Cleary et al., 2010; Jönsson & Olsson, 2003; Jönsson et al., 2005).

PERCEPTUAL ACCOUNTS OF ODOR IDENTIFICATION FAILURES

The perceptual accounts of odor identification failures all concern *odor quality discrimination* (OQD) as an underlying ability-limiting function. There is rather broad consensus that most, if not all, tests of olfactory performance are limited by the property of discrimination (Cain, 1979; Schab & Cain, 1991; Wise, Olsson, & Cain, 2000). For example, de Wijk and colleagues stated that "all subsequent higher order processing, including recognition memory and identification, can only be as accurate as the resolution of the sensory system" (1995, p. 24). Eskenazi, Cain, and Friend similarly stated that "the ability to discriminate must underlie the ability to identify" (1986, p. 204) an odor.

What, then, characterizes OQD, per se? OQD is often regarded as very good in humans, based on our large number of olfactory receptors that could be combined to code for an almost infinite number of odorants, and the finding that very small changes of a molecular structure can result in identifiable differences in odor quality (Laska, Ayabe-Kanamura, Hubener, & Saito, 2000; Laska & Freyer, 1997). Moreover, odor discrimination can also improve with repeated exposure (Jehl, Royet, & Holley, 1995; Rabin, 1988; but see Olsson, Faxbrink, & Jönsson, 2002) or through conditioning (Li, Moallem, Paller, & Gottfried, 2007). Yeshurun and Sobel (2010) even argue that OQD is "outstanding," and perhaps even more so for ecologically valid odors in kin recognition studies. However, a closer look at the kin recognition literature reveals moderate performance levels. For instance, in one experiment, 16 mothers out of 20 could identify their own offspring in a binary choice by smell alone (i.e., chance = 10). In a second experiment, 13 out of 17 mothers were correct when given three choices (chance = 8.5) (Porter, Cernoch, & McLaughlin, 1983). Another study showed that participants could identify their own T-shirt among nine other participants' shirts (worn 24 hours) in only 75 percent of the cases (Lord & Kasprzak, 1989).

For nonbody odors, Olsson and Cain (2000) attempted to quantify an OQD threshold. They assessed the degree to which an odor (A) needed to be substituted (in liquid phase) with another fairly dissimilar odorant (B) to reach a just noticeable difference in perceived odor quality for odor A. The substitution required for this just noticeable difference averaged as high as 30 percent (see also Wise et al., 2000). In other words, within this experimental protocol, odor A could barely be discriminated from a mixture of 70 percent of odorant A and 30 percent of odorant B. Nonetheless, it is worth bearing in mind that the particular task used to establish discriminative performance can have a large bearing on whether a difference is detected. Thus, detecting subtle differences in milk products (with cows fed different types of silage) is not possible using a two-alternative forced choice discrimination test, but is possible using an authenticity test, in which participants are asked whether the stimulus represents an authentic example of a particular category (Frandsen, Dijksterhuis, Brockhoff, Nielsen, & Martens, 2007).

A number of studies have indicated that discrimination is indeed a problem in odor identification and naming. In the first experiment by Cain and colleagues (1998), participants tried to name the same set of odors in four sessions, each separated by about two days. The overall naming accuracy increased over time, but the naming performance varied across the sessions: an odor that was correctly named on one day was sometimes incorrectly named on another. The hit rate varied between 42 percent and 47 percent across the sessions, but only 33 percent of the odors were correctly named in all sessions, indicating errors of discrimination. In another study by Cain and colleagues (1998), participants' discrimination ability for one odor set was highly correlated with their naming ability for another set (see also Eskenazi, Cain, Novelly, & Friend, 1983; Rabin, 1988, for similar findings). De Wijk and Cain (1994a) further showed that odor naming performance follows an inverted U-shaped function with age, reflecting higher performance in young adults than in children and the elderly. Discrimination ability showed the same pattern and was correlated with naming ability. In another study, de Wijk and Cain (1994b) found significant correlations between discrimination and naming performance for both free and cued naming (see also Eskenazi et al., 1986), as well as with consistency in applying the same label to a given odor with different intensities. In these studies, the correlation between discrimination and naming performance varied from moderate (.48) to high (.80), clearly tying OQD with odor identification ability. Further, the odor naming errors people make often reveal errors of discrimination (e.g., Engen, 1987), such as when the name *lemon* or *lime* is used to describe the smell of an orange. Researchers of olfaction, therefore, often find it meaningful to separate two measures of naming performance: a strict measure of accuracy (the odor label has to be fully correct), and a measure that includes "near misses" that reveal some level of knowledge about the odor. An example of the latter would be to name an orange as either *lemon* or *lime* or as the generic label *citrus fruit*. To conclude, our ability to discriminate between odors seems closely connected to our ability to identify and consequently name odors.

How, then, does odor quality discrimination ability affect odor naming? Odor presentation will often fail to activate the odor name, but if the name is provided, odor perception instantly becomes unambiguous (see de Wijk et al., 1995, for similar reasoning). The clarity with which an identified odor is perceived can be contrasted with the more fuzzy (unclear) perception of the odor before correct (or incorrect) identification has occurred. We call this the *fuzzy perception account* of odor identification. The basic idea of this perceptual account is that as long as an odor is not identified, the perception of it is *fuzzy*, like a blurred image that is not clearly perceived until you get some contextual clues (as is typical during everyday life) or are told what it represents. The consequence of this lack of clarity is that it is harder to discriminate between unidentified than between identified odors (e.g., de Wijk & Cain, 1994b; Jönsson et al., 2011), as seen in the correlation between OQD and odor naming ability. However, when additional information is available, the correct association between the perceptual representation and the identity can be made (Jönsson et al., 2005).

WHAT DO WE KNOW ABOUT ODORS THAT WE
CANNOT NAME?

Places, things, and people are sometimes hard to name, but even when this occurs we still usually know a lot about them (e.g., Hodges & Greene, 1998; Yarmey, 1973; Young, Hay, & Ellis, 1985). This phenomenon has been explored in several different ways. Methods include studying tip-of-the tongue states (e.g., Yarmey, 1973), failures to recall a target word from a cue during paired associate learning (e.g., Koriat, Levy-Sadot, Edry, & de Marcas, 2003), and naming failures during day-to-day life (e.g., Young et al., 1985). All of these approaches have confirmed that knowledge about an item can be recovered in the absence of a name (e.g., Burton & Bruce, 1992; Yavuz & Bousfield, 1959). In contrast to these findings from the visual and auditory domains, with olfaction relatively little information may be available if the odor's name is absent (Jönsson & Olsson, 2012).

Researchers have used several different techniques to explore what can be known about an odor that one cannot name. The first to address this question were Lawless and Engen (1977), who had participants smell a range of odors. When they encountered a smell that felt familiar but that they could not name, participants were asked additional questions about that odor. While Lawless and Engen (1977) did not verify the accuracy of their participants' judgments, participants claimed to know either the source of the odor or where it might commonly be located on 50 percent of occasions. Participants were also asked to judge how similar the familiar but nameless odor was to two comparison odors. Responses were similar to those obtained from control participants, suggesting that the odors' perceptual qualities were apparent even in the absence of a name. In still another task, participants were asked to provide information about the odor's name (e.g., length, sounds like, etc.). Here participants were unable to provide the type of information typically obtained in TOT states (e.g., details of the first letter, number of syllables; Brown, 1991).

More recent work suggests that what is known about a familiar odor that cannot be named is perhaps more limited than Lawless and Engen's (1977) findings suggest. Jönsson and Olsson (2003) also asked participants whether they knew the likely source and location of familiar odors. This was often not known, but they too did not assess the accuracy of participants' reports. However, in a further study, Jönsson and colleagues (2005) compared what participants knew about familiar odors they could not name and famous people they could not name. For famous people that could not be named, the participants usually knew the person's profession.

However, for familiar odors that people could not name, people were rarely able to provide any details about the odors' probable source or location.

Two more recent studies have also probed olfactory knowledge for familiar odors using two further techniques. One way to determine what a participant knows, irrespective of whether it is true or not, is to see if that information can be recovered consistently across different test occasions. This procedure was used to test people who report synesthetic experiences (e.g., Simner et al., 2005). For example, Baron-Cohen, Wyke, and Binnie (1987) found synesthetes' reports to be more consistent over time than those of non-synesthetic controls. Stevenson and Mahmut (2013a) recently applied this approach to odors. Participants smelled an odor, evaluated its various properties, attempted to name it, and then repeated this same process at a later point in time. This allowed a comparison of the consistency for different types of information given for three classes of odors: identically named on both occasions, given similar names on both occasions, or given different names on both occasions. The only information consistently preserved for odors given different names on each test was hedonic tone. Other information – activity, potency, familiarity, intensity, redolence ratings (e.g., smells like …) – was unreliable when the odor was named inconsistently (or not at all). This suggests that only odor hedonic information can be reliably known independent of a name.

In another approach to determine what can be known about odors that are familiar but cannot be named, Stevenson and Mahmut (2013b) borrowed a test format previously used in neuropsychology. Some neuropsychological disorders are characterized by a loss of ability to name everyday objects (i.e., aphasia). Such a deficit might be specific to names or it could include other semantic information – but how does one go about testing this when a patient cannot name common objects? One way around this is the Pyramid and Palm trees test, which assesses semantic knowledge via pictorial associations (Howard & Patterson, 1992). For example, participants are presented with a target picture of a pyramid, and test pictures of a palm tree and a pine tree, and they then have to pick which test picture best goes with the target. We adapted this conceptual association test to odors in two ways. In our odor picture test, participants smelled a familiar odor and then picked which of two test pictures went best with it. For example, the smell of banana was followed by pictures of a koala and a monkey. Our second approach was to use an odor triad test. Here participants were presented with a target smell, followed by two test smells, and they had to pick the test smell that best matched the target. To illustrate, the smell of mushroom was followed by the odors of wet soil and tea. On the odor picture test, participants were generally very good at selecting the correct picture, *unless* the odor could not be named. On the odor triad test, participants were generally very bad at selecting the correct test odor, *unless* the odor could be named. Together, these findings suggest that access to the various types of semantic knowledge necessary to correctly answer the odor picture and odor triad tests was only available when the odor could be named.

In sum, nameless familiar odors would appear to have some discrete perceptual properties, as well as having consistent hedonic tone. Beyond that, people know remarkably little about such odors – in contrast to faces, places, and other visual and auditory objects.

SUBJECTIVE KNOWLEDGE ABOUT ODORS THAT WE CANNOT NAME

What, then, do we think we know about odors that we cannot name? Although we are sometimes unable to name an odor, we can still have knowledge about it. This knowledge can be objectively measurable, if you can give a general category for an odor (e.g., fruit) or the context in which the odor is typically experienced (e.g., grandmas' kitchens). As reviewed earlier, this knowledge generally seems to be rather sketchy for odors in the absence of a name. However, whether there is knowledge in the absence of proper odor identification can also be inferred from metacognitive measures. For example, you can feel quite strongly that you know an odor and if just given the possibility to think a bit longer you believe you would retrieve the name of the object from which the odor emanates. Or alternatively, you think you do not have a clue what odor it is. A reliable relationship between such metamemory judgments with actual knowledge about the odor is also an informative measure of odor knowledge. Actual knowledge can be measured by a recognition test following the metamemory judgment, or the extent to which the judgments relate to free retrieval of the odor name if given sufficient time.

In the verbal domain, it is well documented that we can monitor the availability of a memory at above chance levels, even though we might fail to retrieve it (Hart, 1965; Koriat, 1993, 1994, 1995; Koriat & Levy-Sadot, 2001; Metcalfe, 2000; Nelson, 1996; Nelson & Narens, 1990), and this is typically referred to as the *feeling-of-knowing* (FOK) experience. Indeed, we are even able to tell whether an answer to a general information question is in memory (or not) faster than we can articulate the answer (Nhouyvanisvong & Reder, 1998; Reder, 1987). Reder and Ritter (1992) argued that FOK is a general process that operates whenever memory is queried and varies from a strong feeling of *not* knowing to a strong feeling of knowing.

The most common way of investigating FOK judgments is to present participants with general information questions (e.g., what is the capital of Australia?). For all questions where the answer is not remembered, participants make an FOK judgment that is followed by a multiple choice recognition test (Sydney, Melbourne, Canberra, Perth).[1] FOK ratings are then correlated with actual recognition performance, and an extensive body of FOK data shows that people are moderately accurate in monitoring their knowledge (see Metcalfe, 2000, for a review). However, few studies have examined FOK in olfaction (Cain et al., 1998; Jönsson & Olsson, 2003; Jönsson et al., 2005). Cain and colleagues compared the predictive validity of FOK for verbal and olfactory material. Whereas they replicated the common finding that FOKs for answers to semantic general knowledge questions were predictive of later multiple choice recognition performance, this was not the case for FOK judgments about odor names. In a follow-up study by Jönsson and Olsson (2003; Experiment 1), participants were asked to name a set of common odors. If they could not name the odor, they rated how confident they were that they would recognize the correct odor name. When presented with a name, participants accepted the correct name on 72 percent of trials and rejected an incorrect name on 86 percent of trials. The participants' FOK judgments were moderately, and significantly, correlated with their recognition of the correct odor name (.34), as measured by the Goodman-Kruskal gamma correlation (Nelson, 1984). For other modalities, the gamma correlation typically ranges between .45 and .55 (Metcalfe, 2000). In a later study, Jönsson and colleagues (2005) directly compared the accuracy (i.e., predictive validity) of FOK for the labels of common odors with FOK for names of famous persons. Although both were reliably related to actual ability to retrieve an accurate label, FOK responses for person names were superior. Hence, even when we fail to immediately name an odor, we still have enough knowledge of the odor to somewhat accurately say whether we can later recognize it or retrieve it from memory, but to a lesser extent than is demonstrated with other modalities. A special case of FOK is the strong and imminent feeling of retrieval people can have when a word they cannot remember is on the tip of their tongue.

TIP-OF-THE-TONGUE EXPERIENCES

Brown and McNeill (see Brown, 1991, 2012, and Schwartz, 2002, for reviews) were the first to perform a systematic investigation of the tip-of-the-tongue (TOT) experience, and described it as follows: "If you are unable to think of the word, but feel sure that you know it and that it is on the verge of coming back to you, then you are in a TOT state" (1966, p. 327). Most subsequent studies have relied on this description or some version of it. Typical ways of eliciting TOT states in the laboratory are to present participants with word definitions or to show pictures of famous persons. The TOT state seems to occur universally across different languages (Schwartz, 1999, 2002). The TOT state is also closely related to the FOK experience and, most probably, any FOK study includes some TOT states that are defined as strong FOK experiences. However, all strong FOK states are not TOT experiences. For example, Yaniv and Meyer (1987) found instances of high FOK ratings for items not reported to be on the tip of the tongue (see Brown, 2012). In addition, the research methodology typically differs between FOK and TOT experiments. Whereas a person in an FOK experiment is merely asked about the likelihood of being able to recognize (or retrieve) the missing answer at a later time, independent of the strength of the FOK, TOT experiments only target the stronger feelings of imminent retrieval people have following retrieval failures (Nhouyvanisvong & Reder, 1998).

"Perhaps the most striking aspect of the TOT experience is that while hanging in linguistic limbo, unable to pull up the missing word, bits and pieces of it often come to mind" (Brown, 2012, p. 81). These words illustrate one of the major attributes of having something on the tip of the tongue; you can't access the sought-for word, but yet have partial access to it. More specifically, when we fail to retrieve the name of an object (e.g., a person or an odor), the relevant and irrelevant information that appears as a by-product of our memory search can be subdivided into two categories (Koriat et al., 2003): structural-phonological information and semantic information. Examples of the latter would be "yellow" and "fruit" for lemon, or if the name of a person is missing you may still know the person's profession (e.g., dentist). Structural-phonological information includes the first letter/phoneme of the sought-for word (e.g., the missing word begins with a C as in "carrot"), other letters, similar-sounding words, number of syllables, and so forth (Brown, 1991, 2012). Although the availability of structural-phonological information has attracted the most attention when investigating TOT experiences, TOTs also trigger a multitude of other semantic clues (Brown, 1991, 2012; Koriat et al., 2003; Lovelace, 1987; Yarmey, 1973), and the distinction between these two kinds of information seems especially important when investigating odor-induced TOTs.

The third experiment in Lawless and Engen (1977) used odors to trigger TOT experiences for names of the odor sources. If participants were unable to name an odor, but gave a high familiarity rating and felt a TOT for the odor name, they filled out a questionnaire asking for partial information about the sought-for odor name (e.g., first letter, number of syllables) and other associated information (e.g., a visual image of the odorous object, or a plausible odor category such as "spice" for black pepper). In contrast to verbal TOTs, where partial access to such information is common (Brown, 1991, 2012), Lawless and Engen (1977) found that the participants had virtually no partial odor name access at all, and coined the term "tip-of-the-nose" experience to differentiate the olfactory version of the verbal TOT experience. The almost complete lack of structural-phonological information accompanying a very strong feeling of knowing for an odor that you cannot name was later replicated by Jönsson and Olsson (2003; Experiment 2). When reporting a TOT experience, Jönsson and Olsson asked about (i) similar-sounding words, (ii) words with similar meaning, (iii) accented syllable, (iv) number of syllables, and (v) letters in the sought-after word. They evoked a TOT experience in 17.3 percent of the trials, but the amount of correct partial name access was virtually nil at 0 percent to 2.3 percent across the five questions.

Participants can sometimes categorize the odor correctly (e.g., spice for black pepper), or have access to other semantic information (Lawless & Engen, 1977). For example, Jönsson and Olsson (2003) found that when reporting a TOT experience, 20 percent of the participants could name a place from which the odor might have come, 13 percent could name an object from which it might have come, 17 percent could name a general category for the odor, and 8 percent could name a similar odor (Jönsson & Olsson, 2003). As in the Lawless and Engen study, responses were not scored for accuracy, but rather indicate what categories of semantic information participants think they have about the odor. In a more recent study of the tip-of-the-nose experience, Yeshurun and Sobel (2012) had participants smell an odor and then tell whether the odor identity was (i) known, (ii) on the tip of the tongue, (iii) familiar, or (iv) not known. They found brain activation in areas related to olfactory perception (bilateral piriform cortex and orbitofrontal cortex), memory (bilateral hippocampus), and verbal (inferior frontal gyrus and superior temporal gyrus) functions. Most important, only left piriform cortex discriminated between degrees of feeling of knowing, with higher activation for "know," "TOT," and "familiar" responses than for "don't know" responses. The authors concluded that the feeling of knowing for an odor is reflected in olfactory and memory regions, whereas verbal-related regions are not involved. These imaging data converge nicely with the behavioral data showing a lack of partial word access when participants report having an odor "on the tip of the nose." Indeed, odor-elicited TOTs apparently deserve the separate term invented by Lawless and Engen (1977), as they lack one key aspect of the TOT experience – they simply do not seem to involve partial word access.

Jönsson and colleagues (2005; Experiment 1) further investigated why odor naming sometimes fails or, more precisely, where in the naming process it fails. They let participants try to name a set of common odors and a set of famous people, of comparable difficulty levels. If the participants could not name the item, they were asked to indicate whether they: (i) lacked the name and the identity of the odor or person, or (ii) lacked the name but had identified the stimulus (i.e., they knew who or what it was; here referred to as *subjective identification*). If the participants thought they knew the identity of the odorous object, they were asked whether they were having a TOT experience (resolution of the sought-for name felt imminent). If they did not know the identity, they judged how certain they were that they would be able to retrieve the exact name or describe the item (i.e., an FOK judgment) if given more time. If odor naming failures associated with very strong feelings of imminent retrieval were due to name-activation failures, we would expect (i) the rate of subjective identifications to be high and (ii) the odor-elicited TOT rate to be high or at least comparable to the TOT rate for the names of famous people. In addition, (iii) if the subjective identification rate is high, the odors should also activate a high degree of semantic information during the memory search (i.e., the amount of semantic information triggered by an odor should follow the subjective identification rate). These predictions failed on all accounts. Only 8 percent of the naming failures for odors were associated with subjective identifications; significantly lower than for the person names (43%). Further, whereas 24 percent of the person naming failures led to a TOT state, only 7 percent of the odor naming failures did. Instead, odor naming failures often led to strong or very strong FOK judgments (i.e., the participants had not identified the odors but felt that that they were very familiar). Finally, the participants' general knowledge of the unsuccessfully named odors and pictures showed the same pattern as the subjective identifications, namely, they had reliably less semantic information about the odors than the people.

For TOTs, the predictive validity is often referred to as the *resolution rate*, or how often TOT states are resolved by retrieval of the sought-for word without help from other cues. Hence, it is a measure of the predictive validity of TOTs as an index of later retrieval. Of the items for which a TOT state was reported in the Jönsson and Olsson (2003) study, only 23.8 percent were correctly resolved within the allotted 90 seconds. Also symptomatic of odors is that naming attempts following TOTs are often incorrect (34.9%). Jönsson and Olsson also let their participants distinguish between strong and very strong TOT states, and more of the former (36.7%) than the latter (19.0%) were correctly resolved. Although odor-elicited TOTs are sometimes resolved, the rate is lower than what is normally found for verbal stimuli (Brown, 2012), congruent with the somewhat lower predictive validity of FOKs for odors.

The apparent difficulty in naming even familiar odors would seem to make olfaction the perfect modality for triggering TOTs in the lab. How frequently TOTs occur is referred to as *TOT incidence*, and in the lab this translates into the percentage of items that elicit a (self-reported) TOT state. Jönsson and Olsson (2003, Experiment 2) reported a TOT incidence of 17.3 percent, whereas Cleary and colleagues (2010) found a considerably higher TOT incidence (41–49%), and Lawless and Engen (1977) discovered a much lower rate (6.4%). Averaged across these few studies using odor as stimuli, the percentage of trials that lead to TOTs is fairly comparable to 13±5 percent typically found for verbal stimuli (cf. Brown, 1991).

CONCLUDING COMMENTS

Lawless and Engen's (1977) findings concerning tip-of-the-nose experiences have received very frequent citation in the olfactory literature, but have not been followed up by much additional empirical work. Until 2005, the scientific literature consisted of the single article by Lawless and Engen (1977; but see also Engen, 1987), which is surprising as the paper is one of the more cited empirical papers in the olfactory cognition literature (> 100 citations, 1977–2004; ISI Web of Science). Some studies have since investigated the TOT (or tip-of-the-nose) experience for odors (Cleary et al., 2010; Jönsson & Olsson, 2003; Jönsson et al., 2005; Yeshurun & Sobel, 2012). The available evidence converges on the finding that when we have a strong feeling that we know a familiar odor that we cannot name, we know virtually nothing about it in terms of partial word access. Indeed, we seem to have little knowledge in general about unnamed odors (e.g., Stevenson & Mahmut, 2013a, 2013b). If odor naming failures were similar to other types of name activation failures, we would expect odors to trigger a similar amount of partial word information (see Brown, 2012, for a review), but they do not. In addition, as tip-of-the-nose experiences are typically triggered by very familiar, well-encoded, everyday items (e.g., juniper, banana, or coffee), name activation failures seem implausible. Rather, when people report that they have a strong feeling that they will soon resolve the name of the odor, what they are actually searching for is the identity of the object that smells. To conclude, whereas a TOT is "the phenomenological experience that a currently inaccessible word is stored in memory and will be retrieved" (Schwartz, 1999, p. 1), the tip-of-the-nose experience should more properly be defined as the phenomenological experience that a currently unidentified odor source stored in memory will soon be identified.

NOTES

1. The correct answer is Canberra.

REFERENCES

Baron-Cohen, S., Wyke, M., & Binnie, C. (1987). Hearing words and seeing colors: An experimental investigation of a case of synesthesia. *Perception, 16,* 761–767.

Brown, A. S. (1991). A review of the tip-of-the-tongue experience. *Psychological Bulletin,* 109, 204–223.

(2012). *The tip of the tongue state.* New York: Psychology Press.

Brown, R., & McNeill, D. (1966). The "tip of the tongue" phenomenon. *Journal of Verbal Learning and Verbal Behavior,* 5, 325–337.

Burton, A. M., & Bruce V. (1992). I recognize your face but I can't remember your name: A simple explanation? *British Journal of Psychology,* 83, 45–60.

Cain, W. S. (1979). To know with the nose: Keys to odor identification, *Science,* 203, 467–470.

(1982). Odor identification by males and females: Predictions vs performance. *Chemical Senses,* 7, 129–142.

Cain, W. S., de Wijk, R., Lulejian, C., Schiet, F., & See, L. C. (1998). Odor identification: Perceptual and semantic dimensions. *Chemical Senses,* 23, 309–326.

Cain, W. S., Goodspeed, R. B., Gent, J. F., & Leonard, G. (1988). Evaluation of olfactory dysfunction in the Connecticut Chemosensory Clinical Research Center. *Laryngoscope,* 98, 83–88.

Cleary, A. M., Konkel, K. E., Nomi, J. S., & McCabe, D. P. (2010). Odor recognition without identification. *Memory & Cognition,* 38, 452–460.

Davis, R. G. (1981). The role of nonolfactory context cues in odor identification. *Perception & Psychophysics,* 30, 83–89.

Degel, J., & Köster, E. P. (1999). Odors: Implicit memory and performance effects. *Chemical Senses,* 24, 317–325.

De Wijk, R. A., & Cain, W. S. (1994a). Odor identification by name and edibility: Life-span development and safety. *Human Factors,* 36, 182–187.

(1994b). Odor quality: Discrimination versus free and cued identification. *Perception and Psychophysics,* 56, 12–18.

De Wijk, R. A., Schab, F. R., & Cain, W. S. (1995). Odor identification. In F. R. Schab & R. G. Crowder (Eds.), *Memory for odors* (pp. 21–37). Mahwah, NJ: Lawrence Erlbaum Associates.

Desor, J. A., & Beauchamp, G. K. (1974). The human capacity to transmit olfactory information. *Perception & Psychophysics,* 16, 551–556.

Distel, H., & Hudson, R. (2001). Judgment of odor intensity is influenced by subjects' knowledge of the odor source. *Chemical Senses,* 26, 247–251.

Doty, R. L., Shaman, P., Kimmelman, C. P., & Dann, M. S. (1984). University of Pennsylvania Smell Identification Test: A rapid quantitative olfactory function test for the clinic. *Laryngoscope,* 94, 176–178.

Engen, T. (1987). Remembering odors and their names. *American Scientist,* 75, 497–503.

(1991). *Odor sensation and memory.* New York: Praeger Publishers.

Eskenazi, B., Cain, W. S., & Friend, K. B. (1986). Exploration of olfactory aptitude. *Bulletin of the Psychonomic Society,* 24, 203–206.

Eskenazi, B., Cain, W. S., Novelly, R. A., & Friend, K. B. (1983). Olfactory functioning in temporal lobectomy patients. *Neuropsychologia,* 21, 365–374.

Frandsen, L. S. W., Dijksterhuis, G. B., Brockhoff, P. B., Nielsen, J. H., & Martens, M. (2007). Feelings as a basis for discrimination: Comparison of a modified authenticity test with the same-different test for slightly different types of milk. *Food Quality and Preference,* 18, 97–105.

Hart, J. T. (1965). Memory and the feeling-of-knowing experience. *Journal of Educational Psychology,* 56, 208–216.

Herz, R. S., & Engen, T. (1996). Odor memory: Review and analysis. *Psychonomic Bulletin and Review,* 3, 300–313.

Hodges, J. R., & Greene, J. D. W. (1998). Knowing about people and naming them: Can Alzheimer's disease patients do one without the other? *Quarterly Journal of Experimental Psychology,* 51A, 121–134.

Howard, D., & Patterson, K. (1992). *Pyramids and palm trees: A test of semantic access from pictures and words.* Bury St. Edmunds, UK: Thames Valley Test Company.

Holley, A. (2002). Cognitive aspects of olfaction in perfumer practice. In C. Rouby, B. Schaal, D. Dubois, R. Gervais, & A. Holley (Eds.), *Olfaction, taste and cognition* (pp. 16–26), Cambridge University Press.

Jehl, C., Royet, J. P., & Holley, A. (1995). Odor discrimination and recognition memory as a function of familiarization. *Perception and Psychophysics,* 57, 1002–1011.

Johnson, C. J., Paivio, A., & Clark, J. M. (1996). Cognitive components of picture naming. *Psychological Bulletin,* 120, 113–139.

Jönsson, F. U., Møller, P., & Olsson, M. J. (2011), Olfactory working memory: Effects of verbalization on the 2-back task. *Memory & Cognition,* 39, 1023–1032.

Jönsson, F. U., & Olsson, M. J. (2003). Olfactory metacognition. *Chemical Senses,* 28, 651–658.

(2012). Knowing what we smell. In G. M. Zucco, R. S. Herz, & B. Schaal (Eds.), *Olfactory cognition: From perception and memory to environmental odours and neuroscience* (pp. 115–136). Amsterdam, The Netherlands: John Benjamins Publishing Company.

Jönsson, F. U., Tchekhova, A., Lönner, P., & Olsson, M. J. (2005). A metamemory perspective on odor naming and identification. *Chemical Senses*, 30, 353–365.

Kobal, G., Hummel, T., Sekinger, B., Barz, S., Roscher, S., & Wolf, S. (1996). "Sniffin' Sticks": Screening of olfactory performance. *Rhinology*, 34, 222–226.

Koriat, A. (1993). How do we know that we know? The accessibility model of the feeling of knowing. *Psychological Review*, 100, 609–639.

   (1994). Memory's knowledge about its own knowledge: The accessibility account of the feeling-of-knowing. In J. Metcalfe & A. P. Shimamura (Eds.), *Metacognition: Knowing about knowing* (pp. 115–135). Cambridge, MA: Bradford.

   (1995). Dissociating knowing and the feeling of knowing: Further evidence for the accessibility model. *Journal of Experimental Psychology: General*, 124, 311–333.

Koriat, A., & Levy-Sadot, R. (2001). The combined contributions of the cue familiarity and accessibility heuristics to feelings of knowing. *Journal of Experimental Psychology: Learning, Memory, and Cognition*, 27, 34–53.

Koriat, A., Levy-Sadot, R., Edry, E., & de Marcas, S. (2003). What do we know about what we cannot remember? Accessing the semantic attributes of words that cannot be recalled. *Journal of Experimental Psychology: Learning, Memory, and Cognition*, 29, 1095–1105.

Köster, E. P. (2002). The specific characteristics of the sense of smell. In C. Rouby, B. Schaal, D. Dubois, R. Gervais, & A. Holley, (Eds.), *Olfaction, taste, and cognition* (pp. 27–43). New York: Cambridge University Press.

Laska M., Ayabe-Kanamura S., Hubener F., & Saito S. (2000). Olfactory discrimination ability for aliphatic odorants as a function of oxygen moiety. *Chemical Senses*, 25, 189–197.

Laska, M., & Freyer, D. (1997). Olfactory discrimination ability for aliphatic esters in squirrel monkeys and humans. *Chemical Senses*, 22, 457–465.

Lawless, H., & Engen, T. (1977). Associations to odors: Interference, mnemonics, and verbal labeling. *Journal of Experimental Psychology: Human Learning and Memory*, 3, 52–59.

Li, W., Moallem, I., Paller K. A., & Gottfried J. A. (2007). Subliminal smells can guide social preferences. *Psychological Science*, 18, 1044–1049.

Lord, T., & Kasprzak, M. (1989). Identification of self through olfaction. *Perceptual and Motor Skills*, 69, 219–224.

Lorig, T. (1999). On the similarity of odor and language perception. *Neuroscience and Biobehavioral Reviews*, 23, 391–389.

Lovelace, E. (1987). Attributes that come to mind in the TOT state. *Bulletin of the Psychonomic Society*, 25, 370–372.

McCauley, C., Parmelee, C. M., Sperber, R. D. & Carr, T. H. (1980). Early extraction of meaning from pictures and its relation to conscious identification. *Journal of Experimental Psychology: Human Perception and Performance*, 6, 265–276.

Metcalfe, J. (2000). Metamemory: Theory and data. In E. Tulving and F. I. M. Craik (Eds.), *The Oxford handbook of memory* (pp. 197–211). New York: Oxford University Press.

Nelson, T. O. (1996). Consciousness and metacognition. *American Psychologist*, 51, 102–116.

(1984). A comparison of current measures of the accuracy of feeling of knowing predictions. *Psychological Bulletin*, 95, 109–133.

Nelson, T. O., & Narens, L. (1990). Metamemory: A theoretical framework and some new findings. In G. H. Bower (Ed.), *The psychology of learning and motivation* (pp. 1–45). New York: Academic Press.

Nordin, S., Brämerson, A., Lidén, E., & Bende, M. (1998).The Scandinavian odor-identification test: Development, reliability, validity and normative data. *Acta Otolaryngology*, 118, 226–234.

Nordin, S., Nyroos, M., Maunuksela, T., Niskanen, T., & Tuorila, H. (2002). Applicability of the Scandinavian odor identification test: A Finnish-Swedish comparison. *Acta Otolaryngology*, 122, 294–297.

Nhouyvanisvong, A., & Reder, L. M. (1998). Rapid feeling-of-knowing: A strategy selection mechanism. In V. Y. Yzerbyt, G. Lories, & B. Dardenne (Eds.), *Metacognition: Cognitive and social dimensions* (pp. 35–52). Thousand Oaks, CA: Sage Publications.

Olsson, M. J., & Cain, W. S. (2000). Psychometrics of odor quality discrimination: Method for threshold determination. *Chemical Senses*, 25, 493–499.

Olsson, M. J., Faxbrink, M., & Jönsson, F. U. (2002). Repetition priming in odor memory. In C. Rouby, B. Schaal, D. Dubois, R. Gervais, H. Rémi, & A. Holley (Eds.), *Olfaction, taste, and cognition.* (pp. 246–260). New York: Cambridge University Press.

Olsson, M. J., & Fridén M. (2001), Evidence of odor priming: Edibility judgments are primed differently between the hemispheres. *Chemical Senses*, 26, 117–123.

Olsson, M. J., & Jönsson, F. U. (2008). Is it easier to match a name to an odor than vice versa? *Chemosensory Perception*, 1, 184–189.

Porter, R. H., Cernoch, J. M., & McLaughlin, F. J. (1983). Maternal recognition of neonates through olfactory cues. *Physiology & Behavior*, 30, 151–154.

Rabin, M. D. (1988). Experience facilitates olfactory quality discrimination. *Perception and Psychophysics*, 44, 532–540.

Reder, L. M. (1987). Strategy selection in question answering. *Cognitive Psychology*, 19, 90–138.

Reder, L. M., & Ritter, F. E. (1992). What determines initial feeling of knowing? Familiarity with question terms, not with the answer. *Journal of Experimental Psychology: Learning, Memory and Cognition*, 18, 435–451.

Schab, F. R., & Cain, W. S. (1991). Memory for odors. In D. G. Laing, R. L. Dory, & W. Breipohl (Eds.), *The human sense of smell* (pp. 217–240). New York: Springer.

Schwartz, B. L. (1999). Sparkling at the end of the tongue: The etiology of tip-of-the-tongue states: A diary study. *Psychonomic Bulletin & Review*, 6, 379–393.

(2002). *Tip-of-the-tongue states: Phenomenology, mechanism, and lexical retrieval.* Mahwah, NJ: Lawrence Erlbaum Associates.

Simner, J., Ward, J., Lanz, M., Jansari, A., Noonan, K., Glover, L., & Oakley, D. A. (2005). Non-random associations of graphemes to colours in synaesthetic and non-synaesthetic populations. *Cognitive Neuropsychology*, 22, 1069–1085.

Stevenson, R. J., & Mahmut, M. (2013a). Using response consistency to probe olfactory knowledge. *Chemical Senses*, **38**, 237–249.

(2013b). The accessibility of semantic knowledge for odours that can and cannot be named. *Quarterly Journal of Experimental Psychology*, **66**, 1414–1431.

Sulmont-Rossé, C., Issanchou, S., & Köster, E. P. (2005). Odor naming methodology: Correct identification with multiple-choice versus repeatable identification in a free task. *Chemical Senses*, 30, 23–27.

White, T. L., & Kurtz, D. B. (2003). The relationship between metacognitive awareness of olfactory ability and age in people reporting chemosensory disturbances. *American Journal of Psychology*, 116, 99–110.

Wise, P. M., Olsson, M. J., & Cain, W. S. (2000). Quantification of odor quality. *Chemical Senses*, 25, 429–443.

Yaniv, I., & Meyer, D. E. (1987). Activation and metacognition of inaccessible stored information: Potential bases for incubation effects in problem solving. *Journal of Experimental Psychology: Learning, Memory, and Cognition*, 13, 187–205.

Yarmey, A. D. (1973). I recognize your face but I can't remember your name: Further evidence on the tip-of-the-tongue phenomenon. *Memory & Cognition*, 1, 287–290.

Yavuz, H., & Bousfield, W. (1959). Recall of connotative meaning. *Psychological Reports*, 5, 319–320.

Yeshurun, Y., & Sobel, N. (2010). An odor is not worth a thousand words: From multidimensional odor to unidimensional objects. *Annual Review of Psychology*, 61, 219–241.

(2012). *Where is the tip of the nose in the brain?* Poster presented at the XIV International Symposium on Olfaction and Taste, Stockholm, Sweden, June 23–27, 2012.

Young, A. W., Hay, D. C., & Ellis, A. W. (1985). The faces that launched a thousand slips: Everyday difficulties and errors in recognising people. *British Journal of Psychology*, 76, 495–523.

15

What Do We Know When We Forget?

ASHER KORIAT AND RAVIT NUSSINSON

The tip-of-the-tongue (TOT) state has attracted special attention because it combines two seemingly inconsistent features: we are unable to retrieve the solicited word or name but are convinced that we know it and feel that its recall is imminent. Several researchers have stressed the emotional and motivational distress that accompanies the TOT. The frustration from the memory blockage is particularly strong when we are able to retrieve partial clues about the elusive memory target although we fail to retrieve the target in full.

BLOCKED MEMORY FOR NAMES

In the lion's share of the studies, the TOT has been elicited by providing participants with word definitions and asking them to retrieve the corresponding word (A. Brown, 2012, table 3.2). Several questions about the TOT have been investigated using this procedure. The present chapter focuses on one question that has received some empirical evidence: What kind of partial fragments of information can participants report when they are stuck in a memory blockage state? In their pioneering study, R. Brown and McNeill (1966) asked participants in a TOT to make several guesses about the elusive memory target. They demonstrated that, while in the TOT and prior to recall, participants were successful in guessing some of the letters in the elusive word, the number of syllables in it, and the location of the primary stress. Other studies also showed that participants in a TOT have access

The preparation of this chapter was supported by the Max Wertheimer Minerva Center for Cognitive Processes and Human Performance at the University of Haifa. We are grateful to Ornit Tzuri for her help in copyediting.
Correspondence concerning this chapter should be addressed to Asher Koriat, Department of Psychology, Haifa University, Haifa 31905, Israel. E-mail: akoriat@research.haifa.ac.il.

to information about the length of the word, its frequency of occurrence, number of syllables, first letter, final letter, ending sound, and beginning sound (Brown & Burrows, 2009; Caramazza & Miozzo, 1997; Ecke, 2004; Koriat & Lieblich, 1974, 1975; Lovelace, 1987; Yarmey, 1973). These findings laid the ground for a general model of how words are stored in the mental lexicon and retrieved from it. The general conclusion was that "the lexical network is organized along lines of phonemic (and to some degree orthographic) similarity" (Collins & Loftus, 1975, p. 413).

The thesis advanced in this chapter is that an understanding of the TOT can benefit from an analysis of memory blockage states within the perspective of goal-oriented behavior. We propose that the kind of partial information that participants are most likely to access during memory blockage depends largely on the goal that was active when memory was blocked. According to goal-systems theory (Kruglanski et al., 2002), when a certain goal is pursued, various goal-related constructs are activated, such as the means for achieving that goal. Indeed, research indicates that the accessibility of a goal results in the activation of goal-related knowledge (Aarts, Dijksterhuis, & De Vries, 2001; Balcetis & Dunning, 2006; Fishbach & Ferguson, 2007; Förster, Liberman, & Higgins, 2005; Moskowitz, 2002). For example, Aarts and colleagues (2001) have shown that thirsty participants (those asked by the experimenter to consume salty snacks) responded faster to beverages or to items associated with drinking (e.g., soda, juice, bottle) as compared to control words and compared with non-thirsty participants.

In the case of the TOT, memory search is cued by a definition that specifies the meaning of the solicited word. The person's goal is to name the word that fits that definition. The intention to retrieve the word narrows the memory search (see Koriat & Lieblich, 1974), activating fragmentary phonemic information that is part of the program of retrieving the complete word. In the terminology used in discussions of word production (Levelt, 1989; Roelofs, Meyer, & Levelt, 1998), the TOT represents a failure in the transition from *lemma* to *lexeme*. *Lemma* refers to the abstract semantic and conceptual representation of the word, whereas *lexeme* refers to a representation that specifies the phonological form. When the retrieval of the lexeme is thwarted, the person can still provide information about some of the phonemic attributes that are activated (see Gollan & Acenas, 2004), which constitutes the next step toward the completion of the goal – producing the word. Thus, the TOT, as defined by R. Brown and McNeill (1966), represents what we shall term a *Blocked Memory for Name* (BMfN) state. As several authors have noted (e.g., Dale & McGlaughlin, 1971; Norman, 1969; Yarmey, 1973), because TOT are precipitated by word definitions, and the corresponding word is solicited, participants tend to generate primarily acoustically related words.

BLOCKED MEMORY FOR MEANING

Consider the following situation: When reading a text, you encounter a rare word whose meaning is not immediately clear to you (Durso & Shore, 1991; Shore & Durso, 1990). Several associations come to mind as you search for the meaning. In this situation, the word is given and your goal is to retrieve the meaning of the word relying on these associations. Retrieval failure in this case may be said to represent *Blocked Memory for Meaning* (BMfM). Therefore, when complete retrieval fails, the partial information accessed is likely to concern semantic and associative features that constitute the next stepping stone toward the retrieval of the meaning of the word. Indeed, this is what happened in several studies in which memory was cued by the word itself. For example, in the study of Koriat, Levy-Sadot, Edry, and De Marcas (2003), participants studied the Hebrew translations of pseudo-Somali words and were tested by having to recall the Hebrew word in response to the Somali cue. When they failed, they were asked to judge the word's meaning with respect to one of the three dimensions of the semantic differential (Osgood, 1952) – evaluation (good-bad), potency (strong-weak), and activity (active-passive). Participants' judgments about the attributes of the irretrievable word were significantly accurate for each of the three dimensions. For example, participants who could not recall the translations of Somali words that signified "pleasure," "feather," or "boredom" could still judge the connotation of the word as good, weak, and passive, respectively. Access to the semantic attributes of the irretrievable word is also suggested by the observation that when participants made commission errors, the Hebrew word that they reported had the same polarity on the respective dimension as the correct word (e.g., responding "happy" instead of "health"). Such a tendency for consistent polarities between commission errors and targets was observed for all three dimensions. Similar results supporting access to the connotative attributes of words whose full meaning could not be retrieved was also reported by Yavuz and Bousfield (1959), Schacter and Worling (1985), and Koriat (1993).

It is interesting to note that in Koriat and colleagues (2003), partial recall exhibited a slower rate of forgetting than complete recall. Also, whereas complete recalls were predominantly associated with *remember* responses, attribute judgments were predominantly associated with *know* and *guess* responses. These observations were taken to suggest that access to partial information is based, in part, on implicit memory (Durso & Shore, 1991), and that source monitoring is more difficult for partial recall than for complete recall. Indeed, several studies indicated that participants are accurate in making semantic judgments about a rare word even when they deny any knowledge of that word (Durso & Shore, 1991; Eysenck, 1979; Shore & Durso, 1990).

Several studies that used memory pointers other than word definitions also indicated that participants experiencing memory blockage could provide accurate information about semantic and associative features of the solicited target. For example, Yarmey (1973) presented participants with photographs of celebrities. When they failed to retrieve the person's name but felt sure that they knew it and that it was on the verge of coming back, they were able not only to guess correctly phonemic features of the name, but were also accurate in guessing the person's profession, and where he had been most often seen (newspapers, television, movies, etc.). Thus, when participants are specifically requested to report information about non-acoustic features (e.g., profession), they are generally accurate in providing generic information. Caramazza and Miozzo (1997) provide evidence showing that during TOTs, Italian speakers correctly guessed the gender of the searched-for words. Lovelace (1987) asked participants questions that required the recall of a name. Participants in a TOT could provide some structural attributes of the name, but also the country or language associated with the name, descriptive attributes, and situational attributes. Riefer, Kevari, and Kramer (1995) presented their participants with theme songs of TV shows and asked them to identify the show. While in TOTs participants recalled a character from the show, a leading actor's name, or plot outline.

BLOCKED MEMORY FOR ACTION

Consider next a third kind of memory blockage that is characterized by a different goal. This will be referred to as *Blocked Memory for Action* (BMfA): You walk into the kitchen to do something. You are stuck in the middle of the kitchen not knowing what you came for. What kind of partial information can you access in this situation?

In such BMfA states, the original intention is to reach a certain end by executing a series of behavioral acts. The goal representation typically activates behavioral programs designed to reach (or move closer to reaching) a desired end state. BMfA states are often characterized by *intention loss* (Reason, 1984): during the course of executing a goal-directed behavior, one discovers that the intention or some aspects of it have suddenly been forgotten. Subjectively, this type of memory lapse is characterized by a feeling of "What am I doing here?" (see Reason, 1984). The person is aware of the fact that the goal of one's actions was known a while ago but was somehow lost. Loss of intention can also occur before any intention-related action has been initiated ("I meant to do something, what was it?"). What do people know when intention is lost? Over the years, the senior author has collected reports of BMfA states from students in memory classes. The students were asked to keep a record of BMfA states when they occurred. In particular, they were asked to note all the information that they could access immediately when in a BMfA state, and before the blockage was resolved. When the blocked memory was resolved, they were asked to describe what they could remember. Despite the limitations of this procedure (Reason & Lucas, 1984), the reports seem to converge in providing some insights.

Here is one example for which we had a verbatim report:

> I was doing something just before my wife and I were about to leave home. It suddenly occurred to me that I had to lock the back door of the apartment. I stopped what I was doing and went to lock the door. Then I realized that there was something that I had been doing before I went to lock the door but I could not remember what it was. The only thing I could recall was that I had to "insert something into something" and, in fact, I felt the movement in my own hand. I recalled what it was when I saw a dossier on my desk and a bill next to it. What I had intended to do was to file the bill in the dossier by inserting it into an envelope within the dossier.

The reports suggest that in a BMfA state, participants are most likely to retrieve partial information about the intended action. Sometimes participants can mimic aspects of the intended actions with their hands. Two specific aspects are sometimes notable: location and size. For example, when a person walks into a room to obtain something, he may point in the general direction where the object lies in relation to the body (e.g., above or below). Possibly, location reflects the general direction where one should be heading. Also, sometimes participants can tell that the object is small, and can even shape their hands or palms to suggest the kind of movement needed to grab or hold the object. Sometimes people could convey semantic or associative information. For example, some people recalled that the lost intention had to do with food or eating, or with a telephone call that they had just received. Such semantic or associative information was generally accessed as people tried to retrieve the lost intention by attempting to reconstruct the events that had given rise to the intention (e.g., feeling hungry).

Another situation that is somewhat similar to the BMfA state just described involves a prospective memory in which some information about a to-be-performed task is lost. For example, while in the supermarket you may remember that there was some additional item that you wanted to buy but cannot remember what it was. Here the abstract retention is retrieved but not its specifics. In an unpublished study on prospective memory, we left the keys to the room on the table and told participants to do something with them (e.g., put them in a drawer) when they have completed a certain task. Some participants remembered that they had to do something with the keys but could not remember what.

Studies on the tip-of-the-finger (TOF) phenomenon also indicate access to gestural rather than oral or written word production. In a study by Thompson, Emmorey, and Gollan (2005), deaf participants were presented with a list of written English words and were asked to translate them into their corresponding American Sign Language signs. When participants reported experiencing a TOF, they were asked if they could recall any properties of the sign. In most cases, participants were able to correctly retrieve some structural features of the hand sign such as hand shape, hand location, hand orientation, and hand movement.

Similarly, in the tip-of-the-pen (TOP) phenomenon, Chinese writers who lose momentarily the visual representation of a Chinese character depicting a certain concept are able to provide orthographic information about the inaccessible character (structural features such as the number of strokes and radicals), and they do so more than during a non-TOP situation (Sun, Vinson, & Vigliocco, 1998). In a somewhat related phenomenon – the slip of the pen (SOP, see Brown, 1991) – participants inadvertently substitute the intended word with another word in written word production. High levels of correspondence are found between the SOP and the intended target, especially for their first and final letters (Hotopf, 1980; Wing & Baddeley, 1980).

A GOAL-DIRECTED PERSPECTIVE ON MEMORY BLOCKAGE STATES

Several features of the TOT, emphasized by many writers, are consistent with our analysis of memory blockage states within a goal-directed framework. First, the TOT is often accompanied by frustration with not being able to retrieve the elusive target (Schwartz, 2001a), and by the experience of relief when the sought-for target is retrieved. The frustration is particularly intense when the person succeeds in accessing partial fragments of the solicited target. It was proposed that the memory pointer (e.g., word definition) initially activates a large number of candidates that satisfy the retrieval description only grossly (Koriat & Lieblich, 1977). The activations emanating from these candidates exert two conflicting effects: They interfere with accessing the correct target but at the same time enhance the subjective feeling that the target is about to emerge into consciousness. These conflicting effects contribute to the feelings of frustration accompanying TOTs (Koriat, 1994, 1998; Schwartz & Smith, 1997; Smith, 1994). Several researchers proposed that the difficulty in retrieving the solicited target in the TOT results precisely from the interfering effects of "interlopers" or "blockers" and that these compelling but wrong candidates must be first suppressed before the correct target can be retrieved (see A. Brown, 1991; Jones, 1989; Reason & Lucas, 1984).

The second feature of the TOT that supports its analysis within a goal-driven perspective lies in the motivation to bring that state to an end by retrieving the sought-for target (A. Brown, 2012). Schwartz (2001b) proposed that TOTs have both monitoring and control functions. The monitoring function is reflected in the strong feeling of knowing associated with a TOT, whereas the control function is reflected in the greater motivation for an extended memory search during TOTs than during non-TOT states.

The motivational function of the TOT is supported by findings indicating longer retrieval latencies of the target during a TOT (Gruneberg, Smith, & Winfrow, 1973; Schwartz, 2001b). It is also supported by the observation of Litman, Hutchins, and Russon (2005) that participants were more likely to open an envelope containing the target word during a TOT compared to a don't know (DK) state. It was also proposed that the extended search for the elusive target during a TOT diminishes cognitive resources, as suggested by the poorer performance on a secondary task of participants in a TOT compared to that of participants in a non-TOT state (Ryan, Petty, & Wenzlaff, 1982; see Schwartz, 2002).

The TOT has the qualities of an interrupted task, as discussed by Kurt Lewin (1935). Lewin proposed that the intention to perform a task creates a tension system (a "quasi need") that presses toward task completion. Completion of the task results in the discharge of the tension system associated with the quasi-need. When the activities used to fulfill the intention are interrupted, the unreleased tension can have cognitive and behavioral consequences. In particular, this tension can result in a strong tendency to resume the task, and in a better memory for the unfinished task (the so called Zeigarnik effect, see Van Bergen, 1968).

The TOT can be seen to involve a kind of interrupted or unfinished task (see Yaniv & Meyer, 1987). The intention to retrieve a memory target creates a driving force toward accomplishment, which remains active and perhaps intensifies when retrieval is blocked. Intention-related constructs remain cognitively active, and relief from the tension is reached only when retrieval is successful. Indeed, using both a lexical decision task and a recognition task, Yaniv and Meyer (1987) found that target words that participants were unable to retrieve remained more accessible than control words for up to 30 minutes, and that this was particularly true when the pointers elicited strong feelings of knowing. Other studies indicated that the accessibility of goal-related constructs is reduced after goal fulfillment (see Marsh, Hicks, & Bink, 1998; Marsh, Hicks, & Brian, 1999).

In a naturalistic study of the TOT phenomenon, Reason and Lucas (1984) noted that during TOTs, sometimes incorrect intermediates keep suggesting themselves as possible resolutions of the TOT experience. They suggest that these incorrect responses are comparable to slips of action in which an unintended action that is more habitual under the prevailing circumstances than the one demanded by the current goal plan is executed. Their analysis is compatible with the goal-directed perspective on TOT advocated in this chapter.

In sum, several observations support the analysis of TOTs as an interrupted goal situation. Among these is the annoying frustration that accompanies a TOT, the motivational drive toward task completion, the lingering activation of goal-related constructs, the relief experienced when TOT is finally resolved, and the diminished activation of goal-related constructs after goal accomplishment. Consistent with the goal-directed framework are also the conditions and pointers that precipitate strong TOTs, which seem to involve activations that side track the memory search away from the solicited target (Jones, 1989; Koriat & Lieblich, 1977).

WHAT CAN BE LEARNED FROM THE TYPE OF PARTIAL INFORMATION ACCESSED DURING MEMORY BLOCKAGE?

As noted earlier, some discussions took the results obtained with the TOT to have implications for the organization of the mental lexicon along phonemic features. What should be clear from our analysis, however, is that these implications are specific to the intention activated when memory is blocked. Thus, some of the implications drawn by R. Brown and McNeill (1966) are specific to a BMfN situation in which the intention is to produce a word given its definition. In contrast, when the intention is to retrieve the meaning of a word, the pertinent memory organization is semantic and associative in nature. For example, in Koriat and colleagues' study, the hypothesis was examined that in a BMfM situation, access to the emotional-evaluative dimension of a word is superior to that of other dimensions, consistent with the claimed primacy of emotion (Zajonc, 1984). The results, however, indicated equal access to all three dimensions of the semantic differential – evaluation, potency, and activity – of the word's meaning. The observations pertaining to BMfA situations, in turn, highlight a different organization of memory that is pertinent to intended actions.

Presumably, memory allows for different organizations, each of which becomes activated and shaped by the current intention. The study of the types of partial information that participants access when memory is blocked can shed light on the multiple organizations permitted by memory and the flexibility with which the pertinent organization is adaptively highlighted depending on one's current goals.

ACCESSING DIFFERENT TYPES OF PARTIAL INFORMATION DURING MEMORY SEARCH

So far we classified memory blockage states in terms of the current goal of the person, assuming that that goal determines the type of partial information accessed. However, participants normally access more than one type of information during a memory blockage state. For example, in Yarmey's (1973) study, participants provided both phonemic and semantic partial information. However, in most studies of memory blockage states, participants provided only one type of information. In these studies, two features of the experimental procedure tended to constrain the type of partial information reported, the type of memory pointer used, and the information solicited. For example, in R. Brown and McNeill's (1966) study, like in many other studies, the pointer used to cue memory was the definition of the word, so that there was no point for participants to report semantic information. In addition, in many studies, specific partial information was solicited (first letters, profession, etc.).

To capture the richness of information that is accessed when memory is blocked, it is important to use memory pointers that are less constraining, and also to allow participants to report any information that comes to mind (like in the BMfA study described earlier). In an unpublished exploratory experiment by the senior author, participants were shown a target street on a map, and additional details were provided to make sure that the participants knew which street was the target street. The task was to recall the name of the street, and when unable to retrieve the name, to report any information that came to mind. Participants sometimes reported semantic partial information (e.g., "it is a name of a woman") and sometimes structural or phonological information ("it consists of two words"). Interestingly, the majority of the reports included semantic rather than phonological partial information. What is important to stress is that participants sometimes provided both semantic and phonological information ("it is the name of a person related to Jewish history. It ends with *vitch*"). When pressed, participants could report quite rich partial information that was largely correct.

However, when probed to report all the information that comes to mind, the information reported clearly does not pertain only to the next step toward reaching the retrieval goal. When people experience difficulty retrieving a solicited piece of information, they often probe their memory by deliberately generating a variety of cues that may bring them closer to the desired target information (see Koriat, 2000). For example, in Williams and Hollan's (1981) study, participants were asked to retrieve the names of their high school classmates, and did so for several days. The recall protocols revealed an enormous amount of information that was completely incidental to the task of recalling the names themselves. That information was presumably intended to provide clues that can assist the retrieval of the names. Williams and Hollan (1981) proposed that the retrieval of information from the distant past involves a reconstruction from a variety of bits and pieces of information, and partial retrieval represents a central tool that constraints the reconstructive retrieval process. This is probably true of many everyday memory blockage situations. A personal episode recounted by Nickerson (1981) about the attempt to recall the name of a street discloses the intricacies of the processes that take place when memory is blocked.

To conclude, in this chapter, we proposed a framework for the analysis of blocked memory states in general, and for the TOT, in particular, with a focus on the type of partial information that participants can relay about the elusive target. The goal-directed framework puts an emphasis on the intention of the person when memory retrieval is thwarted. This intention is assumed to constrain the type of partial information that participants can spontaneously access and/or report when complete retrieval is blocked. The study of partial recall can shed light on the memory organizations that are activated and utilized depending on one's current goals and intentions.

REFERENCES

Aarts, H., Dijksterhuis, A., & De Vries, P. (2001). On the psychology of drinking: Being thirsty and perceptually ready. *British Journal of Psychology, 92*, 631–642.
Balcetis, E., & Dunning, D. (2006). See what you want to see: Motivational influences on visual perception. *Journal of Personality and Social Psychology, 91*, 612–625.

Brown, A. S. (1991). A review of the tip of the tongue experience. *Psychological Bulletin*, 109, 204–223.

(2012). *The tip of the tongue state.* New York: Psychology Press.

Brown A. S., & Burrows, C. (2009). Structural knowledge about inaccessible target words during TOTs. *Psychonomic Society Annual Convention*, Boston, MA.

Brown, R., & McNeill, D. (1966). The "tip of the tongue" phenomenon. *Journal of Verbal Learning and Verbal Behavior*, 5, 325–337.

Caramazza, A., & Miozzo, M. (1997). The relation between syntactic and phonological knowledge in lexical access: Evidence from the "tip-of-the-tongue" phenomenon. *Cognition*, 64, 309–343.

Collins, A. M., & Loftus, E. F. (1975). A spreading-activation theory of semantic processing. *Psychological Review*, 82, 407–428.

Dale, H. C. A., & McGlaughlin, A. (1971). Evidence of acoustic coding in long-term memory. *Quarterly Journal of Experimental Psychology*, 23, 1–7.

Durso, F. T., & Shore, W. J. (1991). Partial knowledge of word meanings. *Journal of Experimental Psychology: General*, 120, 190–202.

Ecke, P. (2004). Words on the tip of the tongue: A study of lexical retrieval failures in Spanish-English bilinguals. *Southwest Journal of Linguistics*, 23, 33–63.

Eysenck, M. W. (1979). The feeling of knowing a word's meaning. *British Journal of Psychology*, 70, 243–251.

Fishbach, A., & Ferguson M. J. (2007).The goal construct in social psychology. In A. W. Kruglanski, & E. T. Higgins (Eds.), *Social psychology: Handbook of basic principles* (vol. II, ch. 21, pp. 490–515). New York: Guilford Press.

Förster, J., Liberman, N., & Higgins, E. T. (2005). Accessibility from active and fulfilled goals. *Journal of Experimental Social Psychology*, 41, 220–239.

Gollan, T. H., & Acenas, L. A. R. (2004). What is a TOT? Cognate and translation effects on tip-of-the-tongue states in Spanish-English and Tagalog-English bilinguals. *Journal of Experimental Psychology: Learning, Memory, and Cognition*, 30, 246–269.

Gruneberg, M. M., Smith, R. L., & Winfrow, P. (1973). An investigation into response blockaging. *Acta Psychologica*, 37, 187–196.

Hotopf, N. (1980). Slips of the pen. In U. Frith (Ed.), *Cognitive processes in spelling* (pp. 287–307). San Diego, CA: Academic Press.

Jones, G. V. (1989). Back to Woodworth: Role of interlopers in the tip-of-the-tongue phenomenon. *Memory & Cognition*, 17, 69–76.

Koriat, A. (1993). How do we know that we know? The accessibility model of the feeling of knowing. *Psychological Review*, 100, 609–639.

(1994). Memory's knowledge of its own knowledge: The accessibility account of the feeling of knowing. In J. Metcalfe & A. P. Shimamura (Eds.), *Metacognition: Knowing about knowing* (pp. 115–135). Cambridge, MA: MIT Press.

(1998). Illusions of knowing: The link between knowledge and metaknowledge. In V. Y. Yzerbyt, G. Lories, & B. Dardenne (Eds.), *Metacognition: Cognitive and social dimensions* (pp. 16–34). London: Sage.

(2000). Control processes in remembering. In E. Tulving, & F. I. M. Craik (Eds.), *The Oxford handbook of memory* (pp. 333–346). New York: Oxford University Press.

Koriat. A., Levy-Sadot, R., Edry, E., & de Marcas, G. (2003). What do we know about what we cannot remember? Accessing the semantic attributes of words that cannot be recalled. *Journal of Experimental Psychology: Learning, Memory, and Cognition*, 29, 1095–1105.

Koriat, A., & Lieblich, I. (1974). What does a person in the "TOT" state know that a person in a "don't know" state does not know? *Memory & Cognition*, 2, 647–655.

   (1975). Examination of the letter serial position effect in the "TOT" and the "don't know" states. *Bulletin of the Psychonomic Society*, 6, 539–541.

   (1977). A study of memory pointers. *Acta Psychologica*, 41, 151–164.

Kruglanski, A. W., Shah, J. Y., Fishbach, A., Friedman, R., Chun, W. Y., & Sleeth-Keppler, D. (2002). A theory of goal-systems. In M. P. Zanna (Ed.), *Advances in experimental social psychology* (vol. 34, pp. 331–378). New York: Academic Press.

Levelt, W. J. M. (1989). *Speaking. From intention to articulation.* Cambridge, MA: MIT Press.

Lewin, K. (1935). *A dynamic theory of personality.* McGraw Hill.

Litman, J. A., Hutchins, T. L., & Russon, R. K. (2005). Epistemic curiosity, feeling-of-knowing, and exploratory behaviour. *Cognition and Emotion*, 19, 559–582.

Lovelace, E. (1987). Attributes that come to mind in the TOT state. *Bulletin of the Psychonomic Society*, 25, 370–372.

Marsh, R. L., Hicks, J. L., & Bink, M. L. (1998). Activation of completed, uncompleted, and partially completed intentions. *Journal of Experimental Psychology: Learning, memory & Cognition*, 24, 350–361.

Marsh, R. L., Hicks, J. L., & Bryan, E. S. (1999). The activation of unrelated and canceled intentions. *Memory & Cognition*, 27, 320–327.

Moskowitz, G. B. (2002). Preconscious effects of temporary goals on attention. *Journal of Experimental Social Psychology*, 38, 397–404.

Nickerson, R. S. (1981). Motivated retrieval from archival memory. In J. H. Flowers (Ed.), *Nebraska symposium on motivation* (pp. 73–119). Lincoln: University of Nebraska Press.

Norman, D. A. (1969). *Memory and attention.* Toronto: Wiley.

Osgood, C. E. (1952). The nature and measurement of meaning. *Psychological Bulletin*, 49, 197–237.

Reason, J. T., & Lucas, D. (1984). Using cognitive diaries to investigate naturally occurring memory blocks. In J. E. Harris & P. E. Morris (Eds.), *Everyday memory, actions, and absent-mindedness* (pp. 53–70). London: Academic Press.

Riefer, D. M., Kevari, M. K., & Kramer, D. L. F. (1995). Name that tune: Elliciting the tip-of-the-tongue experience using auditory stimuli. *Psychological Reports*, 77, 1379–1390.

Roelofs, A., Meyer, A. S., Levelt, W. J. M. (1998). A case for the lemma/lexeme distinction in models of speaking: comment on Caramazza and Miozzo (1997). *Cognition*, 69, 219–230.

Ryan, M. P., Petty, C. R., & Wenzlaff, R. M. (1982). Motivated remembering efforts during tip-of-the-tongue states. *Acta Psychologica*, 51, 137–147.

Schacter, D. L., & Worling, J. R. (1985). Attribute information and the feeling of knowing. *Canadian Journal of Psychology*, 39, 467–475.

Schwartz, B. L. (1998). Illusory tip-of-the-tongue states. *Memory*, 6, 623–642.

(2001a). The phenomenology of naturally occurring tip-of-the-tongue states: A diary study. In S. P. Shohov (Ed.), *Advances in Psychology Research*, vol. 8 (pp. 71–84). Huntington, NY: Nova Science Publishers.

(2001b). The relation of tip-of-the-tongue states and retrieval time. *Memory & Cognition*, 29, 117–126.

(2002). *Tip-of-the-tongue states: Phenomenology, mechanism, and lexical retrieval.* Mahwah, NJ: Erlbaum.

Schwartz, B. L., & Smith, S. M. (1997). The retrieval of related information influences tip-of-the-tongue states. *Journal of Memory & Language*, 36, 68–86.

Shore, W. J., & Durso, F. T. (1990). Partial knowledge in vocabulary acquisition: General constraints and specific detail. *Journal of Educational Psychology*, 82, 315–318.

Smith, S. M. (1994). Frustrated feelings of imminent recall: On the tip of the tongue. In J. Metcalfe & A. P. Shimamura (Eds.), *Metacognition: Knowing about knowing* (pp. 27–45). Cambridge, MA: MIT Press.

Sun, Y., Vinson, D. E., & Vigliocco, G. (1998). Tip-of-the-tongue and tip-of-the-pen in Chinese. *Psychonomic Society Convention*. Dallas, TX.

Thompson, R., Emmorey, K., & Golan, T. H. (2005). "Tip of the fingers" experiences by deaf singers: Insights into the organization of a sign-based lexicon. *Psychological Science*, 16, 856–860.

Van Bergen, A. (1968). *Task interruption.* Amsterdam: North-Holland Publishing Company.

Williams, M. D., & Hollan, J. D. (1981). The process of retrieval from very long-term memory. *Cognitive Science*, 5, 87–119.

Wing, A. M., & Baddeley, A. D. (1980). Spelling errors in handwriting: A corpus and a distributional analysis. In U. Frith (Ed.), *Cognitive processes in spelling* (pp. 251–285). San Diego, CA: Academic Press.

Yaniv, I., & Meyer, D. E. (1987). Activation and metacognition of inaccessible stored information: Potential bases for incubation effects in problem solving. *Journal of Experimental Psychology: Learning, Memory & Cognition*, 13, 187–205.

Yarmey, A. D. (1973). I recognize your face, but I can't remember your name: Further evidence on the tip-of-the-tongue phenomenon. *Memory & Cognition*, 1, 287–290.

Yavuz, H. S., & Bousfield, W. A. (1959). Recall of connotative meaning. *Psychological Reports*, 5, 319–320.

Zajonc, R. B. (1984). On the primacy of affect. *American Psychologist*, 39, 117–123.

Author Index

Subject Index

accessibility heuristic hypothesis, 177, 178, 200

aging, 11, 29, 36–38, 44, 45, 55, 59–62, 70, 95, 99, 102–103, 104, 106, 110, 112, 117, 118, 119, 125, 127, 128, 129, 131, 132, 134, 135, 136, 138, 139, 208, 213, 236, 281, 282, 283, 284, 285, 287, 288–289, 290–292, 293, 296–298, 300–301

Alzheimer's, 17, 60, 116–118, 135, 148–149, 282

American Sign Language (ASL), 16, 332

anosognosia, 148

anterior cingulate cortex (ACC), 5, 25, 159, 160–162, 207–209, 222–225

antiepileptic, 175

anxiolytic, 175, 189, 190

aphasia, 5, 17, 61, 103, 110, 315

attention, 27, 111, 118, 126, 129, 145, 152, 166, 205, 211, 236, 239, 242–244, 270, 278

attention deficit/hyperactivity disorder, 145

basal ganglia, 144–145

behaviorist, 2, 6

benzodiazepines, 11, 175, 181–182, 190

bilateral anterior frontal cortex, 207, 209

bilateral parahippocampal gyrus, 222

bilingual, 10, 16, 18, 63

blank-in-the-mind (BIM), 11, 160, 232–261

blocked memory for meaning (BMfM), 329–330

blocked memory for action (BMfA), 330–332, 335

blocking hypothesis, 64, 98

blood oxygenation level dependent (BOLD), 203–204

Boston Naming Test, 47, 150, 157–158

bradykinesia, 144

California Card Sorting Test, 158

California Verbal Learning Test, 126, 129, 148, 150, 154

category,
  coordinate, 108
  subordinate, 108
  superordinate, 108

CHARM model, 20

commission error, 38, 184, 185, 186, 187, 189, 190, 232, 233, 234, 237, 239, 240, 241, 242, 243, 245, 248, 257, 258, 260, 261, 329

conduite d'approche, 110–111

confidence level (CL), 176, 179, 183, 184, 190

context, 65, 67, 68, 97, 112, 183, 266, 267, 284, 305, 306, 307, 310, 313, 316, 322

controlled word association (COWA), 158

cross sectional design, 283

cue-familiarity hypothesis, 22–23, 26, 91, 200

declarative memory, 153

decoupled familiarity, 293, 295–296, 298, 300

déjà vu, 264–278, 281–301

deliberative language processing, 96, 104, 111

demand characteristics, 70, 186, 269, 276, 277

dementia, 116, 117, 118, 121, 132, 135, 136, 144, 145, 160, 166
  frontotemporal, 118
  vascular, 118, 135
  with Lewy bodies, 118, 135

depression, 118, 145, 156, 164, 165, 166

diary studies, 6–7, 17, 37, 52, 54, 55, 60, 62, 63, 65, 100, 185, 200, 201, 299, 300

direct access, 18–20, 22, 23, 25, 27, 28, 69–70, 199

don't know (DK), 11, 26, 27, 34, 35, 38, 39, 40, 43, 45, 59, 124, 157, 186, 207, 208, 209, 210, 211, 212, 213, 214, 215, 216, 217, 218, 219, 220, 221, 319, 333

dopamine, 144, 145, 165

dorsal striatum, 145

double-attractor network, 109–110, 112

353